Management

Leading People and Professional Development

Pippa Riley

Viva Books

New Delhi | Mumbai | Chennai | Kolkata | Bengaluru | Hyderabad | Kochi | Guwahati

First Indian Edition 2011

VIVA BOOKS PRIVATE LIMITED

- 4737/23 Ansari Road, Daryaganj, New Delhi 110 002
  E-mail: vivadelhi@vivagroupindia.net, Tel. 42242200
- 76, Service Industries, Shirvane, Sector 1, Nerul, Navi Mumbai 400 706
  E-mail: vivamumbai@vivagroupindia.net, Tel. 27721273, 27721274
- Jamals Fazal Chambers, 26 Greams Road, Chennai 600 006
  E-mail: vivachennai@vivagroupindia.net, Tel. 28290304, 28294241
- B-103, Jindal Towers, 21/1A/3 Darga Road, Kolkata 700 017
  E-mail: vivakolkata@vivagroupindia.net, Tel. 22836381, 22816713
- 7, Sovereign Park Apartments, 56-58, K. R. Road, Basavanagudi, Bengaluru 560 004
  E-mail: vivabangalore@vivagroupindia.net, Tel. 26607409, 26607410
- 101-102 Mughal Marc Aptt., 3-4-637 to 641, Narayanguda, Hyderabad 500 029
  E-mail: vivahyderabad@vivagroupindia.net, Tel. 27564481, 27564482
- First Floor, Beevi Towers, SRM Road, Kaloor, Kochi 682 018, Kerala
  E-mail: vivakochi@vivagroupindia.net, Tel: 0484-2403055, 2403056
- 232, GNB Road, Beside UCO Bank, Silpukhuri, Guwahati 781 003
  E-mail: vivaguwahati@vivagroupindia.net, Tel: 0361-2666386

Published by arrangement with

BPP Learning Media Ltd.
BPP House, Aldine Place
London W12 8AA

ISBN : 978-81-309-1762-7

Published by Vinod Vasishtha for Viva Books Private Limited, 4737/23, Ansari Road, Daryaganj, New Delhi - 110 002.

Printed and bound by Raj Press, R-3, Inderpuri, New Delhi - 110 012.

Contents

Introduction

Viva-BPP Learning Media's Business Essentials range is the ideal learning solution for students studying for business-related qualifications and degrees. The range provides concise and comprehensive coverage of the key areas that are essential to the business student.

Qualifications in business are traditionally very demanding. Students therefore need learning resources which go straight to the core of the topics involved, and which build upon students' pre-existing knowledge and experience. The BPP Learning Media Business Essentials range has been designed to meet exactly that need.

Features include:

- In-depth coverage of essential topics within business-related subjects
- Plenty of activities, quizzes and topics for discussion to help retain the interest of students and ensure progress
- Up-to-date practical illustrations and case studies that really bring the material to life
- A full index, with key terms highlighted in bold

Each chapter contains:

- An introduction and a list of specific study objectives
- Summary diagrams and signposts to guide you through the chapter
- A chapter roundup, quick quiz with answers and answers to activities

Titles in the Series

- Accounts
- Business Decision Making
- Business Environment
- Business Maths
- Business Strategy
- Economics
- Finance: Management Accounting and Financial Reporting
- Human Resource Development and Employee Relations
- Human Resource Management
- Management: Communications and Achieving Results
- Management: Leading People and Professional Development
- Managing Finance
- Marketing and Promotion
- Marketing and Sales Strategy
- Marketing Principles
- Organisations and Behaviour
- Research Project

Study Guide

This Course Book includes features designed specifically to make learning effective and efficient.

- Each chapter begins with a summary diagram which maps out the areas covered by the chapter. There are detailed summary diagrams at the start of each main section of the chapter. You can use the diagrams during revision as a basis for your notes.
- After the main summary diagram there is an introduction, which sets the chapter in context. This is followed by learning objectives, which show you what you will learn as you work through the chapter.
- Throughout the Course Book, there are special aids to learning. These are indicated by symbols in the margin:

Signposts guide you through the book, showing how each section connects with the next.

Definitions give the meanings of key terms. The *glossary* at the end of the book summarises these.

Activities help you to test how much you have learned. An indication of the time you should take on each is given. Answers are given at the end of each chapter.

Topics for discussion are for use in seminars. They give you a chance to share your views with your fellow students. They allow you to highlight holes in your knowledge and to see how others understand concepts. If you have time, try 'teaching' someone the concepts you have learned in a session. This helps you to remember key points and answering their questions will consolidate your knowledge.

Examples relate what you have learned to the outside world. Try to think up your own examples as you work through the Course Book.

Chapter roundups present the key information from the chapter in a concise format. Useful for revision.

- At the end of each chapter, there is a **chapter roundup** and a **quick quiz** with answers. Use these to revise and consolidate your knowledge. The chapter roundup summarises the chapter. The quick quiz tests what you have learned (the answers often refer you back to the chapter so you can look over subjects again).
- At the end of the book, there is an index.

Part A

Professional Development

Chapter 1 :
SELF-MANAGED LEARNING

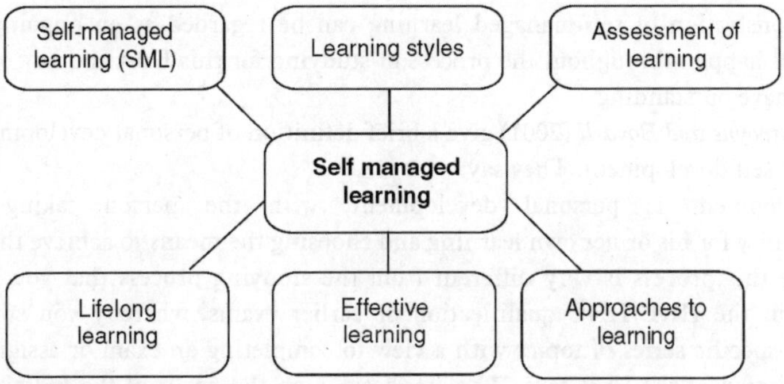

Introduction

Edexcel Specialist Unit 13 is unusual, not just in the context of the HND and HNC Business qualification, but in the context of all exam syllabuses, because it requires you to carry out a detailed self-analysis and self-evaluation. Increasingly this type of self-assessment is a requirement of business-related degree and diploma courses.

This Unit is also unusual in that it is likely that you will develop it throughout the course and your study of other units, so that it reflects your career and personal development over a period of time.

You are required to carry out four different activities in order to achieve the Unit.

- Understand how self-managed learning can enhance lifelong development
- Be able to take responsibility for your own personal and professional development
- Be able to implement and continually review own personal and professional development plan
- Be able to demonstrate acquired interpersonal and transferable skills

The assessment for the Unit consists of three different requirements.

1 For the **personal profile,** you must self-evaluate your current skills and experiences by means of a **skills audit,** and then construct a **personal portfolio**

2 For the **career development** you should keep a **personal journal or skills log** throughout the programme, based on your own personal and career aims and needs

3 Assessment of your **interpersonal and transferable skills** should involve **role play** at your college and the **study of examples of 'real life' situations**

Learning outcomes

On completing this chapter you should be able to:

(a) Evaluate approaches to self-managed learning

(b) Propose ways in which lifelong learning in personal and professional contexts could be encouraged

(c) Evaluate the benefits of self-managed learning to the individual and organisation

The demonstration of self-managed learning can be regarded as an ongoing process, which will happen throughout the process of studying for this Unit and any others that you may have outstanding.

Pedler, Burgoyne and Boydell (2001) give a brief definition of personal development in the context of self development. They say:

'Self-development is personal development, with the person taking primary responsibility for his or her own learning and choosing the means to achieve this.'

Therefore this process is very different from the studying process that you have seen hitherto in the HND/HNC qualification or earlier exams, whereby you studied and learned a specific series of topics with a view to completing an exam or assignment. As the description of the Unit says, 'The emphasis is on the needs of the individual'. The Unit is concerned with your own personal development and enables you, the student, to build on your existing skills to enhance current performance and develop new skills for your future personal and career development.

From that point of view, this Unit is therefore highly personal to you, and although this Course Book can make suggestions and offer guidance, it is up to you to tackle the Unit honestly.

As well as being very personal, this Unit will also have an impact on your role as a member of a team. The description of the Unit stresses that the emphasis is on the needs of the individual but this is 'within the context of how the development of self-management corresponds with effective team management in meeting objectives'.

Note to all students

The chapters in this section on professional development make specific reference to the Edexcel Higher Nationals (HND and HNC) in Business, notably the Edexcel Unit 13 of the Management specialism. Following the requirements of Unit 13 in this way has enabled us to create a structure around which to discuss the ideas that are relevant. You should find that regardless of whatever form of business qualification you are studying, the points made will be equally as valid to you.

Self-managed learning programmes hold numerous advantages over traditional forms of classroom instruction for employees in the workplace, whether they are leaders, managers, or individual contributors. Problem areas with the traditional approaches include: coping with the short life span of useful knowledge; passing down acquired competences to succeeding cohorts; accommodating the demands of productivity while providing for a continuity of learning; and enabling learners to pursue activities that correspond to their learning styles and needs. Self-managed learning includes the learner initiating the learning, making the decisions about what training and development experiences will occur, and how. The learner selects and carries out their own learning goals, objectives, methods and means of verifying that the goals were met.

Probably the most important skill for today's rapidly changing workforce is skills in self-reflection. The highly motivated, self-directed learner with skills in self-reflection can approach the workplace as a continual classroom from which to learn.

1 SELF MANAGED LEARNING (SML)

1.1 Lifelong development

Today emphasis is on lifelong learning and multiple job/career transitions. The aim of lifelong development is for you to understand your potential and help you maximise this potential in the work force today and in the future. From the position you are starting from with this course, you will need to have a clear idea of the kind of career path you would like to follow. People who do not career plan usually get sick from stress working in fields they do not like and students waste time and money pursuing educational areas in which they have no interest. The decisions we make about careers and leisure activities throughout our life span are critical to our sense of well being. Satisfaction in our work can be a key ingredient to our feelings of self-worth. Happiness can be contingent upon a role as productive and worthwhile employer or employee. Conversely, excessive stress on the job can interfere with our health and personal relationships. Many believe that a person who balances work with life roles finds fulfilment in the work place as well as in his or her other life roles as citizen, student, parent, etc. When planning your future you need to understand that career development is often a lifetime project and may require continuous learning.

Personal growth and development is both interactive and incremental. Consequently, all the steps taken along the way - the lifelong learning plans -should be 'living' documents. They should relate to life in the real world, where people and conditions constantly change.

Each part of your development plan, once written, should be revisited from time to time. Just follow these simple guidelines:

- Reflect on the overall process, not just when you first embark on this course but at regular intervals throughout your working life.
- Review your progress regularly and take stock.
- Revise your plan when developments or circumstances so dictate.

Together, these steps will ensure that you do not lose sight of your overall goals and that your development stays on track.

1.2 Self managed learning and self-initiation of learning process

In self managed learning the individual takes the initiative and the responsibility for what occurs. Individuals select, manage, and assess their own learning activities, which can be pursued at any time, in any place, through any means, at any age. Self Managed Learning (SML) is about you managing your own learning. It is a form of development where you take the initiative in learning new skills, knowledge and attitudes with the support of the organisation.

Personal development programmes are highly personalised and tailored to individual needs, involving a mix of different training interventions and a variety of goals to achieve. Support from the organisation may take the form of payment of fees, allowing time off work to attend classes or by setting up a learning resources centre in-house.

Some companies draw up a formal (written and signed) agreement or contract between a learner/manager and a trainer about what the manager will learn and how that learning will be demonstrated. The agreement will also specify an action plan and the resources that will be needed. Popular areas of learning include: finance skills and techniques; IT; interpersonal skills, making presentations; stress management; how to comply with legislation or how to acquire a working knowledge of a foreign language.

The agreement makes explicit use of the stages of the cycle, setting clear targets for development, identifying the relevant theory to be consulted, planning for the manager to take action in the workplace and providing a review and evaluation of the learning.

Whichever route individuals intend to follow, they cannot rely solely on their tertiary education plus the indiscriminate acquisition of knowledge and skills in their professional work to attain their career goal.

In today's working environment, with technology changing rapidly and streamlined organisations offering fewer advancement opportunities, individuals need to take ownership of their careers. They should set time related career objectives. For each stage, a list of the knowledge and skills required should be drawn up and a resultant training plan formulated. This in essence is a Personal Development Plan.

Many learners have found the following five questions a useful starting point:

- Where have I come from - what are my past experiences?
- Where am I now - what strengths and weaknesses do I have? What is the current situation that I am in?
- Where do I want to get to - what goals/targets/objectives do I want to set for myself?
- How will I get there - what programme of study should I design to achieve my goals?
- How will I know if I have arrived - what criteria can I apply to assess my learning.

Activity 1 **(5 minutes)**

Which of the following is a characteristic of self-managed learning?

1 the employee taking the initiative to learn new skills

2 learning from others

3 attending an outdoor training course

4 being sponsored by the employer

1.3 Clear goal setting - an overview

Step 1 The first step is to get the big picture. It will be a statement outlining an idealised description of your life's outcome that will inspire you and create your target.

Step 2 The best way to work out what you really want is to brainstorm your thoughts to come up with a wish-list for each of your relevant life aspects e.g., career, family and friends (see below).

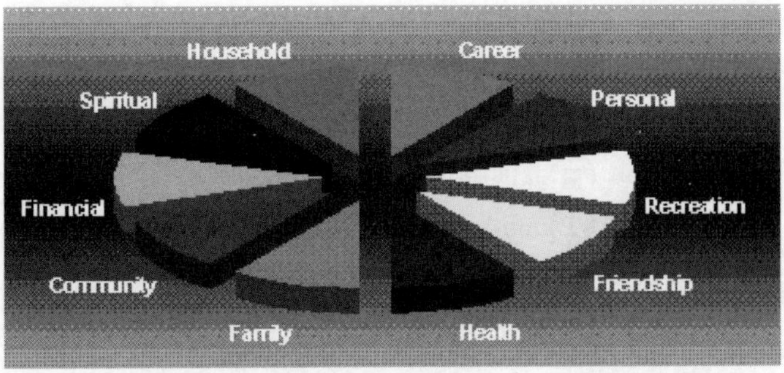

This is the chance for you to picture your perfect life, and put down in writing what it would look like. Written goals are the first step towards commitment, it means you are serious about its achievement. Written goals force you to think - to accept how realistic your goals may or may not be.

Step 3 The aim of goal setting is to set achievable goals, even if that means taking a larger goal or dream and breaking it down into bite-size chunks. A personal SWOT analysis is a great way to work this out.

This will probably be the first of many of these SWOT analyses that you will complete during this course and your career in general.

Strengths	**Weaknesses**
What are your advantages? What do you do well?	What could be improved? What is done badly? What should you avoid?
Opportunities	**Threats**
What are the interesting trends? Does your organisation have a high turnover of managerial staff?	What obstacles do you face?

It is a detailed look at you and your life and will help you identify the most beneficial goals worth pursuing right now based on your current situation, and to identify goals that will help you prepare for the future.

For the purposes of goal setting, it is useful to perform a SWOT analysis on each life aspect as it will help you identify where you need to improve, and therefore help you set goals to make these improvements.

More importantly though, the SWOT analysis allows you to identify your internal strengths that you can capitalise on to seize your opportunities and thwart any external threats.

Step 4 Prioritise - goal setting is a skill, and like all skills, how to set goals takes time and practice to become proficient. So start with a single, easy goal or two to practice on. Once you have achieved this one (or made some progress towards it), you will feel motivated to try the process on some harder goals and confident in applying the process.

Step 5 When you have a set of personal goals that are meaningful to you and will ultimately help you achieve your 'big-picture', all you need to do is develop your chosen goals and make sure they are SMART:

Specific
Measurable
Attainable
Realistic and
Time-bounded

1.4 Preparing a SWOT analysis

To get the best from any development plan for the future it is wise to know the current situation. A SWOT analysis is a simple way to do this: SWOT is an acronym for Strengths, Weaknesses, Opportunities and Threats.

Linked to a strong and powerful goal, it can enable you to take advantage of your skills, talents and abilities to take your career to the next level.

It is often said that there is no point in deciding where you are going until you have established where you are now. As with other areas in business, identifying what you have already achieved (in this case in terms of skills and knowledge) can provide a sound basis for planning for the future.

Select a goal you would like to achieve and then complete the SWOT analysis.

(a) Identify your **strengths,** and your **positive assets**: physical, mental, behavioural and emotional. What are your core skills? What do you do well? You may dress well, have a good memory, be good with the telephone, be honest, calm under pressure, a good listener and so on.

(b) Identify your **weaknesses,** or **liabilities.** Where are your skills/knowledge lacking? What would you like to improve - from your own point of view and from the point of view of other people? You may have no head for numbers, have a tendency to fidget, be subject to stress, or impatient with other people.

(c) Identify the **opportunities** facing you. What are the interesting new trends? Are there changes in markets and professional practice, emerging new specialisms, promotion opportunities or developments in technology?

(d) What **threats** and **obstacles** do you face? Is your professional role changing? Can you foresee competition from other businesses, legislative changes and limited opportunities for progression or threat of redundancy?

There are a number of dimensions to this analysis for individuals.

(a) Do you have the skills necessary to do the job **today?** (You should have – but if not, training is essential.)

(b) Do you have the skills to do the job **tomorrow**? (This may be because of a change in the environment or an expansion of the department – if not, proactive training should be planned to ensure you are prepared.)

(c) Do you have the skills to do **tomorrow's job?** (Will you be promoted? If so, what new skills and knowledge will be needed? This is development and would be a pro-active approach to succession planning, or a personal strategy to increase the chances of promotion.)

(d) Do you have the skills for a **different job tomorrow**? (What will be the alternative employment options in the future and what skills and qualifications will be needed? This is personal career development planning and investment for which many managers are now taking personal responsibility.)

This is a useful exercise. You may gain confidence and set higher goals for yourself as a result of appraising your strengths. You may need to find more realistic goals, or plan to practise/train to minimise your weaknesses. You may decide that you are not in the job – or are not doing enough outside work – to make the most of your strengths. You may identify in your weaknesses the root of certain problems you have had, say, with passing exams or leading a group.

Activity 2 **(20 minutes)**

Draw up a two-columned chart and list some of:

(a) your strengths; *and*
(b) your weaknesses,

that are relevant to your present job, or studies.

Do the strengths outweigh the weaknesses? Can you identify ways in which your weaknesses can be overcome or at least minimised?

It is also important to make a careful assessment of the external environment, including its opportunities and threats. For example, joining an expanding company usually provides more career opportunities than working for a mature company that is not expected to grow. E-learning might make it easier for some people to achieve their qualifications than attending classes at colleges.

Activity 3 **(15 minutes)**

You have already undertaken a personal strengths and weaknesses analysis of your current management competences. You can add to that an **opportunities** and **threats** assessment which will encourage you to think about career prospects and future opportunities. This external analysis of your own personal job market should help you to extend and prioritise the areas of skill development you want to focus on.

1.5 SMART goals - aims and requirements

The following broad guidelines will help you to set effective goals:

- **State each goal as a positive statement**: express your goals positively – 'Execute this technique well' is a much better goal than 'Don't make this stupid mistake.'

- **Be precise**: set a precise goal, putting in dates, times and amounts so that you can measure achievement. If you do this, you will know exactly when you have achieved the goal, and can take complete satisfaction from having achieved it.

- **Set priorities**: when you have several goals, give each a priority. This helps you to avoid feeling overwhelmed by too many goals, and helps to direct your attention to the most important ones.
- **Write goals down**: this crystallises them and gives them more force.
- **Keep operational goals small**: keep the low-level goals you are working towards small and achievable. If a goal is too large, then it can seem that you are not making progress towards it. Keeping goals small and incremental gives more opportunities for reward. Derive today's goals from larger ones.
- **Set performance goals, not outcome goals**: you should take care to set goals over which you have as much control as possible. There is nothing more dispiriting than failing to achieve a personal goal for reasons beyond your control. In business, these could be bad business environments or unexpected effects of government policy. In sport, for example, these reasons could include poor judging, bad weather, injury, or just plain bad luck. If you base your goals on personal performance, then you can keep control over the achievement of your goals and draw satisfaction from them.

EXAMPLE

Set performance goals.

Suppose I have a rigid steel beam that is one foot wide and fifty feet long. I lay the beam on the ground and challenge you to walk the length of the beam without falling off. This is really a very simple task, and anyone with normal coordination would find that they could easily walk those fifty feet without stepping off the beam. If you were faced with this challenge, you would probably be very confident in your ability to complete this task. You would simply focus on the process of placing one foot in front of the other, and trust in your ability to successfully complete the task.
However, suppose I take that same beam and now put it up on posts that are 100ft up in the air. We lift you up those 100ft and deposit you on one end of the beam. Again, I challenge you to walk those fifty feet without falling. How confident would you be that you could successfully walk to the other end without falling off and likely getting yourself killed? Most people would have virtually no confidence and would absolutely refuse to even try walking across that beam. What happens is that you are no longer focused on the process of completing the task and instead are very focused on the potential outcomes!

The reality is that whether the beam is on the ground or way up in the air, the physical task of walking across the beam is essentially the same. What makes trying to cross the beam so difficult when it is high up is that rather than simply focusing on the process of taking a short walk, all of our attention instead becomes focused on the implications of the outcome of our performance!

- **Set realistic goals:** It is important to set goals that you can achieve. All sorts of people (employers, parents, media and society) can set unrealistic goals for you. They will often do this in ignorance of your own desires and ambitions. Alternatively you may set goals that are too high, because you may not appreciate either the obstacles in the way or understand quite how much skill you need to develop to achieve a particular level of performance.

To be useful, goals need to be **SMART**. The acronym S.M.A.R.T. outlines the set of criteria that your goal must follow in order for it to be a well-focused and achievable goal. That set of criteria is:

- Specific: do you know exactly what you want to accomplish with all the details? Is there a description of a precise or specific behaviour or outcome which is linked to a rate, number, percentage or frequency?
- Measurable: are you able to assess your progress? Is there a reliable system in place to measure progress towards the achievement of the objective?
- Attainable/achievable: is your goal within your reach given your current situation?
- Relevant: is your goal relevant towards your purpose in life?
- Time-sensitive: what is the deadline for completing your goal? Is there a finish and/or start date clearly stated or defined

Throughout this text you may also come across SMARTER (specific, measurable, achievable, relevant, time-sensitive, evaluated and reviewed) goal setting.

Aims and requirements

Individuals should be able to establish the ends that they are trying to achieve and the requirements that the work will need to fulfil in order to achieve the stated aims. For example, if you have decided that you want to use a work-related spreadsheet application, then you will need to be able to establish an aim i.e. the level of competence in the use of the package that will be appropriate if successful learning is to take place. You will then need to set out what is required to learn how to use the package i.e. how you will access the training opportunities, resources and how you will prioritise the use of time in order to be successful. You will also need to determine what you will use the package for, bearing in mind that you are seeking to develop a cross-transferable skill.

1.6 Achieving your objectives

Once the direction of your career has been identified, the strategy has to be supported by short-term objectives and action plans. A strategy can be defined as 'a course of action, using specified resources to achieve a defined objective'. The purpose of strategies is to provide a framework for more detailed tactical planning and action.

Tactics and actions are the operational practices that will translate the intention of the strategy into action. They are detailed, short term and subject to immediate control. These can be discussed during the performance appraisal. The objectives must be measurable, e.g. to have completed a part of the HNC/HND Business course by September. The action plans to achieve this objective might be to attend classes, read study guides and text books and submit any coursework on time.

1.7 Personal orientation achievement goals

Goal orientation theories attempt to explain why we pursue achievement tasks and how we view competence and academic success.

Achievement goal orientation is a general motivation theory, which refers to the fact that the type of goal toward which a person is working has a tremendous impact on how they pursue the goal. The theory proposes that people may demonstrate preferences for mastery orientation or performance orientation.

Mastery orientation is described as a person's wish to become proficient in a topic to the best of his or her ability. The person's sense of satisfaction with the work is not influenced by external performance indicators such as grades.

Mastery goal orientation is based on a desire to increase understanding and is found in environments in which people are valued, and where learning and working hard are important; while performance goal orientation is based on a desire to demonstrate competence and is found in environments which emphasise high ability and doing better than others.

Performance orientation is described as a person's wish to achieve highly on external indicators of success, such as grades. The person's sense of satisfaction is highly influenced by grades, and so it is associated with discouragement in the face of low marks. Performance orientation is also associated with higher states of anxiety. In addition, the desire for high marks increases the temptation to cheat or to engage in shallow rote-learning instead of deep understanding.

Performance orientation is thought to increase a student's intrinsic motivation if they perform well, but to decrease motivation when they perform badly.

Within performance goal orientation, Elliot (1999) makes a distinction between performance approach goals and performance avoidance goals. Performance approach goals refer to an orientation towards demonstrating high ability, whereas performance avoidance goals refer to an orientation towards avoiding demonstrating low ability. This suggests that people with performance approach goals are positively motivated to try to do better than others, while those with performance avoidance goals are negatively motivated to try avoiding failure or appearing incompetent.

1.8 Self-reflection

Self-reflection is simply 'thinking over' the data you have gathered. This deceptively simple skill is a key element in the experiential learning cycle. While observation, description, questionnaires and feedback bring our behaviours into conscious awareness, reflection gives them **meaning** and helps to **evaluate** our behaviour and impact on others.

Select areas for reflection and evaluation

How do you decide which areas to reflect on? The areas you choose may be based on:

- **Gathered data.** From your regular observations and descriptions of interpersonal processes, (plus questionnaires, feedback and so on) you identify a pattern of behaviour which does or does not appear to be effective in helping you to achieve your aims.

- **Critical incidents** in which you participated: specific incidents which highlight a given behaviour – for example, by illustrating it particularly clearly, or by eliciting particularly positive or negative outcomes.
- **Examination of goals**. You consider a particular desired outcome or objective which you are or are not (yet) achieving effectively, and identify the behavioural strategies you have been using to pursue it: these may represent potential areas for problem-solving and development.
- **Impressions**: you feel generally satisfied or dissatisfied with your performance in a given area.

Note that the highlighting factors may be positive (indicating a possible strength/opportunity) as well as negative (indicating a possible limitation/threat).

Explore

Reflect on the issues raised by your gathered data in your chosen areas. There is an infinite number of questions you might usefully ask yourself, but as a thought-prompter, you may like to consider:

- your *action tendencies* or patterns of behaviour (how you 'usually' behave or react), and whether you did anything *different* this time;
- what might have *triggered* and *influenced* your behaviour, thoughts or feelings. (Assumptions, perceptions, past experience, expectations? Trait/type preferences?);
- the *outcomes* you wanted from your behaviour – and those you actually got;
- whether the behaviour and its results are the same in all *contexts*, or only in some;
- the *value* and *relevance* of the feedback and assessments you obtained, and how you felt about them;
- any *discrepancies* which emerged between feedback/assessments and your self-perception, and what might account for them.

Incorporate relevant theoretical concepts

Relevant theoretical models and research findings may help you to formulate some ideas as to:

- factors which may be influencing your (and others') behaviour in the situation
- why particular behaviours might be resulting in the observed outcomes
- what you might need or be able to do differently for better outcomes

Theoretical concepts may support or challenge your self perceptions and hypotheses about your behaviours: a useful reality check.

Integrating your practice/observation with theoretical concepts also allows you to move to the next stage of the learning cycle: to draw **conclusions** about your experience. This in turn allows you to **transfer your learning** to different situations. This is the key to genuine learning and on-going development.

Contextualise

This is an opportunity to reflect on the **need** for behavioural change, and its **feasibility**, in the light of:

- your *desired outcomes* and how important they are to you (congruence with your terminal values)
- *opportunities* in the situation, which might be better exploited if you change your behaviour
- *threats* in the situation, which might cause problems if you maintain your present behaviour
- *constraining factors* in the situation which might limit your ability to change your behaviour
- *potential side-effects* of changing your behaviour (impacts on others, change in relationships)
- *restraining factors* within yourself: sources of resistance and reluctance (congruence with instrumental values)

2 LEARNING STYLES

Tell me, and I will forget. Show me, and I may remember. Involve me, and I will understand. - Confucius, 450 B.C.

2.1 Overview of experiential learning

We take in information through our senses, yet we ultimately learn by doing. First, we watch and listen to others. Then we try doing things on our own. This sparks our interest and generates our motivation to self-discover.

Think back to when you learned to ride a bicycle, use a computer, dance, or sing. You took an action, saw the consequences of that action, and chose either to continue, or to take a new and different action. What allowed you to master the new skill was your active participation in the event and your reflection on what you attained. Experience and reflection taught more than any manual or lecture ever could.

2.2 Kolb's experiential learning cycle

Kolb provides one of the most useful descriptive models of the adult learning process available.

The theory presents a cyclical model of learning, consisting of four stages shown below:

- Concrete experience (Do)
- Reflective observation (Observe)
- Abstract conceptualisation (Think)
- Active experimentation (Plan)

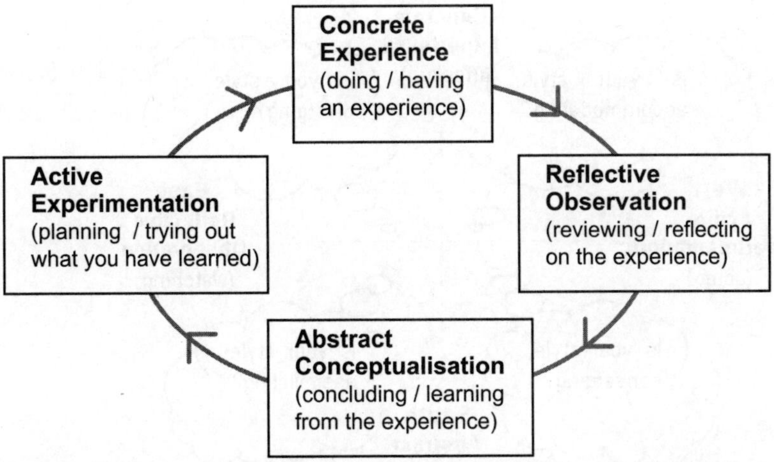

Kolb's four-stage learning cycle shows how experience is translated through reflection into concepts, which in turn are used as guides for active experimentation and the choice of new experiences.

- Concrete experience, either planned or accidental and where the learner actively experiences an activity, is followed by
- Reflection, when the learner consciously reflects back on that experience.
- Abstract conceptualisation is where the learner attempts to conceptualise a theory or model of what is observed.
- Active experimentation is where the learner is trying to plan how to test a model or theory or plan for a forthcoming experience.

Kolb identified four learning styles which correspond to these stages. The styles highlight conditions under which learners learn better. These styles are:

- assimilators, who learn better when presented with sound logical theories to consider
- convergers, who learn better when provided with practical applications of concepts and theories
- accommodators, who learn better when provided with 'hands-on' experience
- divergers, who learn better when allowed to observe and collect a wide range of information.

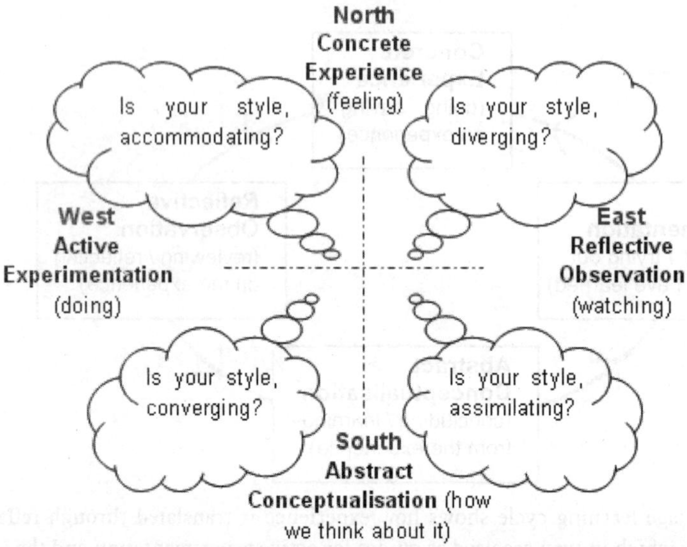

Experiential learning involves doing and puts the learners in an active problem-solving role. It is a form of self-learning which encourages the learners to formulate and commit themselves to their own learning objectives. Kolb sees learning as a continuous cyclical process.

The theory provides useful insights into the nature of learning.

- It demonstrates that there is no end to learning but only another turn of the cycle.
- Learners are not passive recipients but need to actively explore and test the environment.
- It identifies the importance of reflection and internalisation.
- It is a useful way of identifying problems in the learning process.

All this may happen in a flash, or over days, weeks or months, depending on the topic, and there may be a 'wheels within wheels' process at the same time.

Kolb believes that to learn effectively from experience (which includes work placements and practical activities within taught courses) all four stages of the cycle have to be addressed. It doesn't matter where you start on the cycle:

- starting with the activity, and working round to the abstract conceptualisation stage, you would be learning inductively
- starting with theory, and then planning and carrying out some activity, you are working deductively
- if you are observing someone else's activity, drawing conclusions then planning and carrying out your own, then you would be starting at the reflection stage.

2.3 Honey and Mumford's learning styles

Understanding the way that you learn new things - your individual learning style - will help you choose your learning activities to ensure you learn most effectively. This does not mean that you cannot learn from activities that are not specifically suited to your own style - in fact it can be good to choose activities outside your normal style occasionally, to create a balance and help to hone your learning skills.

Kolb (1984) recognised that people tend to have a preference for a particular phase of the cycle, which he identified as a preferred **learning style**.

Honey and Mumford (1992) also noted that 'people vary not just in their learning skills but also in their learning styles. Why otherwise might two people, matched for age, intelligence and need, exposed to the *same* learning opportunity, react so differently?' *Honey and Mumford* formulated a popular classification of learning styles in terms of the attitudes and behaviours which determine an individual's preferred way of learning. They are Activist, Reflector, Theorist and Pragmatist.

Although these are four distinct styles, it is possible that you may have traits from more than one. This is perfectly normal, and means that you will be able to learn well in more than one way. The definitions below will help you to decide which is your preferred style.

If you are an Activist – you will probably want to get involved in a project or specific assignment to develop the skills on the job. Tackling very practical open and flexible learning programmes or activity-based training courses will be most suitable for you.

Activists involve themselves fully and without bias in new experiences. They enjoy the here and now, and are happy to be dominated by immediate experiences. They are open-minded, not sceptical, and this tends to make them enthusiastic about anything new. Their philosophy is: 'I'll try anything once'. They tend to act first and consider the consequences afterwards. Their days are filled with activity. They tackle problems by brainstorming. As soon as the excitement from one activity has died down they are busy looking for the next. They tend to thrive on the challenge of new experiences but are bored with implementation and longer term consolidation. They are gregarious people constantly involving themselves with others but, in doing so, they seek to centre all activities around themselves.

If you are a Reflector – you will appreciate working closely with someone experienced in this area, and learning through observation and discussing your reflections and plans with a mentor. You will also learn much from books, articles and case studies.

Reflectors like to stand back to ponder experiences and observe them from many different perspectives. They collect data, both first hand and from others, and prefer to think about it thoroughly before coming to a conclusion. The thorough collection and analysis of data about experiences and events is what counts so they tend to postpone reaching definitive conclusions for as long as possible. Their philosophy is to be cautious. They are thoughtful people who like to consider all possible angles and implications before making a move. They prefer to take a back seat in meetings and discussions. They enjoy observing other people in action. They listen to others and get the drift of the discussion before making their own points. They tend to adopt a low profile and have a slightly distant, tolerant, unruffled air about them. When they act it is part of a wide picture which includes the past as well as the present and others' observations as well as their own.

If you are a Theorist – you will most value theory-based courses with well-qualified and experienced trainers, well-written books and articles.

Theorists adapt and integrate observations into complex but logically sound theories. They think problems through in a vertical, step-by-step logical way. They assimilate disparate facts into coherent theories. They tend to be perfectionists who won't rest easy until things are tidy and fit into a rational scheme. They like to analyse and synthesise. They are keen on basic assumptions, principles, theories models and systems thinking. Their philosophy prizes rationality and logic. 'If it's logical it's good.'

Questions they frequently ask are: 'Does it make sense?' 'How does this fit with that?' 'What are the basic assumptions?' They tend to be detached, analytical and dedicated to rational objectivity rather than anything subjective or ambiguous. Their approach to problems is consistently logical. This is their 'mental set' and they rigidly reject anything that doesn't fit with it. They prefer to maximise certainty and feel uncomfortable with subjective judgements, lateral thinking and anything flippant.

If you are a Pragmatist – you will find that succinct, practical books and open and flexible learning are good ways of quickly putting new learning to practical use. You will be particularly attracted to working on real-life projects and appreciate the help of someone who can give you some valuable feedback and coaching.

Pragmatists are keen on trying out ideas, theories and techniques to see if they work in practice. They positively search out new ideas and take the first opportunity to experiment with applications. They are the sort of people who return from courses brimming with new ideas that they want to try out in practice. They like to get on with things and act quickly and confidently on ideas that attract them. They tend to be impatient with ruminating and open-ended discussions. They are essentially practical, down to earth people who like making practical decisions and solving problems. They respond to problems and opportunities 'as a challenge'. Their philosophy is 'There is always a better way' and 'If it works it is good'.

Activity 4

Which of the four learning styles identified by Honey and Mumford do you think most closely matches your own? What implications does this have for the way you learn?

2.4 Reflexive modernisation

Ulrick Beck, the German sociologist, argued that we were rapidly entering into a new episode of history where 'simple modernisation' transforms itself into 'reflexive modernisation'. Simple modernisation was characterised by the processes which transformed the 19th century agrarian societies into the industrial societies of the 20th century. Now we witness processes in which the conditions of these classical societies (class, family, neighbourhood, science and democracy) are modernised themselves. This is what Beck calls a 'risk society'. The institutions of modernity are confronted with risks that are their own side effects. For example ecological collapse, global warming, nuclear war, social dislocation, effects of pollution on health or economic system collapse. This is modernity turned back on itself.

The risk society poses new questions and themes for adult education. During the 1970s, when the welfare state reached its peak in the Western world, adult education was aimed at emancipation and the 'empowerment' of people - liberating them from conditions that limited their thinking and acting. In the 1980s we saw a tendency to reduce the impact of these concepts with a 'back to basics' philosophy and adult education reduced to working with deprived groups and developing methods that became closer to social work. What we have now is a world of highly individualistic and consumer-oriented learning. Individual lives are changing and the world of adult learning is being transformed as a result.

In the last few decades there has been a trend in adult education to stress instrumental learning, ie, the transfer of knowledge and skills, giving less attention to fundamental reflection on what is taught. However, predictability and control are no longer the central concepts. The modern information and knowledge society continues to produce escalating quantities of stored cumulative knowledge, but because this knowledge can be stored and retrieved 'outside' the individual, the 'reflexive' forms of knowledge (not know-how but know-how-to-know) are gaining importance. This includes methodological knowledge (knowledge about processes for acquiring, presenting and communicating information), reflexive knowledge (knowledge of how to challenge, criticise, justify and assess the consequences of a concept), as well as personality knowledge (knowledge of how to recognise one's own participation and interpretation in interactions). Unfortunately, most of the educational institutions have not yet begun to take this necessary change into account; planning and teaching still takes place predominantly in material and not in reflexive knowledge categories.

From know-how to know-how-to-know

Material knowledge (know-how)	**Reflexive knowledge (know-how-to-know)**		
Cumulative knowledge Knowledge for storing facts, theories, data etc.	*Methodological knowledge* Knowledge about processes for acquiring, presenting and communicating information.	*Reflexive knowledge* Knowledge of how to challenge, criticise, justify and assess the consequences of a concept.	*Personality knowledge* Knowledge of how to recognise one's own participation and interpretation in interactions.

Contemporary society is also a consumer society where the market transforms individual members of society into consumers who endeavour to satisfy their desires. In other words there can be no market economy unless there are consumers who want to purchase the products that are being produced.

Consequently, it may be seen that education is a form of production whereas learning is a form of consumption. This has tremendous implications for the future of established providers. In a world of unbounded adult learning, the role of the specialised adult education institution with its workforce of specialised teachers is far from clear. Now it is possible to learn everything you want to know by purchasing your own multi-media personal computer and surfing the web, watching the television learning zone programmes, buying your own 'teach yourself' books and magazines and even purchasing your own self-directed learning courses. Increasingly, people across the world are being exposed to global events, as informational technology penetrates more cultures.

Activity 5 **(30 minutes)**

Think about a learning experience that you are planning to undertake to demonstrate self-managed learning in a professional context.

(a) How will the learning activity relate to the four stages of Kolb's learning cycle?

(b) In carrying out the learning, what styles of learning will you concentrate on in terms of Honey and Mumford's activist, theorist, pragmatist, reflector classification?

(c) What do you see as the principal advantages and drawback of employing your chosen approach?

3 APPROACHES TO LEARNING

3.1 Facilitating learning

Training and development methods vary tremendously depending on the person, the job, the resources, the organisation and the economic environment. You can divide them into on-the-job and off-the-job training methods, structured or unstructured, participatory or self development, sitting in front of a computer screen or 'sitting with Nellie'. The methods that you might be looking at include: training courses, both external and in-house; on-the-job training; mentoring; coaching; computerised interactive learning; planned experiences; and self-managed learning.

3.2 Learning through research

An important part of modern independent learning is the ability to use the Internet because it can provide up-to-the-minute data from a range of sources. It is an invaluable source of research information.

Krol and Ferguson *(The Whole Internet)* suggest that 'Once you're connected to the Internet, you have instant access to an almost indescribable wealth of information. Through electronic mail and bulletin boards [newsgroups] you can use a different kind of resource: a worldwide supply of knowledgeable people, some of whom are bound to share your interests, no matter how obscure'.

A Personal Learning Environment is comprised of all the different Internet tools we can use for learning. Many of these tools will be based on social software - a type of software that lets people rendezvous, connect or collaborate by use of a computer network. It supports networks of people, content and services that are more adaptable and responsive to changing needs and goals.

Social software adapts to its environment, instead of requiring its environment to adapt to software. It underpins what is loosely referred to as Web 2.0 technologies. Whereas

Web 1 was largely implemented as a push technology - to allow access to information on a dispersed basis, Web 2.0 is a two way process, allowing the Internet to be used for creating and sharing information and knowledge, rather than merely accessing external artefacts.

Social software is increasingly being used in education and training through such applications as web logs, wikis, tools and applications for creating and sharing multi media and tools for sharing all kinds of different personal knowledge bases including bookmarks and book collections.

Social software offers the opportunity for narrowing the divide between producers and consumers. Consumers become producers, through creating and sharing. One implication is the potential for a new ecology of 'open' content, books, learning materials and multi media, through learners themselves becoming producers of learning materials.

Social software has already led to widespread adoption of portfolios for learners bringing together learning from different contexts and sources of learning and providing an on-going record of lifelong learning, capable of expression in different forms.

Examples of the software you can use for your personal learning environment include a word processor, an e-mail client for communication, a Web browser, search engines, a diary for managing work and sharing with others, audio for making podcasts, video editor for making multi media presentations, a content management system for creating web sites, a photo editing programme and sharing service, instant messaging and VOIP and a number of other services from different social software companies. And, of course, the operating system itself for managing and storing files - a lot of software.

3.3 Learning from others

Coaches and mentors both work one-on-one, but mentors tend to offer specific content as well as contacts, while coaches focus on processes to support clients in doing their own learning.

Coaching can be defined as 'bringing out the best in a person, improving a person's skills'. It is a specialised form of communication, which is useful when there is a need to extend the depth and range of an employee's knowledge very quickly for reasons which may range from the introduction of new techniques to the need to train for a particular job, perhaps on the unexpected retirement of the present job holder.

A coach is concerned with deep personal and professional development - the emphasis is on personal. The most effective coaches are external to the company, where they are independent of organisational pressure and political influence and free to offer more-or-less objective counsel and guidance. It is difficult to create the necessary confidential space and trust with an executive if his or her coaching relationship is embedded within the organisation's formal structure.

Mentoring is a process where one person offers help, guidance, advice and support to facilitate the learning or development of another. It is used by organisations to show junior employees how things are done. The mentor is expected to guide the new recruit through a development programme and 'socialise' them into the culture of the enterprise. It is a route for bringing on 'high flyers' by allowing them to make mistakes under supervision. Mentoring focuses on learning and offers support for the learner through the learning process to maximise learning. It is a good way of breaking down internal barriers between departments or groups and promoting equal opportunities.

The mentor provides continuous personal support and motivation, helping the learner to solve real problems and make real decisions.

The benefits to the learner	The benefits to the organisation
• opportunity to learn from role model • integration of work activities with learning and development • quicker learning about the way the organisation works • greater clarity of development goals • increased self confidence from feedback • insight into senior management roles • access to sources not usually available	• development of staff for more senior roles • supports introduction and implementation of change • breaks down barriers that can deter individual progress • introduces self managed learning • helps develop skills outside the usual sphere of practice • breaks down occupational barriers • helps personal and professional development • supports high potential managers on educational programmes.

3.4 Secondments

A secondment is where an employee temporarily changes job roles within the same company or transfers to another organisation for an agreed period of time. This can be within the private or public sector, or to a non-profit making organisation, such as a charity or government body, and usually last between 3 to 24 months.

Secondments within an external organisation can range from management staff being seconded to an external company to give them experience of managing a different organisation, to technical staff taking secondments with suppliers or customers to gain experience of the supply chain.

Secondments benefit all parties involved; the employee, the employer and the host organisation.

- Employees benefit from taking secondments as they are an excellent way to explore different career possibilities without them leaving their current job. They are a valuable way of offering employees professional development and career opportunities, especially within flat organisational structures where promotion may be limited.

  Professional placements give employees the opportunity of acquiring new skills whilst continuing their employment with the same organisation. They often acquire valuable experiences whilst on placement and generally gain a broader outlook.

  Taking a secondment also demonstrates an employee's flexibility and adaptability, both of which are desirable qualities to future employers. Most importantly secondments give employees the opportunity to improve their career possibilities by developing their CVs.

- Employers benefit from allowing employees to take secondments in many ways. Employees that have taken a secondment acquire transferable skills and knowledge that they can put into practice once they return to their original position. These skills can then be communicated across the team and other departments within the organisation to improve and enhance the skill set of other staff.

Secondments also give the organisation the opportunity to build a wider network if the secondment is taken in an external company.

- Host organisations also benefit where the employee is taking a secondment in an external organisation. The main benefit to them is that they gain assistance with projects, usually from skilled personnel. They also get an external perspective and transferable skills from person on secondment, which can be beneficial for the project and the organisation.

3.5 Interviews

You know from your own experience what an interview is, but if you had to define it, you might call it a **planned interaction** at work, characterised by **objectives**. It is conducted in order to achieve a specific **purpose** for at least one of the parties involved, such as information gathering, problem solving or behaviour change.

An interview must be **planned** if it is to be effective. An agenda can be drawn up on the basis of objectives, and should be structured with an introductory phase, main body and concluding phase. Knowing what the opening will be (to start the interview off fluently), and knowing what you want from the close (to achieve objectives) are as important as drafting questions and topics for the main part of the interview.

An interview is an interaction, not a monologue.

(a) During an investigation, the interviewer must ask questions that elicit useful answers and listen to them.

(b) Interviews usually involve interaction between people in their roles as, for instance, representative and customer, superior and subordinate. In addition, there is a role difference between interviewer and interviewee: the interviewer should take control of proceedings.

(c) The degree of formality in the interview will depend on the circumstances and personalities involved, but the interaction of roles implies some formality in the work context. The fine line between formality and tension will need to be managed.

First of all, the **objectives** of the interview must be determined. The basic framework of the interview can then be planned, with ideas for any points that must be made or information that must be obtained or given; there should be enough flexibility, however, so that the interviewer can listen and respond to the interviewee's input and questions where relevant. It is particularly important to anticipate how the interviewee will react at the start of the interview and at key stages during it, and how the interviewer's approach may have to be modified as a result.

There may be some **preparation** to do for the content of the interview: information to be gathered on the interviewee or the topic under discussion. Interviews for appraisal, grievance and discipline require considerable prior information and thought if they are to be handled constructively.

Physical preparations include obtaining suitable time and accommodation for the interview, usually somewhere private and free from distraction. The setting can be imposing and intimidating or informal and reassuring, as can the physical appearance of the interviewer.

The purpose of the interview should be clearly laid out as a preliminary to engaging in any discussion.

The tone and atmosphere of the interview will also be established by the first impressions the parties have of each other, and the interviewer's opening remarks. The interviewer should clarify the purpose of the interview. It is usually desirable to put the interviewee at ease, but the interviewer's strategy may be to maintain or even increase the tension, perhaps to test a candidate under pressure, to underline the seriousness of a disciplinary interview, or to assert control in other situations.

In less extreme conditions, even the desk alone can distance the interviewer from the interviewee. If this is felt to be undesirable, for example in a customer interview, the physical setting may be changed or the interviewer may take particular care to set a positive, supportive and welcoming tone in opening the interview.

Ask the right questions. Listen to the answers.

Questions should be paced and put carefully. The interviewer should not try to confuse the interviewee; nor should he allow the interviewee to digress or gloss over important points. The interviewer must retain control over the information-gathering process.

Open questions should be used, so that interviewees have to put together their own responses in complete sentences. This is a lot more revealing than using **closed questions** which invite 'yes' or 'no' answers. **Closed questions** have several disadvantages.

(a) They elicit answers only to the question asked: there may be other questions and issues that have been anticipated but will emerge if the interviewee is given the chance to speak.

(b) They do not allow interviewees to express their personalities so that interaction can take place on a deeper level.

(c) They make it easier for interviewees to conceal things ('you never asked me....')

(d) They make the interviewer work very hard.

The interviewer should not ask **leading questions**, giving the interviewee ideas about how to respond: the response may be adjusted to please or impress.

The interviewer must listen to and evaluate the responses, to distinguish between what the interviewee wants to say; is trying not to say; is saying but doesn't mean, or is lying about and is having difficulty saying. It is also necessary to distinguish between what the interviewer needs and does not need to know.

Interviewers must also be **self aware**. They must recognise when they are being told what they wish to hear and ensure that their own attitudes do not colour their perception of what interviewees say.

Non-verbal signals or body language should also be taken as relevant feedback. The interviewer should look for signs of stress (nervous movements, pallor), dishonesty (failure to meet the eye), irritation (frown, tapping foot), positive response (smile, nod, leaning forward) and so on. The interviewer can also *use* non-verbal signs to create a desired impression (smart appearance, smile, firm handshake) and to provide feedback (raised eyebrow, encouraging nod).

A **summary of proceedings or findings** is usually a good way of confirming information, signalling the extent to which objectives have been achieved, and 'winding down' the interview towards closure. If a decision is required, it should be given: but only if the interviewee has the authority and has acquired the information to do so. The general 'position' of the parties should be clarified, especially if a compromise or agreement has been reached, or if one or both parties is not yet satisfied. Further action required should be agreed or communicated to the interviewee. A courteous closure (handshake, goodbye) should end the proceedings.

Once the interviewee has left, the interviewer should complete a permanent record of the interview and initiate any actions agreed at or required by the interview.

3.6 Seminars and conferences

A seminar is a lecture or presentation delivered to an audience on a particular topic or set of topics that are educational in nature. It is usually held for groups of 10-50 individuals. A seminar is frequently held at a hotel meeting space or within an office conference room.

A conference is a type of meeting held between members of often disparate organisations to discuss matters of mutual interest. Conferences are held for a variety of reasons, including resolving problems, making decisions, developing cooperation, and publicising ideas, products, and services. They may take place within an organisation but often draw people together regionally, nationally, or internationally, and involve a large number of speakers and delegates. Many conferences are organised for commercial profit.

It is quite difficult to distinguish between certain types of meetings. They include conference, forum, congress, symposium, seminar, and workshop.

- A workshop would usually be a relatively small/intimate event with some sense of involvement by all in creating something particular such as a new policy or a solution to an issue.
- A forum suggests some sort of discussion/talking point/learning from other people in the same field.
- Congress sounds grand and very academic.
- Conference covers a multitude of types and fields.
- A symposium suggests that more than one person is speaking.
- A seminar is often one person giving perhaps an hour-long lecture, although there could be more than one speaker.

3.7 Internet, Intranets and Extranets

The **Internet** is a global network of computers accessed with the aid of a modem. It includes Web sites, e-mail, newsgroups, and other forums. It is a public network, although many of the computers connected to it are also part of intranets. It uses the Internet Protocol (IP) as a communication standard.

An **intranet** is a private computer network that uses Internet Protocol technologies to securely share any part of an organisation's information or network operating system within that organisation. The term is used in contrast to *internet*, a network between organisations, and instead refers to a network within an organisation. Sometimes the term refers only to the organisation's internal website, but may be a more extensive part of the organisation's information technology infrastructure. It may host multiple private websites and constitute an important component and focal point of internal communication and collaboration.

Intranets are used for:

- Performance data: linked to sales, inventory, job progress and other database and reporting systems, enabling employees to process and analyse data to fulfil their work objectives.
- Employment information: online policy and procedures manuals (health and safety, disciplinary and grievance), training and induction material, internal contacts for help and information.
- Employee support/information: advice on first aid, healthy working at computer terminals, training courses offered and resources held in the corporate library and so on.
- Notice boards for the posting of message to and from employees: notice of meetings, events and trade union activities.
- Departmental home pages: information and news about each department's personnel and activities to aid identification and cross-functional understanding.
- Bulletins or newsletters: details of product launches and marketing campaigns, staff moves, changes in company policy – or whatever might be communicated through the print equivalent, plus links to relevant databases or departmental home pages.
- E-mail facilities for the exchange of messages, memos and reports between employees in different locations.
- Upward communication: suggestion schemes, feedback questionnaires.
- Individual personnel files, to which employees can download training materials, references, certificates and appraisals.

An **extranet** is a private network that uses Internet technology and the public telecommunication system to securely share part of a business's information or operations with suppliers, vendors, partners, customers, or other businesses. An extranet can be viewed as part of a company's intranet that is extended to users outside the company.

Whereas an intranet resides behind a firewall and is accessible only to people who are members of the same company or organisation, an extranet provides various levels of accessibility to outsiders.

Only those outsiders with a valid username and password can access an extranet, with varying levels of access rights enabling control over what people can view. Extranets are becoming a very popular means for business partners to exchange information. They can share data or systems to provide smoother transaction processing and more efficient services for customers.

An extranet may be used to:

- provide a 'pooled' service which a number of business partners can access.
- exchange news which is of use to partner companies and clients.
- share training or development resources.

3.8 Newsgroups

A Usenet newsgroup operates rather like a free public notice board with access to lots of up-to-date research information. If you post an item on the 'notice board' everyone who uses that particular newsgroup can read it. They can post a reply or email you personally but you cannot tell who reads your messages unless they post a reply. The amount of time an item stays on the notice board depends on the news provider's system. You will also find discussion groups which are referred to by different names such as bulleting boards, e-groups and forums. Like newsgroups they allow you to post notices for others to read. Thousands of these are indexed at www.tile.net/lists/

3.9 Bulletin boards

A bulletin board system (BBS) is a computer or an application dedicated to the sharing or exchange of messages or other files on a network. Originally an electronic version of the type of bulletin board found on the wall in many kitchens and work places, the BBS was used to post simple messages between users. The BBS became the primary kind of online community through the 1980s and early 1990s, before the World Wide Web arrived.

Most bulletin boards are devoted to a particular subject, although some are more general in nature. Despite the vastly greater reach of the Internet, the bulletin board system is still fairly common in parts of the world where the Internet is less established and is still valued by many with Internet access for its ability to foster a sense of community.

4 EFFECTIVE LEARNING

4.1 Personal assessment

Learning has happened when people can demonstrate that they know something that they did not know before (insights and realisations as well as facts) and/or when they can do something they could not do before (skills).

Effective learning focuses on **how** we learn. It means:

- recognising the importance of 'achieved' learning
- understanding the learning process - the learning cycle and learning style preferences
- taking best advantage of learning opportunities

- creating and implementing a personal development plan
- encouraging and managing a learning culture

For effective learning to take place it is essential that activities are well planned with clear objectives and time schedules. Activities need to be well organised in a clear structure designed to achieve learning objectives. Finally the learning that takes place needs to be evaluated. What have you learned? What have you learned about yourself? For example, are you a good planner, a good organiser? What is your preferred learning style? What improvements could you make to your planning and organising?

4.2 Planning

You should plan to focus on learning in more than one way. Instead of just reading a book or listening to a podcast, which involves auditory learning, find a way to rehearse the information both verbally and visually. This might involve describing what you learned to a friend, taking notes or drawing a mind map. Educators have long noted that one of the best ways to learn something is to teach it to someone else. Start by translating the information into your own words. This process alone helps solidify new knowledge in your brain. Next, find some way to share what you have learned. Some ideas include writing a blog post, creating a podcast or participating in a group discussion. By learning in more than one way, you are further cementing the knowledge in your mind. The more regions of the brain that store data about a subject, the more interconnection there is. This cross-referencing of data means you have learned, rather than just memorised.

Another great way to become a more effective learner is to use relational learning, which involves relating new information to things that you already know. For example, if you are learning about Romeo and Juliet, you might associate what you learn about the play with prior knowledge you have about Shakespeare, the historical period in which the author lived and other relevant information.

For many of us, learning typically involves reading textbooks, attending lectures or doing research in the library or on the Web. While seeing information and then writing it down is important, actually putting new knowledge and skills into practice can be one of the best ways to improve learning. If you are trying to acquire a new skill or ability, focus on gaining practical experience. If it is a sport or athletic skill, perform the activity on a regular basis. If you are learning a new language, practice speaking with another person and surround yourself with immersive experiences.

4.3 Evaluation

While it may seem that spending more time studying is one of the best ways to maximise learning, research has demonstrated that taking tests actually helps you remember what you have learned, even if it was not covered on the test. Students who had extra time to study but were not tested had significantly lower recall of the materials.

Another great strategy for improving your learning efficiency is to recognise your learning habits and styles. There are a number of different theories about learning styles, which can all help you gain a better understanding of how you learn best. Howard Gardner's theory of multiple intelligences describes seven different types of intelligence that can help reveal your individual strengths.

Intelligence type	Capability and perception
Linguistic	words and language (as in a poet)
Logical-Mathematical	logic and numbers (as in a scientist)
Musical	music, sound, rhythm (as in a composer)
Bodily-kinesthetic	body movement control (as in an athlete or dancer)
Spatial-Visual	images and space (as in a sculptor or airplane pilot)
Interpersonal	other people's feelings (as in a salesman or teacher
Intrapersonal	self-awareness (exhibited by individuals with accurate views of themselves)

Intelligence is a mixture of several abilities (Gardner explains seven intelligences, and alludes to others) that are all of great value in life. But nobody is good at them all. In life we need people who collectively are good at different things. A well-balanced world, and well-balanced organisations and teams, are necessarily comprised of people who possess different mixtures of intelligences.

Gardner was one of the first to teach us that we should not judge and develop people (especially children, young people, and people at the beginnings of their careers) according to an arbitrary and narrow definition of intelligence. We must instead rediscover and promote the vast range of capabilities that have a value in life and organisations, and then set about valuing people for who they are, what they can be, and helping them to grow and fulfil their potential.

5 LIFELONG LEARNING

5.1 Self-directed learning

Lifelong learning is a broad concept involving an individual's education that is flexible, diverse and available at different times and places throughout life. The scale of current economic and social change, the rapid transition to a knowledge-based society, and demographic pressures resulting from an ageing population in Europe are all challenges which demand a new approach to education and training, within the framework of lifelong learning.

Self-directed learning is based on the principle that people learn and retain more if they find things out for themselves. Harrison (1992) emphasises the need to create a climate of awareness about the opportunities for learning and development and to design training events to develop training styles and skills.

In particular, the organisation can encourage self-directed learning by ensuring that learners:

- Define for themselves, with whatever guidance they may require, what they need to know to perform their job effectively.
- Are given guidance on where they can get the material or information which will help them learn.
- Prepare a learning plan and programme as part of a learning contract.

- Prepare a personal development plan setting out what they need to learn, how they should develop and the actions they need to take to achieve learning and development goals.

5.2 Continuing professional development

Continuing Professional Development (CPD) is a part of the lifelong learning process. It is the systematic and continuous updating, maintenance and enhancement of your professional and personal skills. It will generally, although not exclusively, walk hand in hand with your personal development plans. Personal development plans will identify training gaps and needs but other unexpected opportunities may come up which will also contribute towards CPD.

Learning and development becomes planned, rather than accidental.

- CPD is **continuing** because learning never ceases, regardless of age or seniority.
- It is **professional** because it is focused on personal competence in a professional role.
- It is concerned with **development** because its goal is to improve personal performance and enhance career progression and is much wider than just formal training courses.

Planning, recording and reflecting are the real key to successful CPD so before starting you will need to decide the means of recording your plan and achievements that will suit you best. Remember, as important as record keeping is, it is only a means to an end. It is the process of planning, reviewing, learning and reflecting that matters, not the particular method or format you adopt. However, the very process of writing will help to distil experiences, recognise patterns and discern trends. It enables you to remember what has gone before and capture lessons for the future. It also becomes a valuable and objective measure of your professional competence and, as such, it can be useful when preparing for staff appraisals or tailoring your CV for a specific promotion or career move.

It is important to keep records in two key areas.

(a) A **personal development plan** – this looks ahead and sets out your objectives and the action and activities you plan to take to achieve them.

(b) A **record of achievements** – this is a full record of the action and activities you have undertaken, together with their respective outcomes.

Your records demonstrate you have thoroughly reflected on your accomplishments to date, carefully assessed your present situation and coherently planned your future professional development.

5.3 Linking higher education with industry

There are three ways in which higher education links with and supports industry and national economic performance:

(a) Supply of highly qualified people - the higher education system is the major source of supply for industry and the economy of highly qualified personnel. Some industries, that are heavily dependent on supplies of graduates from particular disciplines, work together with educational institutions to obtain a more secure source of supply through sponsorship of students, sharing of costs and integration of industrial experience within courses such as sandwich courses.

(b) Research and development - with their breadth and depth of technical and professional knowledge, universities and colleges are uniquely well-placed to assist industry in carrying out applied research. More widely, consultancy work in sales and marketing, design, finance and administrative systems is a mainstay of higher education. Research work carried out by higher education institutions for industry is not confined to the largest institutions or the largest firms. Some higher education institutions are specifically targeting their consultancy efforts on medium sized firms which cannot hope to carry out the work in-house.

(c) Technology transfer - links between companies and specific higher education institutions. In the UK, the government have funded a network of **Regional Technology Centres (RTCs)** based on collaborative ventures between companies and higher education institutions. These centres aim to provide an effective information and training support system for emerging and rapidly developing technologies.

Science parks, with their formal and operational links with a university, college or major research centre, also play an active role in technology transfer.

5.4 Further education

Further education (FE) covers the types of education that go beyond what has been achieved in compulsory education, but which are not at degree level (Higher Education). Typically, further education includes A levels, AS levels and vocational qualifications.

16 and 19 year olds make up the largest group of people in further education, but many other people undertake full-time or part-time further education.

The further education sector includes:

- Further education colleges, sixth form colleges and specialist colleges
- Work based learning providers - organisations who deliver learning in the workplace, 'on the job' or in a training centre
- Adult and community learning providers - organisations who deliver learning through a local authority or voluntary organisation, or in a community setting
- Offender learning providers

Activity 6 **(10 minutes)**

Find out where your nearest Regional Technology Centre is and how it links higher education and industry.

5.5 Recognition of Prior Learning (RPL)

As the value of learning (as opposed to formally recognised education and training) is increasingly recognised through the promotion of lifelong learning, social inclusion, wider participation and employability, it has been increasingly acknowledged that adults have 'prior learning' that is of value to individuals, companies and society at large.

Prior learning can be learning acquired formally, non-formally and/or informally. However, it is learning that has not been fully acknowledged or accredited. Subject to reflection, articulation and/or accreditation this learning may be recognised and/or accredited. This recognition might take the form of awarding credits that count towards a qualification, or it might refer to a simple acknowledgement that such learning has taken place, thereby allowing the learner to be admitted to a programme of study or employment.

- **Accreditation of Prior Experiential Learning** (APEL) is the process by which non-certificated learning achieved in a range of learning contexts is recognised in relation to meeting the credit requirements for a qualification. This would include all cases where evidence of learning is available – for example from the workplace or from voluntary/community work – but no qualification has been achieved. In this process, credit is awarded in relation to the qualification in recognition of learning achievement and learners do not have to repeat the units for which equivalent achievement has already been demonstrated. It will therefore contribute to the credits that learners require to complete the qualification. Evidence of learning must be included in the learner's portfolio and mapped against one or more units within the qualification.

- **Recognition of Prior Certificated Learning** – also referred to as Exemption - is the process through which previously assessed and certificated learning is recognised as meeting the requirements for the achievement of a qualification. This would include all cases where an award or qualification has been achieved and a certificate awarded through a recognised awarding body. Where previous learning has already been certificated, no credit is awarded in relation to the qualification, but learners are exempted from relevant credit requirements. It will not therefore contribute to the credits that learners require to achieve the qualification.

If a provider does wish for allowance to be made for prior learning, this request must be highlighted at the beginning of the programme so that the external moderator can be advised. The external moderator will then need to see the relevant certificate(s) (for exemption) and/or evidence of the previous non-certificated learning mapped against the unit(s) (for APEL).

Activity 7 **(15 minutes)**

What are the benefits of recognising prior learning?

5.6 Apprenticeships

Apprenticeship programmes can be designed to include structured opportunities for learning on and off-the-job. The 'dual system' operated in Germany is perhaps the best known example of this approach. In the UK, apprenticeships which offer this model are most commonly found in sectors such as engineering that have a long-standing history of apprenticeship provision, and which include day or block release at college to pursue vocational qualifications. At its best apprenticeship represents an integrated model of work, study and qualifications which can foster progression, including higher education. A key component of the provision made available in such programmes is the existence of an employee with training and supervisory experience who has responsibility for supporting the young person's 'learning journey' and for developing links between the on- and off-the-job components.

Unfortunately, the government supported apprenticeship programme available in the UK (known as the Modern Apprenticeship), is not always committed to providing such an opportunity. The central reason for this is that the National Vocational Qualification that Modern Apprentices are obliged to pursue is a competence-based certificate delivered in the workplace. This award is rarely accepted as sufficient for university entrance. Sectors, such as engineering, which include attendance at college to enable young people to obtain the knowledge-based qualifications that are necessary for career progression and access to higher level educational opportunities, go beyond the Modern Apprenticeship's mandatory requirements. In so doing, they provide an example of how combining the opportunity to learn at work and formal study offers a platform for progression and a foundation for lifelong learning.

There are more than 180 Apprenticeships available in approximately 80 sectors of industry and commerce. These range from accountancy to football, engineering to veterinary nursing, business administration to construction.

There are two levels of Modern Apprenticeship available - standard and advanced:

- **Standard apprenticeships** are equivalent to five good GCSE passes. Apprentices work towards a work-based learning qualification such as a National Vocational Qualification to Level 2, Key Skills, and in some cases a relevant technical certificate.
- **Advanced Apprenticeships** are equivalent to two A-level passes. Apprentices work towards a work-based learning qualification such as a National Vocational Qualification to Level 3, Key Skills, and in some cases a relevant technical certificate.

5.7 Credit Accumulation and Transfer Scheme (CATS)

Credit Accumulation and Transfer Scheme (CATS) is used by many universities in the UK to monitor, record and reward passage through a modular degree course and to facilitate movement between courses and institutions. Typically a university course of 10 to 20 2-hour sessions would, on successful completion, be worth between 10 and 20 CATS points, at one of Levels 1 to 3.

To qualify for an honours degree 360 points need to be accumulated (240 points at level 2 or above and 120 points at level 3). A foundation degree is broadly equivalent to 240 points, and a 'pass/ordinary degree' equivalent to 300 points. A postgraduate Master's degree is equivalent to 180 points at Level M.

6 ASSESSMENT OF LEARNING

6.1 Learning achievements and disappointments

Specifying assessment measures and carrying out some form of assessment are integral parts of the agreement set up with the company or of your own self-managed learning plan. Assessment enables progress to be evaluated and success to be recognised and rewarded. The methods of assessment include demonstration of the skill, written report, witness statements and feedback, products and outcomes and interviews. The actual method will depend on the particular agreement and also the context in which it is undertaken

The learning cycle represents an ongoing process of learning and development. Our experience forms the basis for reviewing, drawing conclusions and planning future learning. Learning can arise just as easily from lack of success as from succeeding in activities. Failure is a word that has an unfortunate negative meaning associated with it. Who would wish to have the word applied to them? However, failure nearly always brings with it the opportunity to learn. It is only when failure is not used for learning that there is really true failure. Alternative words to failure include stall, cessation and discontinuance. These words imply that some event or progress has not taken place. In many situations when you find out that something you set out to accomplish does not work out as planned, you have the opportunity to learn not only how you might have set about it differently but also how you might act in future situations. It is called learning from experience.

6.2 Improved ability range with personal learning

The following diagram is based on the learner completing a self-assessment questionnaire using 'learning power' profiles, which are automatically generated in the form of a spider diagram (Harlen and Deakin-Crick 2002). These locate the individual's average score on each learning dimension along the 'leg' of the spider. This form of feedback suggests a profile of the whole person with many parts, rather than a set of scores that imply a pass or a fail. For this reason no numbers are given to the scores.

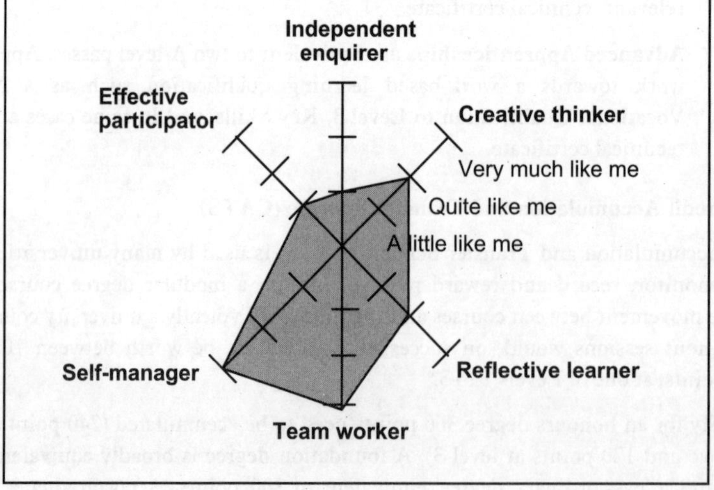

6.3 Feedback

Feedback is simply communication which offers information to an individual or group about how their behaviour is *perceived* by the feedback-giver and how it *affects* him or her.

The purpose of feedback is to help people learn by increasing their awareness of what they do, how they do it and its impact on other people. Learners need to know how well or how poorly their learning is proceeding, where they might be going wrong, and in what ways and what aspects of their learning can be improved.

There are two main types of feedback, both of which are valuable in enhancing performance and development.

- **Motivational feedback** is used to reward and reinforce positive behaviours and performance by praising and encouraging the individual. Its purpose is to increase *confidence.*
- **Developmental feedback** is given when a particular area of performance needs to be improved, helping the individual to identify what needs to be changed and how this might be done. Its purpose is to increase *competence.*

Motivational feedback may contribute to people's development. They may not realise all the skills they have, and receiving positive feedback on performance may help to highlight areas of under-utilised potential.

Constructive feedback is designed to widen options and encourage development. This does *not* mean giving only positive or 'encouraging' feedback about what a person did well: feedback about undesirable behaviours and their effects, given skilfully, is in many ways more useful.

Activity 8 **(15 minutes)**

Aim: to help you to identify areas of difficulty in giving feedback.

Instructions: Consider a situation in the past when you have had to give feedback to someone about their performance or behaviour.

(a) How did you feel about it?

(b) What do you think makes giving:

- positive feedback on good performance and
- negative feedback on poor performance

difficult for you (and others)?

Characteristics of constructive feedback:

- **Informative** - identifying strengths, weaknesses and ways to improve
- **Criterion-referenced** - relating to subject objectives
- **Motivating** - giving encouragement whenever possible
- **Timely** - as soon as possible

Although feedback is often thought of as being given in response to assessment, there are many forms of feedback on learning, which do not relate to assessment at all, ranging from feedback on work in progress (eg. during lab work) to more generic feedback on how effective a student is performing their studies overall (end of year study advice). This paper, however, concentrates on providing feedback on assessment, both coursework and exams.

Feedback on assessment can be given to sum up the final judgement of the quality of the work (summative feedback), or to help improve the student's work in future (formative feedback). A further, but in higher education less common, form of feedback helps the learners identify their aptitude and ability for a particular kind of learning (diagnostic feedback).

6.4 Difference between feedback and assessment

There is a difference between feedback and assessment. Giving feedback to subordinates is similar to assessing their performance, but different in several important ways. Both require subordinates to do something e.g., remember, recognise, design or process. Both also apply criteria and standards to performance in order to evaluate the quality of their work. However, assessment stops at that point and simply announces the results of the assessment to the subordinate eg, 'you have passed' or 'you got a C' or whatever the grading format calls for.

Feedback differs from assessment in three ways:

(a) In feedback, the manager and the subordinate engage in dialogue about what distinguishes successful from unsuccessful performance ie, they talk about criteria and standards.

(b) In feedback, the subordinate performance is done without grading consequences. In this sense, he or she is in a 'practice situation'.

(c) Feedback is done for two purposes that are different from the primary purpose of assessment:

(i) It is done primarily to enhance the quality of subordinate performance – not to grade that performance.

(ii) It also has the potential to help subordinates learn how to assess their own performance in the future.

Feedback relates closely to goal setting. Goals serve as targets for performance. When employees understand how they are attaining those goals, they can adjust their behaviour to perform more. Recognition, praise and encouragement create feelings of confidence, competence, development and progress that enhance the motivation to learn.

Chapter roundup

- In self managed learning the individual takes the initiative and the responsibility for what occurs. Individuals select, manage, and assess their own learning activities, which can be pursued at any time, in any place, through any means, at any age.
- An approach to self-development based on increasing self-awareness allows managers to take responsibility for relevant, flexible and continuous experiential learning. It can be expressed as a learning cycle, incorporating four stages: having an experience; reviewing the experience; concluding from the experience; planning the next steps.
- Kolb's experiential learning cycle presents a cyclical model of learning, consisting of four stages: concrete experience reflective observation, abstract conceptualisation and active experimentation.
- Kolb identified four learning styles which correspond to the four-stage learning cycle: they are assimilators, convergers, accommodators and divergers.
- People tend to have a preference for a particular phase or phases on the learning cycle, or a preferred learning style(s). Honey and Mumford (1992) identify four learning styles: Activist, Reflector, Theorist and Pragmatist.
- To get the best from any development plan for the future it is wise to know the current situation. A SWOT analysis is a simple way to do this: SWOT is an acronym for Strengths, Weaknesses, Opportunities and Threats.
- The acronym S.M.A.R.T. outlines the set of criteria that your goal must follow in order for it to be a well-focused and achievable goal.
- Learning approaches vary tremendously depending on the person, the job, the resources, the organisation and the economic environment. The methods that you might be looking at include: learning through research, learning from others, mentoring/coaching, seminars, conferences, interviews, use of the Internet, social networks, use of bulletin boards and newsgroups.
- Continuing Professional Development (CPD) is a part of the lifelong learning process. It is the systematic and continuous updating, maintenance and enhancement of your professional and personal skills.
- As the value of learning is increasingly recognised through the promotion of lifelong learning, social inclusion, wider participation and employability, it has been increasingly acknowledged that adults have 'prior learning' that is of value to individuals, companies and society at large.
- The learning cycle represents an ongoing process of learning and development. Our experience forms the basis for reviewing, drawing conclusions and planning future learning. Learning can arise just as easily from lack of success as from succeeding in activities.

Answers to activities

1 Self-managed learning is characterised by the employee taking the initiative to learn new skills.

2 Examples of strengths and weaknesses:

Strengths	Weaknesses
Compulsive Strong follow-through Articulate Write well Balanced work-life perspective Many interests Ambitious	Strong need to 'get things done and off my list' with consequence of getting it done right away, thereby undermining the benefits of more careful deliberation over time. Stress of many tasks and need to do each carefully can lead me to think unkindly about the people and/or the circumstance creating the task. Can be impatient - suffer fools poorly. Time pressure causes stress and can lead to emotional 'hijacking'.

3 Examples of opportunities and threats

Opportunities	Threats
To engage others in providing feedback about their experience of me To receive coaching in service of improving my leadership skills To learn from others in similar roles to mine To enhance my ability to manage the need to complete task quickly in order to be able to deliberate more carefully	Time pressure, which can derail my plan for self-improvement because it catapults me back to my 'usual' habits The multitude of everyday demands, which conspires against self-reflection

4 **If you are an Activist -** you will probably want to get involved in a project or specific assignment to develop the skills on the job. Tackling very practical open and flexible learning programmes or activity-based training courses will be most suitable for you.

If you are a Reflector - you will appreciate working closely with someone experienced in this area, and learning through observation and discussing your reflections and plans with a mentor. You will also learn much from books, articles and case studies.

If you are a Theorist - you will most value theory-based courses with well-qualified and experienced trainers, well-written books and articles.

If you are a Pragmatist - you will find that succinct, practical books and open and flexible learning are good ways of quickly putting new learning to practical use. You will be particularly attracted to working on real-life projects and appreciate the help of someone who can give you some valuable feedback and coaching.

5 There is no 'answer' to this activity – other than to attempt it.

6 According to their Web site, the Farnborough centre helps businesses of all sizes by:

- identifying skills gaps within companies and providing Information, Advice and Guidance on how to fill these gaps
- providing funding to enable companies to further the professional development of their employees
- liaising with local commercial and academic institutions and recommending suitable long and short courses and training
- building, funding and implementing bespoke training schemes for Aerospace and Space related companies.

They are in partnership with Farnborough Aerospace Consortium, BAE Systems, TAG Aviation, Flight Safety International, QinetiQ, EADS Astrium, Farnborough College of Technology, Northbrook College University of Surrey, and Highbury College amongst others.

7 The benefits of recognising prior learning include the following:

- Facilitates access for 'non-traditional' students - people who may not have the opportunity to do further study can obtain higher qualifications
- Acknowledges value of learning outside a formal setting, e.g. values and recognises learning in the workplace
- Validates the worth of learning students have achieved by themselves
- Enables progression to other programmes of study
- Eliminates unnecessary repetition and duplication of material already familiar to the student. Public (and private) money is better used because people who already have skills and knowledge are not re-trained.
- Shortens the time necessary to earn a qualification - this motivates students who might otherwise be discouraged by the length of time required to complete a college level course or a particular programme of study
- Enhances students' pride and self-esteem for what they have accomplished as learners
- Enhances students' perception and understanding of learning as a lifelong process

8 You may have come up with some of the following difficulties or barriers.

Positive feedback: disliking giving compliments (embarrassment?); the fear of sounding insincere or as if you want something from the other person; the feeling that the person is 'only doing their job', so why should they get praise (perhaps some hostility?); the fear of being thought to have 'gone soft' (clinging to a 'hard' image?)

Negative feedback: fear of being disliked, and even disrupting the relationship; dislike of 'causing a scene'; not wanting to hurt the person's feelings; convincing yourself that the problem is not important or will go away by itself.

Note that many of these difficulties are based on a misconception about what giving feedback is for, and that it can be done in a skilled and appropriate manner.

Chapter 2 :

INTERPERSONAL AND TRANSFERABLE SKILLS

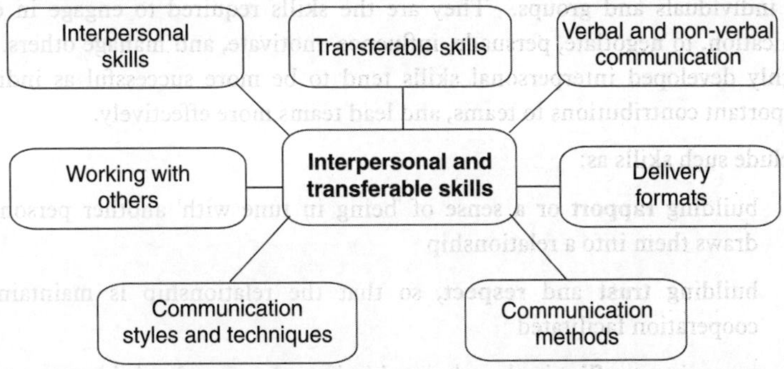

Introduction

The efficient running of organisations requires that all the members of the organisation work together towards the achievement of the organisation's objectives. This working together requires the adequate understanding of what others are doing. It requires a high level of co-ordination and control, and fundamentally it requires communication, which is efficient and effective.

One of the main objectives of Unit 13 is to develop your abilities to organise, manage and practise a range of approaches to improve your performance as a self-organised learner. In this chapter, we look at a variety of interpersonal and transferable skills which will be of value both in your HND studies and in your professional career beyond.

Learning outcomes

On completing this chapter you should be able to:

(a) Select solutions to work-based problems.

(b) Communicate in a variety of styles and appropriate manner at various levels.

1 INTERPERSONAL SKILLS

1.1 What are interpersonal skills?

Definition

> **Interpersonal skills** are the skills used in interactions and relationships between two or more people.

Interpersonal skills determine the effectiveness of interactions between individuals, and between individuals and groups. They are the skills required to engage in effective communication, to negotiate, persuade, influence, motivate, and manage others. People with highly developed interpersonal skills tend to be more successful as individuals, make important contributions to teams, and lead teams more effectively.

They include such skills as:

- building **rapport** or a sense of 'being in tune with' another person, which draws them into a relationship
- building **trust** and **respect**, so that the relationship is maintained and cooperation facilitated
- managing **conflict** in the relationship in such a way that it is preserved.
- **persuading** or **influencing** another person, to do what you want them to do or to share your beliefs
- **negotiating** or bargaining in order to reach mutually acceptable or compromise solutions to problems
- communicating **assertively**, so that you uphold your rights and get your needs met – without violating the rights or ignoring the needs of others
- communicating **informatively**, so that you give (and receive) relevant and timely information
- communicating **supportively**, so that you encourage the other person

These are essentially communication skills. We discuss many aspects of communication in this chapter, including some of the particular 'styles' mentioned above.

1.2 Why are interpersonal skills important?

You need interpersonal skills in order to:

- Understand and manage the **roles, relationships, attitudes** and **perceptions** operating in any situation in which two or more people are involved
- **Communicate** clearly with other people
- Achieve your **aims** from any interpersonal encounter (ideally, allowing the other parties to emerge satisfied as well).

In a business context, interpersonal skills are particularly important for processes such as:

- **Motivation**: persuading and inspiring employees to committed performance (often identified with 'leadership')

- **Team-building**: building trust, encouraging communication, forming cooperative relationships and managing conflict
- **Customer care** (including internal customers): winning trust, managing conflict, exchanging information and persuading
- **Negotiation**: maintaining relationships despite conflicting interests, working towards mutually acceptable solutions
- **Workload management**: being able to delegate effectively, negotiate assistance, and say 'no' assertively.

Activity 1 **(10 minutes)**

Using the following grid, monitor all the various conversations or interactions you have at work in the course of one day. For each one, put a tick in the appropriate column.

	Technical/ work-related with colleagues	*Technical/ work-related with customers/ clients/ enquirers*	*Organisational/ team/ 'membership'*	*Asking for help or advice*	*Getting support/ encouragement /challenge*	*Non work-related: just friendly/ courteous*
During work time						
During breaks/ lunch/ after work etc						
	Total:	Total:	Total:	Total:	Total:	Total:

What does this information tell you about the contexts in which your interpersonal skills are required?

Interpersonal skills are the ones that involve the way you interact with others on your educational course or in the workplace. Transferable skills are ones that can be transferred between one situation and another e.g., the ability to communicate clearly is transferable across a range of contexts: at college or in different types of workplace.

2 TRANSFERABLE SKILLS

2.1 Categories of skills

Transferable skills are general skills you can use in many jobs. You gain these skills from previous jobs, projects, voluntary work, sport, your home life, hobbies, and interests. They enable you to be adaptable and flexible in case you need to change your job.

As well as numeracy and languages, employers want their staff to be experienced in the following categories of skills:

People skills	
Leadership	The ability to take responsibility for a situation and to lead by enabling others to have the skills to follow. This is about having the initiative and skills to move forward, taking others with you.
Teamwork	Demonstration of your ability to work with others. Experience of this can be found in most jobs. The key here is to recognise when you have worked in a team and to identify examples where you have motivated others in the team by your own influence through negotiation
Influencing / Negotiating	This is related to the skill of effective oral communication. It is a demonstration of your ability to talk to all levels of industry; ask the right questions, listen to the answers and make your mark with the other person in a positive, non-arrogant way. Contacts in all walks of life could be useful to your future, so remember that everyone you meet is important.
Customer skills	An employer needs to know that you can interact positively with customers. You may be expected to carry out research, telesales, or run discussion groups and if you have had previous experience working with customers it will be a bonus.
Communication	Written work is expected to be clear and accurate and well presented - most students have examples of projects, reports and essays. Oral communication needs to be clear and articulate - being able to talk to people is vital in most management positions. Also remember that what you communicate is important - being able to prioritise and recognise what needs to be passed to others is a skill too

Self-reliance skills	
Reliability	Being predictable, able to be trusted and dependable are skills associated with reliability that are highly prized.
Self-awareness	The ability to understand what you don't know is as important as recognising the skills you do have. The ability to know what you still have to learn, how you may be able to improve and the awareness to confidently approach these shortcomings in a positive manner is vital to future success.
Self-management	The recognition that in order to improve skills some action planning may be required in terms of training or further study. Recognition that it is important to follow workplace rules and ethics without compromising your own creativity
Motivation and Enthusiasm	Employers like to recruit people who choose to work for them. If you have done some work experience elsewhere in the sector you will be able to show that you have an interest in their business in general, and an enthusiasm for making your career there.
Initiative	Initiative is seeing or knowing what needs to be done and doing it. It is the ability to think for yourself, make your own decisions and have confidence in them. Think of examples from course work, personal life and work experience. For example, networking for jobs/work experience, starting a new group or resurrecting an old one, creating your own website, coping well with a sudden crisis and volunteering.
Resourcefulness	Employers like to employ people who are able to 'bring them solutions, not problems'. This is linked to using initiative, but it is also about using your own past experience, knowledge and skills to solve problems and deal with difficult situations

General skills	
Numeracy	Understanding and use of basic statistics and arithmetic. Some experience will provide good evidence, particularly if you've worked with figures or money
Flexibility	Employers look for graduates who will be able to recognise possible areas of failure in their planning and can consider contingencies in advance. This skill also covers the willingness to try new tasks and be flexible in methods and hours of working
Adaptability	All organisations undergo change and they are seeking employees who are able to cope with change in a positive way. If you can give examples of situations where you have affected or dealt with change in the past this will be a bonus
Problem solving	Employers look for evidence of the ability to overcome problems positively and calmly. Often work experience which has involved dealing with the public will provide examples. Problem solving is not about 'being able to get your own way', but looking for a solution to best suit the circumstances
Planning	The skill of recognising priorities and planning time available so all tasks can be completed. Most students will be used to planning work to meet deadlines, but this skill will need to be adapted a little to meet the requirements of a commercial organisation

Specialist skills	
IT Skills	Most employers will expect you to have the ability to use a word processor. You can develop this by a part time course or job if your study demands little IT involvement. You may be expected to produce graphs using spreadsheets, presentations using PowerPoint, interrogate a database, and have a general understanding of and ability to use the Internet
Commercial awareness	This should really be the most obvious employability skill for a prospective employee – but often it is overlooked by an expectation that you will be 'trained' in this and will not need to understand the business prior to joining. It is, conversely, probably the most essential skill in most cases as it is vital that any new recruit has an awareness of the need for efficiency, cost effectiveness, good time management, and recognition of customer importance and a general knowledge of the marketplace in which the organisation operates. Commercial awareness can be gained by working for commercial organisations at any level. Particularly valuable is working in a customer-oriented organisation as awareness will develop very quickly.

2.2 Personal effectiveness

Personal effectiveness is at the heart of best practice and excellence. It means making the most of all the personal resources at your disposal - your personal talents, energy and time relative to what is most important to you. It is like money management or investment - you want to get the best return on your resources. As with managing money, you can either drift through life making ad hoc decisions or you can set time aside periodically to review your investments. It's not about sacrificing spontaneity or opportunism to be super organised if this is not your style. It's more a matter of taking whatever steps fit your style to give you the feeling that you are making best use of your resources.

Personal effectiveness covers a range of tasks and activities such as teamwork and presentation skills, ability to manage stress, to influence others, to plan, to relate to others and to prioritise objectives.

One precondition for personal effectiveness is better self-awareness.

A useful framework for looking at self-awareness, blind spots, and perception-checking is the 'Johari window' (*Luft* 1961). It classifies behaviours on a simple matrix: the horizontal axis representing what is known and unknown to self and the vertical axis representing what is known and unknown to others.

The Johari Window

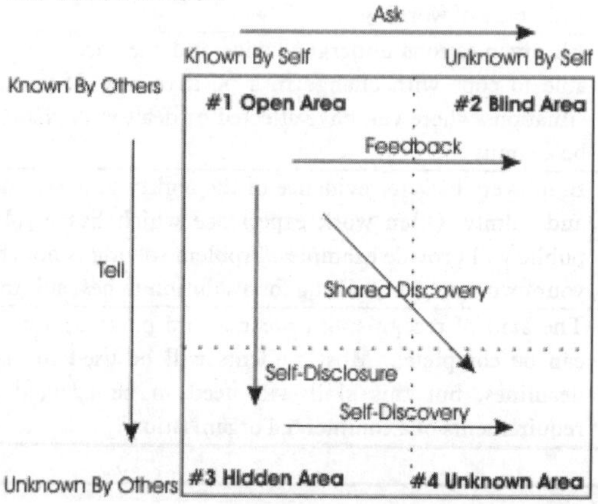

1 **The open area** contains things that are openly known and talked about - and which may be seen as strengths or weaknesses. This is the self that we choose to share with others. These **public** behaviours can be used effectively in interpersonal interactions because both parties are able to perceive and take them into account.

2 **The blind area** contains things that others observe that we don't know about. **Blind** behaviours are often non-verbal behaviours and action tendencies: patterns of behaviour and habitual mannerisms. For example, you do not realise that you adopt a sarcastic tone of voice in conflict situations. Blind behaviours can limit interpersonal interactions, because they may undermine your conscious intentions and messages.

3 **The hidden area** contains aspects of our self that we know about and keep hidden from others. These **hidden** behaviours include private feelings and thoughts which you decide not to share, or which you fail to convey effectively. For example, you don't show your anger, or don't express it in a way people understand, so others don't 'know' that you are angry. Hidden behaviours can limit interpersonal interactions, because they create potential for misunderstanding and neglect opportunities for feedback.

4 **The unknown area** contains things that nobody knows about us - including ourselves. This may be because we have never exposed those areas of our personality, or because they are buried deep in the subconscious. **Unknown** behaviours are a potential wasted resource in interpersonal interactions: not currently available for use, e.g. you may have leadership abilities that neither you nor others are aware of.

The process of developing self-awareness involves:

- Reducing *unknown* behaviours, by bringing them into your awareness through **self-observation, reflection** and **assessment** (for example, using self-report questionnaires).
- Reducing *blind* behaviours of others' perceptions of you through **feedback-seeking.**
- Managing *hidden* behaviours, through more – or less – **self-disclosure** to others, as relevant to the requirements of the interaction and appropriate to the level of trust and intimacy in the relationship.

Note that while the general aim is to increase public behaviours, we are not advocating indiscriminate self-disclosure! It is possible to disclose too little, and so limit both the collaborative and learning potential of an interaction. It is, however, possible to disclose too much and this may be irrelevant to the information needs of others.

FOR DISCUSSION

How far do you think you should seek to increase your 'public' behaviours? Are there situations in your work context in which it would be advisable to keep certain behaviours hidden?

2.3 Self-discipline

Self-discipline involves acting according to what you think instead of how you feel in the moment. Often it involves sacrificing the pleasure and thrill of the moment for what matters most in life. Therefore it is self-discipline that drives you to:

- Work on an idea or project after the initial rush of enthusiasm has faded away
- Go to the gym when all you want to do is lie on the couch and watch TV
- Say 'no' when tempted to break your diet
- Only check your emails a few times per day at particular times

It means behaving according to what you have decided is best, regardless of how you feel in the moment. Therefore the first trait of discipline is self-knowledge. You need to decide what behaviour best reflects your goals and values. This process requires introspection and self-analysis, and is most effective when tied to written expression.

Self-discipline depends upon conscious awareness as to both what you are doing and what you are not doing. If you are not aware your behaviour is undisciplined, how will you know to act otherwise?

Developing self-discipline takes time, and the key here is you are aware of your undisciplined behaviour. With time this awareness will come earlier, meaning rather than catching yourself in the act of being undisciplined you will have awareness before you act in this way. This gives you the opportunity to make a decision that is in better alignment with your goals and values.

It is not enough to simply write out your goals and values. You must make an internal commitment to them. Otherwise when your alarm clock goes off at 5am you will see no harm in hitting the snooze button for 'just another 5 minutes.' Or, when the initial rush of enthusiasm has faded away from a project you will struggle to see it through to completion.

If you struggle with commitment, start by making a conscious decision to follow through on what you say you are going to do - both when you said you would do it and how you said you would do it..

2.4 Problems and problem solving

A problem is a condition that's not acceptable. It may involve tangible and/or intangible elements such as people, processes, systems, states of affair, products, circumstances, or any business or personal situation.

Problems can be defined broadly as situations in which we experience uncertainty or difficulty in achieving what we want to achieve, e.g.

- Stopping smoking is a problem when you decide you want to stop but cannot.
- A computer malfunction is a problem if it prevents you completing work on time.
- An excessive workload is a problem when it interferes with your ability to work effectively.
- Poor communication is a problem when it reduces the efficiency of an organisation.

Problems can be divided broadly into two groups:

1. Those where the current situation is not what was expected (known as closed or maintenance problems)
2. Those where we want to change our current situation in some way but there is an obstacle preventing us doing so (known as open-ended or achievement problems).

Closed problems occur when something has happened that should not have happened, or something we expected to happen has not happened, i.e. there is a deviation from the normal or expected state of affairs. For example, it could be the unexpected resignation of a key member of staff, or the failure of the principal speaker to arrive at a conference. The cause (or obstacle) may be known or unknown, but something needs to be done about it.

Open-ended problems occur when we want to achieve a specific objective but there are certain obstacles blocking our progress. They can be subdivided into three groups:

- where we are unable to reach our current objective, e.g., failing to meet a sales target
- where our current objective could be exceeded, e.g., improved efficiency
- where a new objective could be achieved through problem solving, eg creating a new product or service.

Solving a problem involves finding ways to overcome any obstacles and to achieve our objective.

Although each problem is unique in terms of the information involved, and requires a unique blend of thought processes to find a solution, all successful problem solving follows a basic pattern and goes through these stages:

- defining the problem;
- finding possible solutions;
- choosing the best solution; and
- implementing the solution.

Defining open-ended problems involves identifying and defining your objectives and any obstacles which could prevent you reaching them. Try to specify the problem in as few words as possible and to set out the likely causes of the problem. Data may need to be collected and analysed to give a better understanding of the problem and its causes. For example, if customer satisfaction targets are not being met it will make sense to keep a record of customer complaints and then to analyse them to see where the major problems lie.

It is helpful to present the problem using a range of techniques such as written reports and diagrammatic means - charts, graphs and diagrams. For example a pie chart may be used to show a breakdown of the main sources of customer complaints and a line graph to show trends over time in customer satisfaction.

Brainstorming involves generating a lot of ways of dealing with the problem. They can be crazy ideas because at this stage they are not going to be followed through. However, sometimes crazy ideas can be structured into sensible solutions.

In a brainstorming session participants simply suggest as many ideas as they can without justifying them or having them questioned.

Mind mapping can be used to set out a graphic representation of a problem and its solutions. Every mind map has a central point. This could be a brief description of a problem. The ways of solving the problem can then be set out as branches emanating from the problem at the centre.

There are two stages in the process: a free thinking stage and an organising stage - these should not be done together.

Stage 1: brainstorming

Write your topic or area of study in the centre of a blank page. Use colours, pictures, words and symbols to record any other ideas, topics, authors, theories or anything else associated with the topic. You can put these anywhere on the page. Associate freely and do not filter out ideas; at this point anything and everything is OK.

Stage 2: mind mapping

Map the relationships between the ideas or key points using lines, arrows, colours and words to link them. Identify the type of relationship between points: contrast/similarity/cause/effect. Write these along the linking lines.

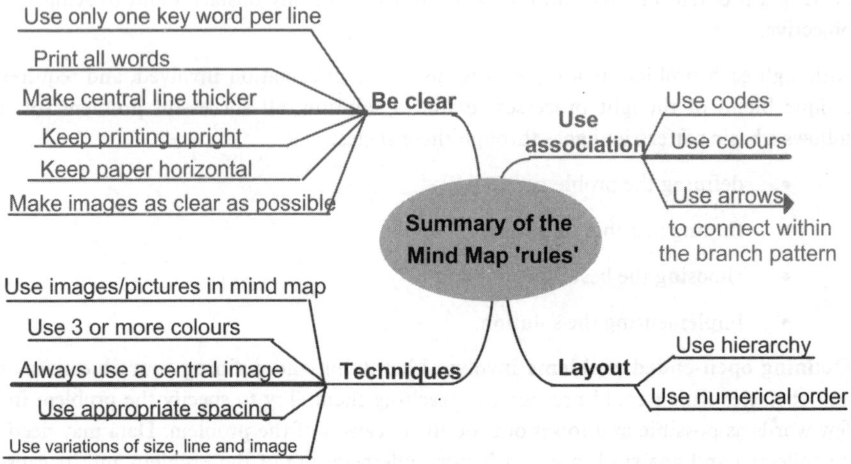

Finding possible solutions - closed problems generally have one or a limited number of possible solutions, while open-ended problems usually can be solved in a large number of ways. The most effective solution to an open-ended problem is found by selecting the best from a wide range of possibilities. Finding solutions involves analysing the problem to ensure that you fully understand it and then constructing courses of action which will achieve your objective. The more ideas you have to work with, the better your chances of finding an effective solution.

Choosing the best solution - the stage at which you *evaluate the possible solutions* and select that which will be most effective in solving the problem. It is a process of decision making based on a comparison of the potential outcome of alternative solutions. This involves:

- identifying all the features of an ideal solution, including the constraints it has to meet
- eliminating solutions which do not meet the constraints
- evaluating the remaining solutions against the outcome required
- assessing the risks associated with the 'best' solution
- making the decision to implement this solution

The solution should include the following elements:

- a timescale - often this will involve setting out short-term (definite) solutions, medium-term goals and long-term projections of outcomes.
- stages - breaking down the achievement of the solution into relevant components where appropriate
- resources - including the finance required to achieve and implement the solution
- critical path analysis - when it is possible to quantify the time required to carry out a project and the sequence of steps in which the project will be carried out, it is then possible to set out the critical path.

A problem is only solved when a solution has been implemented. In some situations, before this can take place, you need to *gain acceptance of the solution by other people,* or get their authority to implement it. This may involve various strategies of persuasion.

Implementing the solution - involves three separate stages:

1 planning and preparing to implement the solution

2 taking the appropriate action and monitoring its effects

3 reviewing the ultimate success of the action

Implementing your solution is the culmination of all your efforts and requires very careful planning. The plan describes the sequence of actions required to achieve the objective, the timescale and the resources required at each stage. Ways of minimising the risks involved and preventing mistakes have to be devised and built into the plan. Details of what must be done if things go wrong are also included.

Once the plan has been put into effect, the situation has to be monitored to ensure that things are running smoothly. Any problems or potential problems have to be dealt with quickly. When the action is completed it's necessary to measure its success, both to estimate its usefulness for solving future problems of this type and to ensure that the problem has been solved. If not, further action may be required.

These stages provide *a very flexible framework which can be adapted to suit all problems.* With closed problems, for example, where there is likely to be only one or a few solutions, the emphasis will be on defining and analysing the problem to indicate possible causes. Open-ended problems, on the other hand, require more work at the idea generation stage to develop a large range of possible solutions.

At any stage in solving a problem it may be necessary to go back and adapt work done at an earlier stage.

Problem solving requires two distinct types of mental skill, analytical and creative.

Analytical or logical thinking includes skills such as ordering, comparing, contrasting, evaluating and selecting. It provides a logical framework for problem solving and helps to select the best alternative from those available by narrowing down the range of possibilities (a convergent process). Analytical thinking often predominates in solving closed problems, where the many possible causes have to be identified and analysed to find the real cause.

Creative thinking - is where problem solving is used as a creative tool to generate new ideas for doing things, starting with a blank sheet. This type of problem solving requires the most flexible approach.

Often problem solving involves creative thinking. We sometimes refer to this as thinking 'out of the box'. Thinking inside the box means coming up with 'tried and tested' solutions to problems that do not require a lot of imagination. In contrast, creative thinking involves developing novel solutions that nobody has thought of before.

2.5 Creativity and creative thinking

Creativity means using your imagination in problem solving. Creativity can include innovation, synthesis and development. Innovation is where you find a completely new way of thinking about, or doing something. If you can improvise quickly at work e.g., use an alternative material for a job in an emergency, find a quicker way around a job or work out a new procedure, then you are being innovative or creative. Synthesis is where you take ideas from different sources and combine them. Development occurs when you take a basic idea and extend it.

Creative thinking is a divergent process, using the imagination to create a large range of ideas for solutions. It requires us to look beyond the obvious, creating ideas which may, at first, seem unrealistic or have no logical connection with the problem. There is a large element of creative thinking in solving open problems.

The creative thinking skills can be divided into several key elements:

- fluency - producing many ideas
- flexibility - producing a broad range of ideas .
- originality - producing uncommon ideas
- elaboration - developing ideas.

Effective problem solving requires a controlled mixture of analytical and creative thinking.

Research has shown that, in general terms, each side or hemisphere of the brain is specialised to serve one of these groups. Left-brain thinking is more logical and analytical, and is predominantly verbal. Right-brain thinking is more holistic and is concerned with feelings and impressionistic relationships. The left side of your brain deals with a problem or situation by collecting data, making analyses, and using a rational thinking process to reach a logical conclusion. The right side of your brain approaches the same problem or situation by making intuitive leaps to answers based on insights and perceptions. The left brain tends to break information apart for analysis, while the right brain tends to put information together to synthesise a whole picture.

To be a good problem solver you need to be able to switch from one group of skills to the other and back again, although this is not always easy. Traditional education gives far greater encouragement to the development and use of left-brain thinking. This is reinforced in the way we are required to work, where emphasis is placed on rational, logical analysis of data in drawing conclusions.

2.6 Six Thinking Hats

Edward de Bono, in his book Six Thinking Hats, suggests that there are different types of thinking and that we can switch from one to another, particularly if we are aware of these different modes of thinking and can get into the habit of applying whichever is the most appropriate to each problem. Each 'thinking hat' is a different style of thinking. These are explained below:

White Hat – with this thinking hat, you focus on the data available. Look at the information you have, and see what you can learn from it. Look for gaps in your knowledge, and either try to fill them or take account of them.

Red Hat – signifies feelings, hunches and intuition. When using this hat you can express emotions and feelings and share fears, likes, dislikes, loves, and hates.

Black Hat – when using black hat thinking you look at things pessimistically, cautiously and defensively. Try to see why ideas and approaches might not work. This is important because it highlights the weak points in a plan or course of action. It allows you to eliminate them, alter your approach, or prepare contingency plans to counter problems that arise. It is probably the most powerful and useful of the hats but a problem if overused.

Yellow Hat – the yellow hat helps you to think positively. It is the optimistic viewpoint that helps you to see all the benefits of the decision and the value in it, and spot the opportunities that arise from it. Yellow Hat thinking helps you to keep going when everything looks gloomy and difficult.

Green Hat – focuses on creativity; the possibilities, alternatives, and new ideas. It is an opportunity to express new concepts and new perceptions. It is a freewheeling way of thinking, in which there is little criticism of ideas.

Blue Hat – is used to manage the thinking process. It's the control mechanism that ensures the Six Thinking Hats guidelines are observed. This is the hat worn by people chairing meetings. When running into difficulties because ideas are running dry, they may direct activity into Green Hat thinking. When contingency plans are needed, they will ask for Black Hat thinking, and so on.

Six Thinking Hats is a good technique for looking at the effects of a decision from a number of different points of view.

It allows necessary emotion and scepticism to be brought into what would otherwise be purely rational decisions. It opens up the opportunity for creativity within decision making. It also helps, for example, persistently pessimistic people to be positive and creative.

Plans developed using the '6 Thinking Hats' technique are sounder and more resilient than would otherwise be the case.

Hats may be used in some structured sequence depending on the nature of the issue. Here is an example agenda for a typical 6 hats workshop

1 Present the facts of the case - white hat

2 Generate ideas on how the case could be handled - green hat

3 Evaluate the merits of the ideas. List the benefits - yellow hat - and the drawbacks - black hat.

4 Get everybody's gut feelings about the alternatives - red hat

Activity 2 **(20 minutes)**

The directors of a property company are looking at whether they should construct a new office building. The economy is doing well, and the amount of vacant office space is reducing sharply. As part of their decision they decide to use the 6 Thinking Hats technique during a planning meeting.

Identify which hat is being used in each of the following stages of the meeting:

1 They analyse the data they have and examine the trend in vacant office space, which shows a sharp reduction. They anticipate that by the time the office block would be completed, that there will be a severe shortage of office space. Current government projections show steady economic growth for at least the construction period.

2 Some of the directors think the proposed building looks quite ugly. While it would be highly cost-effective, they worry that people would not like to work in it.

3 They worry that government projections may be wrong. The economy may be about to enter a 'cyclical downturn', in which case the office building may be empty for a long time. If the building is not attractive, then companies will choose to work in another better-looking building at the same rent.

4 They argue that if the economy holds up and their projections are correct, the company stands to make a great deal of money. If they are lucky, maybe they could sell the building before the next downturn, or rent to tenants on long-term leases that will last through any recession.

5 They consider whether they should change the design to make the building more pleasant. Perhaps they could build prestige offices that people would want to rent in any economic climate. Alternatively, maybe they should invest the money in the short term to buy up property at a low cost when a recession comes.

6 The meeting's chairperson may have needed to keep other members of the team from switching styles, or from criticising other peoples' points

3 VERBAL AND NON-VERBAL COMMUNICATION

3.1 Why we communicate

Communication is the basis of our relationships with other people. It is the means whereby people in an organisation exchange information regarding the operations of the enterprise. It is the interchange of ideas, facts and emotions by two or more persons.

Definition

Communication in business can be defined as 'the transmission of information so that it is received, understood and leads to action'.

The general purpose of most communications will be as follows.

- **To inform**: to give people data that they require
- **To persuade**: to get somebody to do something
- **To request**: to ask for something
- **To confirm**: to check that information is correct and that both parties have the same understanding of it
- **To build the relationship**: giving information in such a way as to acknowledge and maintain the relationship between the sender and receiver – mutual trust, loyalty, respect, benefit and so on

In addition, you may have a specific purpose for communicating. Think in terms of the **outcome** that you want from the communication event: what do you want to happen, and when?

Knowing the **purpose of your communication** – what you want to achieve – is the first step in planning any message.

3.2 The communication process

Effective communication is a two-way process, often shown as a 'cycle'. Signals or messages are sent by the communicator and received by the other party who sends back some form of confirmation that the message has been received and understood. The process of communication can be modelled as shown in the following diagram

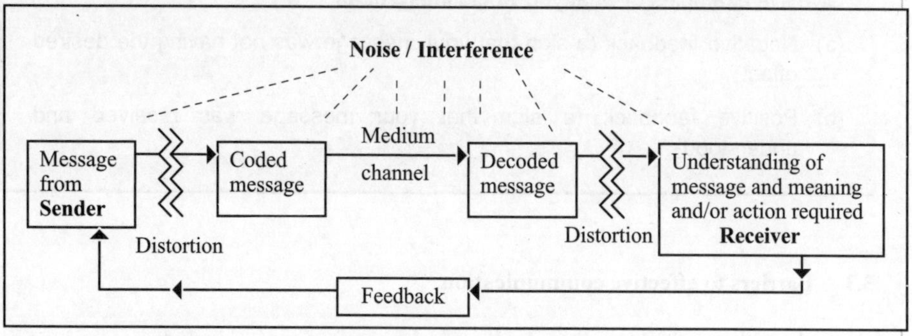

The communication process involves six basic elements: sender (encoder), message, channel, receiver (decoder), noise, and feedback.

The sender initiates the communication process. The code or language of a message may be spoken or written or it may be non-verbal e.g., in pictures, numbers or by body language. The choice of medium (letter, memo, e-mail, report, presentation, telephone call) and channel of delivery (telecom system, notice board, postal system, World Wide Web) depends on a number of factors:

- **Speed** - a phone call is quicker than a letter
- **Complexity** - a written message allows the use of diagrams and figure working with time for perusal at the recipient's own pace
- **Need for a written record** - for the confirmation of business or legal transactions

- **Need for interaction** or the immediate exchange of information or questions and answers. Face-to-face and phone discussion is often used to resolve conflicts, solve problems and close sales for this reason.
- **Confidentiality** e.g., a private interview or sealed letter or conversely the need to disseminate or spread information widely and quickly e.g., via a notice board, public meeting or web site.
- **Cost** - for the best possible result at the least possible price (taking into account all the above).

Because there may be distortion at the coding or decoding stage i.e., the meaning of the message may be lost in handling, feedback is an important way to gauge the receiver's reaction and make sure the message is understood. Feedback can range from a smile or a nod to a blank look or a shrug or from the desired action being taken.

Within the communication process it is also important to note the problem of 'noise' i.e., anything in the environment that impedes the transmission of the message, is significant. Noise can arise from many sources e.g., factors as diverse as loud machinery, status differentials between sender and receiver, distractions of pressure at work or emotional upsets. The effective communicator must ensure that noise does not interfere with successful transmission of the message.

Activity 3 **(10 minutes)**

Give five examples of what you would interpret as:

(a) Negative feedback (a sign that your message was not having the desired effect)

(b) Positive feedback (a sign that your message was received and understood)

3.3 Barriers to effective communication

General problems which can occur in the communication process include:

(a) **Distortion**: a process by which the meaning of a message is lost 'in translation'. Misunderstanding may arise from technical or ambiguous language, misinterpretation of symbols etc

(b) **Noise**: interference in the environment of communication which prevents the message getting through clearly e.g. due to physical noise, technical interference, or interpersonal differences making communication difficult

(c) **Misunderstanding** due to lack of clarity or technical jargon

(d) **Non-verbal signs** (gesture, facial expression) contradicting the verbal message

(e) Failure to give or to seek **feedback**

(f) **'Overload'** – a person being given too much information to digest in the time available

(g) **Perceptual selection:** people hearing only what they want to hear in a message

(h) **Differences** in social, racial or educational background

(i) **Poor communication skills** on the part of sender or recipient

Additional difficulties may arise from the **work context,** including:

(a) **Status** (of the sender and receiver of information)

   (i) A senior manager's words are listened to closely and a colleague's perhaps discounted.

   (ii) A subordinate might mistrust his or her superior's intentions and might look for 'hidden meanings' in a message.

(b) **Jargon.** People from different job or specialist backgrounds (eg accountants, HR managers, IT experts) can have difficulty in talking on a non-specialist's wavelength.

(c) **Priorities.** People or departments may have different priorities or perspectives so that one person places more or less emphasis on a situation than another.

(d) **Selective reporting.** Subordinates may give superiors incorrect or incomplete information (eg to protect a colleague, to avoid 'bothering' the superior). A senior manager may, however only be able to handle edited information because he does not have time to sift through details.

(e) **Use.** Managers may be prepared to make decisions on a 'hunch' without proper regard to the communications they may or may not have received.

(f) **Timing.** Information which has no immediate use tends to be forgotten.

(g) **Opportunity.** Mechanisms, formal or informal, for people to say what they think may be lacking, especially for upward communication.

(h) **Conflict.** Where there is conflict between individuals or departments, communications will be withdrawn and information withheld.

(i) **Cultural values** about communication. For example:

   (i) **Secrecy.** Information might be given on a need-to-know basis, rather than be considered as a potential resource for everyone to use.

   (ii) **Can't handle bad news.** The culture of some organisations may prevent the communication of certain messages. Organisations with a 'can-do' philosophy may not want to hear that certain tasks are impossible, for example.

Activity 4 **(10 minutes)**

Suggest the most effective medium for communication in the following situations.

(a) New printer cartridges are urgently required from the office goods supplier.

(b) The managing director wants to give a message to all staff.

(c) Fred Bloggs has been absent five times in the past month and his manager intends to take action.

(d) You need information quickly from another department.

(e) You have to explain a complicated operation to a group of people.

3.4 Direction of communication flows

Formal communication channels are normally established as part of the organisation's structure (the organisational chart displays these channels.) The channel is the path a message follows from the sender to the receiver. In a hierarchical structure the channels are largely vertical chains designed to allow effective communication between managers and subordinates. Communication flows can be:

Vertical channels go up and down the scalar chain from superior to subordinate. Managers use downward channels as a basis for giving specific job instructions, policy decisions, guidance and resolution of queries. Such information can help clarify operational goals, provide a sense of direction and give subordinates data related to their performance. Three forms of downward communication are manuals, handbooks, and newsletters.

Employees use upward channels to send messages to managers. Upward communication provides management with feedback from employees on results achieved and problems encountered. Three forms of upward communication are suggestion systems, grievances, and attitude surveys.

Horizontal or lateral channels are used when communicating across departmental lines, with suppliers, or with customers. Horizontal communication between 'peer groups' is usually easier and more direct then vertical communication, being less inhibited by considerations of rank. Four of the most important reasons for lateral communication are:

(a) task co-ordination – department heads may meet periodically to discuss how each department is contributing to organisational objectives

(b) problem-solving – members of a department may meet to discuss how they will handle a threatened budget cut

(c) information sharing – members of one department may meet with the members of another department to explain some new information or study

(d) conflict resolution – members of one department may meet to discuss a problem, e.g., duplication of activities in the department and some other department.

In every organisation there are **informal communication networks** as well as the formal channels. This is often referred to as 'the grapevine', which has been defined as 'the network of social relations that arises spontaneously as people associate with one another. It is an expression of people's natural motivation to communicate'.

Grapevine activity is likely to flourish in many common situations, for example:

- Where there is a lack of information about a situation and people try to fill in the gaps as best they can.
- Where there is insecurity in the situation.
- Where there is a personal interest in a situation e.g., when a supervisor disciplines a friend, people may well gossip about it.
- Where there is personal animosity in a situation and people seek to gain advantage by the spreading of rumours.
- Where there is new information that people wish to spread quickly.

3.5 Patterns of communication

Communication networks structure the flow of information among network members. They influence decision quality, member satisfaction, message quality, and other variables. The patterns of communication that develop depend, in part, on the structure of the group. If there is little structure in a group, members communicate with anyone they want to. If the group is highly structured, group members might only communicate with certain other members.

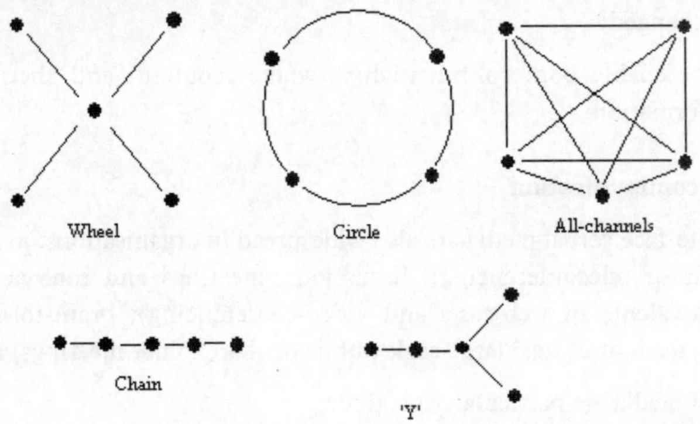

We are most familiar with the **all-channel** network of a small group, where everyone can communicate to everyone else in the group. Another common network is the **inverted Y**, the normal hierarchy where each member communicates to the person above and the person(s) below, but levels are not skipped when communicating up or down the organisation.

Three other networks that have been studied are the wheel, the chain, and the circle. In the **wheel network** a central person can communicate with every other person, but they cannot talk to each other except through the centre. A taxi dispatcher, for instance, occupies the centre of a wheel and has a high degree of central control over information. Drivers who equip themselves with cellular telephones and take calls directly from their regular customers can bypass the dispatcher and create their own communication network.

In a **chain network**, individuals can communicate only to the two people next to them in the chain (or only one other person for the person at the end of the chain). For example, people on an assembly line may be restricted in whom they can talk to by their physical location on the line. A **circle network** is a closed chain. Though all members do not communicate with every other member, no one person controls the communication.

Which type of network is better depends upon the type of task the group is working on. If the task is simple and there is only one right way to perform it, then a more structured group works best, because a central leader is necessary. If there are several ways to accomplish the task, a less structured group works better, because this allows members to generate ideas freely. Group members usually get the most satisfaction from the all channels network, because it gives them greater freedom and a feeling of control.

3.6 Written communication

A range of written communication media is used in business contexts, for one-to-one and one-to-group communication. Examples include: letters, reports, forms, notice boards, e-mail, information leaflets, manuals and handbooks, the minutes of meetings and so on.

The key advantages of written formats are that:

(a) they focus the attention of sender and receiver;

(b) they enable subsequent and repeated reference to information and agreements;

(c) they provide legally acceptable evidence of information and agreements exchanged;

(d) they enable both confidentiality (where required) and sharing/copying of information.

3.7 Verbal communication

Oral and face-to-face verbal media are also widespread in organisations, in forms such as: telephone calls or teleconferencing; discussions, meetings and interviews (and their electronic equivalents in web-casts and video-conferencing); brainstorming sessions, quality circles, team briefings; large-scale public or shareholder meetings; and so on.

These kinds of media are particularly good for:

(a) Generating new ideas, because of their real-time information sharing and interactivity (as in brainstorming).

(b) Interactive feedback, exchange of views and questioning (without the lead time required for responses in writing).

(c) The availability of non-verbal cues (including tone of voice and, in face-to-face communication, body language) to support interpretation of underlying meaning and messages.

(d) Personal interactions and relationship building (because of the ability to build rapport and be sensitive to the audience's needs and responses).

(e) Spreading information informally to large groups of people, with opportunities for interactive feedback and questions (as in briefings and public meetings).

Confirmation and reference material can often be provided in writing for, or following, conversations and meetings, in order to support more detailed and repeated reference, where necessary.

3.8 Non-verbal communication

Non-verbal communication is, as its name implies, communication without words, or other than by words. It is often called **body language** and consists of facial expression, posture, proximity, gestures and non-verbal noises (grunts, yawns etc).

Consciously or unconsciously, we send messages through body language during every face to face encounter. We can use it deliberately to **confirm** our verbal message – for example, by nodding and smiling as we tell someone we are happy to help them – or to **contradict** it, if we want to be sarcastic (saying 'How interesting!' with a yawn, for example).

More often, however, our body language contradicts our verbal message *without* our being aware of it, giving a 'mixed message' like your saying you understand an instruction while looking extremely perplexed. Body language can also 'give away' messages that we would – for social or business reasons – rather not send, such as lack of interest, hostility or whatever.

If you can be aware of other people's body language, and interpret its meaning, you can:

- Receive feedback from listeners and modify your message accordingly
- Recognise people's real feelings when their words are constrained by formalities (politeness or dishonesty)
- Recognise interpersonal problems (e.g. an angry silence, refusal to look someone in the eye)
- Read situations so you can modify your communication/response strategy. (Is the boss irritated by a delay? Reassure - and hurry. Is a colleague on the point of tears? Support and soothe.)

What is it that we see and interpret when we say 'He looked upset', 'I could tell he was nervous', or 'She didn't say anything, but I could tell she was pleased'?

Sign	Meaning and interpretation
Facial expression	The eyebrows, eyes, nose, lips and mouth, jaw and head position all contribute to the expression on someone's face: lips can be tight or slack, eyes narrowed or widened, the eyebrows lowered or raised, the whole face moving or still, pale or flushed.
Gestures	People make gestures unconsciously: jabbing a finger in the air for emphasis, tapping the fingers when impatient. They also make conscious gestures – and not only impolite ones: a finger against the lips for silence, a jerk of the head to indicate a direction, a shrug to indicate indifference.
Movement	Watch how people move, at what pace, and to what effect. Someone who walks briskly conveys determination; someone who shuffles along, laziness or depression; someone who can never sit still, nervousness or impatience.

Sign	Meaning and interpretation
Positioning	You will probably find you sit closer to the people you like and trust, face them directly, or even lean towards them. You may keep a 'respectful' distance between yourself and someone with whom you have a more formal relationship.
Contact	Shaking hands is acceptable for transmitting greeting in most contexts but, for example, nudging or prodding for emphasis, or clapping on the back, implies familiarity and ease.
Posture	Consider the way you sit and stand. Lounge, hunch or sit/stand up straight and you convey relaxation, negativity or alertness. Lean forward when you listen to someone, and you transmit interest: lean well back and you convey weariness or boredom.
Sounds	A sceptical grunt, a sympathetic murmur and a delighted whoop are particularly useful non-verbal feedback signals.

Be aware that no non-verbal cue by itself is enough to make an accurate diagnosis of someone's meaning or mental state! A frown may be caused by irritation *or* perplexity *or* a headache! Consider the whole body language of the person, take the context into account – and test out your theories before acting on them!

You should also be aware that body language means different things in different cultures. An assertive level of steady eye contact, for a Westerner, would be regarded as aggressive and offensive to some Eastern cultures – just to give one example. Beware of making assumptions!

Activity 5 **(10 minutes)**

How might you interpret (or use) the following non-verbal cues?

(a) A clenched fist

(b) Stroking the chin slowly, with furrowed brow

(c) Head in hands

(d) Sitting elbow on knee, chin resting on fist

(e) Tapping toes

(f) Turning or leaning away from another person while talking

(g) A sigh, whole facial muscles relax and mouth smiles

(h) A sigh, while body sags and face 'falls'

3.9 Electronic communication

The introduction of personal computer networks facilitates new sorts of communication, of which **email** is probably by far the most prevalent. It is particularly useful in organisations which are widely dispersed over several sites in one or more countries.

Email has many **advantages** over the telephone and paper memos, which explains why it has been so widely adopted.

(a) Emails can be sent to large numbers of people at the same time without having to be physically distributed on paper.

(b) Email messages need not interrupt the recipient's flow of work, unlike a phone call.

Email also has **drawbacks**, however.

(a) Some people use email when face to face contact is more appropriate.

(b) Although email can feel as informal as a spoken conversation, email records can be used in legal proceedings, eg for former employees suing the company for unfair dismissal. They may also be cited in defamation. *Asda* were successfully sued by a disgruntled customer because untrue rumours that a customer was guilty of fraud had been circulated via the company's email system, for example.

(c) They contribute to information overload: there is a temptation to copy email to people that do not really need to see it.

(d) If email is the main means of communication with external parties, the company's corporate identity may be compromised if people send emails in a variety of formats.

These problems emphasise the need for **internal guidance** on how email should be used. If email is used to communicate with other customers or suppliers, it should be treated in the same way as other business correspondence, including obtaining appropriate authorisation. The guidance should prohibit defamatory or other abusive messages. Above all employees should be made aware that communication by email is permanent and not transitory in nature.

Electronic data interchange (EDI) is a form of direct communication between computers and may be used between organisations. For instance, production scheduling software may send orders directly to a supplier's stock handling computer via a telephone link.

We will now go on to look in detail at some of the main communication methods you might use at work: written communication - letters, memos, e-mails, faxes and other documents, visual communication - including various charts and graphs and oral communication including the telephone

4 COMMUNICATION METHODS

4.1 Written communication - the letter

The letter is a very **flexible and versatile medium of communication**. It can be used for many different purposes.

- Request, supply and confirm information and instructions
- Offer and accept goods and services
- Convey and acknowledge satisfaction and dissatisfaction

The elements of a standard business letter are:

- **Return address:** If you have company letterhead you can skip this section. Include your full business address and correct legal business name. You can also include your email address or phone number if needed by your recipient.
- **Date:** Follow the month, day and year format. Make your date current to the actual mailing date of the letter.
- **Recipient's name and address:** Include the full name and address of the contact you are sending the letter to. The person's title can be added along with the phone number if needed.
- **Greeting:** For the greeting use the person's formal name and end with a colon for your business letter.
- **Subject:** Clearly stating the subject of the letter helps you recipient quickly know the context of what your letter is about.
- **Body:** Your letter body should start with a general introduction of who you are and the letter purpose. Include specific paragraphs to outline the issue or problem. Close the body with a call to action. Every business letter should be short and concise taking into account your reader's limited time.
- **Closing:** Here you can choose any formal format such as 'Yours faithfully' or 'Yours sincerely.'
- **Signature:** Sign your name as the same as in your letter. Name & Title: Include your full name and job title.
- **Enclosures and CC:** If you are sending additional documents include an enclosure line and if someone else is receiving a copy of the letter include cc. or carbon copy of the other receiver or receivers.

You can simplify the entire process of creating a properly formatted business letter by using your word processing program. In Microsoft Word, you can use the letter wizard by going to the 'Tools' function, select 'Letters & Mailings' and click on the Letter Wizard. The wizard will prompt you through each field and allow you to choose a format.

On the next page is an example. (Later we shall see some alternative layouts.) (Remember, these are only common conventions: be sure to follow the **guidelines** and **house style** of your own organisation.)

Hi-Tech Office Equipment Ltd

Micro House, High St, Newtown, Middlesex NT3 0PN
Telephone: Newtown (01789) 1234 Fax: (01789) 5678

Directors:	Registered Office:
I. Teck (Managing)	Micro House, High St, Newtown
M. Ployer	Middlesex NT3 0PN
D. Rechtor	Registered No 123 4 56 789
N. Other	Registered in England

Our Ref: IW/cw
Your Ref: JB/nn 7th June 20X0

Private & Confidential

J. M. Bloggs, Esq
Administrator
Toubai Forze Timber Yard
Wood Lane Industrial Estate
SUSSEX
SX1 4PW

Dear Mr. Bloggs

WORD PROCESSING EQUIPMENT

Thank you for your letter of 3rd June 20X0, in which you request further details of Hi-Tech's range of personal computers with word processing software packages. I am delighted to hear that our earlier discussions were of some help to you.

Please find enclosed our list of hardware and software with current prices. I have also included our leaflet entitled 'Desktop', which outlines some of the options for word processing on PCs: I trust this will answer your questions and give you an idea of the exciting possibilities.

I would also take this opportunity to remind you that two of your old printers are currently under maintenance contract with us, and that both of them become due for routine servicing within the next month. Perhaps you would contact my secretary to arrange a convenient date for our engineer to call at your offices.

I look forward to hearing from you when you have thought about the word processing option. If you have any queries or need further information on accessories do not hesitate to let me know.

Yours sincerely

I. M. Wright
SALES MANAGER
Enc

Greeting and complimentary closes

By convention, the following greetings and complimentary closes should be used together:

Greeting	Close	Context
Dear Sir/Madam/Sirs (*Name not used*)	Yours faithfully	Formal situations Recipient not personally known
Dear Dr/Mr/Mrs/Miss Cake Dear Sir Keith/Lady Jane (formal name used)	Yours sincerely	Established relationships
Dear Joe/Josephine	Yours sincerely	Close, informal relationships
My dear Joe/Josephine	Kind regards Best wishes Affectionately	More various, because more personal

Signature

If an assistant or secretary is signing a letter on behalf of the writer, the writer's name is preceded by 'For' (or its equivalent from legal terminology 'pp.' which stands for per procurationem).

For I Cantwell

Accounts Manager

Enclosure reference

If you are putting something other than the letter in the same envelope, such as a cheque, price list or leaflet, use an enclosure reference to make sure that the reader or the person opening the mail does not overlook (and possibly discard) it: 'Enc' (or Encs for more than one item) is the standard form.

Copy reference

If a duplicate of a letter has been sent to an interested third party, it is courteous to acknowledge the fact to the letter's recipient with a similar footnote:

Copies to (3rd party names) *or* cc: (3rd party names)

Follow-up sheets

The second sheet, and all subsequent sheets, of a letter will be on plain (un-headed) paper. In case they should get detached or confused, therefore, continuation sheets are headed as follows.

Name of recipient, page number in letter, date.

Alternative layouts

Simplicity and attractiveness are general guidelines to good layout, and there are two main styles currently in use.

FULLY BLOCKED style is the easiest to type and therefore increases the typist's productivity. Everything starts at the left-hand margin. This style is becoming increasingly common.

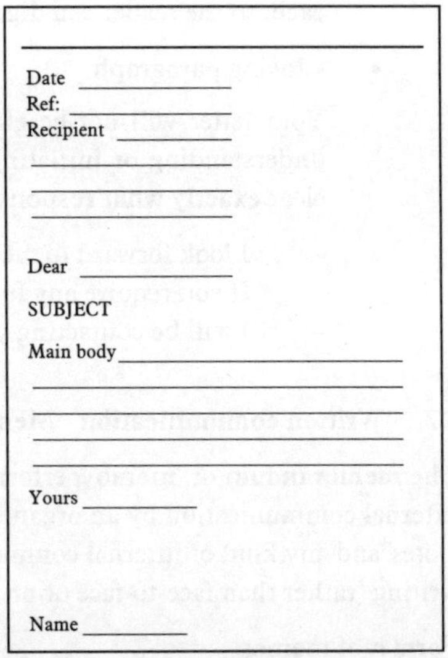

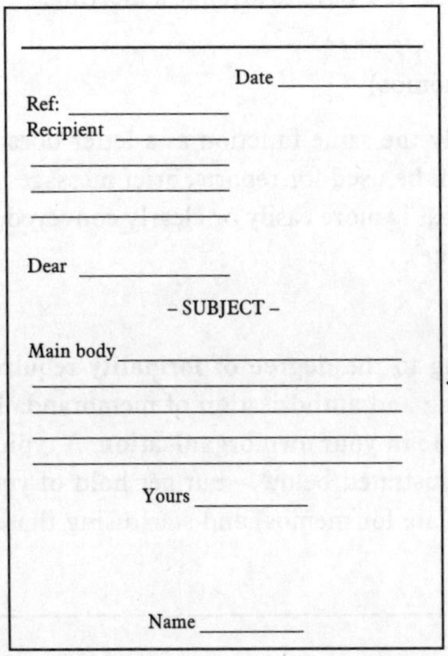

SEMI-BLOCKED style is much like fully blocked, but selected elements are moved over for balance. The date is against the right hand margin: the *complimentary close* starts from the centre: the subject header may be centralised.

Letter content

A letter (and indeed, any written message) should have a beginning, a middle and an end.

- **Opening paragraph**

  The reader will not be as familiar with the context of the message as you are. Offer:

  - A brief **explanation** of why you are writing. ('Thank you for your letter of 3 March, in which you requested information about auditing services.')
  - An **acknowledgement** of relevant correspondence received. ('As requested [or agreed] in our telephone conversation [or meeting] of 4 September, I am sending you our brochure of services.')
  - Important **background** details. ('I have been asked by my colleague, George Brown, to contact you in regard to your enquiry about auditing services.')

- **Development of the message**

  The middle paragraph(s) should contain the substance of your response to a previous message, details of the matter in hand, or the information you wish to communicate. If you are making several points, start a new paragraph with each, so the reader can digest each part of your message in turn.

- **Closing paragraph**

  Your letter will not be effective unless it has the desired result of creating understanding or initiating action. Summarise your point briefly – or make clear **exactly what response is required.**

  – I look forward to meeting you to discuss the matter in more detail.
  – If you require any further information, please call me.
  – I will be contacting you in the next few days to arrange a meeting.

4.2 Written communication - Memoranda (memos)

The **memorandum** or '**memo**' performs internally the same function as a letter does in external communication by an organisation. It can be used for reports, brief messages or 'notes' and any kind of internal communication that is more easily or clearly conveyed in writing (rather than face-to-face or on the telephone).

Format of memos

Memorandum format will vary slightly according to the **degree of formality** required and the organisation's policy on matters like filing and authorisation of memoranda by their writer. **Follow the conventions of house style in your own organisation**. A typical format, including all the required elements, is illustrated below – but get hold of your own organisation's memo pad (or computer template for memos) and start using that, if you do not already do so.

Organisation's name (optional)

MEMORANDUM

To: (recipient's name or designation) **Ref**: (for filing)

From: (author's name or designation) **Date**: (in full)

Subject: (main theme of message)

The message of the memorandum is set out like that of a letter: good English in spaced paragraphs. Note that no inside address, salutation or complimentary close is required.

Signed: (optional) author signs/initials

Copies to: (recipient(s) of copies)

Enc: to indicate accompanying material, if any

Forrest Fire Extinguishers Ltd

MEMORANDUM

To: All Staff **Ref:** PANC/mp

From: P A N Cake, Managing Director **Date:** 13 January 2009

Subject: Overtime arrangements for January/February

I would like to remind you that thanks to Pancake Day on and around the 12 February, we can expect the usual increased demand for small extinguishers. I am afraid this will involve substantial overtime hours for everyone.

In order to make this as easy as possible, the works canteen will be open all evening for snacks and hot drinks. The works van will also be available in case of transport difficulties late at night.

I realise that this period puts pressure on production and administrative staff alike, but I would appreciate your cooperation in working as many hours of overtime as you feel able.

Copies to: All staff

Activity 6 **(30 minutes)**

You were made responsible for ordering stationery in The Accounts Department of Modus Operandi Ltd a month ago. The system requires anybody who notices that stationery stocks are running low or are exhausted to fill in a standard requisition form and pass it to you in room 32. This is clearly stated in a notice on the door of the stationery cupboard. You have not received any requisition forms during your month in office but you have frequently been interrupted in your work by heads popping round the door making remarks like 'Why aren't there any yellow highlighters in the cupboard?' and 'Who is it that does the stationery then?'

This is annoying and you have decided to send a memo to all staff in your department reminding them of the system.

Required:

Draft the memo, using your own name.

4.3 Written communication - E-mail messages

Many organisations now conduct both internal and external communications via e-mail systems. E-mail can be used for a wide variety of communication purposes, in place of letters, circulars, internal memos, notes and other brief messages. Lengthier messages (such as briefs and reports) and graphic messages (such as diagrams and maps) can be attached as file attachments.

Most organisations have guidelines for the use of e-mail.

- E-mail messages have a legal effect. Firms can be sued for libellous, offensive or misleading remarks made in e-mail, and e-mail messages can be cited as evidence in court.
- E-mail can be used excessively, to the exclusion of other forms of communication which might be more appropriate. Excessive personal use (or abuse) is also an issue for many organisations (as it has been with the telephone).
- E-mail is not private, and remains on the server. There are thus dangers in using it to send confidential messages.

Using e-mail software

The most common e-mail software is Microsoft Outlook. In Outlook, depending on which version you use, a new (empty) mail message looks something like this

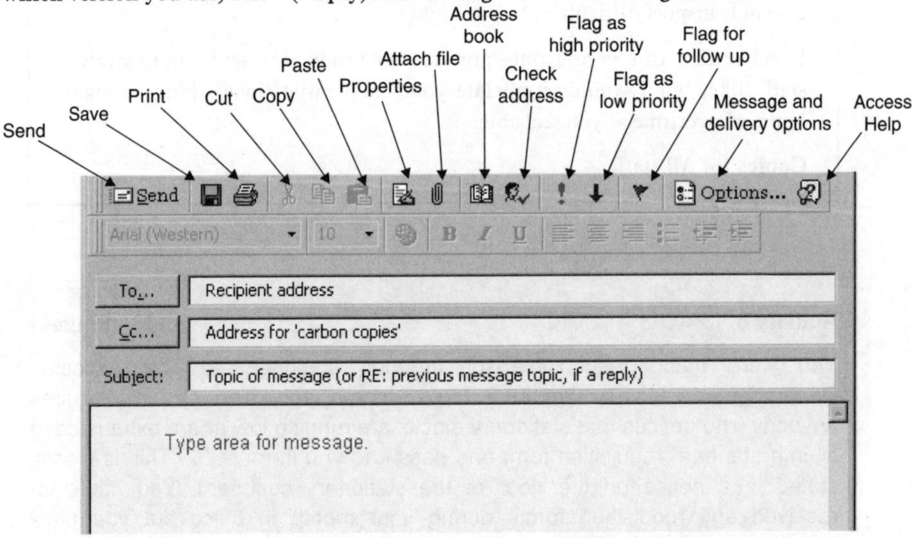

You will need to become familiar with the functions and capabilities of whatever software your organisation uses.

Composing effective e-mail messages

The following are general hints on composing e-mail messages.

Do not commit to e-mail any message that is private or confidential. As mentioned above, it is not a secure medium in general: a co-worker may cover someone's e-mail while (s)he is absent, the system administrator may access messages and companies may monitor e-mail.

Do not send illegal or offensive messages. (This should not be on your agenda anyway – especially for marketing purposes – but abusive, discriminatory and harassing messages do get sent.) E-mails can be traced to their source, and systems administrators can be liable for the misdeeds of users.

Beware of informality. Writers of e-mails may dash off a friendly note, but the recipients may (quite rightly) regard it as a written (and legally valid) response which may imply contract terms.

Beware of 'tone of voice'. Sarcasm and irony do not come across well in brief, typed, computer-mediated messages. If you wish to be humorous (in an informal context), there are conventions: adding 'emoticons' such as 'smiley faces' (☺) or the typed equivalent :).

Use mixed case letters. All uppercase (ie capitals) IS INTERPRETED AS SHOUTING!

Keep the line-length reasonably short, to ensure that it displays effectively on most recipient terminals.

Ensure that you give the recipient's address correctly and that you state a subject. The first will avoid getting the message returned to you (remember that computers are very literal) and the second will avoid getting the message deleted by the recipient as possible junk or virus mail.

Remember that sending e-mail is instant and that you cannot usually re-call a message. Check your message carefully before you click on 'send'.

Activity 7 **(15 minutes)**

How often do you use e-mail at work, and for what purposes?

What guidelines are there in your organisation for:

(a) how to use the e-mail software?

(b) how to format and compose e-mail messages (disclaimers, signatures, style)?

(c) restricting the use of e-mail?

4.4 Other written formats

There are a number of other formats you may need to use in the course of your work, including a variety of:

- **notices** or posters
- **reports**: highly-structured formal reports, or short informal reports (which may be submitted as memos or e-mails, say)
- **forms**: eg accident reports forms, payroll forms, expenses sheets

In addition, there will be different **technologies** available for **producing** and **transmitting** written messages.

- **Handwriting** of messages: a personal letter or telephone message, say
- **Word-processing** for the **production** of documents (including letters, memos, notices, reports and forms) which may be:
  - Typed on a computer using a word-processing package
  - Saved to computer disk for storage and retrieval
  - Printed out if hard copy is required and

 - Sent either electronically (via e-mail) or physically (via internal or external post or delivery)

- **Facsimile transfer (fax)** of documents. Any **hard-copy** message (letter, memo, report, form, diagram or chart) can be **transmitted** via fax, which allows it to be printed out as an exact copy, almost instantaneously, at the remote fax machine.

  Make sure that you prepare (or use) a **fax header sheet** approved by your organisation, setting out:

  - The target recipient (name, position, organisation, fax number)
  - The sender (name, position, organisation, contact details)
  - The date
  - The number of pages being sent (including the header) in case of loss or damage
  - Any accompanying notes (like a covering letter) to explain or direct attention to the documents being faxed

- **E-mail** of documents. Any message produced on (or scanned into) a computer can be attached to an e-mail message and **transmitted** via the Internet or computer network to a remote computer, even faster and more cheaply than fax.

The guidelines given in this chapter will be useful in composing any written message effectively.

4.5 Visual communication

If you are preparing a report or giving a presentation, you may need to use **visual aids** of some kind:

- to convey large amounts of data more accessibly. ('A picture paints a thousand words.')
- to add interest and appeal

Examples of visual communication you might use include:

- The **presentation** of text in documents: using layout, colour, spacing, different typefaces, logos and so on.
- **Tables** of data: a simple way of presenting **numerical information**.
- **Illustrations**: from technical drawings to simple pictures which **highlight basic lines and features** of an object.

- **Bar charts**: a visually appealing way of **showing or comparing magnitudes** of an item (eg amount of money, hours, sales) according to the length of the bars on the chart.

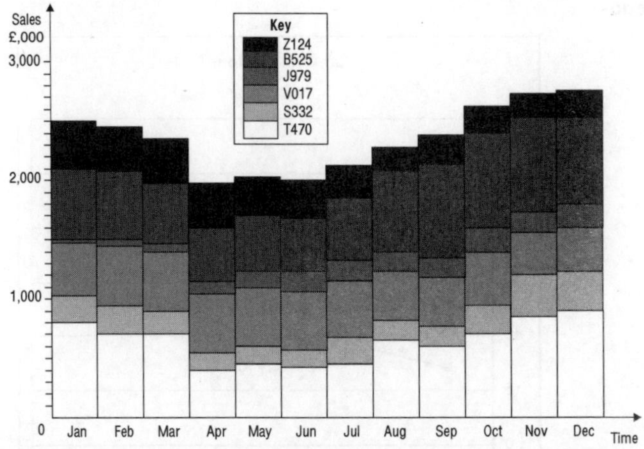

- **Pie charts**: a visually effective way of showing the relative sizes of **component elements** of a total value or amount (represented by the 360 degrees of the circle or 'pie').

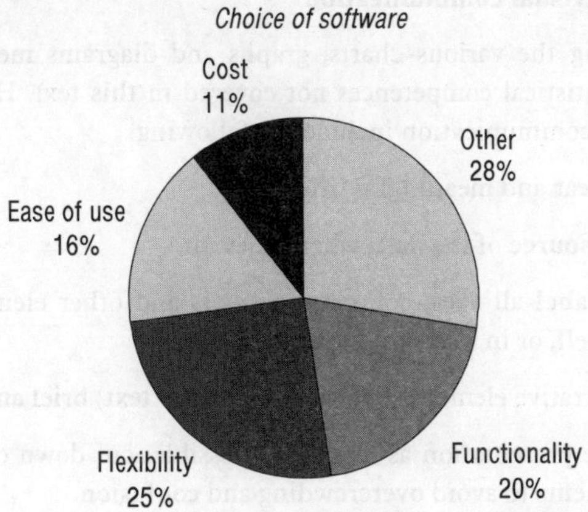

- **Line graphs**: showing the **relationship between two variables** (represented by horizontal and vertical axes) by plotting points and joining them by straight or curved lines. These are particularly useful for demonstrating **trends**.

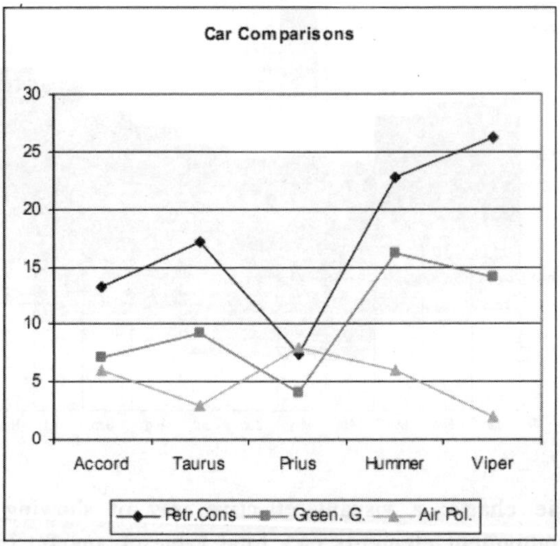

Basic principles of visual communication

Of course, preparing the various charts, graphs and diagrams mentioned above (and others), requires statistical competences not covered in this text. However, the general principles of visual communication include the following.

- Give a clear and meaningful **title**.
- Cite the **source** of the data, where relevant.
- Clearly **label** all axes, columns, symbols and other elements: either on the visual itself, or in a separate 'key'.
- Keep narrative elements (labels, explanatory text) brief and simple
- Keep the presentation as **simple** as possible: cut down on unnecessary lines and elements to avoid overcrowding and confusion.
- Use the **size** and **spacing** of the visual to make it easy to read.

Activity 8 **(45 minutes)**

The table below shows a company's sales figures for 2009.

Prod	*Jan*	*Feb*	*Mar*	*Apr*	*May*	*Jun*	*Jul*	*Aug*	*Sep*	*Oct*	*Nov*	*Dec*	*Total*
	£'000	£'000	£'000	£'000	£'000	£'000	£'000	£'000	£'000	£'000	£'000	£'000	£'000
T470	800	725	725	400	415	405	410	605	590	700	845	900	
S332	210	210	180	170	175	160	195	200	195	210	220	230	
V017	480	510	510	510	520	515	510	385	420	475	460	465	
J979	25	50	60	95	125	140	145	145	165	180	190	190	
B525	615	600	505	430	445	430	485	560	650	700	695	610	
Z124	370	360	370	385	370	350	380	375	375	360	325	355	

Tasks

Add up the columns and rows and then (making your presentation as simple or elaborate as you wish) construct the following.

(a) A graph of the year's sales

(b) A bar chart of the year's sales

(c) A pie chart, showing whatever information you think is most appropriate for this form

(d) Which method did you find most effective in presenting this information?

4.6 Oral communication – the telephone

The telephone is still the most used item of office equipment. There are bound to be many situations in which you find yourself having to communicate via the phone with internal – and external – customers.

The following guidelines may seem obvious: good! Make sure that you use them – or any guidelines given by your organisation: they ensure that you promote a positive and consistent image, as well as being efficient and effective.

Know what result you are aiming at. What action or information will satisfy you, and where and when must you get them? (You might *say* 'I was just wondering…' to sound tactful, but make sure you have done all your wondering before you pick up the receiver.)

Know to whom you should be talking. Find out names and extension numbers if possible, and keep them handy in a personal directory.

Know what you want to say, and the order and style in which you want to say it.

- A **checklist** of points will be a helpful reminder
- Have all relevant **documents** and **reference material** to hand.

Make sure you will not be **interrupted, distracted or disturbed** once you have dialled the number.

Tactics and techniques

When you get through to the dialled number, wait for a greeting and identification from the answering party. **Seek** the identification if necessary. ('Good morning. To whom am I speaking?') It is time-wasting and embarrassing to launch into the subject of your call, only to be interrupted two minutes later by: 'I'm sorry. You need to speak to ... ' or even 'Thank you. I'll put you through.'

If the target recipient of your call is out or otherwise unavailable, carry out your 'Plan B', which may be any one of the following.

- Ask to speak to **someone else** who might be knowledgeable enough to help you.
- Leave a **message** with the secretary, or switchboard operator. Make it a brief one, but dictate clearly all essential details of who you are, where you can be contacted, and what the main subject of your call was to be. State whether you wish to be called back.
- Arrange to **call back** at a convenient time, when it is anticipated that the target will be available.

Once through to the appropriate person, the business of the call should be covered as **succinctly** as possible (consistent with rapport-building and courtesy).

Greet the other person by **name**: if you do not already know it – find out first!

Prepare the ground by briefly explaining the context of your call, what it is about, any relevant details.

Remember that the other person **cannot see you** to lip-read, judge your facial expression, or see you nod your head. Speak clearly, spell out proper names and figures; use your tone of voice to reinforce your message.

Pace your message so that the other person can refer to files or take notes.

Check your own notes as you speak and make fresh ones of any information you receive.

You may easily be **misheard** or misinterpreted over the telephone line, so you will have to seek constant feedback. If you are not receiving any signals, ask for some ('Have you got that?', 'Can you read that back?', 'Am I going too fast for you?', 'OK?')

Close the call effectively. Emphasise any action you require, and check that the other person has understood your expectations.

Receiving calls

It is very important that those who **answer** the telephones in an organisation should be **efficient, courteous and helpful**. A voice on the telephone may be the **first** or only **impression** of the organisation that an outsider receives: remember that you will have to create the impression you make with your voice and responsiveness alone.

Give a **courteous greeting** and **identify yourself** in whatever way is appropriate (name, department and organisation): there may be 'house rules' about this.

Identify and **note** the caller's name and organisation as soon as possible

---

Listen carefully to the message: it may require instant action or response.

Check your understanding. If the other person speaks too fast, or you do not catch something, are not sure that you have heard it right, or simply do not understand, say so: a courteous interruption to ask for a repetition or spelling is helpful to the caller.

Never leave callers hanging. If you have to transfer them to another extension or put them on hold, tell them what you intend to do.
Speak clearly and with a certain **formality**, and keep your **tone** appropriately helpful, courteous and alert. (It is easy to sound brusque when you intend to sound efficient).
Take **concise notes** of any details you may require in order to follow-up the conversation. If you are giving information, pace it so that the caller can also take notes.
Co-operate with the caller. If you can resolve the matter in the course of the call, for example, by providing information, do so. If there are still matters to be resolved – further action to be taken or information to be sent to the caller by post – make sure that you are both clear as to what is required, and within what timeframe.

5 COMMUNICATION STYLES AND TECHNIQUES

5.1 Introduction

Communication styles include speaking, effective listening, respect for others' opinions, influencing, being assertive, negotiating, persuading, presentation, consulting and counselling as well as the use of information and communications technology (ICT). The techniques and skills associated with these styles are outlined below.

5.2 Speaking skills

The following are key skills in effective spoken communication – whether face-to-face or on the phone.

- **Clear articulation** is vital: not because it is associated with a particular region, section of society or level of education, but because you want to be understood immediately and unambiguously by *any other person*, in order to get a response that you require. Be **considerate** to the recipient of your message: don't use or pronounce words in a way that he or she will not understand, and don't speak too quickly. If you are satisfied that your speech is clear, unambiguous and not mannered just for the sake of it: fine.
- If you are articulating clearly, you will be much more audible, but you will also have to consider how to **project your voice**. Speaking softly or even at a normal **volume** will be ineffective in a large room with a high ceiling and heavy curtains.
- **Intonation** affects *how* your message reaches its recipient, as much as volume affects *whether* it does. Be aware of how the placing of **emphasis** on different words alters the meaning of a sentence: the stress *implies* something to the listener. How does your voice sound? Cheery? Gloomy? Disapproving? Encouraging? Affectionate? Enthusiastic? Indifferent? Hostile? Stay alert: if your voice is not **expressive**, you may come across as bored or indifferent.
- **Pace and pauses** are further elements in fluent but clear delivery. Don't garble your words or string together long breathless sentences. Avoid excessive use of 'um' or 'er' and phrases like 'sort of' and 'I mean'.

5.3 Listening skills

Listening is not the same as hearing. Effective listening involves really paying full attention to others: their words, speech, demeanour and body language. It means asking appropriate questions so as to understand what they are trying to communicate.

Effective listening is hard work and requires considerable skill; in social settings individual listeners often fail to listen to the messages that are being expressed because they are distracted by other things, such as the impression they are making and a wish to put their point across. To be a good listener requires that sometimes you just sit back and concentrate very hard on the message being put across. You can then prompt the person talking to clarify the meaning of what they say by asking brief questions: 'can you tell me more about ..? Do you mean that....?

Many benefits are available from effective listening.

- It is a **quick, direct source of information**, which may be useful to you.
- It offers the opportunity to use the speaker's **tone of voice** to help you interpret underlying messages. (One example is knowing when someone is serious or joking.)
- It is **interactive** and **flexible**, so you can ask questions or add information of your own, to make the communication process more effective.
- It **builds relationships**, by encouraging (and demonstrating) understanding of another person's feelings and point of view.

The following are some guidelines on being a good listener.

What to do	How to do it
Be ready	Get your attitude right at the start, and decide to listen. You might even be able to do some background research so that you have established a context for the message you intend to receive.
Be interested	Don't try to soak up a message like a sponge: make it interesting for yourself by asking questions: how is this information relevant to me and how can I use it?
Be patient	Try to hold yourself back from interrupting if you disagree with someone, and don't compete to get your view in before the speaker has properly finished. Wait until a suitable opening (ie while your point is still relevant to the immediate discussion, but not while the speaker is just drawing a breath between phrases). Don't be so preoccupied with how you're going to respond that you forget to listen to what is being said.
Keep your mind on the job	Concentrate. It is very easy to switch off as attention wanders or you get tired. Don't get side-tracked by irrelevancies in the message: cooperate with the speaker in getting to the point of what he is trying to say.
Give feedback	For example, try an interested and attentive look, a nod, a murmur of agreement or query ('Yes... Really?'). If there are opportunities, use some verbal means of checking that you have understood the message correctly: ask questions, referring to the speaker's words in a way that demonstrates your interpretation of them ('You said earlier that...' 'You implied that...'). The speaker can then correct you if you have missed or misinterpreted something.

5.4 Respecting the opinion of others

Another important communications skill is that of respecting the opinions of others. We can save a lot of time and effort by considering what other people are saying, and forgetting for the time being our own point of view.

Respecting the opinion of others is particularly important in team work situations. Sometimes you will have to listen to views you do not like, do not understand or to which you cannot relate. A good listener is someone who tries to get a better understanding of views that are different from their own in order to see if there is merit in them. The best way of dealing with this is to keep an open mind and ask the speaker, in a non-threatening way, to clarify their ideas e.g. by saying 'that sounds interesting but could you explain how it will work in practice?' or 'can you explain to me how that is better than other ideas that have been put forward?' A good listener is constantly seeking to find out the best ideas and solutions even though these may contradict his or her starting position. However, this does not mean that you have to accept someone else's ideas, but you do need to consider them.

5.5 Influencing techniques

Influencing successfully means getting a result which meets the needs of both you and your customer - often called a win-win situation. It might be persuading a company to take a course of action i.e. purchase your product or use your service or it could be to persuade someone within the company of your point of view. Lee Bryce (*The Influential Woman*) suggests that there are two types of influencing techniques – push and pull:

Pull	Push
1. State your view of the problem/ opportunity.	1. Identify the problem/opportunity and propose your solution.
2. Clarify how the other person sees the situation.	2. Invite reactions.
3. Work towards agreement on the nature of the problem/opportunity	3. Check that you understand each other's arguments.
4. Look for solutions, using as many of the other person's ideas as possible.	4. Deal with objections: a) by persuasion (if you want commitment) b) by authority (if you only need compliance)
5. Come to joint agreement on outcome and action plan.	5. Agree on the outcome and action plan.

Influencing behaviours can be conveniently split into pull or push and this helps us to determine which style we may have used in the past and which we would want to use more of in the future.

Pull influencing involves motivating people, using your personality to its full effect to pull people towards your viewpoint, using benefits to help solve problems and issues. It means dragging someone to your goal which also satisfies their goals as well. Success factors to be able to use pull influencing techniques involve:

- The quality of the questions used to obtain information and check understanding
- The ability to put yourself in the customer's shoes
- The skill to build on your customer's proposals.
- The ability to forge relationships and coalitions to influence people

Pull influencing can bring extensive results often culminating in a long term relationship and a trusted adviser status being achieved

Push influencing is the opposite and uses your skills to persuade and move the customer to the position of change which brings about the win-win relationship - using logical arguments and facts to persuade, bargaining and negotiating, using punishment or rewards to coerce the customer or authority to move them.

Success factors for push based influencing come down to:

- The quality of your ideas and reasoning
- Your credibility and authority
- Your ability to get the right people to support your proposal

Push based influencing has its place but is not as effective as pull based influencing because power forms the basis of much of pull influencing and power can be too forceful in many situations.

5.6 Being assertive

Assertive behaviour involves standing up for your own rights and needs but also respecting the rights and needs of others. Assertive people stand up for their own rights in such a way that they do not violate another person's rights. They express their needs, wants, opinions, feelings and beliefs in direct, honest and appropriate ways.

Assertive behaviour must be carefully distinguished from aggressive behaviour – this is standing up for yourself at the expense of other people and involves:

- standing up for your own rights but doing so in such a way that you violate the rights of other people;
- ignoring or dismissing the needs, wants, opinions, feelings or beliefs of others;
- expressing your own needs, wants and opinions in inappropriate ways.

Aggression is some form of attack and may be verbal or physical. A frustrated employee may attack his or her supervisor or kick a machine that has broken down. Verbal aggression can take such forms as shouting, name-calling, and sarcasm, swearing or making snide remarks.

Assertive behaviour must also be distinguished from passive or non-assertive behaviour – a 'flight' reaction that takes the form of giving in to others demands:

- Failing to stand up for your rights, or allowing others to disregard them
- Expressing your needs, wants, opinions and feelings apologetically or vaguely
- Failing to express honestly your needs, feelings and opinions.

Activity 9 **(10 minutes)**

Think about incidences of conflict you have observed or been involved in at your work-place or college.

What can you see as the (a) immediate or apparent benefits ('payoffs') and (b) the actual longer term results of:

- Behaving passively or non-assertively?
- Behaving aggressively?
- Behaving assertively?

Techniques of assertion

Asking for what you want

(a) **Decide what it is you want or feel, and express it directly and specifically**. Don't assume that others will know, or work out from hints, what it is that you really want.

(b) **Stick to your statement.** If you are ignored, refused or responded to in some other negative way, don't back down, 'fly off the handle', or enter into arguments designed to deflect you from your purpose. Stick to your position, and repeat it calmly, as often as necessary: repetition projects an image of determination and reinforces your own confidence and conviction.

(c) **Deflect responses from the other person.** Show that you have heard and understood the other person's response, but are not going to be sidetracked.

Saying no without upsetting yourself or your colleagues

Saying 'no' can be very difficult for people: they feel it is selfish, or will cause offence.

(a) **Don't be pushed.** If you are at all hesitant about whether to say 'yes' or 'no' try asking for time to decide, to think or obtain more information. Why should you make an instant decision? Acknowledge your doubts: ask your questions. Feel free to change your mind.

(b) **Say 'no' clearly and calmly, if that is your answer.** Explain why, if you think it appropriate – not because you are anxious to excuse yourself, as if it were not your right to say 'no'. Don't express regret unless you feel regretful. Remember that when you say 'no', you are refusing a request, not rejecting a person.

(c) **Acknowledge your feelings.** If you feel awkward about refusing, or under pressure to accept, say so: the other person will be reassured that you are giving him or her due consideration.

(d) **Watch your body language.** If you have said 'yes' when you wanted to say 'no', don't start giving 'no' signals by sulking. If you are saying 'no', don't give contradictory signals by smiling ingratiatingly, lingering as if waiting to be talked out of it etc.

Receiving criticism and feedback

Distinguish between **valid criticism** (which you know to be legitimate), **invalid criticism** (which you now to be untrue) and a **put down** (intended to be hurtful or humiliating).

(a) **Invalid criticism and put-downs** should be handled simply and assertively with a straightforward denial: 'I don't accept that at all'.

(b) **Valid criticism** should be regarded positively as a potentially helpful experience.

  (i) **Negative assertions**: learning how to agree with a criticism if it does in fact apply to you, without growing defensive or abjectly apologetic. You simply acknowledge the truth in what the critic is saying, together with your response to the situation.

  (ii) **Negative enquiry**: learning how to take the initiative, to **prompt** specific criticism, in order to use the information if it is constructive **or** expose an attempt to put you down or be negative.

Giving criticism

Expressing negative feelings to others so that they hear what you are saying but do not feel personally attacked or rejected is not easy. Effective communication will be impossible if you make the other person defensive or aggressive, or if you let your own feelings get in the way. Guidelines are as follows.

(a) Describe the **behaviour** and express your feelings about the behaviour – to the individual personally.

(b) **Ask for a specific change of behaviour**. Being specified separates constructive criticism (which involves give and take) from attack or complaint.

(c) **End on a positive note**. This does not mean backing off your criticism ('it's not that important, really: I just thought I'd mention it'), but stating something positive that you feel. For example: 'I'm glad I've had a chance to say this', or 'In all other areas, you're doing fine, so I hope we can get this sorted out'.

Activity 10 **(10 minutes)**

A colleague telephones you when you are working on some invoices that you particularly want to finish. He says he wants to talk about next week's safety meeting. You prefer to discuss it later.

Give (a) an assertive response and (b) an aggressive response

5.7 Negotiating techniques

Negotiating is an activity that seeks to reach agreement between two or more starting positions. It is a process of:

(a) Purposeful persuasion: each party attempts to persuade the other to accept its case, by marshalling persuasive arguments.

(b) Constructive compromise: each party accepts the need to move closer towards each other's position, so that they can explore common ground and areas where concessions and compromises can be made while still meeting the key needs of both parties.

Everyone negotiates (almost every day) and certain principles seem to be present which anyone can learn.

- Ask questions – before stating a position or making proposals, it is very helpful to inquire about the other side's interests and concerns. This will help you understand what is important to the other side and may provide new ideas for mutual benefit. Ask clarifying questions to really understand the other's concerns in this negotiation. This will also help you determine their approach to negotiations: win-lose or win-win. You can then make more realistic proposals.
- 'Win-win' negotiations involve understanding each other's interests and finding solutions that will benefit both parties. The goal is to co-operate and seek solutions so both parties can walk away winners. If you come to the table thinking only one person can win (win-lose), there won't be an effort to co-operate or problem solve. By the same token, if you come to the table expecting to lose (lose-win), you play the martyr and resentment builds.
- Respect – when the other side feels that you respect him or her, it reduces defensiveness and increases the sharing of useful information -- which can lead to an agreement. When people feel disrespect, they become more rigid and likely to hide information you need.
- Trust – people tend to be more generous toward those they like and trust. An attitude of friendliness and openness generally is more persuasive than an attitude of deception and manipulation. Being honest about the information you provide and showing interest in the other side's concerns can help.

The skills of a negotiator can be summarised under three main headings:

(a) Interpersonal skills – the use of good communicating techniques, the use of power and influence, and the ability to impress a personal style on the tactics of negotiation.

(b) Analytical skills – the ability to analyse information, diagnose problems, to plan and set objectives, and the exercise of good judgement in interpreting results.

(c) Technical skills – attention to detail and thorough case preparation.

There are behaviours that are typical of successful negotiators and distinguish them from the less successful:

Successful negotiators	Less successful negotiators
Skilled negotiators avoid criticising or attacking the other person and concentrate instead on 'attacking' the problem in a no nonsense but constructive way.	Less skilled negotiators are more likely to get locked into an attacking spiral where one side attacks the other, which provokes a counter attack and so on.
Skilled negotiators ask many more questions than the less skilled. The skilled negotiator asks questions not only to gain more information and understanding but also as an alternative to disagreeing bluntly, and as a means of putting forward suggestions.	The less skilled tend to assume that they understand the other person's point of view and that the other person has the same basic information. This makes asking questions redundant.
Skilled negotiators keep the emotional temperature down by sticking to the facts.	Less skilled negotiators are inclined to exaggeration, using expressions such as 'an offer you can't refuse' and 'mutually beneficial'.
The skilled negotiator is more likely to say things that reveal what he or she is thinking, intending and feeling than the less skilled.	The less skilled negotiator feels vulnerable to losing the argument and is more likely to 'keep his cards close to his chest'.
Disagreements are inevitable during the course of a negotiation. The skilled negotiator gives the explanation first and rounds off the explanation by saying that they were in disagreement. This has a more constructive effect because the explanation becomes the focus for the other person's reaction rather than the fact of a disagreement.	Less skilled negotiators disagree first and then go on to give reasons. This often provokes a negative reaction from the other person who bridles at the explicit disagreement and therefore fails to listen to the reasons.

Activity 11 **(30 minutes)**

Get together with fellow students (or friends) in pairs or teams to prepare and role-play a negotiation.

Scenario:

You want to go on holiday with the whole family to a coastal resort this summer. Your (role-play) partner wants to have some quiet time at home redecorating the bathroom, knowing that the two teenage (role-play) kids are keen to spend time with friends. These projects are important to both (or all four) of you. Negotiate! If you really can't find role-play partners, make notes on the possible strategies, win-win potential and best-realistic-worst positions for all participants.

5.8 Presentation skills

A presentation is a combination of both verbal and visual form of communication that is used by managers at some meetings, training sessions, lectures and conferences.

Before any presentation is made it is necessary to establish the objectives of the presentation, why it is being done and what you want it to achieve. Once these things have been identified, the best way to achieve the objectives can be established. Compiling a presentation that holds the audience's interest and drives the point home with clarity is not as easy as it looks. Some professional presenters advise that you divide your presentation into three sections

(a) The *introduction* summarises your overall message and should begin with a title slide, or transparency, that succinctly states the purpose of the presentation.

(b) The *main section*, sometimes called the *rationale*, delivers your main points. In general, each point should be made in a simple, powerful text slide and then bolstered with more detail from charts and subsidiary text slides. For some reason, three items of supporting data for each main point seems to work best for most audiences and most arguments.

(c) Section three winds up with re-emphasis, starting with a summary, moving on to a *conclusion* and leaving the audience with a message that will persuade them to act – this may be to applaud your department's progress or to buy your scheme. The final line of the presentation must be a definite close.

The presentation must be summarised throughout, because you cannot rely on the audience having read any handouts prior to the presentations.

The audience should be given the opportunity to ask questions and whether this is done at regular intervals or at the end of the presentation will depend upon the topic of the presentation and the audience to which it is addressed.

Graphics, in the form of still or moving pictures, can be a particularly effective method of communication. They have *advantages* in that they are attention-catching, have a dramatic impact, they facilitate the understanding of complex material and are comprehensive to those of poor linguistic ability.

Key elements of a successful presentation are those of:

- thorough preparation
- good knowledge of subject
- understanding the needs of the audience
- selection and use of appropriate communications media.

5.9 Consultation techniques

Definition

> **Consultation** is where one party seeks the views of another party before either party takes a decision.

Consultation is the process where, on a regular basis, management genuinely seeks the views, ideas and feelings of employees before a decision is taken.

Consultation is not the same as negotiation. Negotiation implies acceptance by both parties that agreement between them is required before a decision is taken. Consultation implies a willingness to listen to the views of another while reserving the right to take the final decision, with or without agreement on both sides.

For the effective manager, using his or her interpersonal skills, a way of consulting subordinates is to discuss proposals with them. The 'I have decided to give you X approach is nowhere near as effective as the 'I've been thinking – do you feel that you can tackle X approach?'

Consulting implies decisions are only made after consultation. However, the final decision may not include any or all of the ideas put forward. Subordinates may feel cheated and not truly involved.

5.10 Counselling techniques

Counselling is client-centred and involves the client in solving the problem. A shorter definition is 'helping a person to help themselves'. Counselling is a specialist term and must be distinguished from telling, advising and manipulating.

- *Telling* is where the person giving help by telling the client what to do is problem centred and excludes the client from the problem-solving process.
- *Advising* is also a problem-centred person giving help and excluding the client in problem-solving. The process usually involves the adviser identifying options and getting the client to select the one which the adviser favours.
- *Manipulating* is when the client is excluded from the problem-solving process and the person doing the manipulating is satisfying his or her own needs.

Effective counselling shows an organisation's commitment to and concern for its staff and is likely to improve employee loyalty and enthusiasm. The techniques include:

- helping others to identify problems, issues and possible solutions for themselves;
- using a non-directive approach rather than advising or making specific suggestions;
- encouraging reflection and talking around issues;
- allowing others to lead and determine the direction;
- using open questions to help others explore ideas, feelings and thoughts;
- having more of a passive role, listening very actively and carefully;
- speaking only to clarify and probe.

5.11 Information and communication technology (ICT)

Information and Communication Technology (ICT) is concerned with the electronic collection, organisation, analysis, presentation, and communication of information. It encompasses all media types and formats as well as all relevant tools.

Skills in using information and communication technology are increasingly useful for obtaining and analysing information, for organising your ideas, and for communicating and working with others. A good place to start if the approach is completely new to you is with your personal development planning. If you are already proficient, you will have automatically developed your own files and spreadsheets. It is recommended you use a word processing file for your narrative and examples, together with an electronic spreadsheet of objectives and timescales for your personal development planning.

5.12 Changing communication

In the last few years, the infrastructure and tools of communication have radically changed. The phone is swiftly being overtaken by e-mail as the most popular method of remote interpersonal communication. The Internet has changed the way people access information. Even 'old' media like the television and telephone are being transformed by new data transmission infrastructures and integration with computer systems.

Broadly, communication has changed in the following ways.

(a) **Higher speed** – the development of 'facsimile transfer' (fax) was breakthrough in its day: enabling documents, which previously had to be posted, to be transferred down a phone line. Now, messages can be transferred via a local computer network or the Internet almost instantly, to the point where real time conversations can be held using online messaging and chat rooms. Recent infrastructure innovations such as ISDN (Integrated Systems Digital Network), DSL (Digital Subscriber Lines), satellite transmission (for telephone and television signals), fibre optic cabling and increased 'band width' (allowing more data to pass through networks more swiftly) have supported this process.

(b) **Wider access to information** – once you are connected to the Internet, you have instant access to an almost indescribable wealth of information. Through electronic mail and bulletin boards (newsgroups) you can use a different kind of resource: a worldwide supply of knowledgeable people, some of whom are bound to share your interests, no matter how obscure... There are also more (and better) resources, including museums, exhibitions, art galleries and shops.

(c) **24–7 global communication** – information and communications technology (ICT) has enabled 24-hour 7-day global communication: across working or office hours, time zones and geographical distances. Telex, fax and answer machines were a start in this direction – but they required (possibly delayed) human intervention to initiate a response. The Internet allows users to access information/services and perform transactions at any time of any day. Nor is there any distinction between local and international sites, in terms of speed or cost of access. (Physical delivery of products ordered will, of course, re-erect some of the geographical barriers.)

(d) **Interactivity and multi-media** – Interactivity is mutual responsiveness. Consumers are increasingly demanding in terms of interactivity in accessing and responding to promotional messages. Consumers are also increasingly demanding in terms of the stimulation provided by promotional messages. Multi media communication implies the use of written, visual and audio elements to enhance a message's impact and interest. The Internet and related technologies have habituated people (particularly young media and IT consumers) to multi-media presentations, high-level animated/video-based graphics and interaction with material. Although the impact of such trends may be limited by the power of the individual user's PC and the speed of the modem, printed matter may seem relatively uninteresting in comparison: some of the features of online and multi-media presentation are being added to traditional print advertising and information: simulated 'links' and buttons, multi-directional graphics and so on.

(e) **Personalisation** – database, document generation and web technologies have improved the ease and sophistication of targeting and personalisation of contact between organisations and customers. Examples include:

(i) Allowing users to customise web pages for their personal interests and tastes

(ii) Making individually-targeted product offers and recommendations based on browsing/buying behaviour

(iii) Sending personally addressed and targeted-content messages to customers

(iv) Encouraging users/customers to form 'virtual communities' (for example, using chat rooms, discussion boards and newsgroups)

6 DELIVERY FORMATS

6.1 Demonstrate acquired interpersonal and transferable skills

Transferable skills are skills you have acquired through any number of activities - such as courses, clubs, volunteering, and working full or part-time that can be used in any new activity. Major categories for marketable transferable skills are: communication, research and planning, human relations, organisation, management and leadership, and general work behaviours.

Talents, traits and practical knowledge are all part of the skills spectrum. Some of these skills have more transfer value than others for employment opportunities. So it is important to think about your skills and their value to what you want to do or are applying for. Skills are not stagnant so it is always possible to build the ones that you are good at, and to strengthen or develop the ones you are not so good at in your work, volunteering or education.

Skills can be divided into different subsets:

1 working with people

2 working with things

3 working with information and data

For example, some transferable skills can be used in every workplace setting (e.g., organising or public speaking) while some are more applicable to specific settings (e.g., drafting or accounting).

The following are examples of skills often acquired through the classroom, jobs, athletics and other activities. Use these examples to help you develop your own list of the transferable skills you have acquired.

Working with people

Selling	Training	Teaching	Supervising
Advising	Motivating	Negotiating	Organising
Mediating	Delegating	Representing	Entertaining

Working with things

Repairing	Designing	Driving
Building	Surveying	Negotiating
Sketching	Machining	Drafting
Constructing	Organising	Keyboarding

Working with data/information

Calculating	Computing	Testing	Developing databases
Writing	Filing	Sorting	Working with spreadsheets
Accounting	Budgeting	Analysing	Gathering data

When planning your future, it may be useful to do a skills audit. A skills audit is a self-reflective process where you identify the skills and strengths that you already have that affect your employability. They might include some of the core transferable skills listed above.

A good way to start a skills audit is to draw a table with your skills listed by row. Against each skill, note your level of competency and think of examples or evidence that demonstrate your ability. Finally, identify areas where you may need further knowledge or training to reach the skill level that you need.

Consider the following when you conduct your skills audit:

- specific skills you have developed as a result of your qualification;
- work experience you have completed;
- job-specific and transferable skills you have acquired;
- skills you have developed through extracurricular activities, such as volunteering, art, sport, music, drama, etc.;
- positive feedback you have received throughout your course and activities.

The skills audit will help you:

- recollect skills which you may not have thought of or which you may not have considered to be important or relevant;
- think of good, real-life examples to demonstrate your skills. The following example may be useful for interviews with universities or employers.

EXAMPLE

Michael, project engineer

'I have worked in the rail engineering industry for the past 20 years. I have had a range of technical roles, from trainee technician to project engineer. I have been responsible for multi-disciplinary projects, ranging from small infrastructure renewals through to major multi-million pound infrastructure investment projects.

A couple of years ago I decided I needed to gain experience and qualifications in business, so I decided to take an HND course in Business Management. I chose this particular course for its modular structure and content. It was based around the fundamental aspects of business instead of purely engineering or rail-orientated activities.

The module subject matter involved a broad range of business subjects including accountancy, strategic management, human resource management and web design, plus other modules. I felt the topic content would help me better understand the mechanics of project and business management.

The course helped me relate expenditure to project plans. I also learned about tools that managers use to change and adapt work procedures. The course taught me how to work with staff to maximise cooperation, productivity and manage change.'

6.2 Mastering the 'soft' skills

When employers consider job candidates, they do not simply look at academic credentials and past work experience. In order to ensure that candidates have what it takes to make a valuable contribution to the company, a whole range of skills that go beyond the technical requirements of a job need to be considered. Meeting the specifications outlined in a job posting is obviously a must, but do you possess some of the intangible skills that can convince prospective employers of your potential?

Transferable or 'soft' skills can enhance your career mobility and increase your chances of success in landing the job you want. As the name implies, transferable skills can be taken with you from job to job and are therefore an important aspect of your career development. The following skills can help give you a competitive edge when applying for a position.

People skills - personalities and needs of co-workers can vary enormously. A good leader can manage the wide range of people's expectations with fairness, tact, and understanding, while keeping an eye on organisational goals. Good people skills are critical when dealing with difficult colleagues - bullies, underachievers and incompetent managers. Successful team members are able to clearly assert their own expectations while remaining empathetic to others' needs.

Good people skills are very important to employers, who typically look for well-rounded employees who work well in teams, are diplomatic, resourceful, and are able to build networks among their peers. When applying for a job, try to demonstrate how you have been able to bring out the best in the people around you.

Communications skills - in the daily operations of any enterprise many messages are passed back and forth. Being able to pass on information in a clear and concise manner is incredibly important to the achievement of a company's goals. The tone and delivery of your communications can also have a marked impact on motivation levels of fellow team members. Solid writing skills are a huge plus in any job, and if you can communicate in more than one language, you definitely have an edge over unilingual job candidates.

In knowledge industries such as pharmaceutical, the ability to make effective presentations is very important. As in most things, practice and preparation make perfect. If you have little experience in this area, you should definitely consider enrolling in a public speaking course. Familiarity with presentation and word processing software and other electronic communications media is a necessity for many jobs.

Negotiation skills - whether they take the form of getting a better price from a supplier, dealing with complex industrial relations issues, or getting a colleague to help you on a project, negotiations are a part of daily life. Learning to give and take in order to achieve goals is a skill that employers value highly. Show prospective employers examples of past achievements and some of the tactics you employed to successfully negotiate your way toward a goal.

Business skills - are highly transferable and the more you acquire, the more marketable you become. Employers highly value employees who possess the ability to manage a budget, make financial projections, and recognise business opportunities. Make a habit of keeping an eye on the bottom line and being aware of the business realities surrounding the pharmaceutical industry.

Experience is king in business, so make sure you let employers know what kind of skills you have acquired over the years. A previous job in sales may have taught you to think on your feet, and more importantly, to understand that the customer always comes first. Even in a research lab environment, a customer service orientation (substitute 'customer' with 'shareholder') is important in keeping a focus on profitability.

Creative and strategic thinking - ability to apply lateral thinking to come up with unique and innovative solutions to problems help give you (and your company) a competitive edge. Pharmaceutical companies have a particular need for workers who can quickly adapt to changing circumstances. In interview situations you should be prepared to give examples of challenges that you have faced and creative solutions that you have come up with to help save the day.

Just as important as the ability to generate creative solutions is the wisdom to attack the right problems. Companies value employees who understand how their work fits into the big picture. An aptitude for strategic thinking is the mark of a good manager.

Time management - employers give top marks to candidates with a proven ability to juggle multiple priorities and responsibilities. Time is money and companies love people who are efficient in their use of time and who are effective at helping co-workers eliminate waste and duplication of effort. Employees who meet deadlines and deliver projects on time (and on budget) are huge assets. This is especially true in pharmaceutical companies where time to market is critical and money is lost with every tick of the patent expiration clock.

Motivation and commitment - successful companies strive to align employees' personal goals with corporate objectives and they are eager to hire candidates who put a great deal of pride and personal effort into their work. Again, giving examples of past achievements is the best way of underscoring your high personal standards and drive to succeed. Just as important is the ability to bring out these qualities in others. Leadership skills are always in high demand, especially as companies rely more and more on self-directed teams and project-oriented work organisation.

Personal image and self-awareness - you should be aware of the image you present to co-workers and clients, making sure that it fits the context in which you find yourself. If your glasses are patched up with sticking plaster it might lead people to believe that you use the same approach to resolve work-related problems. Understanding how people perceive you is important in a variety of areas such as negotiations, managing workplace relationships, and selling your company to prospective business partners.

Your CV and job interview should leave no doubt in the employer's mind that you either possess the above skills and qualities or are taking steps to gain the experience and training necessary to fill any gaps. Try to highlight various ways in which your skills, knowledge, and experience in these areas have led to concrete achievements. Lifelong learning is an important part of anyone's career, so paying attention to developing your transferable skills is a strategy that will serve you well throughout your working life

Your knowledge and skills

All your experiences are valuable - personal and work-related experience.

Knowledge about your transferable skills makes it possible for you to make links between where you are now and where you would like to be.

Transferable skills are skills you have acquired during any activity in your life that are transferable and applicable to what you want to do in your next job. For example, during your volunteer work at a community centre, you helped the social worker to organise play activities for children. This experience helped you to develop your planning skills - a skill that is necessary for your next position as a facilitator of youth activities at another community centre.

Knowledge of your transferable skills is important in compiling your career portfolio, curriculum vitae, and cover letters and for devising interview strategies. You need to be able to identify your skills, assess how you can demonstrate them, determine how you can develop them and communicate them to employers.

Think of everything you have done and how this is transferable to what you want to be doing. If you are replying to an advertisement in the newspaper, emphasise the skills that the employer is asking for. Analyse any jobs (full-time, part-time, and voluntary), your studies (formal and informal), projects, parenting, hobbies, or sports in terms of skills that you have acquired. Remember that no experience is insignificant.

7 WORKING WITH OTHERS

7.1 Achieve shared goals

Working with others will help you to understand the best ways to work with other people to achieve shared goals. You will learn how to:

- figure out what needs to be done;
- discuss and decide who will be responsible for which task and be clear about what everyone is going to be doing;
- decide on timescales and resources to get your tasks done on time;

- get together and talk about how you are progressing - what went well and what didn't;
- agree with the others on ways you might be able to improve;
- find ways of working together that work;
- support each other;
- take on different roles;
- deal with difficult situations and difficult relationships;
- know where to go to for help.

By working with others, you can use the skills of the whole of your group to get a job done successfully. You will be able to share your skills and learn new skills and new ways of working from other people. You will also get to share ideas

7.2 Develop a strategy for working with others

In your portfolio you need to present the outcomes from your work in a group/team situation. This will include

- A description of the group activity, noting those involved. Include details of the work you did in a one-to-one situation and group situation, and the particular activity where you took a leading role.
- The outcomes of the group work, or part of it. For example, a written report, web site, video recording or poster presentation.

7.3 Team player

Because so many jobs involve working in one or more work-groups, you must have the ability to work with others in a professional manner while attempting to achieve a common goal. The skills involved in teamwork are:

- ability to work with others
- achieve a common goal
- resourceful
- building trusting relationships
- negotiating (developing a mutually beneficial solution among parties)
- responding to feedback (changing your behaviour when supervisors and others you respect make suggestions)

By being a team player - departmental or cross-functional - it becomes even more important to:

- share successes with your team
- avoid pointing your finger when there are failures
- build your reputation and
- increase your value to the organisation

- adjust your priorities to those of the team when necessary
- multicultural understanding (the experience of a positive relationship with someone different from yourself in terms of culture, language, social condition, or history)

7.4 Flexibility/adaptability

Adaptability/Flexibility deals with openness to new ideas and concepts, to working independently or as part of a team and to carrying out multiple tasks or projects.

Adaptable-flexible values include the following:

Dedication	Reliability	Get job done
Ready to work	Positive attitude	Enthusiasm
Prodessionalism	Fair	Self-confidence
Unique mix of skills	Self-motivated	Work independently
Willingness to learn	Openness to grow	Resilient

Adaptability suggests making positive adjustments to changing social situations and events. The skills include:

- habit of curiosity
- think creatively
- solve problems effectively and quickly
- work well with those who are different from you
- positive adjustments to changing social situations and events
- innovation (using information from a variety of different sources to create unique solutions to a problem)

Flexibility: employers need to know that the people they hire can expand and change as their companies do - especially in today's rapidly changing economy. Applicants who are receptive to new ideas and concepts are highly valued by employers. Are you capable of changing and being receptive to new situations and ideas?

7.5 Social skills

Social networking competency is defined as socialising informally. It includes developing contacts with people who are a source of information and support and maintaining those contacts through periodic visits, telephone calls, correspondence, and attendance at meetings and social events. Illustrative behaviours include:

- Relays relevant experiences and passes on knowledge unselfishly.
- Maintains contacts with people in other areas of the company or in different organisations who can be useful sources of information or resources.

- Does favors (e.g., provides information, assistance, political support, or resources) to maintain good working relationships with people whose cooperation and support are important.
- Attends meetings and social events to continually solidify and grow his or her network.
- Uses his or her network to solve problems efficiently and effectively.
- Actively designs his or her network in anticipation of future needs or plans (e.g., has clear goals in mind when building his or her network).

Chapter roundup

- Interpersonal skills for building and maintaining relationships include: rapport building, influencing, building trust and cooperation and managing conflict. These are underpinned by skills in communication.
- Communication in an organisation flows downwards, upwards, sideways and diagonally.
- Barriers to communication include 'noise' (from the environment), poorly constructed or coded/decoded messages (distortion) and failures in understanding caused by the relative positions of senders and receivers.
- Written communication formats include letters, memoranda, fax, e-mail and reports. Each has specific requirements for:
  - the suitability of the medium for its intended use and recipient
  - the format and structure of the message
  - competent use of any equipment involved in the medium
- Verbal communication is the least formal, most common way of communicating. It includes face-to-face and telephone discussions. There are particular techniques involved in:
  - using the telephone efficiently
  - being an effective listener
- Non-verbal communication (including tone of voice and body language) can support or undermine verbal messages: it needs to be carefully interpreted and managed.
- It is important to adapt the content and style of your communication to your purpose and the likely response of the other person. Different styles of communication include:
  - information
  - influence
  - assertion
  - negotiation
- Social networking competency is defined as socialising informally. It includes developing contacts with people who are a source of information and support and maintaining those contacts through periodic visits, telephone calls, correspondence, and attendance at meetings and social events.

Quick quiz

1 Give three processes which rely heavily on the person's interpersonal skills

2 Which area of the Johari window represents what is known by others but not yourself?

A Open area
B Blind area
C Hidden area
D Unknown area

3 In your classroom / study area how might there be barriers to communication?

4 The appropriate 'complimentary close' to the salutation 'Dear Sir' is:

A Yours sincerely
B Yours faithfully
C To whom it may concern
D Dear Sir or Madam

5 From your knowledge of body language, what might be conveyed by the following?

(a) clenched first
(b) drumming fingers on the table
(c) stroking the chin

Why might you use caution in making this diagnosis?

6 The best means of conveying bad news to someone is via e-mail. True or false?

7 Your manager comes to you late on a Friday afternoon and tells you that she needs a piece of work from you 'urgently'. You are in the middle of something else. You say (loudly): 'There is no way I can do it now: I'm busy. Get someone else to do it!'

This would be defined as:

A an assertive response
B a non-assertive response
C an aggressive response
D an informative response

8 What type of chart is used to show pictorially the relative sizes of component elements of a total value or amount, as a proportion of the 360% of a circle?

9 Effective listening means not thinking your own thoughts until the other person has finished speaking. True or false?

Answers to quick quiz

1 In a business context, interpersonal skills are particularly important for processes such as motivation, team building, customer care, negotiation and workload management.

2 **The blind area** contains things that others observe that we don't know about. **Blind** behaviours are often non-verbal behaviours and action tendencies: patterns of behaviour and habitual mannerisms. For example, you do not realise that you adopt a sarcastic tone of voice in conflict situations.

3 Disruption from class mates, forgotten books, do not understand teacher, mind on other things, boredom.

4 B.

5 (a) Anger (b) Boredom or impatience (c) Deep in thought or perplexity. Caution is required because these signals by themselves cannot be accurately diagnosed, and may mean different things in different cultures.

6 False, in general. Face-to-face would be preferable, allowing sensitivity and supportive communication. If the news was very urgent, a telephone call would still be preferable to e-mail, which can come across as very cold and abrupt.

7 C. Many people confuse 'assertive' with 'aggressive': make sure you know the difference!

8 Pie chart.

9 False. You may have had to think carefully about this. The point is not to *distract* yourself or *interrupt* the other person with your thoughts (or your impatience to say them). However, you need to *keep thinking*: consider whether what you are hearing is true/relevant, come up with questions, further information requests, feedback signals etc.

Answers to activities

1 Your answer will reflect your interpersonal activities on the day you chose: no two answers will be alike.

What could you learn from this data? You would expect technical/work-related conversations to dominate during work time and friendly/courteous conversations during breaks. (If not, are you wasting the organisation's time? Or becoming a workaholic?)

You would expect to ask for advice and help sometimes, but not as a large proportion of your interactions. (If not, are you avoiding seeking help when you ought to do so? Or are you constantly in crisis, or asking for help needlessly?)

You would expect to receive some supportive and encouraging words occasionally. (If not, where can you get some?)

2 Looking at the problem with the **White Hat**, they analyse the data they have. They examine the trend in vacant office space, which shows a sharp reduction. They anticipate that by the time the office block would be completed, that there will be a severe shortage of office space. Current government projections show steady economic growth for at least the construction period.

With **Red Hat** thinking, some of the directors think the proposed building looks quite ugly. While it would be highly cost-effective, they worry that people would not like to work in it.

When they think with the **Black Hat**, they worry that government projections may be wrong. The economy may be about to enter a 'cyclical downturn', in which case the office building may be empty for a long time.

If the building is not attractive, then companies will choose to work in another better-looking building at the same rent.

With the **Yellow Hat**, however, if the economy holds up and their projections are correct, the company stands to make a great deal of money. If they are lucky, maybe they could sell the building before the next downturn, or rent to tenants on long-term leases that will last through any recession

If they are lucky, maybe they could sell the building before the next downturn, or rent to tenants on long-term leases that will last through any recession.

With **Green Hat** thinking they consider whether they should change the design to make the building more pleasant. Perhaps they could build prestige offices that people would want to rent in any economic climate. Alternatively, maybe they should invest the money in the short term to buy up property at a low cost when a recession comes.

The **Blue Hat** has been used by the meeting's Chair to move between the different thinking styles. He or she may have needed to keep other members of the team from switching styles, or from criticising other peoples' points.

3

Positive feedback	Negative feedback
Action taken as requested	No action taken or wrong action taken
Letter/memo/note confirming receipt of message and replying in an appropriate way	No written response where expected
Accurate reading back of message	Incorrect reading back of message
Statement: 'Yes, I've got that.'	Request for clarification or repetition
Smile, nod, murmur of agreement	Silence, blank look, frown etc

4 (a) Telephone, confirmed in writing later (order form, letter) – or e-mail order (if both parties have access)

(b) Noticeboard (or employee Web page, if available) or general meeting: depending on the sensitivity of the topic and the need for staff to ask questions.

(c) Face-to-face private conversation – but it would be a good idea to confirm the outcome in writing so that records can be maintained.

(d) Telephone, email or face-to-face (if close by).

(e) Face-to-face, supported by clear written notes. You can then use visual aids or gestures to help explain. This will also give you the opportunity to check the group's understanding – while the notes will save the group having to memorise what you say, and enable them to focus on understanding

5 (a) Anger or tenseness
(b) Perplexity or thoughtfulness
(c) Despair or exhaustion
(d) A rather negative (tired? bored?) attempt to show attention
(e) Impatience
(f) Unease or coldness, even hostility
(g) Relief, relaxation
(h) Sadness, wistfulness

6

MEMORANDUM

To: All staff in The Accounts Department Ref: STAT/1

From: Your name Date: 24 September 2007

Subject: Stationery

Please note that I am now responsible for ordering stationery for The Accounts Department.

The normal procedure appears to have lapsed and as a gentle reminder I attach a copy of the standard stationery requisition form. I should be grateful if you would complete a form and pass it to me whenever you become aware that stocks of any item are running low.

I shall ensure that there is always an ample supply of requisition forms and pens in the stationery cupboard.

7 We have provided no solution to this activity, as it depends on your own organisational practices and policies. Make sure that you are aware of any guidelines that exist in regard to: security, liability (e.g. disclaimer messages), presentation (e.g. signatures, stationery), content (e.g. non-offensive) and usage (e.g. work use only).

8 The totals you should have arrived at are as follows.

Product	*T470*	*S332*	*V017*	*J979*	*B525*	*Z124*
Total	7,520	2,355	5,760	1,510	6,725	4,375

Month	*Total*
	£'000
January	2,500
February	2,455
March	2,350
April	1,990
May	2,050
June	2,000
July	2,125
August	2,270
September	2,395
October	2,625
November	2,735
December	2,750
	28,245

Tutorial note. We have laid out the answer like this to make you aware that it is more difficult to check information presented in one way against information presented in another. It would have been kinder of us if we had simply reproduced the table with totals. Note, also, how much more effectively the table uses space.

(a)

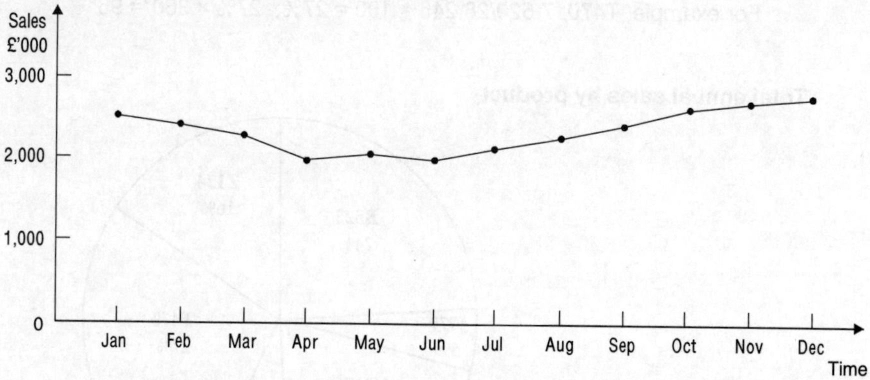

(b) We have divided our bar chart into segments for each product. Do not worry if you did not think of this, but notice how much more information you get if you present the data in this way.

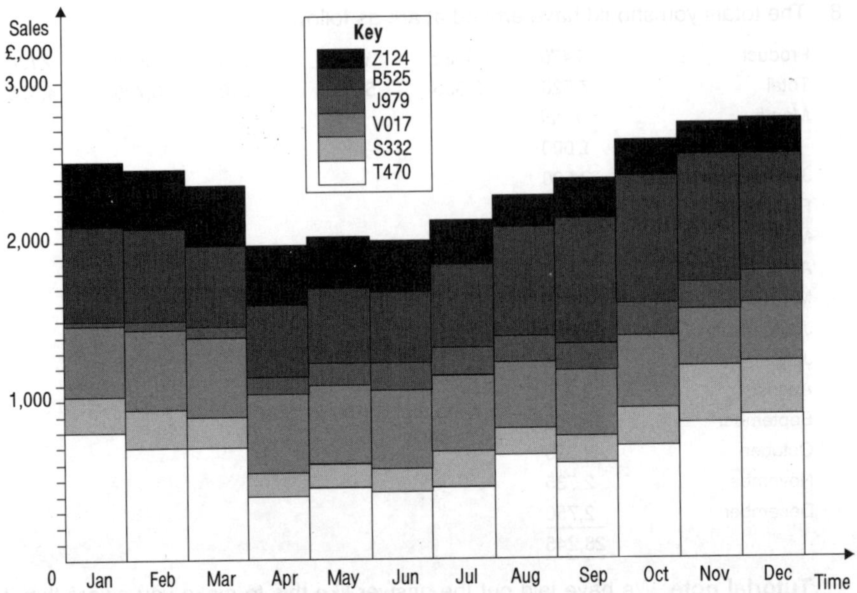

(c) We think that the share of total sales by product is the most appropriate information to show in pie-chart form. To arrive at the percentages for each segment divide the total for each product by the overall total and multiply by 100. To arrive at the number of degrees take the relevant percentage of 360°.

For example, T470: 7,520/28,245 × 100 = 27%; 27% × 360°= 96°

Total annual sales by product

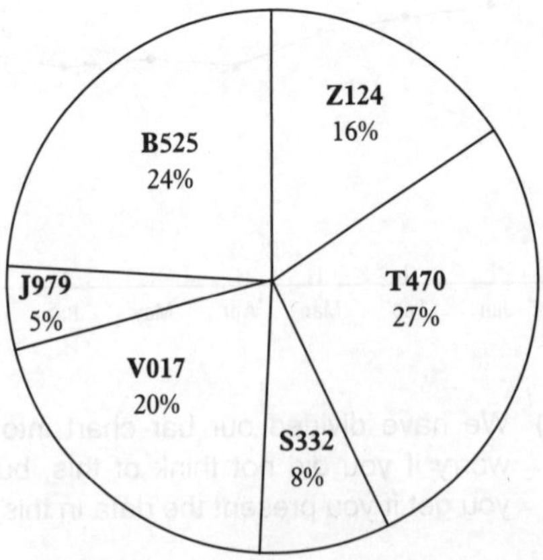

We do not think that any of the methods show the full range of information completely effectively. The graph is perhaps the worst (individual lines for each product could have been plotted but the graph would have been very crowded). The bar chart is probably the best method.

In practice, of course, there is no reason why all four methods (including the table) should not be used.

9 This activity should have made you think.

You may have come up with some of the following points. Note that assertiveness is an effective strategy for interpersonal relations!

Passive behaviour

Apparent/immediate payoffs: you avoid conflict and unpleasantness; you get to feel good for sacrificing your needs to others; people may like you.

Longer-term results: you do not get your needs met; you may feel angry and resentful later; others may lose respect for you; dominant people may feel they can exploit you whenever they wish

Aggressive behaviour

Apparent/immediate payoffs: you get your way; you may enjoy dominating people; you can let off some steam or anger; you may be respected for your 'forthrightness'.

Longer-term results: others may resent or fear you; others may withdraw from relationship with you; if others are equally dominant, conflict may escalate; you may feel guilty later; you may suffer anger-related problems such as high blood pressure.

Assertive behaviour

Apparent/immediate payoffs: you get your needs met; you have the satisfaction of expressing your feelings; you don't need to feel guilty or resentful later; interpersonal relationships are maintained or improved; new solutions to problems can be reached.

Longer-term results: as apparent/immediate payoffs, precisely because assertive behaviour takes this into consideration in deliberately managing communication for long term benefits.

10 An assertive response might be 'Fine. I'm happy to talk about the safety meeting, but right now I'd like to finish these invoices. How about me ringing you back later this afternoon?

An aggressive response might be ' You can't expect me to think about a safety meeting. I'm in the middle of doing some invoices. You'll have to ring me back later.'

11 We have provided no solution to this activity – use your imagination!

Chapter 3 :

TIME MANAGEMENT

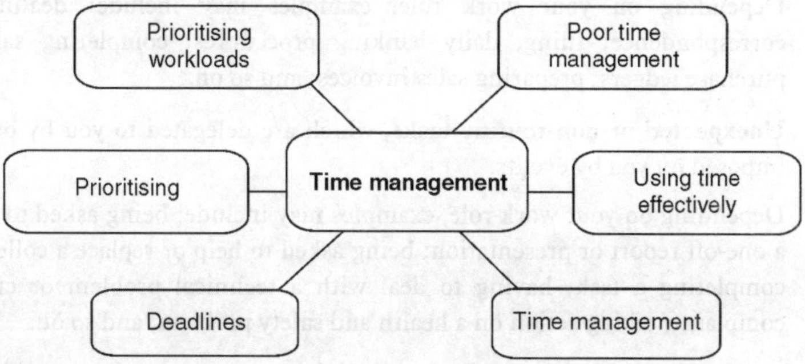

Introduction

This chapter should help you to focus on the way you manage your own workload. How you plan, prioritise and organise both routine and non-routine work is of critical importance to how efficient and effective you will be. With good time management skills you are in control of your time and your life, of your stress and energy levels. You make progress at work. You are able to maintain balance between your work, personal, and family lives. All time management skills are learnable. More than likely you will see much improvement from simply becoming aware of the causes of common personal time management problems. After you have read the chapter you should be aware of the importance of anticipating problems before they arise and asking for assistance where necessary. Identifying any weaknesses in your own skills, level of experience, or ability to meet deadlines is critical to working effectively as a member of a team.

Learning outcomes

On completing this chapter you should be able to:

(a) Select solutions to work-based problems.

(b) Evaluate and use effective time management strategies.

1 PRIORITISING WORKLOADS

1.1 Work planning

On any given working day, you might have a large number of tasks to perform: your 'work load'.

- **Routine tasks**, which you perform on a regularly daily, weekly or monthly cycle, according to well-defined procedures.

  Depending on your work role, examples may include: dealing with correspondence; filing, daily banking procedures; completing sales and purchase ledgers; preparing sales invoices; and so on.

- **Unexpected or non-routine tasks**, which are delegated to you by others or imposed on you by events.

  Depending on your work role, examples may include: being asked to prepare a one-off report or presentation; being asked to help or replace a colleague in completing a task; having to deal with a technical problem or customer complaint; taking action on a health and safety problem; and so on.

Some tasks can be planned in advance into a schedule or routine – and some will require one-off or urgent attention. Some tasks will be easily placed in an 'in-tray', presenting themselves for your attention - and some may emerge from situations as more complex problems without a clear-cut 'to do' list. Some tasks can be completed and filed – and some may require complex problem solving over a long period.

How do you know what **order** to tackle these tasks in? Which are more **important**? Do you interrupt your routine tasks to handle **unexpected** tasks? How do you keep track of complex **on-going** tasks without their getting lost in the flow of smaller, clearer tasks? How do you **keep up**? How do you know if you are **falling behind** – and what do you do about it?

If you are to manage your work load efficiently and effectively, there needs to be some kind of **framework of planning, decision-making and problem-solving** which will enable you to:

- Assign relative importance and urgency to different tasks, so you know what order you need to tackle them in, and which tasks take precedence when non-routine matters crop up: this process is called **prioritisation**
- Set or take into account target dates by which given tasks must be completed: these dates are called **deadlines.**
- Schedule work time and coordinate relevant resources so that tasks can be completed by the deadline, allowing for unforeseen events where necessary: this process is called **work planning**.
- Make the most efficient use of your available time, by prioritising, planning and methodical working: this is called **time management**.

1.2 Working methodically

A well-organised employee should endeavour to ensure that as a general guideline the following factors are considered:

- **Neatness and tidiness** – if the desk, shelves, cabinets, etc are tidied, it aids retrieval and efficiency as well as having the advantage of pleasing appearance.
- **Order** – there are advantages to be gained from ensuring that tasks are tackled in some semblance of order, be it chronological or priority. Efficiency is improved if work is grouped into batches of the same type and carried out at the same time.
- **Routine** – it is important that routine in all aspects of the employee's work should be established. For those tasks that need to be done each day, a routine should be established so that they are done at the same time each day. Important and difficult tasks should always be attempted when the employee is fresh, normally during the morning. Tasks, requests and instructions should be written down; memory often proves defective. The adage 'never put off until tomorrow what can be done today' should be put into action. The regular routine, once established, should be written down. This will enable the employee to use it as both a reminder and a checklist. Additionally, if the employee is absent or leaves the organisation the written routine will enable a substitute or replacement to function more effectively.

1.3 Schedules

There are two aspects to scheduling – activity and time.

- **Activity scheduling** may be used for any task that involves a number of actions, which must necessarily be undertaken in some sequence. It involves identifying key factors and assembling them on a checklist. Activity scheduling is concerned with the determination of priority and the establishment of the order in which tasks are to be tackled.

  Establishing the order in which tasks are to be tackled is not as easy in practice as it appears in principle because some tasks:

  - must be completed before others may be commenced
  - may need to be carried out at the same time as others
  - may need to be completed at the same time as others but factors such as finance or manpower may prevent this.

  A problem that is suited to activity scheduling is the arrangement of an interview where, say, three panel members are required and six candidates have been short-listed for interview. Obviously mutually convenient dates must be found when all six parties are available and to add to the burden the room that is to be used for the interview must be available on the days when the six parties are available.

- **Time scheduling** follows the preparation of an activity schedule and involves the determination of time required for each activity. Effectively, a time schedule determines the order in which activities are scheduled on a checklist with the time required for each activity also being shown alongside each item.

The process of time scheduling commences with the determination of the time required to perform each activity. The total of the individual activity times, with allowances for simultaneous activities, will produce the time allowed for one complete group of activities. It is particularly useful in the process of planning especially as it enables deadlines to be set.

1.4 Action sheets

This system is a natural progression from activity and time scheduling. Action sheets really represent a summary of the time each stage of a particular task should take and the relationship of that time both to the total time necessary to complete the task and to the time of individual stages.

The example below depicts an action sheet for a celebration such as a wedding:

Activity number	Detail	No. of weeks in advance
1	Book church	26
2	Book reception hall	26
3	Send out invitations	12
4	Receive replies	4
5	Order food/refreshments	3
6	Check arrangements	2
7	The big day	-

1.5 Other systems

Planning charts and boards – usually show information in summary form. Their main feature is that any required item of information may be seen at a glance. They are often used to show details of future events that affect departments, for example, to plan staff holidays.

Work requisition forms – a requisition form is essentially a document that itemises work that needs to be done. It usually requests the recipient of the form to carry out certain tasks as clearly indicated on the form. It is essential that careful thought goes into the design of such forms to ensure that all the necessary information required to complete any particular task is included.

Arranging appointments – the failure to note down full and appropriate information regarding a particular appointment could have serious repercussions for the organisation, particularly if an appointment is missed altogether. It is sensible to have a routine for making appointments and that the following information is obtained:

- the full name and title of the person you intend or are required to see
- the full and precise name and address of the relevant organisation
- the telephone number and the extension of the person you must see
- the time, date and anticipated length of the meeting

- the location of the meeting e.g. which room on which floor in which block
- outline details of the matter to be discussed
- travel directions and details of entrance points and security procedures.

It is, of course, equally important for those details to be sent to people who may be intending to visit you.

2 USING TIME EFFECTIVELY

2.1 The importance of time management

Time Management (TM) implies planning the best use of time, including cutting down on time wasted, devoting more time to the really important issues, or jobs on hand, and completing more in the time available. Failure to manage your time can leave you so short of it that you have a 'last minute rush' to get a really important job done. Inevitably, something gets overlooked, causing yet another crisis, which, in turn, takes yet more time to put right.

An essential objective of looking at time management is to enable you to save at least some of the time you presently waste in one way or another at work, and to use this time better in tackling jobs, which really require your undivided attention and effort. It is of course unlikely you will never waste time in the future, but even a 10% saving in the first year could give you up to 4 hours a week extra productive time.

2.2 Principles of effective time management

Time management is a set of principles, practices, skills, tools, and systems working together to help you get more value out of your time with the aim of improving the quality of your life.

Time, like any other resource, needs to be managed, if it is to be used efficiently (without waste) and effectively (productively).

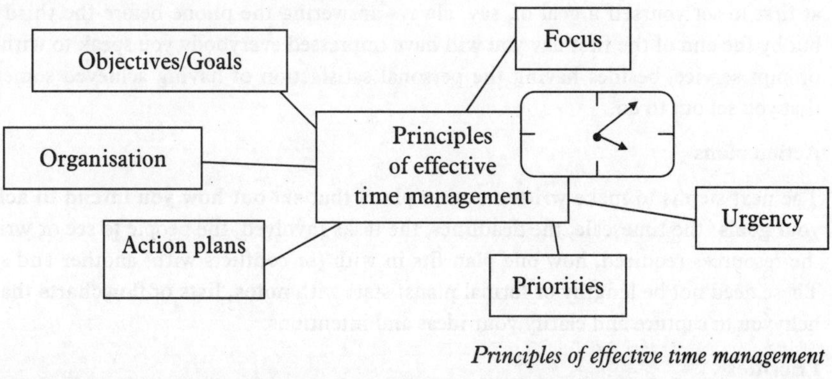

Principles of effective time management

To be a truly effective time manager you must apply these principles to your personal life with the same enthusiasm that you apply them to your job.

Time management is the control of activities towards particular goals/objectives. Once we have our goals we must then devise strategies and tactics for our plan. Time management is really a key part of a greater aim.

Setting work objectives/goals

If you have no idea what it is you are supposed to accomplish, or only a vague idea, all the time in the world will not be long enough to get it done. Nor will you know whether it is done or not.

To be useful, objectives need to be SMART:

- **S**pecific
- **M**easurable
- **A**ttainable
- **R**ealistic
- **T**ime-bounded

We looked at SMART goals in Chapter 1.

In work terms you could probably set **specific goals** by reference to your job description: 'prepare and despatch invoices for all goods sold'; 'issue monthly statements'; 'monitor slow paying customers' and so on.

However, **measurable** and **time-bounded goals** are very important for **effective time management.** If you say 'My goal is to see that invoices are issued and despatched for all goods sold *on the day of sale*' you have a very clear and specific idea of what it is that you have to achieve and whether you are achieving it or not.

The same applies to personal goals. 'I'd like a promotion' is just a wish. 'I aim to be promoted to General Manager by the end of my first year' is a goal, but not a realistic or attainable one. 'I aim to be promoted to supervisor of my section by the end of next year' gives you something to aim at.

Set SMART objectives for all aspects of your work, large and small. It may seem silly at first to set yourself a goal of, say, always answering the phone before the third ring, but by the end of the first day you will have impressed everybody you speak to with your prompt service, besides having the personal satisfaction of having achieved something that you set out to do.

Action plans

The next step is to make **written action plans that set out how you intend to achieve your goals**: the timescale, the deadlines, the tasks involved, the people to see or write to, the resources required, how one plan fits in with (or conflicts with) another and so on. These need not be lengthy or formal plans: start with **notes, lists** or **flowcharts** that will help you to capture and clarify your ideas and intentions.

Priorities

Now you can set priorities from your plan. You do this by deciding which tasks are the most important – what is the most valuable use of your time at that very moment.

Which task would you do if you only had time to do one task? That is your first priority. Then imagine that it will turn out that you have enough time to do one more thing before you have to leave. What would you do next? That is your second priority. Continue in this vein until you have identified three or four top priorities. Then get on with them, in order. Anything else is a waste of time that could be used in a more valuable way.

Activity 1 **(15 minutes)**

Breakdown the following example of a SMART work objective to show why it is SMART.

Objective

To achieve attendance of at least 150 guests at the national Education conference on 31 March 2011 by sending a promotional email to all relevant Education Professionals within the UK by 30 November 2010

Focus: one thing at a time

Work on **one thing at a time** until it is finished, where possible.

- If a task cannot be completely finished in one 'session', complete everything that it is in your power to complete at that time and use a **follow-up system** to make sure that it is not forgotten in the future. Correspondence, in particular, will involve varying periods of delay between question and answer, action and response.
- **Make sure that everything that you need is available before you start work.** If it isn't, you may not be able to do the task yet, but one of the things on your to do list will be to order supplies of the necessary forms or stationery, or to obtain the required information or do whatever it is that is holding you up.
- **Before you start a task clear away everything from your desk that you do *not* need for that particular task.** Put irrelevant things where you will be able to retrieve them instantly when you come to deal with the tasks that you need them for. If they are not needed by anyone throw them away.

  It is quite hard to discipline yourself to do this because it might take some time, initially, and you might feel that that time could be spent doing other things. However, once tidy working becomes a habit, it will take no time at all, because your desk will always be either clear or have on it only the things you are using at that precise moment. Moreover, one of the best ways of helping yourself to concentrate and handle things one at a time is to remove less important distractions.

Urgency: do it now!

Do not put off large, difficult or unpleasant tasks simply because they are large, difficult or unpleasant. If you put it off, today's routine will be tomorrow's emergency: worse, today's emergency will be even *more* of an emergency tomorrow. Do it now!

Think for a moment about how you behave when you know something is very urgent. If you oversleep, you leap out of bed the moment you wake up. If you suddenly find out that a report has to go out last post today rather than tomorrow afternoon, then you get on with it at once. We are saying that you should develop the ability to treat everything that you have to do in this way. Procrastination is a natural tendency – fewer than 2% of people are reckoned to have a true sense of urgency - but procrastination really is the thief of time.

Organisation

Apart from working to plans, checklists and schedules, your work organisation might be improved by the following.

- **An ABCD method of in-tray management**. When a task or piece of paper comes into your in-tray or 'to do' list, you should never merely look at it and put it back for later. This would mean you would handle it more than once – usually over and over again, if it is a trivial or unpleasant item! Resolve to take one of the following approaches

  Act on the item immediately

  Bin it, if you are sure it is worthless, irrelevant and unnecessary

  Create a definite plan for coming back to the item: get it on your schedule, timetable or 'to do list'

  Delegate it to someone else to handle

- **Organise your work in batches** of jobs requiring the same activities, files, equipment and so on. Group your filing tasks or word processing tasks, for example, and do them in a session, rather than having to travel to and fro or compete for equipment time for each separate task.

- **Take advantage of your natural work patterns**. Self-discipline is aided by developing regular hours or days for certain tasks, like dealing with correspondence first thing, or filing at the end of the day. If you are able to plan your own schedules, you might also take into account your personal patterns of energy, concentration, alertness etc. Large or complex tasks might be undertaken in the mornings before you get tired. Friday afternoon is usually not a good time to start a demanding task in the office...

Activity 2 **(20 minutes)**

Which of the statements overleaf apply in your case and which do not? Add explanatory notes where applicable.

	True	*False*	*Explanatory notes*
I work with a tidy desk.	☐	☐	
All my drawers, shelves and cabinets are tidy.	☐	☐	
Items that I use frequently are always ready to hand.	☐	☐	
Whenever I have finished with a file or a book I put it back where it belongs immediately.	☐	☐	
I write everything down and never forget anything.	☐	☐	
I work on one task at a time until it is finished.	☐	☐	
I do daily tasks daily except in very exceptional circumstances, in which case I catch up the next day.	☐	☐	
Every routine task that I do is done at a regular time each day.	☐	☐	
I never pick up a piece of paper without taking action on it (writing a reply, filing it, binning it, whatever).	☐	☐	
I organise my work into batches and do all of one type of work at the same time.	☐	☐	
I never run out of stationery that takes a while to obtain: I keep an eye on this and order in advance.	☐	☐	
My routine work could easily be taken over by someone else if I were unavoidably absent because I keep proper notes of what I am doing.	☐	☐	
I try to anticipate likely work and I ask my boss what is expected of me over the next week or so, so that I can plan out my work.	☐	☐	
I am able to estimate how long any task will take fairly accurately.	☐	☐	
I never miss deadlines.	☐	☐	
I do not panic under pressure.	☐	☐	

3 PRIORITISING

3.1 What makes a piece of work 'high priority'?

Prioritising basically involves arranging all the tasks which may face an individual at the same time (this week, or today) in order of '**preference**'. Because of the individual's responsibility to the organisation, this will not just be what he would 'like' to get done (or do first), but what will be most valuable to the attainment of his immediate or long-term goals.

A piece of work will be **high priority** in the following circumstances.

- **If it has to be completed by a deadline.** The closer the deadline, the more urgent the work will be. A report which is to be typed for a board meeting the following day will take precedence in planning the day's work over the preparation of an agenda to be circulated in a week's time: **routine work comes lowest on the list,** as it can usually be 'caught up with' later if necessary.
- **If other tasks depend on it**: if the preparation of a sales invoice, or notes for a meeting, depends on a particular file, the first task may be to send a request for it to the file registry. Work can't start unless the file is there. Begin at the beginning!
- **If other people depend on it**. An item being given low priority by one individual or department – for example, retrieval or reproduction of a particular document – may hold up the activities of others.
- **If it is important**. There may be a clash of priorities between two urgent tasks, in which case relative **consequences** should be considered: if an important decision or action rests on a task (for example, a report for senior management, or correction of an error in a large customer order) then that task should take precedence over, say, the preparation of notes for a meeting, or processing a smaller order.

Activity 3 **(20 minutes)**

Devise a mnemonic, using the letters 'P-R-I-O-R-I-T-Y', that will help you remember when a piece of work is high priority.

3.2 Routine and unexpected priorities

Routine priorities or regular peak times include:

- Preparation of the weekly payroll
- Monthly issue of account statements
- Year end accounts preparation

They can be planned ahead of time, and other tasks postponed or redistributed around them.

Non-routine priorities occur when **unexpected demands** are made: events crop up, perhaps at short notice, or errors are discovered and require corrective action. If these are also **important** (as well as sudden) they should be regarded as high priority.

3.3 Priority and urgency

Just because a task is **urgent** (that is, its deadline is close), it does not necessarily mean it is **high priority**. A task may be urgent but **unimportant**, compared to a task which has a more distant deadline.

On the other hand, as we noted earlier, you should **treat all important tasks as if they were urgent**.

In other words, you need to be aware of changing priorities. You need to:

- **Monitor** incoming work for unexpected or non-routine demands.
- Immediately **prioritise** each new task in relation to your existing list of tasks: it may not belong at the bottom of your 'to do' list but at the top!
- **Adapt your schedule** accordingly.

  This may simply involve changing the order of your 'to do' list in order to tackle new priorities before lesser ones.

  If your schedule is 'tight', however, there may be less room to manoeuvre. You may find that if you tackle the new high-priority task first, you will have difficulties completing a lesser-priority (but potentially still important) task by your target or deadline. In this case you may need to:

  – Ask your supervisor to confirm that your priorities are correct.

  – Notify your supervisor, and any other people affected, of potential difficulties in meeting previously-arranged commitments.

  – Request assistance with meeting the new or previous demands.

- Adapt any relevant resource allocations accordingly.

  Again, this may simply involve re-allocating your own time (or that of others under your authority), machine hours or services (eg secretarial support) to the new priority. Again, however, this may have to be authorised and/or negotiated with your supervisor and others affected by the change.

Eliminate the urgent - urgent tasks have short-term consequences while important tasks are those with long-term, goal-related implications. Too often the urgent and unimportant jobs get done to the detriment of the important. One way of resolving the dilemma is to use the Urgent versus Important matrix, shown below. Tasks that are both important and urgent should get top priority (A). The ones that are urgent but not very important (B) need to be done soon, but spend as little time as possible on each. Important but not urgent tasks (C) should be started as soon as possible as they have disaster potential i.e. they could suddenly become both important and urgent. Tasks that are neither important nor urgent (D) go to the back of the queue.

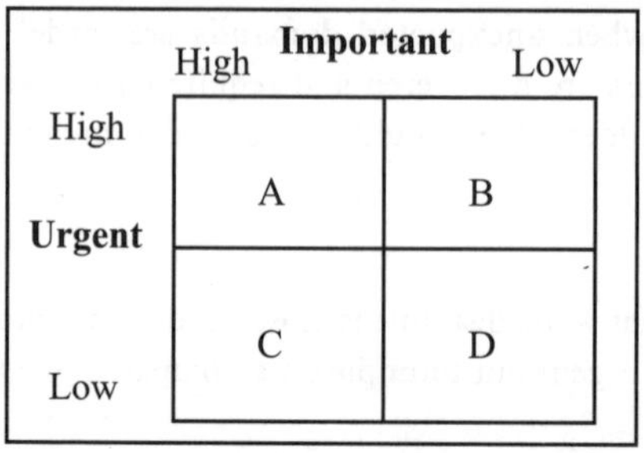

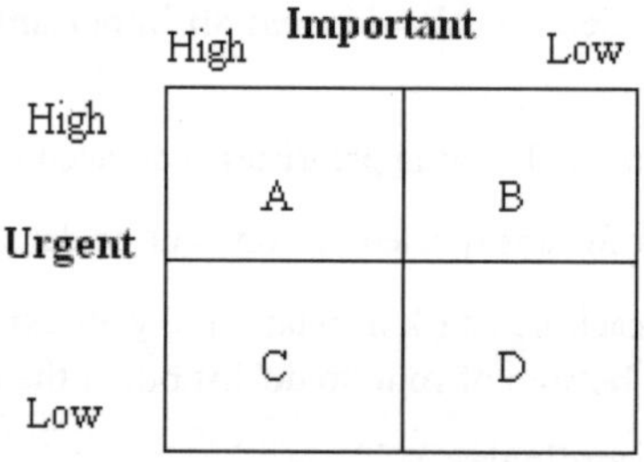

Time management grid

What people tend to notice is that they regularly do the urgent but not important jobs before the important but not urgent jobs. This is quite wrong. Prioritisation is all about ensuring important jobs are done first. Therefore the jobs that fall into the top part of the graph - the important jobs, are those that should be focused on.

Review each day's work - at the end of each day, take five minutes to review what you have done, and how successful the day has been. Make a note of anything not achieved, or which still needs completion. Put it on the list for tomorrow. Clear your desk before you leave.

Make yourself unavailable - when you have a task on hand that is both urgent and important, use any subterfuge to prevent interruptions.

Learn to delegate - each task you do should be critically examined from time to time. Many of your preferred tasks could be candidates for delegation. Let a member of your team enjoy doing them; it saves your time and develops and motivates subordinates.

Conquer procrastination - find out what causes you to put off doing something and remedy it. Maybe it is a feeling of inadequacy due to lack of information, lack of a particular skill or lack of training. When you are avoiding something, break it into smaller tasks and do just one of the smaller tasks or set a timer and work on the big task for just 15 minutes. By doing a little at a time, eventually you will reach a point where you will want to finish.

3.4 The 'Must', 'Ought' and 'Prefer' principle

The 'Must', 'Ought' and 'Prefer' principle involves listing all the tasks, duties and activities you need to do within a given day then assessing the approximate time each is likely to take and allocating one of the MOP categories to each task.

M is a 'must' task, one which simply has to be completed in whole or part on that day, (and probably by a particular time, too). These jobs are best tackled first in any given day, when you have sufficient discretion over your time. When you are under time constraints imposed by others, M jobs should be done at the earliest opportunity.

O or 'ought', tasks, are those which you decide are highly desirable to be completed during the day, but as a last resort could be delayed. These need to be attempted after the M tasks are under way.

P, or 'preferred', tasks are those jobs you like doing because you find them pleasurable and satisfying. Additionally, such jobs will normally contribute to the good of the organisation - provided you do not spend too much time on them. However, by the very nature of P tasks, the tendency is to spend time on them to the detriment of Ms and Os, unless you have carried out the approximate time assessment mentioned above (an M task!), and kept to it.

After working out all the tasks and jobs to be done during a day, you may want to add 'cushion time', a further period of time to cover for unscheduled interruptions, and breaks for tea, coffee and lunch. Now you may find the total time available is insufficient to do every job listed. Several strategies might help here.

One way out is to start work earlier. Another is to enter only the Ms and Os into the schedule then reassess the Ps. Perhaps some can wait; others can be delegated sideways, downwards or upwards. Yet others will just not get done at all.

Work through the day in an orderly way - now you have a plan for the day: the jobs and tasks to be done have been established, and the order in which they are to be done. You have made sufficient time available to accomplish the work. You can now focus on one job at a time, giving your whole attention to the task in hand. Avoid whenever you can, lots of short work periods. Spend say two hours with M jobs, two with Os, and the rest of the time with fixed appointments (eg regular meetings), interruptions and P tasks.

The advantage of this type of approach is that, provided the tasks determined by others do not come too often in the early part of the day, the 'must' ones are done when you are fresh, and more able to cope with demanding activities. At the end of the day, when your energy level is lower, it is easier for you to have to deal with the preferred tasks.

Activity 4 **(30 minutes)**

Write down a list of at least 8-10 jobs that you must do. Try to categorise them as important or urgent and rank them on a scale of 1 to 10 (with 10 being least important or urgent). Now look at the grid given in the answer, which shows how prioritisation can be illustrated graphically.

4 DEADLINES

4.1 What is a deadline?

A deadline is the **latest date or time** by which a task **must be completed** in order for its objectives to be fulfilled.

The important points about deadlines are:

- They have been set for a reason
- They get closer!

The need to 'meet specific demands and deadlines' (Element 23.1) effectively underlies **all** the elements of competence and performance criteria. If you are the type of person who is so 'in the moment' that you are not aware of time passing or deadlines approaching, do whatever it takes – alarm clocks, diary follow-up systems, daily work checklists, visualisations of time lines or charts – to get you deadline-minded!

4.2 Reasons to avoid missing a deadline

Delay on your part delays other people from getting on with their work, and creates a bad impression of you and the organisation you work for.

If you are late in producing a piece of work then you will tend to hurry it as the deadline draws near or passes, and its **quality will suffer.**

You will have **less time to do your next piece of work.** That too will be late or below standard.

You may get a **reputation** as someone who misses deadlines, and may not be trusted with responsibility in future.

On the other hand, there may be a problem if you find that you get a reputation as being someone who always **beats his or her deadlines**: you may find that you end up with a much larger workload than slower colleagues. This will have to be discussed with your superior: perhaps you are ready for more responsibility!

4.3 How to meet your deadlines: basic principles

Different people approach their work in different ways. You may like to get the easy tasks out of the way first. On the other hand you may prefer to get the difficult bits out of the way first.

As soon as possible after you are allocated a task and a deadline think it through (with a colleague if necessary) from beginning to end.

Then you can plan out how you are going to achieve it in the time specified. If you set aside one day for gathering information, say, two days for inputting and processing, and one day for analysing and preparing the results for presentation, you would comfortably meet a Friday deadline for a task allocated on Monday morning. This planning stage is the time to renegotiate the deadline if it appears that the work cannot be done in the time that has been allocated.

Your plan should indicate what input, if any, you will need from others. Before you do anything else, make sure that others are aware of the deadline you are working to and how their work fits in with your overall plan.

Batch together any tasks that are similar and routine and do them all in one go. For example, you may have to write to those buyers of a certain product who share a certain characteristic. It is likely to be more efficient to identify all of the customers with the characteristic first, and then to write to them all, rather than writing to each customer as you come across his case.

Monitor your progress constantly. Something may take far longer than you anticipated: how will this affect your ability to complete the task on time?

Activity 5 **(20 minutes)**

You are the accounts assistant at Modus Operandi Ltd.

It is three o'clock on a Friday afternoon, and you are performing your routine end-of-week tasks, including issuing pay slips to staff, printing them out on the department's one printer and planning to distribute them to workers' departmental pigeon holes prior to the end of work at 5.00. (The office is closed over the weekend.)

The department manager, Mrs Tancredi, comes to you and requests a print out of a confidential report that she will need by lunch time on Monday for a meeting. You calculate that the report will take three hours to print.

What will you do?

4.4 Difficulties meeting deadlines

If an individual feels that they are not up to the demands of a particular job or that a deadline cannot be met then this is likely to be due to either a lack of time, or a lack of skills or a lack of experience. A lack of time is almost impossible to deal with unless large amounts of overtime are to be worked. Lack of skills or experience however can be overcome if assistance is sought.

As soon as you know or can anticipate that a deadline is likely to be missed tell the person who is relying on you and explain why.

- If you are being delayed because you are awaiting input from others, the person you report to may have the authority to hurry them along.
- If unforeseen difficulties have arisen, your manager may be able to arrange for your workload to be shared, to make sure that the job comes in on time.
- If you are late because you have not worked hard enough you will naturally be reluctant to explain this to your superior. Own up earlier rather than later, while there is still a chance of salvaging the situation.

The appropriate person to whom you need to report anticipated difficulties may be:

- The line manager to whom you are responsible for the task's completion – and the one who retains ultimate responsibility for seeing it done. The line manager has the authority to:
  - adjust the plan (eg by extending the deadline)
  - mobilise extra resources (eg allocating more machine time or extra staff to help you)
  - influence other people (especially in other teams or departments) whose performance is causing your difficulties
  - communicate with other people (especially in other teams or departments) whose performance will be affected by your difficulties

- The project manager, if you are a member of a project team and the task is part of a project rather than routine departmental work. The project manager will have similar authority to the line manager, within the scope of the project: in addition, (s)he may be able to negotiate with your line manager to free you from departmental duties while the difficulties are met.
- Any colleagues who may be relying on your completion of the work, and whose schedules and deadlines may be coordinated with yours. These colleagues may not have authority to help you with your difficulties, but they may be in a position to adjust their plans – or to inform their own line and project managers of a possible delay. Be realistic about revising your target deadline – or about the likelihood of overcoming the difficulties in time to make the original deadline: *repeated* changes of plan swiftly erode working relationships!

Activity 6 **(20 minutes)**

You are a member of the Accounts Department of Modus Operandi Ltd, headed by the Chief Accountant, Mrs Tancredi.

For a three-week period, as part of the Development Plan agreed at your last performance appraisal, you have been seconded to a Task Force auditing the organisation's data security practices and compliance with Data Protection requirements. The head of this task force is the IT manager, Mr Sproule. You have been given a work area in the IT department and your routine accounting duties have been re-allocated for the three weeks.

It is coming up to the end of week two of your secondment, and you are aware that you are going to have problems completing your report on the employee database, as agreed, by the end of week three. You are having trouble obtaining the information you require on Personnel Records from the Human Resources (HR) assistant, Jenny Gomez: she has been busy preparing an induction course. Jenny is unable to say when she will have time to prepare your data – but without it, you can go no further in preparing your report.

Meanwhile, your colleague Parvinder in the Accounts Department, who has been undertaking your routine accounting duties while you have been on secondment, is due to go on his annual holiday the day after you return to the department, giving him a day to brief you on what has been going on and what tasks are as yet unfinished.

Required:

(a) Outline your problem, and what its effects might be.

(b) Whom do you need to inform – and of what?

(c) Write a brief memo to the person (or each of the persons) you decide to inform.

5 TIME MANAGEMENT

5.1 Improving your time management

What follows is a list of practical suggestions and hints to help you improve your time management.

Spend time planning and organising - using time to think and plan is time well spent. In fact, if you fail to take time for planning, you are, in effect, planning to fail.

For effective time management you should:

- **Establish key tasks** – the six most important tasks you do
- **Set your objectives** – the achievements you are trying to attain in the key post
- **Identify performance standards** – the quantifiable measure of the objectives
- **Identify constraints** – things standing in the way of your objectives
- **Decide on action plans** – ways of removing the constraints.

Set goals - that are specific, measurable, realistic and achievable. They give your life, and the way you spend your time, direction. Your optimum goals should cause you to 'stretch' but not 'break' as you strive for achievement.

Cost your time - take your annual salary, and divide it by the number of working days in a calendar year to give a daily rate. Add about 20% for administrative and other overheads and then divide by the number of working hours in the day (say 7½). The resultant figure is the hourly cost of your time to your employers. Every occasion when you 'save' an hour, or put it to better use, you become more cost-effective.

Identify significant job elements - examine your job description. (If necessary, draw one up for yourself, and get it checked out by a superior or a colleague.) Select from it three or four key activities, or significant job elements. These could be, for example:

- allocate work to teams and individuals agreeing objectives and work plans,
- manage work activities to achieve organisational goals,
- recording or storing information,
- developing and maintaining a healthy and safe working environment.

List the tasks and duties falling under each significant job element then estimate the time taken each month to complete the tasks and duties under each significant job element and cost this time. Assess the corresponding 'payback' to you and the organisation of the time spent on each significant job element. After reviewing the figures, you may decide to increase or decrease this amount of time.

Assess your priorities - there are two kinds of priorities you will need to take into account: long-term priorities and short-term priorities. If you desire promotion, for example, and this means getting a further qualification, then not only may some work time be set aside for study, but a considerable part of your own time as well. Study time becomes a priority activity. Thus you become committed to prioritising your use of time over a long period. Short-term priorities have the advantage of being newer, easier to remember, easier to achieve. The big temptation is to spend more time and effort on the short-term priorities. What is required is for you to strike a balance between the two, on any given day.

Use a planning aid - you may well have gathered by now that you will need a planning aid of some sort (a time/appointments diary, a work-planner or daily schedule form) to assist in planning the day's activities. Only by using such a device will you be able to plan ahead successfully, allocate time, and keep an overall check on what you are doing.

Prioritise - if you do decide to use a planning aid like a daily work schedule, facing you at the start of any day will be a mixture of activities to sort out. Some will be long-term priorities, some short-term priorities, and yet more will have much lower priorities still. Additionally, some activities will be imposed upon you by others e.g. meetings and visitors. These will obviously go into your schedule from the start. Use the 80-20 Rule originally stated by Vilfredo Pareto who noted that 80 percent of the reward comes from 20 percent of the effort. The trick to prioritising is to isolate and identify that valuable 20 percent. Once identified, prioritise time to concentrate your work on those items with the greatest reward

Consider your biological prime time - the time of day when you are at your best. Are you a morning person, a night owl, or a late afternoon 'whiz'? Knowing when your best time is and planning to use that time of day for your priorities (if possible) is effective time management.

Do the right thing right - management expert Peter Drucker says 'doing the right thing is more important than doing things right.' Doing the right thing is effectiveness; doing things right is efficiency. Focus first on effectiveness (identifying what is the right thing to do), then concentrate on efficiency (doing it right).

Learn to speed read - much time is spent reading forms, returns, reports, memos or other paperwork. Savings can be made if you learn to read faster. Read whole phrases, or even whole lines, at a time rather than individual words. Skim quickly through the conventional or routine parts of the document. The average person reads about 300 words a minute - you could aim for 400 and save 15 seconds for every 300 words.

5.2 Making and keeping appointments

An important aspect of time management is to make sure you keep appointments. For this you will need some form of Filofax, diary system or an electronic organiser on a computer. When organising a meeting it is important to arrange both a start and finish time. That way the people at the meeting remain focused on their tasks and can arrange their time after the meeting effectively.

Time management means taking control of your time. The first problem to deal with is appointments. Start with a simple appointments diary. In this book you will have (or at least should have) a complete list of all your known appointments for the foreseeable future. If you have omitted your regular ones (since you remember them anyway) add them now.

Your appointments constitute your interaction with other people; they are the agreed interface between your activities and those of others; they are determined by external obligation. They often fill the diary. Now, be ruthless and eliminate the unnecessary. There may be committees where you can not productively contribute or where a subordinate might be (better) able to participate. There may be long lunches which could be better run as short conference calls. There may be interviews which last three times as long as necessary because they are scheduled for a whole hour. Eliminate the wastage starting today.

For each appointment left in the diary, consider what actions you might take to ensure that no time is wasted: plan to avoid work by being prepared. Thus, if you are going to a meeting where you will be asked to comment on some report, allocate time to read it so avoiding delays in the meeting and increasing your chances of making the right decision the first time. Consider what actions need to be done before AND what actions must be done to follow-up. Even if the latter is unclear before the event, you must still allocate time to review the outcome and to plan the resulting action. Simply mark in your diary the block of time necessary to do this and, when the time comes, do it.

5.3 Reliable estimating of task time

If it is possible, you should estimate the time that will be taken for certain tasks so that you can plan projects and the overall use of your time. Some activities can be broken down into sub-components - called partitionable tasks. With these tasks you can break up the total time allocated to the project into segments.

Usually, you are not able to estimate with much precision how long each task is going to take you, but what you can do is put down how long each specific operation takes you. For example, it takes you 5 minutes to answer an email, 15 minutes to solve a problem or 20 minutes to write a page. So, you can use these numbers to allocate sufficient time to each small operation of the task. If you manage to break down the activity into steps you will really find it more motivating to keep the short deadlines you have set for yourself apart from benefiting from a more precise planning.

Once you have set yourself a goal, start with a mind map with your goal in the middle and then list all of the tasks you will need to do before it's completed. Some might be more urgent than others, or might yield the greatest return. For example, doing a bit of research at the start might reveal some sticking points that you can avoid (and save time). Finally, estimate how long you think each task will take. It's always best to over-estimate these, as there are usually unexpected complications. You might find it helpful to use a time log to record your estimate alongside the task as well as recording how long it actually took so you can calculate better in the future. After a few weeks of using a time log, you can build up an accurate picture of how productive you are being, as well as when your most productive hours are. For example, you might find you are much more productive during the first few hours of the day. Using this information you can optimise your daily performance by scheduling tasks for your most productive hours.

Bearing in mind that our sense of time is highly subjective - look how quickly time flies when you are enjoying a meal with a friend - you could try this straightforward technique.

1. Prepare a typical to do list for the day ahead. From that list, select:

   - One task that you enjoy,
   - One you feel neutral about, and
   - One you dislike.

   Write them down. Next to each item or task, estimate how long you think you will need to finish it. As you complete each task, write down the time it takes next to your estimate. What do you learn?

2. Experiment - shuffle the time of day when you engage in these activities. Again, record the time needed to get each job done. Ask yourself:

- When is the best time to tackle tasks that require creativity? Or focus?
- When is the most efficient time to take on a task you dislike?

3 Experiment - shuffle the time of day when you engage in these activities. Again, record the time needed to get each job done. Ask yourself:

- When is the best time to tackle tasks that require creativity? Or focus?
- When is the most efficient time to take on a task you dislike?

Explore your options until you pinpoint the best time to approach each project, the ideal conditions, and how much time to set aside.

Repeat Steps 1 and 2 with a new set of three tasks. Compare the results.

- If you start out with a project you have felt overwhelmed by, what happens?
- What changes do you make to complete difficult tasks?
- What patterns emerge?

Proceed until you have filled in the information for each thing you do. Your scheduling will be much more successful, now that you can realistically assess how much time you need. If unexpected events eat up a portion of most days, schedule in some buffer time, as well.

This exercise works if you work. It assists you in scheduling tasks during times you can take care of them most efficiently. And you can now set aside the time you genuinely need, not what you think you 'might' need. You will be able to greet each day with a clearer sense of your capabilities and a deeper appreciation of how much you actually accomplish.

6 POOR TIME MANAGEMENT

6.1 The consequences of poor time management

The following are possible consequences of poor TM:

- *Activity mania* - because every day begins without a proper plan, jobs became fragmented, are left unfinished, and have to be picked up again and again. In the end, you are left rushing from one crisis to another, without a moment left for thought and reflection. The law of diminishing returns begins to operate, and yet more activity is required to keep things going.
- *Reacting to, and not controlling, events* - instead of being able to take the initiative, having plans to meet emergencies (so that they are dealt with in the way you prefer), you spend much of your time fending off customers and superiors, or dealing with telephone calls from all and sundry. In what time you have left, you try to cope with the problems, which have emerged.
- *Living in the present, rather than the future* - Charles Handy in his Penguin book *Understanding Organisations* points out that the manager is above all responsible for the future. This means you need to devote time to anticipating and planning for the future: marshalling resources, creating the best possible working environment, recruiting, training and developing staff.

Living in the present means the future is neglected, and more potential problems remain undetected.

- *Becoming less effective* - because a manager with poor TM skills is seen to be inefficient by senior management, advancement and promotion become less likely.
- *Work overload* - being pressed for time as a result of poor TM generally leads to an ever-increasing list of jobs yet to be tackled. Too often, the only perceived way out is to work overtime.
- *Less leisure time* - the more time spent at work the less is available for sport, leisure activities, or for home and family. Interpersonal relationships can be threatened, and job satisfaction diminished.
- *Stress* - all the above consequences of poor TM can lead to stress. This has implications for you, the work team, the organisation at large, as well as family and friends.

6.2 Stress

Stress is a term which is often loosely used to describe feelings of tension or exhaustion - usually associated with too much, or overly-demanding, work. In fact, stress is the product of demands made on an individual's physical and mental energies: monotony and feelings of failure or insecurity are sources of stress, as much as the conventionally considered factors of pressure, overwork and so on.

It is worth remembering, too, that demands on an individual's energies may be stimulating as well as harmful: many people, especially those suited to managerial jobs, work well under pressure, and even require some form of stress to bring out their best performance.

6.3 Symptoms of workplace stress

Harmful stress, or strain, can be identified by its effects on the individual and his or her performance. There are many symptoms of stress, but we can attempt to group them into categories.

(a) **Nervous tension** may manifest itself in various ways: mood swings, irritability and increased sensitivity, preoccupation with details, a polarised perspective on the issues at hand, or sleeplessness. Various physical symptoms including headaches, muscle tension and skin and digestive disorders are also believed to be stress-related.

(b) **Withdrawal** is essentially a defence mechanism which may manifest itself as unusual quietness and reluctance to communicate, or as physical withdrawal in the form of absenteeism, poor time-keeping, or even leaving the organisation.

(c) **Low morale** may lead to low confidence, dissatisfaction, expression of frustration or hopelessness, increased accident rate and poor quality work.

(d) There may be signs that the individual is **repressing the problem**, trying to deny it. Forced cheerfulness, boisterous playfulness or excessive drinking may indicate this.

Some of these symptoms may or may not be correctly identified with stress. There are many other possible causes of such problems, both at work (lack of motivation) and outside (personal problems). The same is true of physical symptoms such as headaches and stomach pains: these are not invariably correlated with personal stress.

6.4 Causes or aggravators of stress

Causes or aggravators of stress in the workplace include the following:

Cause	Comment
Personality	Competitive, sensitive and insecure people feel stress more acutely.
Ambiguity or conflict in the roles required of an individual	If a person is unsure what is expected of him at work, or finds conflict between two incompatible roles (employee and mother of small children, say), role stress may be a problem.
Insecurity, risk and change	A manager with a high sense of responsibility, who has to initiate a risky change, and most people facing career change, end or uncertainty, will feel this kind of stress.
Management style	Unpredictability - constant threat of an outburst Destruction of workers' self esteem - making them feel helpless and insecure Setting up win/lose situations - turning work relationships into a battle for control Providing too much - or too little - stimulation
Job related factors	Awareness of inadequate skill or ability can be stressful, especially if training opportunities are poor. A noisy, dirty, badly lit working environment is clearly undesirable. Where work is not paced by the work technology, as in most technical and professional roles, it is easy for overloads to occur.
Social factors	These include inability to get on with colleagues and the wider range of contacts such as customers and the public and, conversely, isolation from contact.

6.5 Management of stress

Greater awareness of the nature and control of stress is a feature of the modern work environment. Stress management techniques are increasingly taught and encouraged by organisations, and include the following.

(a) Counselling

(b) Time off or regular rest breaks

(c) Relaxation techniques (breathing exercises, meditation)

(d) Physical exercise and self-expression as a safety valve for tension

(e) Delegation and planning (to avoid work-load related stress)

(f) Assertiveness (to control stress related to insecurity in personal relations)

There is also a requirement for management to make arrangements to remove as many causes of stress as possible for employees by, for example, arranging for flexible working hours; improving the work environment; avoiding the management style stresses outlined above; and addressing the other potential causes of stress that may be present.

Chapter roundup

- Work planning involves establishing priorities, scheduling and resource allocation, work programmes and activities schedules are useful in the planning of human resources.
- Activity scheduling is concerned with the determination of priority and the establishment of the order in which tasks are to be tackled
- Time scheduling is an extension of activity scheduling by indicating the required time for each task. It follows the preparation of an activity schedule and involves the determination of time required for each activity.
- Time management is a critical skill in any form of self-managed learning.
- Given that routine tasks may be anticipated and that unexpected demands cannot, this area of priority identification can be divided into routine tasks, which can be accommodated within normal sensible planning, and 'emergency-type' tasks that must be performed at short notice.
- The Time Management Grid is a system of ranking jobs according to their urgency and their importance.
- Stress may be caused by personality type, role ambiguity, insecurity and work, management style and particular job-related and social factors

Answers to activities

1 Breakdown of Objective

- Specific - says what the staff member will do (achieve attendance and send promotional email to all Education Professionals)
- Measurable - states the minimum attendance rate (at least 150 guests)
- Achievable - staff member has a listing of all guests to send invitation and conference is held at a time convenient that does not conflict with other conferences
- Relevant - links into other forums about the Education sector to be conducted later in 2010
- Timely - event to be held on 31 March 2008 & all promotional materials to be distributed by 30 November 2010.

2 There is no answer to this activity – other than to attempt it.

Each of the statements is an ideal of work organisation. Wherever you have ticked the 'False' box you should have some kind of comment explaining why the ideal is not possible in the circumstances under which you work.

Where you have ticked a false box, is there anything you can do about it? For example, if you have said 'I sometimes miss deadlines because others do not deliver their input to me in time', is this really a problem of your relationship with others? If you said 'I am not always able to work on one task at a time until it is finished: sometimes there is a delay because I have to get information from elsewhere', is this the full story? Perhaps you do not plan out your work properly when you start.

This is an opportunity to reappraise the way you work. Take action on any suggestion that strikes you as being a more efficient way of working for you. You will soon begin to appreciate the time and effort saved by good personal organisation.

3 **Note:** Just our suggestion: The devising of the mnemonic was the point of the exercise.

Priority?

Relative consequences

Importance

Other people depend on it

Required for other tasks

Immediacy (urgency)

Time limits (deadlines)

Yes!

4

	Job	Importance ranking	Urgency ranking
1	Bank cheques	9	9
2	Order stationery	2	5
3	Make dental appointment	1	1
4	Send out customer invoices	5	8
5	File supplier invoices	3	2
6	Open post	5	8
7	Make coffee	1	1
8	Holiday application form	1	2
9	Report to Director due next week	10	4
10	Memo to manager re broken window catch	3	7
11	Deal with irate window cleaner	2	10

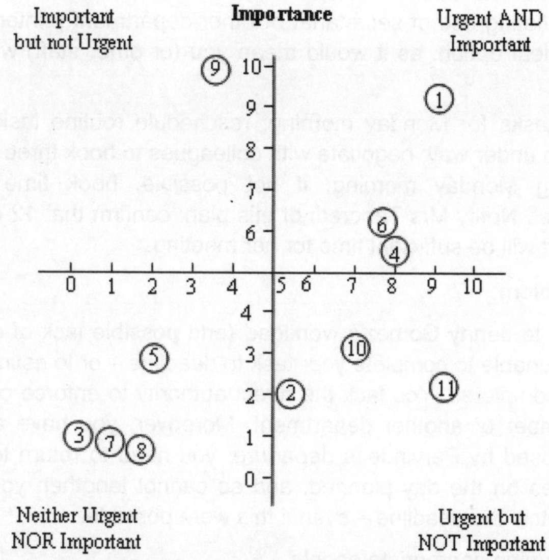

What people tend to notice is that they regularly do the urgent but not important jobs before the important but not urgent jobs. This is quite wrong. Prioritisation is all about ensuring important jobs are done first. Therefore the jobs that fall into the top part of the graph - the important jobs, are those that should be focussed on. In this case, job number ⑨ the report to a director due next week is the job that should be focussed on, bearing in mind any other deadlines that must be met. Of course other people's needs (such as the irate window cleaner) will get in the way of achieving this aim but as a general rule you should focus on the important jobs first, such as the report to the director and banking cheques, slotting in any urgent jobs as best you can. Yet how often do you get to the office, make a coffee, fill in your holiday application form and order some new stationery all because you think they are quick, simple jobs that will only take a minute!

5 **The problem**

Your task of preparing and issuing the pay slips is routine (weekly schedule) – but also high priority because it has to be done by a certain time (distributed by 5 pm) and it is an important matter (since it affects the rights and morale of employees).

The new task is high-priority, in that it has been set by your manager – and the deadline is urgent: given that the office is closed over the weekend, Monday lunchtime is not many working hours away.

Resources are limited for accommodating both priorities: there is only one printer in the department. You are in the middle of printing the pay slips – and the report will require three hours of printing.

Options

Interrupting pay slips and staying late to print the report today? – Not an option (pay slips first priority).

Leaving report printing overnight, for collection Monday? – Not a good option from point of view of security (confidential report left open on the printer)

Raising the matter of limited print resources with Mrs Tancredi: possibility of her negotiating use of secretariat or other department printer for use today? – Not an ideal option, as it would mean you (or other staff) would have to stay very late.

Review tasks for Monday morning: reschedule routine tasks in order to get report job under way; negotiate with colleagues to book three hours printer time first thing Monday morning; if not possible, book time on printer(s) in secretariat. Notify Mrs Tancredi of this plan: confirm that 12 o'clock delivery of the report will be sufficient time for her meeting.

6 (a) **Problem**

Due to Jenny Gomez's workload (and possible lack of cooperation?) you are unable to complete your task to deadline – or to estimate when it might be completed. You lack the direct authority to enforce cooperation from a member of another department. Moreover, you have a further deadline imposed by Parvinder's departure: you need to return to your accounting duties on the day planned, and so cannot lengthen your secondment to 'stretch' the deadline – even if this were possible.

(b) Informing appropriate people

(i) You will need to inform Mr Sproule of the problem with getting the Human Resources (HR) information, as it is his project deadline you are in danger of overrunning – and he may have the authority (as a cross-functional project manager) to influence the HR department.

(ii) You will need to inform Mrs Tancredi that there may be a scheduling conflict that will require you to extend your secondment in order to complete your report. It is up to Mrs Tancredi and Mr Sproule to negotiate how your time will be coordinated between them.

(iii) You should inform Parvinder that there may be a question mark over the date of your return to the department, so that he can make alternative arrangements to brief you, if necessary. (Note that you have not got the authority – or the right – to ask him to postpone his holiday!)

(c) Memoranda

MODUS OPERANDI LTD

MEMORANDUM

From: Your Name

To: Mr Sproule, IT Manager; Mrs Tancredi, Chief Accountant

Date: [Today's date]

Subject Report on Employee Database

I thought it advisable to inform you that I am currently experiencing some delays in accessing the information on Personnel Records which I require to complete my report on the Employee Database.

With six working days remaining until the report deadline, and the end of my agreed secondment, I have been unable to obtain the information from Jenny Gomez, the HR assistant, who is engaged in preparing an induction course. Jenny has been unable to say when she will have time to prepare the Personnel Records information, despite my best efforts to impress upon her the urgency of my task.

I have scheduled five days' work to analyse the information and compile the report. If the information is not immediately forthcoming, my concern is that:

(a) I will be unable to meet the agreed deadline for submitting the report

(b) the period of my secondment will over-run (subject to agreement between you as my project and line managers), conflicting with my commitments to the Accounts Department

(c) any prolonged absence from the Accounts Department will affect my colleague Parvinder, who has been covering my duties.

May I leave it with you both to determine what you think best in regard to the possible prolonging of my secondment? I will personally contact Parvinder to make a contingency plan for the handover of duties.

Meanwhile, Mr Sproule, I would appreciate your advice about how the Personnel Records information might more swiftly be obtained. I would be happy to discuss the matter with you at your convenience.

YN

Chapter 4 :

PERSONAL AND PROFESSIONAL DEVELOPMENT

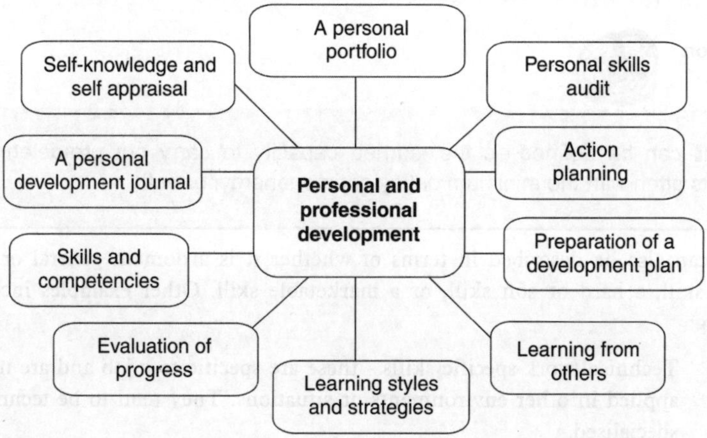

Introduction

Personal and professional development is not a product, devised by training providers and academic institutions. It is a mindset, a habit to acquire. It requires self-directed, independent learning, demanding an active rather than passive approach to learning. It differs from other forms of learning because it requires you to decide what needs to be learned or un-learned, how to learn it, and how to test and assess your learning. This is underpinned by a system of regular appraisal to review progress and plan future actions. Documenting this process in a personal development plan (PDP) helps you to prioritise and monitor the development process.

Learning outcomes

On completing this chapter you should be able to:

(a) Evaluate own current skills and competencies against professional standards and organisational objectives

(b) Identify own development needs and the activities required to meet them

(c) Identify development opportunities to meet current and future defined needs

(d) Devise a personal and professional development plan based on identified needs

(e) Be able to implement and continually review own personal and professional development plan

(f) Discuss the processes and activities required to implement the development plan

(g) Undertake and document development activities as planned

(h) Reflect critically on own learning against original aims and objectives set in the development plan

(i) Update the development plan based on feedback and evaluation

1 SKILLS AND COMPETENCIES

1.1 Explanation

There seems to be some confusion over how we distinguish between a skill and a competence. Some texts assume they are alternative names for the same thing others describe competencies as including more than skills.

Definition

> A skill can be defined as the learned capacity to carry out pre-determined results often with the minimum outlay of time, energy, or both.

A skill can also be described in terms of whether it is a domain general or domain specific skill, a hard or soft skill, or a marketable skill. Other examples include the following:

- Technical/work-specific skills - these are specific to a job and are not easily applied in other environments or situations. They tend to be technical and specialised.
- Functional/transferable skills - these can be applied in most environments and situations. They incorporate various combinations of data, people, and thing skills. Examples of functional skills include communication, planning, organising, managing, analysing, and problem-solving.
- Self-management skills (sometimes referred to as personality traits) are related to how we conduct ourselves and are rooted in temperament. Examples of these skills include taking the initiative, resourcefulness, being good-natured, and reliable.

Definition

> **Competence** can be defined as 'the ability to perform activities to the standards required in employment, using an appropriate mix of knowledge, skill and attitude'.

Competencies are the critical skills, knowledge and attitude that a jobholder must have to perform effectively. To improve competence you need to increase not only your knowledge, but also your understanding of how that knowledge can be applied, your skill in applying it and the attitude to apply it correctly.

Before you can start to work with competences you need to define 4 things:

- What your role encompasses - i.e. what you need to be competent to do. Examples of competence include:
  - exercise of judgement and discretion;
  - communication skills;
  - cost consciousness.
  - personal planning and time management;
  - capacity to meet deadlines or work under pressure;
  - developing teamwork.
- The knowledge, skills and attitude that make up that competence
- At what level you need to be competent - i.e. whether a basic knowledge of the subject is adequate, or do you need to be an expert?
- What you could do to prove that competence - e.g. what evidence you could provide.

For any competence based system the process is the same:

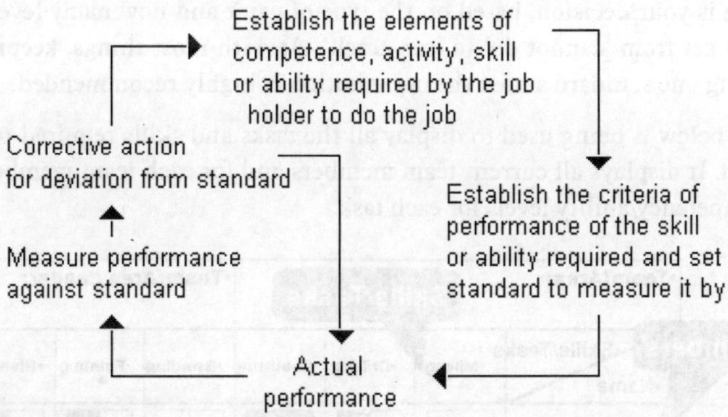

1.2 Skills matrix

The skills matrix is a simple visual tool to aid in the management, control and monitoring of skill levels. It plots a skill and its attendant competencies, referring to performances that classify work output within a continuum of two extremes e.g., superb and mediocre, cannot do and can teach others to do.

The first step is to establish standards. The basic questions you will need to answer are these:

- How many levels of competence will we have?
- What is the description or definition of each level?
- What are the general criteria for these levels?
- Who is capable of teaching at instructor level?
- What is the specific skill or task where the skills matrix will be applied?

The example below shows five levels from zero to four:

Level	Description	Criteria	Symbol
0	Cannot do	Insufficient knowledge or experience to perform to standard	
1	Knows all elements of the task	Has fully reviewed instructions and reference materials and is familiar with tools of the job	
2	Can do the basics	Has received instruction from a level 4 instructor	
3	Can do fully	Qualified by a level 4 instructor	
4	Can teach others how to do	Has taught or audited another person's work within 90 days	

Skill matrices can be as simple as two levels (empty square or circle), full square or circle) and as complex as having seven sections to the pie of a circle. How many sections you will use is your decision, based on the type of work and how many levels you think you need to get from 'cannot do' to 'can teach'. As with most things, keeping it simple and following one standard across the organisation is highly recommended.

The matrix below is being used to display all the tasks and skills required to work in an area or team. It displays all current team members and for each team member it displays current competency/ability levels for each task.

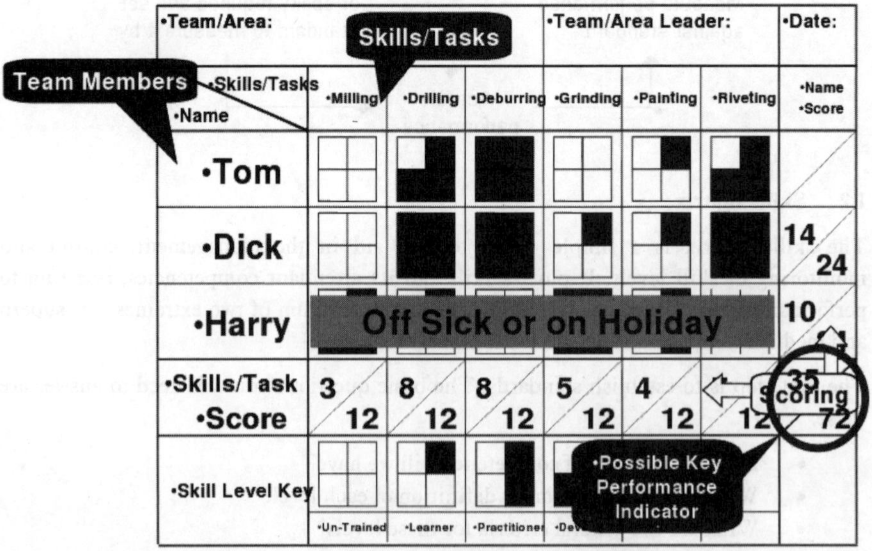

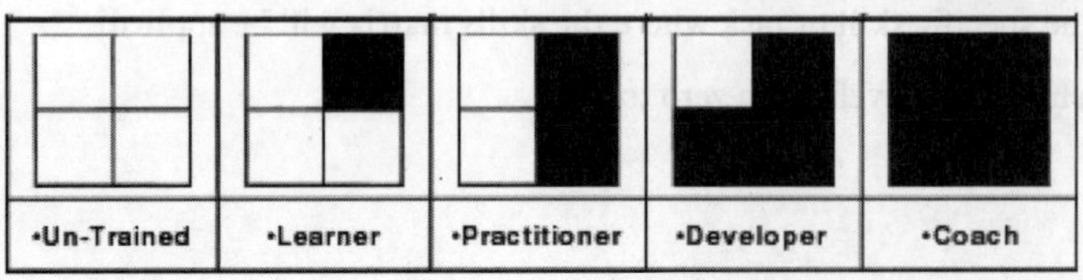

Untrained: No experience of the skill/task/work instruction/package.

Learner: Being taught the skill/task/work instruction/package.

Practitioner: Can carry out the skill/task/work instruction/package:

- Safely.
- To the correct quality standards, first time.
- Without assistance.
- To 1.5 times the standard cycle time i.e. is still not up to speed.

Developer: Can improve the skill/task/work instruction/package:

- Safely.
- To the correct quality standards, first time.
- Work to the standard cycle time.

Coach: Someone who has the skill level of a developer, but can train and develop others in carrying out the skill/task/work instruction/package:

- Safely.
- To the correct quality standards, first time.

Activity 1 **(60 minutes)**

Prepare a skills matrix for your team - or just for yourself

To get the most out of your skills matrix you will need to:

1. Identify the job roles in your team. List your team members in the left-hand column of the blank proforma. Identify up to 8 key tasks or activities that your team must fulfil to be effective and achieve its goals. It might help to refer to Job Descriptions for the team and use National Vocational Qualification standards (NVQs) to help compile your list.
2. Review and code standards of performance - use a coding system to show who has the skills required, and who requires training
3. Assess the requirement for on-the-job training

   To avoid any unnecessary duplication of skills and too many people requiring training use the box at the bottom of each column to show the maximum number of people requiring this skill. Review this number with your team regularly, and according to changing circumstances. Remember to update the Skills Matrix regularly. This is a dynamic document that may change due to changes in priority, personnel, time of year. You can update training as it is completed by each individual and keep track of progress. The maximum number of people required to be able to complete a skill may vary, and will affect the requirement for on-the-job training.

1.3 Gap analysis

A gap analysis is basically the process of matching and comparing the knowledge and skills that you currently have against those that you need for your future role and career and identifying where there are gaps. This matching process can help you to focus better on the skill areas which you need to develop.

For example, if one of your required skills for your future career is 'competency in setting up internet home pages' you may have rated you current ability as a 3 (familiar with and able to use the knowledge or skill yourself - some competency). A friend may have rated you as being a 2 (some awareness but not sufficient to use the skill). Ideally you wish to be a 5 (expert with a high degree of skill and/or comprehensive knowledge - fully competent). You therefore have a gap between your existing competency and your required competency.

If on the other hand you have rated yourself as a 5, and your friend also rated you as being a 5, then you have no current skills gap in this skill area. If you have used a scale of strong/weak/in between then you may wish to identify your gaps as being small gap/large gap/no gap. Note though that not having a current gap does not mean to say that you will not have a gap in, say, 12 months time - this is particularly the case for information technology based skills where new computer programmes and systems are frequently introduced.

1.4 What are 'management skills'?

There is no universally accepted definition of management skills. The demands made on managers differ according to the structure, culture and environment of the organisation *and* over time, with the impact of constant change on the business environment. *Whetten, Cameron and Woods* (2000) surveyed a number of research studies which cite different lists of 'skills' recognised as key contributors to managerial effectiveness and career success. Personal qualities ('enthusiasm' and 'determination') are listed alongside behaviours ('hard work'), activities ('processing paperwork') and 'technical competence'. Even where researchers appear to be talking about the same thing, their terminology varies. Some lists use the phrase 'human relations', while others refer to 'managing people' or 'working well with others'.

How might it be possible to describe 'management skills' in a meaningful way?

FOR DISCUSSION

Independently brainstorm your own answers to the following questions.

- What skills do you need to be an effective manager?
- Can you group these into different categories in any way?
- Can you prioritise which are the most important skills?

If possible, invite at least one other person to contribute his or her own answers to these questions, and compare your views. Consider any differences of viewpoint and where they may come from: your gender or cultural values? personal perceptions? definition of terms? different past experiences of managers or managing?

Whetten and Cameron (2002) suggest that management skills can be differentiated from other kinds of 'managerial characteristics' (such as ambition or integrity) and 'management practices' (such as hiring and firing) because they are:

- *behavioural:* observable and identifiable sets of actions that individuals perform, with certain outcomes;
- *controllable:* able to be consciously demonstrated, practised, improved or restrained by individuals;
- *developable:* amenable to learning, practice and feedback towards higher levels of competency; and
- *inter-related and overlapping:* integrated sets of complex responses, which support one another for behavioural flexibility – rather than simplistic, repetitive behaviours.

Renewed emphasis on management education, training and development has focused attention on specific **skills** and **competences** which are amenable to analysis, modelling, development and assessment. In the UK, competence-based Management Standards, supported by government initiatives such as Investors in People and National Vocational Qualifications (NVQs) are at the forefront of what *Adair and Allen* (1999) identify as:

'a drive towards lifetime learning, flexible self-development, continuous improvement and competence or core skills based training, linked directly to business goals'.

1.5 People skills

Management skills may also be differentiated from purely technical/operational skills (such as using statistics, typing or welding) because they are inherently bound up with *people* and influenced by *personal factors*.

- *Intrapersonal skills* involve processes within people themselves: self awareness, time management, stress management, problem-solving and decision-making.
- *Interpersonal skills* involve interactions between two or more people: communication, leadership, influencing, assertiveness, negotiation, conflict management, team-working and so on.

EXAMPLE

Rosemary Stewart's real-world survey of research into how managers actually behave highlights the 'human dimension' of management.

'The picture that emerges from studies of what managers do is of someone who lives in a whirl of activity, in which attention must be switched every few minutes from one subject, problem and person to another; of an uncertain world where relevant information includes gossip and speculation about how other people are thinking and what they are likely to do; and where it is necessary, particularly in senior posts, to develop a network of people who can fill one in on what is going on and what is likely to happen. It is a picture, too, not of a manager who sits quietly controlling but who is *dependent upon many people*, other than subordinates, with whom reciprocating relationships should be created; who needs to learn how to trade, bargain and compromise; and a picture of managers who, increasingly as they ascend the management ladder, live in a political world where they must learn how to *influence people* other than subordinates, how to manoeuvre, and how to enlist support for what they want to do. In short, it is a much more *human activity* than that commonly suggested in management textbooks.' [Italics ours] (Quoted in Mullins 1999)

Reflection: What impressions of the manager's role have *you* got from 'management textbooks' so far? How do they compare to the real world of work in your own experience?

There are many ways of classifying management roles and skills, and describing how they work together for successful performance. However, it is generally agreed that **interpersonal skills underpin managerial competence** in the key process of 'getting things done through other people'.

1.6 Leadership competencies

As well as the management skills already outlined, effective leaders work at building up and maintaining a series of leadership competencies which they use to do their job. Competency is being described here as something, either natural or learned, which is practiced and used effectively to achieve a desired goals. For example, someone may be charismatic, but this is only a 'competency' if they are consciously aware of this attribute, and use it purposefully to influence others positively. Competency covers knowledge, skills, practices and processes of the effective leader.

The following is the top 7 groups of key working competencies. This is what experienced, successful leaders actually do.

1. **Influence others.** Leaders must have the ability to get others to act in the desired way. They have the ability to win respect from those who must be influenced, and to build mutual respect. They will give directions and expectations in an appropriate way to influence others to act, and they are also open to ideas and listen actively to others. They walk the talk, influencing others by modelling the behaviour, and they reinforce the appropriate attitude, behaviour and performance in others. They communicate to the group in a way that sways the group towards behaving in the desired way.

2. **Foster accountability.** Leaders establish in their team members a commitment to achieving results by building a culture of accountability. Again, they model this with their behaviour, displaying accountability for themselves, their own areas of accountability and their team. They use fair processes and they organise action plans for sharing workload and effort. They have open team process for identifying stress points and for accessing help from other team members. They promote accountability and hold each team member personally responsible for their area. They react to deadlines and targets with positive or corrective feedback.

3. **Build positive working relationships.** Leaders actively build a network of positive working relationships, both internally with other departments and colleagues, and externally with clients. They take responsibility for ensuring that a relationship is positive and effective, that it works well for both parties. A Leader actively seeks to demonstrate respect for self and respect for others. They investigate the goals, targets and stressors of other departments, and of clients, ensuring they work well with them to achieve common goals. They explore and use various styles, techniques and communication methods to achieve successful results and build good relationships.

4. **Coach for improvement/results.** Leaders develop the potential of every team member and ensure that they are achieving the desired performance. They work with each to ensure each is contributing positively to the team dynamic. They read others - to appreciate their strengths, areas for development, personality style, learning style and motivators. They plan a development strategy for each, and hold effective, motivating coaching sessions.

5. **Communicate effectively.** Leaders PLAN how they communicate, identifying the objectives, the method, the structure etc. They review the outcome of the communication and they learn from this. They use different forms of communication effectively, the right channel for the given task. They lead meetings effectively. They plan, structure and facilitate the meeting to achieve the desired outcome. They use their leadership presence effectively in interactions, to listen, respond, influence and persuade.

6. **Work effectively.** Successful leaders plan their own workload, prioritising key tasks and ensuring the appropriate allocation of time and effort to achieve the required results. They organise and structure, building good working processes, systems and habits so that they can effectively achieve their objectives, goals and targets. They translate objectives/project requirements into an achievable work plan, anticipating obstacles. They prioritise tasks, establishing a clear focus and direction for others to follow. They think ahead to anticipate changing business requirements which could affect priorities and plans. The effective leader continuously improves. They plan what improvements they will introduce, when and how these improvements will be implemented.

7. **Build a high performing team.** Leaders ensure that their team will achieve their team goals and targets, will achieve the desired performance and is well placed to achieve future INCREASED targets. They understand group dynamics and what influences this. They organises the team and build good team processes. They communicate well to the Team, about the business, the team purpose, progress on goal achievement etc. They give feedback, celebrate goal achievement and motivate to improve. They challenge and encourage the team to improve, find new ways of doing things and to develop the desired competencies and team values.

1.7 Developing skills for your HND/HNC

Unit 13 effectively underpins the entire HND/HNC programme by focusing on **self development** in the context of **interpersonal skills and processes.**

- *Pedler, Burgoyne and Boydell* (2001) identify '**balanced learning habits and skills**' as one of the 'meta qualities' which allow managers to develop and deploy *all* the other skills, behaviours and resources they require for successful performance.

- Management involves **working through and with other people**, and interpersonal competence comprises the range of skills required to do this effectively.

- Effective managerial decision-making is not just about making the 'right' decisions, but about effective **management of the processes** by which decisions are made, communicated, implemented and responded to in a given organisation or work group.

This is particularly true in a business environment which increasingly relies on collaborative working in networks, teams and flexible organisation structures – and on continuous learning and adaptation to change.

Self-development, process awareness and interpersonal skills can be applied to all the other units in the HND programme. As you learn and apply strategic planning techniques, for example, you will be taking responsibility for your skill and career development. And you will also need to give attention to your effectiveness in the relevant interpersonal processes of networking, participating in meetings, communicating visions and goals, managing potential for conflict and resistance, negotiating for resources… and so on.

The HND module is designed to help you to develop a double focus, or 'dual channel' awareness, so that ultimately you can monitor and manage interpersonal processes at the same time as working towards any specific business decision or outcome.

1.8 Developing skills for life

Learning how to manage statistical data, market dynamics, business systems and resources is likely to be useful in your professional life. Learning how to manage your behaviours and relationships, and your ongoing development in both areas, is potentially useful in *all* areas of your life – and on a lifelong basis.

Don't leave your skills at the office!

While the aim of Unit 13 is to enhance your competency in a managerial role, the interpersonal and learning skills developed through the module should be applicable in other areas of your life: family, friendships, study and leisure activities. This is explicitly acknowledged in the setting of life – as well as career – goals as the framework for development. Non-work relationships and activities also provide essential scope for practising and applying your developing interpersonal skills – even (and especially) if you are not yet operating professionally in a managerial role.

Learning itself is a life skill

Peter Honey and Alan Mumford (1992) suggest that:

'Learning is perhaps the most important of all the life skills, since the way in which people learn affects everything else. We live in the post industrial 'information' age where data have a shorter shelf-life and where transformational changes are less predictable and occur more rapidly than ever before. Clearly learning is the key, not just to surviving but to thriving on all these changes ...'.

Learning to learn enables you to *keep* on learning far beyond any particular study text, training event – or HND unit! It is a framework for on-going self-development.

Learning is a constant, cyclical process

Research by *David Kolb* (1984) and its implications for management (*Honey and Mumford*, 1992) suggests that effective learning is a cyclical process of experimentation and adjustment.

- We perform an action or have an experience
- We reflect on the experience, its results and any feedback we may have obtained

- We formulate a hypothesis about what we might be able to do differently next time
- We plan to test our hypothesis in action
- We perform the action – and so continue the cycle.

We will cover the learning cycle – and the learning styles associated with each stage – in more detail in Chapter 8 of this Course Book, as we discuss and apply ideas about management development.

New learning needs emerge all the time. Developing the kind of management skills that are needed to manage a business, a team – and, indeed, one's own life and relationships – is a lifelong process: a journey, not a destination. While it is helpful to set goals and yardsticks for measuring your progress along the way, it is important to stay open to further learning and not to become frustrated that you never seem to 'arrive': the journey is in many ways more valuable than the destination itself.

FOR DISCUSSION

'If asked to think about how we have learned, most of us may think first of when attempts have been made to teach us. If, on the other hand, we are asked about problems we have solved, we think about difficult situations we have faced and managed to overcome. However, in solving problems we don't just deal with the immediate difficulty, we discover a solution which we can use again in some form, and we may also become better at solving problems generally. Problem-solving is, to a large extent, learning.' *Pedler, Burgoyne and Boydell* (2001)

How have you learned various interpersonal skills? (Think about communication, leadership, assertiveness, influencing, negotiation and team working – not necessarily in a work setting.) Think about what you have learned through being 'taught', for example courses, workshops etc., and what skills you have learned and developed through experience.

1.9 The HND approach

A focus on behaviour

While the learning objective of content-oriented learning is *knowledge* or *understanding,* the learning objective of skill development is *application:* **intentional behaviour** and **behavioural change.**

This unit is designed to get you to think about how you (and others) behave, so that you can make changes to your behaviour if you wish to do so, in order to achieve your purposes more effectively, efficiently or consistently. While you need to understand the determinants of behaviour – what influences people to behave the way they do – you will be encouraged to focus your development planning on the behaviour itself.

Gillen (1999) defines behaviour as 'the link between what we want and what we get'. He uses the vivid example of learning to play pool or snooker.

Making notes

Observations, impressions and intuitions provide valuable data for self reflection, but in order to make them a durable, flexible and practical source of information, you need to capture and record them! Get into the habit of making notes – verbal or visual, paper or electronic – during or shortly after any meeting or discussion you are involved in.

These will probably not be the kind of notes you might usually make (content-based minutes of the discussion, decisions reached, action to be taken and so on), but **process notes** about:

- repeated patterns of behaviour which you notice in a group or individual
- changes or interruptions to the 'usual' patterns of behaviour, and their effects
- thoughts or feelings that come up for you in response to others' behaviours or changes in behaviour
- how you 'automatically' react to others' behaviour, and what happens
- how you make a controlled and intentional response to others' behaviour, and what happens
- others' responses to your 'usual' behaviours
- others' responses when you experiment with new behaviours
- what happened in the course of *critical* incidents and interactions (those which impact on you and appear to highlight a problem or issue)

These notes will provide the raw material for reflection and self-evaluation. If you rely solely on your memory, you will probably have insufficiently detailed data to go on.

Collecting and filing data

Next, get into the habit of collecting and filing data. If you take notes on loose sheets of paper, put them (as soon as possible) somewhere where you'll find them again! The same applies to:

- the outputs of completed self-report questionnaires and feedback forms
- the outputs of various exercises you undertake as you work through this textbook, your wider reading and other training activities
- copies of reports from performance appraisals or development planning sessions
- feedback-bearing messages of all kinds (for example: commendation or thank-you letters; complaints; personal or employment references)
- draft mind-maps, objectives, action plans and other records of your on-going thinking about your interpersonal skills development
- any other data relating to the impact and effectiveness of your interpersonal skills

If it represents information about your attributes, behaviours or attainments in any area of interpersonal skill – save it! There will be plenty of opportunities to prioritise and organise the data into a more systematic 'portfolio' format as it builds up, and as you get a better sense of what you need.

2 SELF-KNOWLEDGE AND SELF-APPRAISAL

2.1 Reasons

Every manager needs clear images of his or her personal skills and characteristics for the following reasons.

(a) **Interacting with other people and developing interpersonal skills**. People's perceptions of themselves and others, and the roles they play, are crucial in the process of communication and relationship-building. A supervisor will be better able to identify and solve problems with team working and leadership, if he is able to be objective about his own perceptions, role and behaviour.

(b) **Goal-planning and self-development.** An individual will be more able to take control of his future development if he has a realistic picture of his aspirations, capabilities, and potential at a certain point in time. There would be no point planning to take professional exams and become an assistant supervisor in five years, if you did not have the ambition, capacity for hard work or leadership qualities required. On the other hand, many people have a low opinion of themselves and do not attempt to plan a positive course for their careers and lives – which an objective appraisal of their strengths and weaknesses might indicate.

(c) **Motivation and performance**. If you do not know what you are capable of, you may not be motivated to fulfil your potential to perform at a higher level. If you are not performing well, it is too easy to shift the blame on to 'fate', 'the system' or other people. You could be aware of weaknesses in yourself that contribute to the problem – and overcome them.

The organisation obviously has an interest in assessing its employees' skills and characteristics as well: for selection, training, promotion planning and pay awards. Formal performance appraisal is a critical and well-established part of this, and you should be aware that the process can be used to further self-knowledge and is therefore of value to the individual as well as to the organisation.

(a) An appraisal report, for example, may require the employee's assessor to grade him on a number of personal characteristics and skills, to assess particular strengths and weaknesses which affect his job performance and to recommend areas for development. If the employee accepts the assessment (and he should have opportunity to discuss it in an interview or counselling session), he can add the information to his own picture of himself.

(b) Potential assessment techniques are designed to gauge:

   (i) the employee's strengths and weaknesses in existing skills and qualities;

   (ii) potential for improvement, correction and development; and

   (iii) the goals, aspirations and attitudes of the appraisee, with regard to career advancement and the acceptance of responsibility.

   Various techniques can be used, including written tests, simulated desk-top tasks or case studies, interviews and personality tests.

(c) **Group assessment** and training techniques are particularly useful to help supervisors and managers to gain an accurate picture of how they relate to other people, and how people react to them. Role-play exercises allow people to participate in situations requiring negotiating or influencing skills, conflict resolution or team leadership, with subsequent feedback from the trainer and other group members: participants are made aware of their own patterns of behaviour and how these affect others, how they are perceived and what responses they get.

(d) **Assessment centres**. An assessment centre is a place where a person's behaviour and performance in job-related tasks and activities can be conveniently evaluated. Candidates are brought to a central location such as an hotel for a period and are tested and observed by a panel of assessors: exercises include leaderless group discussion, role play and business games. They are used in recruiting outsiders and assessing existing employees for advancement.

There are ways, however, in which an individual can engage informally in the same process of developing self awareness, which may involve two broad activities:

(a) compiling a personal dossier in order to build up an accurate self-image;

(b) carrying out a strengths and weaknesses analysis.

These are the procedures that are an essential part of this Unit.

2.2 Building an accurate self-image

Humans are self-conscious creatures: we behave partly in accordance with the image or concept that we have of ourselves. That self-image is something we mainly learn from interacting with other people; a reflection of their behaviour and attitudes towards us. It is formed by experience over time and is constantly adjusted. For example, repeated failure or criticism at work might tend to create a low self-image spreading into other areas of the individual's life, where it may be completely unjustified. Every individual has a self-image, but very few people attempt to confirm, refute or change their self-image in any systematic or objective fashion. In other words, they are not self-aware.

2.3 Developing self-awareness

In order to become more self-aware, you might try out the ideas below.

(a) Acquire knowledge about human beings and their behaviour in general. Your own studies of motivation, people in groups, interpersonal skills etc will help you to observe and understand what is going on when you act or interact with other people.

(b) Gather the opinions of trusted individuals who know you well. On the basis that, in dealing with other people, 'you are what they think you are', this is a practical way of finding out about yourself. For example, even if you have low self-confidence, you may appear to others to be aggressive and overbearing, perhaps because you try to cover up your lack of confidence.

(i) In this process, you are using other people as a mirror which reflects your image back to you. You see yourself as others see you. This can be quite a daunting prospect, so you would need to talk to someone whom you could trust to be honest but supportive: bolstering – or crushing – your ego is not only unhelpful, but downright dangerous, since your self-image will get further distorted. The other person also needs to trust you: they will not be honest with a criticism if they think you will never speak to them again!

(ii) A friend or partner, relative or colleague might be consulted. They would be in a position to help you with those aspects of your personality and behaviour that are displayed in contact with other people in various situations ('you tend to snap at people when you are under pressure'; 'you're not a good listener in meetings'; 'you're a good person to have around in a crisis').

(c) Compare yourself to role models in your life. All individuals consciously or unconsciously select models or ideals for themselves, for the various roles that are relevant to their lives. Parents, school teachers, colleagues or superiors at work are often influential in giving the individual a picture of what he should aspire to be like at different stages in his life. You may choose your model because of your view of his or her charisma, knowledge or expertise (the appeal of the teacher or more experienced colleague); success (as with a hero or celebrity or tycoon); or dominating personality. Festinger suggested that most people seek to evaluate their own performance through comparison with other individuals rather than by using absolute standards. So having a role model to measure yourself against helps to formulate your self-image and your aspirations to change and grow.

(d) Take tests – independently, or as part of the appraisal or training processes of the organisation. Tests for intelligence, aptitude, personality and proficiency are all examples of psychometric testing, which is the science of measuring mental capacities and processes. Intelligence tests include memory tests, ability to think quickly and logically and problem solving skills. Aptitude tests measure and predict a person's potential for doing a job or learning new skills. Personality tests measure characteristics such as ambition, motivation and emotional stability and proficiency tests measure the person's ability to do the job.

(e) Analyse incidents at work or outside work. A particular problem with the work group, for example, may give you insight into your own behaviour in that situation. A new challenge might bring out in you a quality you had not displayed before.

Activity 2 **(30 minutes)**

Who do you look up to – at work or outside work, whether you know them personally or not? Do you want to be like them – and if so how? Compare yourself to this 'role model': what areas of yourself would you have to change in order to be more like them – and how could you go about it?

Does your employer have a system of mentoring? If you do not have, or are not yourself, a mentor, ask your superior whether there is mentoring at more senior levels. If there is, what is the mentor expected to do? How useful is it in practice?

It is a good idea to compile the findings from such an investigation into a written self profile. You could start with information from your discussions with others, and your own observations. Take *Rodger's* 'Seven-point plan' personnel specification, which includes such features as aptitude, disposition, interests and physical attributes – or consider what aspects are likely to be important to you in your own life: your impact on other people, your motivation, your confidence level, whether you are introvert or extrovert and so on. Test results and copies of assessment reports can be added to the file as they are acquired, along with any changes, for instance, if you gain some further insight from a particular incident, or you get training in some area which enhances your skills or attributes.

2.4 Self-appraisal: strengths and weaknesses analysis

To construct your own SWOT analysis you need to examine your current situation. What are your strengths and weaknesses? How can you capitalise on your strengths and overcome your weaknesses? What are the external opportunities and threats in your chosen career field?

- Strengths need to be maintained or built upon.
- Weaknesses need to be remedied, changed or stopped.
- Opportunities need to be prioritised, captured, built on and optimised.
- Threats need to be countered or minimised and managed.

Consider the overall picture of where you think you are now, and where you want to be. What personal skills, experience and behaviours will help you (list under Strengths), and which will require some work (list under weaknesses)? What external factors (things not within your direct control) may help you (opportunities) or hinder you (threats)?

Strengths

- What advantages do you have that others don't have (for example, skills, certifications, education, or connections)?
- What do you do better than anyone else?
- What personal resources can you access?
- What do other people (and your manager, in particular) see as your strengths?
- Which of your achievements are you most proud of?
- What values do you believe in that others fail to exhibit?
- Are you part of a network that no one else is involved in? If so, what connections do you have with influential people?

Weaknesses

- What tasks do you usually avoid because you don't feel confident doing them?
- What will the people around you see as your weaknesses?
- Are you completely confident in your education and skills training? If not, where are you weakest?
- What are your negative work habits (for example, are you often late, are you disorganised, do you have a short temper, or are you poor at handling stress?

- Do you have personality traits that hold you back in your field? For instance, if you have to conduct meetings on a regular basis, a fear of public speaking would be a major weakness.
- Do other people see weaknesses that you don't see? Do co-workers consistently outperform you in key areas? Be realistic – it's best to face any unpleasant truths as soon as possible.

Opportunities

- What new technology can help you? Or can you get help from others or from people via the Internet?
- Is your industry growing? If so, how can you take advantage of the current market?
- Do you have a network of strategic contacts to help you, or offer good advice?
- What trends (management or otherwise) do you see in your company, and how can you take advantage of them?
- Are any of your competitors failing to do something important? If so, can you take advantage of their mistakes?
- Is there a need in your company or industry that no one is filling?
- Do your customers or vendors complain about something in your company? If so, could you create an opportunity by offering a solution?

You might find useful opportunities in the following:

- Networking events, educational classes, or conferences.
- A colleague going on an extended leave. Could you take on some of this person's projects to gain experience?
- A new role or project that forces you to learn new skills, like public speaking or international relations.
- A company expansion or acquisition. Do you have specific skills (like a second language) that could help with the process?

Also, importantly, look at your strengths, and ask yourself whether these open up any opportunities – and look at your weaknesses, and ask yourself whether you could open up opportunities by eliminating those weaknesses.

Threats

- What obstacles do you currently face at work?
- Are any of your colleagues competing with you for projects or roles?
- Is your job (or the demand for the things you do) changing?
- Does changing technology threaten your position?
- Could any of your weaknesses lead to threats?

Performing this analysis will often provide key information – it can point out what needs to be done and put problems into perspective.

Activity 3 **(10 minutes)**

Update your personal SWOT that you completed in an activity in chapter 1 and put it into your organiser.

3 PERSONAL SKILLS AUDIT

The personal skills audit and self-appraisal requires you to identify, review and assess your own performance of current management skills.

3.1 The importance of transferable skills

When reflecting on your skills remember that employers aren't only interested in the subject-specific knowledge gained through study. They are also looking for the kinds of skills that can be acquired through all sorts of activities and adapted in different contexts.

Looking at current job adverts to identify the kinds of key skills employers are looking for is a useful exercise. You will frequently come across phrases like: 'good communicator', 'team player', 'excellent interpersonal skills', 'analytical skills', 'works well under pressure', 'deliver to tight deadlines', 'ability to prioritise effectively', 'experience of handling budgets', 'able to work with minimum supervision', 'good IT skills', 'excellent organisational and communication skills'

Transferable skills are non-job specific skills that you have acquired during any activity or life experiences. Student activities and experiences include college and community activities, class projects, and assignments, hobbies, athletic activities and summer part-time jobs.

Transferable skills fall into three groups: working with people, working with things, and working with data/information. These terms are defined below:

1. Working with people skills happen when people sell, train, advise, and negotiate.
2. Working with things skills occur when people repair, operate machinery, sketch, survey, or troubleshoot
3. Working with data/information skills involve budgeting, researching, and analysing.

3.2 Why do I need to identify my skills?

Understanding your skills is an important aspect of career development and can help you in the following ways:

- clarify your career focus;
- develop your motivation and self-confidence;
- help you refine and focus your job search techniques;
- improve your employability.

Careers guidance and psychometric testing can be useful methods of identifying skills and can raise your self-awareness. The more self-aware and confident you are of your skills, the more likely you are to attract employment of your choice.

When planning your career, it may be useful to undertake a skills audit. A skills audit is a self-reflective process enabling you to identify your skills, strengths and qualities which may affect your employability. They might include some of the core transferable skills listed above.

Activity 4 **(10 minutes)**

Look at the following list of skills and for each identify why you think it is important or relevant for the business manager

Skill		*Importance*
1	Time Management	
2	Prioritisation	
3	Delegation	
4	Communication	
5	Negotiation	
6	Leadership	
7	Motivation	
8	Team Building.	

3.3 Self-appraisal

Take each of the headings listed in the exercise above, and consider to what degree you have each of the skills. You should spend at least five minutes on each one, and jot down your thoughts on each one on a fresh sheet of paper. Consider these factors about each one:

- Is it relevant to you in your current job? If it is not relevant now, is it likely to be in the future?
- If it is a skill which is relevant now, how well do you think that you exercise it?
- Think of specific examples of ways in which you have used that skill
- Could you use the skill better than you do at the moment, or differently?
- Would it improve your ability to do your job if you improved your use of that skill?
- What impact would it have on your management skills generally if you exercised this skill better
- In summary, do you use that skill effectively or is there room for improvement?

- Do you use or have any other management skills which are not included in our list? Think of the nature of your own job, and consider whether you carry out any tasks which are unique to your own role.

You may find it helpful to take a short break after each one so that you tackle the next one with a refreshed mind.

It is vital that you are honest in assessing your skills! You will only be deluding yourself and wasting your time if you are not honest.

Once you have thought through each of the skill headings, and made rough notes, make a more formal record of your deliberations. This will be useful for two reasons:

- It will form a key part of journal or skills log and provide important evidence which can be assessed as part of the Unit
- It may form the basis of the personal development plan which you will need to draw up with your line manager as part of this Unit.

Activity 5 **(20 minutes)**

Aim:

To help you to identify your priority development needs in the light of your career goals.

Instructions:

- Write down your highest priority career goal.
- List the *three* interpersonal skills which you feel are most relevant to successful achievement of this goal.
- Identify and list any *five* specific strengths *and* weaknesses you perceive or have identified in your behaviours or skills in these areas. (If you highlighted 'listening' as a key interpersonal skill, for example, you might identify strengths such as 'patience' and 'open-mindedness' and weaknesses such as 'passive listening behaviours' and 'insufficient feedback giving'.)
- Now restate these strengths and weaknesses as *development needs*: behaviours that need to be adjusted or skills that need to be improved in order for you to achieve your goal. (If your strength is 'patience', for example, you might restate it as a need 'to maintain patience in conflict situations' or 'to be assertive where patience allows discussion to get off track'. If your weakness is 'passive listening behaviours', for example, you might restate it as a need 'to adopt active listening behaviours'.
- Rank your development needs in order of (a) urgency, (b) importance and (c) leverage, by assigning each a score from 1 (least urgent, important, cost-effective) to 10 (most urgent, important, cost-effective).

Goal: ____

	How urgent? (1-10)	How important? (1-10)	How cost-effective? (1-10)	Total
Development needs: building on interpersonal strengths				
1	☐	☐	☐	....
2	☐	☐	☐	....
3	☐	☐	☐	....
4	☐	☐	☐	....
5	☐	☐	☐	....
Development needs: overcoming interpersonal limitations				
1	☐	☐	☐	....
2	☐	☐	☐	....
3	☐	☐	☐	....
4	☐	☐	☐	....
5	☐	☐	☐	....

- Total the ranking scores for each development need. Those with the highest scores may represent your highest priorities for obtaining that goal.

3.4 Skills audit

A skills audit is a review of your existing skills against the skills you need both now and in the future. It can help you to identify your existing skills, identify what skills you may need to carry out your existing work and role more effectively and to plan, develop and improve the skills and knowledge needed for your future career.

Carrying out a skills audit is a five stage process.

Stage 1 - Existing skills and knowledge identification

First you write down, as a bullet point list, the knowledge and skills which you consider to be important for your current work. You may find it useful to refer to your 'job description' (if there is one for your work).

Stage 2 - Future skills and knowledge identification

Next write down as a bullet point list, the knowledge and skills which you consider to be important for your future career.

Each list should comprise roughly between fifteen to twenty bullet points.

Stage 3 - Rating your ability

Once you have produced your lists you need to rate your current ability against each one. This may be done via a 3 point rating of strong, weak and somewhere in-between, or you may find it more useful to use a five point scale such as the one below.

1	No current knowledge or skill (no current competency)
2	Some awareness but not sufficiently competent to use it
3	Familiar with and able to use the knowledge or skill (some competency)
4	Proficient in the knowledge or skill and able to show others how to use it (high level of competency)
5	Expert with a high degree of skill and/or comprehensive knowledge (fully competent).

Stage 4 - Review your ability ratings

Next ask a friend or your supervisor, or tutor to review your list and give you feedback. Try to ensure that you choose someone who is honest and not afraid to tell you the truth. There is no point in asking a close friend if they are unwilling to be honest for fear that they may hurt your feelings by telling you that you are possibly not as good at something as you think you are.

Stage 5 - Your future development

The final stage is simply that of using the information to concentrate on developing the skill and knowledge areas where you have a low score or have identified that you are not fully competent.

The **Edexcel Guidelines** require you to carry out a skills audit, evaluating your:

- self-management
- leadership and
- personal and interpersonal skills

Examples of each of these categories are listed below.

Use the audit to self-assess your skills on a five point scale:

1 = wide experience	3 = a little experience	5 = don't know
2 = some experience	4 = no experience	

Self-management skills	Rating	Who, where, what will help me improve in this area
Manage time effectively		
Set realistic objectives, priorities and standards		
Listen actively and with purpose		
Show intellectual flexibility and creativity		
Take responsibility for acting in a professional/ethical manner		
Plan/work towards long-term aims and goals		
Purposely reflect on own learning and progress		
Take responsibility for own learning/personal growth		
Demonstrate awareness of learning processes		
Clarify personal values		
Cope with physical demands/stress		
Monitor, evaluate and adapt own performance		

Personal and interpersonal skills	Rating	Who, where, what will help me improve in this area
Work well with men and women from diverse backgrounds		
Generate new ideas		
Specify goals and constraints, generate alternatives, consider risks, and evaluate and choose best alternatives		
Recognise problems and devise and implement plan of action		
Use efficient learning techniques to acquire and apply new knowledge and skills		
Exert a high level of effort and perseverance towards goal attainment		
Belief in own self-worth and maintain a positive view of self		
Demonstrate understanding, friendliness, adaptability, empathy, and politeness in group settings		
Assess self accurately, set personal goals, monitor progress, and exhibit self-control		
Choose ethical courses of action		
Contribute to a spirit of teamwork and cooperation		
Involve others in problem-solving and		

decision-making		

Leadership skills	Rating	Who, where, what will help me improve in this area
Willing to take risks to propose new ideas and support those of others		
Develop and nurture effective working relationships		
Share expertise and knowledge to help others develop		
Remain positive and productive during times of uncertainty and change		
Support personal and work practices that promote health and wellness		
Show appreciation for a job well done		
Contribute to a spirit of teamwork and cooperation		
Involve others in problem-solving and decision-making		
Help others develop ways to overcome barriers to personal effectiveness		

Consider the following when you conduct your own skills audit:

- specific skills you have developed as a result of your qualification;
- work experience you have completed;
- job-specific and transferable skills you have acquired;
- skills you have developed through extra-curricular activities, such as volunteering, art, sport or music;
- positive feedback you have received throughout your course and activities.

The skills audit will help you to recollect skills which you may not have thought of or which you may not have considered to be important or relevant. It will also help you to consider relevant real-life examples to demonstrate your skills. These examples may be useful for interviews with universities or employers.

Activity 6 **(5 minutes)**

Allocate each of the skills in the list below to one of the headings:

Self-management *Leadership* *Interpersonal*

Time management

Delegation

Communication

Prioritisation

Motivation

Negotiation

Leadership

Team building

4 PREPARATION OF A DEVELOPMENT PLAN

The Edexcel Guidelines say you must prepare a development plan covering:

- Career and personal development
- Current performance
- Future needs
- Aims, objectives and targets
- Review dates
- Achievement dates
- Learning programme/activities
- Action plans

A Personal Development Plan (PDP) is a document that you fill in, which outlines what development objectives you have for the next year (or agreed period) and what development activities you plan to help you achieve those objectives. The PDP will help you to take a broader and more structured approach to your development and should encourage you to take responsibility for your learning.

Your PDP should:

- Outline the agreed development need
- Identify the actions to meet the need
- Identify timescales for completion
- Indicate responsibility for implementation
- Contain suggested review dates

4.1 Career and personal development

PDP is not an end itself; it is a cyclical process. This means that you can start your development at any point in the cycle. PDP also allows you to evaluate your performance, to identify training or development needs and to think about future plans. In essence, PDP is about lifelong or continuous learning in the workplace.

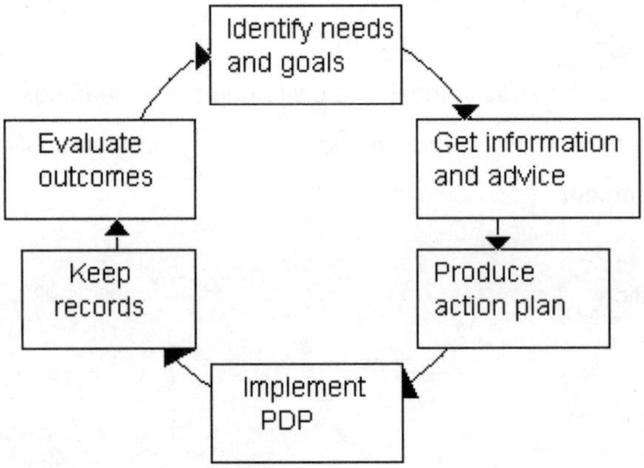

Key benefits of PDP include the following:

- It identifies routes for personal progression
- It revitalises technical skills
- It identifies existing skills that need updating or new skills that need to be acquired
- It builds on and reinforces transferable skills
- It promotes continuous learning
- It helps you to make the most of opportunities at work
- It increases levels of motivation and job satisfaction
- It provides individuals with a mechanism for reflecting and monitoring own performance.

The objectives of your PDP should be SMARTER:

Up to now we have outlined the 'SMART' framework for formulating effective business objectives. However, *Adair and Allen* (1999) suggest that objectives need to be SMARTER.

- **Specific.** What exactly do you hope to achieve, and in what contexts? Can it be broken down into smaller, more specific steps?
- **Measurable.** How will you recognise success in pursuing the objective? How will you measure your progress along the way?
- **Agreed.** Whose support or authority do you need to pursue the objective? (Note for planning stage: arrange an opportunity to discuss it with them.)
- **Realistic.** Are you able to achieve the objective within the constraints of your current abilities and commitments, your available time and resources?
- **Time-bounded.** By what date do you want to achieve the objective?
- **Evaluated.** Is the objective worth pursuing, given the investment in time or effort it will require?
- **Reviewed.** When and how will you review your progress?

In other words, objectives should be stretching but achievable. It should be clear when the objective has been achieved. Large objectives can be broken into steps or sub-objectives that are clear and actionable with realistic dates for completion.

Objectives do not always have to be directly related to specific work tasks. For example, a PDP goal might be to improve language skills.

4.2 Current performance

The ultimate goal of your plan is to analyse and develop the following:

- where are you now (listing your achievements so far, how you achieved them and the skills and knowledge you possess)
- where you want to be (critical to know where you want to be as you can't develop a plan if you don't know where you are going - rather like a car journey)
- how you are going to get there

Analysing your current strengths

Conduct a self-assessment to determine current skills, interests, and values (you can use the personal SWOT analysis already completed). In addition to an assessment of current job strengths and areas of improvement, ask questions such as:

What do I value?	How do others see me?
How satisfied am I in my current job?	How do I want to be seen?
How well does my job meet my needs?	What kind of person do I want to be?
If I wanted to make a change, what would it be?	What makes me happy?

So you can work out what type of additional skills, help or knowledge you need you will need to first state what you currently possess.

Outline your current success under the following headings:

- My personal achievements
- My work achievements
- My qualifications
- Training courses attended
- My financial status

4.3 Future needs

Few people are lucky enough to start life knowing what they want to be when they grow up, and sticking to that idea throughout their education and subsequent career. Even fewer are able to follow a precisely defined career path where development and promotion occur at pre-determined stages.

In the 21st century professionals are responsible for their own careers and have to make decisions about where they want to go next. They must be able to adapt to sudden career changes, whether these result from new opportunities or redundancy. This may seem to rule out the need to plan where you want your career to take you, but in reality strengthens the case for assessing your future needs and planning how to gain the competence you will need to meet them.

In terms of your future needs, you should also give some thought to the type of support which might help you to achieve your plan. For example, will you require a mentor at some stage? If so, when, and where would you look for one? What other types of supporters would you want? If you are thinking of gaining NVQs you will need to identify assessors and verifiers. You may also need financial support and/or flexible working arrangements if you are planning to study for a further qualification.

4.4 Aims, objectives and targets

Aims - having a clear aim begins to define the plan. For example: a large-scale short-term aim requires a plan with detail and strict timescales, whereas a goal to achieve a personal life change within five-to-ten years requires much less detail and scheduling, provided the crucial causes and effects stages are identified.

Objectives - an objective is something which you plan to do or achieve. It may be part of ongoing service delivery ('business as usual') or improvements, or a one-off improvement initiative. It can be something very simple or quite complex. The best way to organise your work into manageable chunks is to set short, medium and long-term objectives. Always remember, short, medium and long are all relative terms and will mean different things to different people. Some plans may only last over a 1 year period, others may last up to 6 years, and it all depends on you and your own circumstances.

It is also important to remember that these short, medium and long term objectives are fluid and must be reviewed on a regular basis to ensure that they are still relevant.

An objective may have a series of actions or tasks associated with it and it is structured in stages. You can add more stages and elements (in other words the factors which cause things to happen) as necessary. If any element is too big to imagine realistically achieving in one go, then break it down into further elements. Even the most ambitious goals and plans are achievable when broken down and given time.

A plan to achieve an objective is normally best developed by working backwards from the aim. Ask yourself at each stage of the plan: 'What must happen before this?' And then plan to achieve each element, working back in realistic bite-sized elements, to where you are today.

Prioritise - once you have established a list of objectives, allocate numbers to them to indicate how important they are, with 1 as the highest, 2 as the next highest and so on.

You may find it difficult to decide which order they should go in. They could be prioritised in terms of

- Importance to your job
- Importance to you as an individual
- How much you want to achieve them
- How quickly you need to achieve them
- Cost to you or your employer
- Pleasure and potential satisfaction arising
- How realistic it is that you will achieve them

The order in which you put your objectives may change a number of times before it is finalised. You may want to prioritise improving your command of French, but if you do not use the language at work it would not be regarded as a high business priority. However, if it is something which you personally have a burning desire to do it should not necessarily be consigned to the bottom of the heap, as it would pay dividends in terms of personal satisfaction and sense of achievement.

Similarly, you may well want to be promoted or given the chance to work in a different department before a certain date, but that may not be realistic from a business planning point of view. Alternatively, your promotion may depend on your passing exams and gaining qualifications, or on someone ahead of you being promoted themselves, so that the matter is not entirely under your control.

Targets - a target is a level of performance which you aim to achieve or maintain and is usually quantitative – therefore, is numerically measurable. In some cases, it is difficult to set a quantitative target and therefore a broader desired outcome may be set, based upon something qualitative - for example, an improvement in perceptions

Ideally, an objective should have a target associated with it and visa versa.

Plans can be structured in different ways according to individual preference and the various planning tools and methods which exist. Detailed people prefer detailed plans. Intuitive people prefer broader more flexible plans.

Choose a planning format that you are comfortable using - and adapt and develop it as you need. There is no point in adopting a complex spreadsheet if you will not enjoy using it. Conversely, if you want to analyse lots of details, then choose a format which will accommodate this.

Whatever planning format you prefer, all plans begin as a simple outline. It could just be a table drawn on a piece of A4 paper. Beyond this you can add more detail and structure to suit your aims and preferences, but you must begin with a clear aim, and an outline of what will make it happen.

1 Write down your aim. Describe it. Clearly define it so that a stranger could understand it and know what it means.

2 Attach some measures or parameters or standards (scale, values, comparative references, etc) to prove that it is achieved. Commit to a timescale - even if it is five or ten years away. Then ask yourself and identify what factors would directly cause the aim to be achieved.

3 Consider realistically and identify the factors which would cause the aim to be achieved. If necessary research this - you will only be fooling yourself if you guess or ignore an unavoidable aspect. Write these factors down and clearly define them, again so that even a stranger could understand them.

4 Attach measures or parameters or standards as necessary (scale, values, comparative references, etc).

5 Attach timings.

6 When you have completed your plan, you can then start to work through the levels - from the bottom to the top. Adapt your plan as required - especially add new factors as you discover them, and plan how each can be achieved by incorporating them into this model.

A natural way to develop this outline planning method is to use project management tools, such as Critical Path Analysis, or a Gantt chart, or another of the various computerised project tools now available.

4.5 Review dates

It is important to set either target dates for the achievement of goals or review dates to monitor progress. These targets should be agreed with your manager, as your successful development will be heavily dependent on these reviews. Unless clear deadlines can be set, it may be better to set a review date, which allows sufficient time for development to occur.

Where regular one-to-one meetings are the norm, the PDP can be scheduled as an item for discussion. It may be useful to prepare a short progress report, summarising what has been achieved and what remains to be done. This could also to reflect on your learning and demonstrate to your manager what you have achieved.

On average, the PDP should be reviewed quarterly, though more frequent reviews might be needed in the early stages to ensure it gets off the ground.

Key points

- Record plans
- Monitor progress
- Seek support, feedback and encouragement
- Make your development a priority
- Be prepared to redraw plans
- Anticipate and be prepared for problems
- Make it enjoyable
- Keep your development plan stretching and achievable – not too big

4.6 Achievement dates

How do you measure your success? Achievement may be measured in two ways: the first is by completing the task in the time allowed and the second is completing the task to your stated satisfaction. The target time for completion you set yourself should be the easiest to tick off but the evidence required for satisfactory completion may not be as easy as it sometimes depends on criteria outside your control.

Objectives need clear indications of success if they are to retain their motivating power. These can be expressed in terms of both improved job performance and direct benefits to you e.g. promotion, more leisure time.

Some of the best rewards might be less tangible ones, e.g. having less stress on the job, feeling a sense of achievement, or receiving recognition for a job well done.

Ask yourself the questions 'What evidence do I need to convince me that I am making progress against my objectives?' This will help you identify the signs of improvement, which indicate progress.

Also ask yourself 'What factors will confirm my improvements in the eyes of my manager?' In other words, clearly agree the practical evidence that will provide tangible evidence of improvement.

What about **contingency plans**?

Unforeseen obstacles can bring a plan to a complete stop. However, with some forethought, many obstacles can be anticipated and contingency plans can be put into place to reach the objective by a different route.

It is also important to ensure your PDP is realistic, for example the timescales you have set to achieve your objectives.

Once you have completed your Learning Development Plan you can then begin to work towards the achievement of your learning outcomes. The development of your portfolio of evidence of achievement should start as soon as you commence your learning activities.

4.7 Development activities

Once you have decided in which area you want to develop you can use certain criteria to help you decide the best development activity for you.

Some of these are listed below. You may be able to think of other criteria you would wish to use. If so, add yours to the list.

- Prior knowledge - what do you already need to know, or be able to do to benefit from the activities?
- Career relevance - can the activity be readily integrated into your work schedule, or does it demand disruptions to the schedule?
- How appropriate is the activity to your current position, aspirations and potential?
- Support required - does the activity need substantial support from managers or colleagues, or can you initiate and manage the activity alone? To avoid the obvious dangers of adopting a self-reliant approach, it is important to ensure support is obtained. You must continually ask the questions 'What help do I need to ensure I am making progress?'
- Pace - do you decide on the pace and speed of learning, or is this dictated by the activity itself?
- Transfer - how easily is the learning transferred to the work situation?
- Group - does the learning take place in a group setting, with mutual support and feedback, or is it a solo activity?
- Feedback - does the activity itself provide unambiguous feedback to you on progress, or must this be obtained from other sources, e.g. by applying it on the job, or from managers' or colleagues' observations?
- Costs - what is the actual cost of the training, e.g. a book on 'delegating' may cost £15; a course on the same subject may cost £500?
- Payoff - are the costs incurred justifiable in relation to the benefits obtained?
- Timescale - over what length of time does the activity take place to achieve competence, e.g. a day-release course of one day per week for 18 months?
- Time consumed - how much time is actually spent on the activity, e.g. day-release course might take 70 days?

- On-the-job - can the activity be carried out as part of your normal work schedule or does it require time away from normal duties?
- Planning and organising - how much planning and organising is required to set up and run the activity?
- Preferred learning style - is the activity best suited to your learning style?

Selecting the development activities that work for you

Learning opportunities come in many guises. They are not restricted to the workplace or formal training courses. If you cannot find opportunities in the workplace, think creatively. Look at your leisure activities or use your networks to find people who can help elsewhere.

Work-related learning opportunities

- Practice and reflection
- Observing other colleagues (e.g. to learn a new technique)
- Giving a presentation to your team members
- Collaborative working
- Teaching
- Giving a seminar
- Organising, attending or chairing meetings
- Attending conferences
- Work shadowing (a valuable way for anyone to gain insight into new or unfamiliar work environments)
- Mentoring a student or more junior colleague, or being mentored

Formal training/development

Typically this would be attending a course, either at your institution, externally, or online. Courses cover transferable skills such as presentation, writing reports, grant applications, CV and job search skills, time management, or project management. They may also be subject- or discipline- specific on e.g. research techniques. Another option is online or distance learning where you can work at your own pace and in your own time.

Professional and specialist magazines and journals often contain valuable articles, features or series on the knowledge and skills your have identified as areas for improvement. Attending local events, such as a lecture, will help your understanding, and provide a chance for you to meet with other professionals.

Recreational

Taking part in social/leisure activities or volunteering may offer opportunities for development that are not available in the workplace, for example, organising a sponsored hike, membership of social club committees, playing team sports.

Other examples you might consider are:

- involvement in local or national government, which would widen your understanding of major issues, help you to appreciate the complexity of decision making, and enhance your skill in negotiation and persuading others.

- contributing to a voluntary service, such as St John's Ambulance, which would give you vital first-aid skills

4.8 How do I successfully manage my PDP?

Having put your PDP together, there are a few suggestions you can follow to help you manage it effectively:

- Sharing your plan with a colleague can give them an opportunity to help you
- If you do get other people involved it's a good idea to keep them regularly updated on your progress
- Different people can help you in different ways. A good listener is ideal to talk to about your plans and your progress. Someone you know to have a lot of knowledge and experience makes a good technical sounding board. Someone whose feedback you value as specific and non-judgemental can help you objectively assess your progress
- Watch out for significant differences between your planned and actual progress. Check the reasons and decide if you need to take action
- You may need to be methodical when monitoring your progress. It may be a good idea to schedule time for this in your diary
- Whenever the unexpected occurs, take time to look at the development plans you have made. There may be changes to make, activities to cancel or reschedule or new opportunities to take that can help you get nearer to your goals
- Remember to take time to think and review
- Always ask for feedback at every opportunity and use it to review the progress of your plan
- Learn from the things that go wrong, analyse them to do better next time and whatever happens don't be put off
- Make a point of enjoying the success you achieve. However at the same time make a point of analysing your success and building on it

5 ACTION PLANNING

5.1 An action plan

Again, you may have your own preferences in regard to formatting and recording action plans: timetables, diaries, checklists and so on. Feel free to use whatever works for you.

We recommend a simple, systematic format such as the following.

Objective	Methods	Timescale	Monitoring and review
Statement of SMARTER behavioural objective	List of specific methods/activities selected	Target completion date for each listed method/activity	How, with whom and how often you will check your progress?

We show an example of a completed action plan, using this simple framework, in Section 5.4 below, following a brief discussion of some of the key issues.

5.2 Defining realistic time scales

It is generally unrealistic:

- to attempt massive behavioural changes in a short time frame; and
- to attempt to work on too many areas of change at a time.

It may take time to acquire the underpinning knowledge and concepts relevant to a given skill; to arrange to receive coaching, or feedback on your competence; to practise the skill repeatedly in low-risk environments (perhaps in study settings), learning by trial and error; to find an opportunity to apply the skill at work; to repeat the application in order to consolidate your learning; and to gather feedback through which you can evaluate your success. Set realistic time scales for each stage of this process.

Remember that this is likely to be only one of the plans and schedules operating in your life – and in the lives of those whose help, counsel and feedback you may require. There will be other demands on your time, attention and resources – and theirs. Some of the steps in your plan may be dictated by external events: scheduled meetings (for example, with your mentor), or opportunities arising to put skills into practice (an interview, negotiation or team meeting).

There is nothing wrong with planning for **gradual, incremental changes** or improvements over time. Indeed, it may be beneficial to make one or two small, realistic steps towards your goal, and to consolidate them before moving on to the next steps. *Whetten and Cameron* (2000, p. 125) call this a 'small wins' strategy. It is a valid, confidence-building and stress-reducing approach to problem-solving, particularly when tackling large and complex tasks. It is also central to the concept of continuous improvement (in Japanese, *kaizen*): a way of sustaining on-going development over time.

5.3 Identifying ways to monitor and review progress

In order to benefit from any development activity, you need to know:

- whether your progress is on schedule in relation to your plans.

  Your activity or resources may need adjusting in order to bring them into line with your schedule or performance targets.

- whether, or how far, your planned activity is effective in achieving your objectives.

  Your plan may need adjusting in order to achieve the objective more effectively. The objective itself may need adjusting if it turns out to have been unrealistic or unattainable in its original form.

The control process may involve *regular monitoring* of your activity and/or *periodic review* of your results.

- What **progress markers** are built into your objectives, which you can check for in your performance? What are your criteria for success at each stage of your plan?
- What types of **information** will you use for monitoring? Your own observations and reflections? Performance results? Feedback from other people?
- What **other people** might you involve in the monitoring and review process? A mentor? Your line manager or appraiser? Selected feedback-givers? Your learning partners or study group?
- How **often** will you review/sample your activity and its results? Periodically? By random sampling? At key stage deadlines? At completion date?

Illustrated below is an example of an action planning sheet.

ACTION PLANNING SHEET

SMART objective: ____
____

Identified strengths which will facilitate my attaining the objective

-
-
-
-
-

Identified limitations which may hinder my attaining the objective

-
-
-
-
-

Rewards/payoffs for achieving the objective (rank in terms of value):

1
2
3
4
5

SMART objective: ____
____

Blockages/barriers/risks/downsides to achieving the objective	Strategies for overcoming blockages/barriers/ risks/downsides
•	•
•	•
•	•
•	•
•	•

Steps for achieving the objective (starting now)	Time deadline
•	•
•	•
•	•
•	•
•	•

Indicators that you have achieved the objective	How/when evaluated?
•	•
•	•
•	•
•	•
•	•

5.4 Example of a completed action plan

The figure below is an example of the kind of action plan you may formulate using the framework suggested in section 5.1 above.

Objective	Methods	Timescale	Monitoring and review
To be able to utilise a range of influencing strategies and styles to achieve successful outcomes: by end December.	*Reading:* Gillen Agreed: Improve your powers of influence'	End March	Review progress in June and December with manager
	Coaching: Meet with manager. Discuss key decision makes in the organisation. Identify examples of successful strategies.	By end March	Monthly meetings with mentor
	Project: Take responsibility for agreeing franchise arrangements with prospective partners	Agreement reached by October	Seek feedback on influencing style from management team colleagues
	Reflect on day-to-day influencing experiences: note in PDJ and discuss with mentor.	Monthly	
To remain calm when faced with aggressive behaviour (not raise voice, use sarcastic tone or make un-controlled gestures): by end August	Meet with John before next marketing meeting ask him to observe and give feedback on my behaviour. At marketing meeting, try to implement assertiveness skills (broken record, count to 10) if Paula becomes aggressive.	Meet with John by end April	Seek regular meeting with John for on-going feedback.
	Meet with John after the meeting to get feedback. Identify from this meeting further action points.	Further action points by mid May	Reflect on marketing meetings in PDJ: evaluate results of assertiveness behaviours.

Figure 4.2: Example of a completed action plan

Activity 7 **(20 minutes)**

Draw up an action plan sheet, using the columns shown in our example. Select one immediate training need for yourself (perhaps related to some aspect of the HND syllabus) and formulate an action plan.

We will now look at two key managerial tools for developing self awareness: a personal development journal and personal portfolio.

6 A PERSONAL DEVELOPMENT JOURNAL (PDJ)

6.1 What is a 'PDJ'?

A 'journal' is a book (or note pad, or whatever) in which you regularly record your experiences and actions, events and interactions in which you have participated *and* your reflections on them.

A PDJ is a structured approach to recording your experience, providing you with data which will enable you:

- to bring your experience into your conscious awareness, opening up the possibility of different and more intentional behaviours;
- to reflect on and analyse your behaviours and their outcomes, enabling you to learn consciously and intentionally from your experience, maximising your learning opportunities;
- to monitor and track your development.

Recording your external and internal observations of events and interactions on a regular basis captures your experience while it is fresh in your mind. If you do not do this, you will be relying on longer-range memories, which are likely to be less detailed, coherent and accurate – and will accordingly make a lesser contribution to your development.

6.2 Structuring your PDJ

A PDJ make take the form of a notebook, loose leaf folder, computerised file or whatever you prefer. However, it is intended to be more than a diary of occasional, miscellaneous jottings: it requires a coherent *structure.*

Pedler et al (2001, p. 80) propose a model which focuses on the following aspects of experience

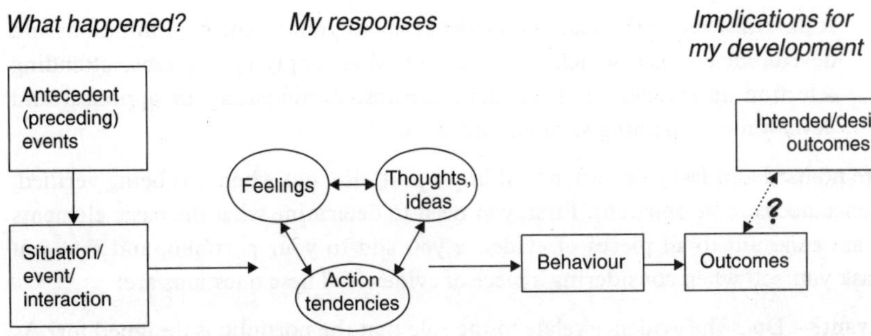

Activity 8 **(20 minutes)**

Aim:

To help you get started on completing a PDJ.

Instructions:

Using the format given above, select a specific interaction or interpersonal activity you participated in recently, and complete one complete journal entry following the guidelines given. What did you find difficult about completing the PDJ? What did you learn about your interpersonal behaviour by completing the PDJ?

7 A PERSONAL PORTFOLIO

There is some confusion surrounding the terms portfolio and profile. A simple analogy would be to consider a portfolio as a photograph album with a collection of photographs and a profile a collection of some of those photos to illustrate a specific point or meet a specific need, for example to prepare for your annual appraisal.

7.1 What is a personal portfolio?

A portfolio is simply a folder for keeping documents, which is organised in its presentation. Designers, architects and artists, among others, have long kept portfolios of their work for systematic storage, easy access, and presentation to interested parties. A portfolio for management education and development works the same way: it represents a filing system *and* a potential résumé.

The intended benefits of compiling a portfolio are as follows.

- It encourages you to become more reflective about your work performance and your impact on other people, heightening your awareness of your personal/interpersonal behaviour and effectiveness. As a conscious gathering of information about your experience, it will increase your self awareness and insight.
- It enables you to evaluate your competence over a period of time, and to plan and evaluate action for your developmer

- It provides you with ideas and evidence about your strengths, limitations and development goals which you can use when applying for jobs, attending selection interviews or assessment centres, participating in appraisal and development planning sessions and so on.

There are no hard and fast rules when building a portfolio, but when it is being verified, the evidence needs to be apparent. First, you need to determine what the basic elements are that are common to all pieces of evidence you add to your portfolio, and that you need to ask yourself when considering a piece of evidence. These questions are:

Is it relevant? – Does the evidence relate to the role that the portfolio is designed for? As an example, if you were once a chef and you held qualifications, will it link in to anything you do now as a manager? If it doesn't, then the advice is to leave it out. If you are including certificates of past achievements, then make sure they are related to the job, i.e. First aid at work, equality and diversity, communication etc – all these would be classed as relevant.

Is it current? – Is the evidence you are adding within a certain time span? Some certificates have a fixed period when they are current for example "Issued 2007 and valid for 3 years" If the certificate has expired there is not much point in including it within your portfolio. This is to ensure that any skills you have are in date and skills decay is not apparent. The portfolio should ideally not have any gaps in it to show consistency.

Is it authentic? – This means that the evidence you are submitting is genuine.

Although normally copies of certificates are requested when submitting a portfolio (for security purposes or in case the portfolio gets lost) there are security marks on certificates to ensure it is genuine, or a number that can be checked with the Body that awarded it in the first place. In the case of other types of evidence, you will need signatures and dates to ensure the authenticity and again be checked with the signatory and cross referenced.

Is it sufficient? – Is there enough evidence to ensure you can carry out the skills required?

Activity 9 **(20 mins)**

Consider the key skills of numeracy, literacy (communication skills) and information technology (IT). Have a look at the standards produced by the Qualifications and Curriculum Authority (QCA) and map yourself against them (www.qca.org.uk). Do you need to develop any of these key skills to progress further?

Also look at the level 3 key skill 'Improving Own Learning and Performance': how do you rate against this? Find out if your college offers you an opportunity to be accredited for any of these skills. You will also find a sample portfolio for assessment against these standards on the QCA website

7.2 What should go in a portfolio?

Portfolios can act as development tools to assist with your career development and enable you to identify and develop a route map to achieve your goals. The portfolio provides a record of interactions and events which you have observed and participated in, and of your development in relevant skills and competences. It is a dynamic document which will develop as you progress through your HND/HNC – and this module in particular.

Your portfolio should include:

- Curriculum Vitae (CV) - this provides a good starting point and gives a basic overview of what you have done within your working and educational life up to the present. As with job interviews, the CV provides a first impression of you as a person and the skills and experience you have gained during school and working life.

- Testimonials - these are letters from certain staff or people that have worked closely with you that can provide evidence that you have made certain decisions/actions that cannot be evidenced in any other way. The Testimonial will contain the details of the work you have done and give an outline of the skills you have undertaken.

  As with other evidence, testimonials are only accepted if they are less than two years old. The only exception to this is if they are providing underpinning knowledge for the portfolio, i.e. events and background leading up to the role you are submitting the evidence for.

  To provide credibility, all testimonials must be written by certain staff to provide an element of sufficiency and authenticity.

- Letters from the public, or thank you notes explaining how you dealt with the 'softer' aspects of your skills such as offering sympathy, diffusing a situation etc.

- Witness statements – these are accounts of events written in a more formal manner on pro formas. Some Services employ Professional Witnesses that are trained to write these specific testimonies which link directly to performance criteria (exact details of what you are expected to do)

7.5 Organising your portfolio

It does not matter how you organise your material – but it does need to be organised, so that you can:

- *Find and access items of information when you want them.* Classify them in any suitable way and label them accordingly, as you put them into the folder, so you can sort them later.
- *Understand the information readily.* 'Raw' notes made during or shortly after interactions and events may need to be re-drafted (while your memory is reasonably fresh) – especially if you have a tendency to use shorthand note forms!

Your portfolio is your personal record which should portray your achievements, qualities, competencies and abilities. Choose a format that best suits your own needs. You may decide to:

- use a lever arch file and coloured file dividers and develop your own record pages.
- use one of the commercial portfolios already available

Suggested format

Contents page – This page contains the main headings with page numbering, ensuring easy access.

Biographical details

Personal details –Name, address, telephone number, e-mail address

Introduction – You should provide a brief introduction about you, why you want to develop your portfolio. What your current role is what your future career and educational aspirations are. Think about where you would like to be in one, three and five years' time. What are your strengths and the potential barriers to achieving this?

General Education – Include name of schools, colleges and universities, dates attended and title of qualification,

Work experience - Start with the most recent and work your way back. Include the name of employer, dates, job title and brief account of key responsibilities.

You may wish to include your certificates of educational and professional achievements, your job description and your CV in this section. Your portfolio will therefore provide a useful resource for when you have to provide this type of evidence.

Activity 10 **(30 minutes)**

Aim:

To get you started on compiling and organising a Personal Portfolio

Instructions:

You were encouraged in Chapter 2 to start collecting evidences and observations immediately. If you undertook this activity, you should have a file of material available.

Review and organise your filed material and turn it into the beginnings of a portfolio.

8 LEARNING STYLES AND STRATEGIES

8.1 Understanding your learning style

Not everyone learns in the same way so it is important to understand how you learn. Are you better in a classroom with other people, sitting down by yourself and reading books or would it be better using some of the online learning systems that are now being developed?

There are many ways to categorise learning styles, but the simplest of them places learners into one or more of three categories:

1 Visual - those who learn best through their eyes and what they see and read. The ideal learning approaches in this case will involve studying magazines and books and learning online.

2 Auditory - those who learn best by hearing things, either on tape or in discussion. Dialogue and discussion is important to their learning process. The ideal learning environment is the classroom, but discussions with colleagues and audio tapes can also be useful.

3 Tactile - those who learn best by 'doing', such as taking their own notes or participating in demonstrations and hands-on projects. Ideal structure: magazine and online learning; classroom that encourages participation.

It is important to analyse the way you learn best before devising the learning strategy/action plan to achieve your goals.

People say things like 'I'm an auditory learner' (meaning that they are comfortable absorbing information which they have heard or discussed); or 'I'm a kinaesthetic (tactile) learner' (if they prefer to learn through practical classes and hands-on activities, rather than by reading books and listening to lectures). In fact, we use all of our senses to absorb information. But you may find it helpful to confirm what your strengths are with regard to perception.

Once you have acquired the information (by listening, reading, etc.), you then process it mentally, as you think about it and memorise it. You will have a natural preference for how you:

- grasp information - do you prefer to deal with abstract concepts and generalisations, or concrete, practical examples?
- order information - would you rather receive facts in a logical, sequential way (to build up a picture one step at a time), or with an overview straight away (to show the big picture first, then the details)?
- engage with information - do you prefer active experimentation or reflective observation?

Finally, there is how you choose to share information with others. You will have a preference for how you:

- *organise information* - with a holistic overview, or with detailed and logical analysis
- *present information* - verbally or using images.

You will need to make the most of your strengths as a learner, and practise strategies that will allow you to build up the weaker areas.

Advice for visual learners

- Use visual materials such as pictures, charts, and maps
- Use colour to highlight texts and own notes
- Take notes or use handouts; look carefully at headings and patterns of topics
- Brainstorm using illustrations, mind maps and models
- Use multi-media where possible (computers; mind maps)
- Study in a quiet place away from visual disturbances
- Visualise information as a picture
- Skim-read to get an overview before reading in detail.

Advice for auditory learners

- Participate frequently in discussions and debates
- Make speeches and presentations
- Use a tape recorder if possible instead of (or as well as) making notes
- Read text aloud
- Create musical jingles and mnemonics to aid memory
- Discuss your ideas verbally
- Dictate to someone else while they write your ideas down
- Speak onto an audio-tape and listen to your own ideas played back.

Advice for tactile / kinaesthetic learners

- Take frequent study breaks
- Move around to learn new things (e.g. read while you are using an exercise bike; model in clay to learn a new concept)
- Stand up to work
- Use bright colours to highlight reading material and turn it into posters or models
- Skim-read before reading in detail.

Honey and Mumford's learning styles

Honey and Mumford (1982) devised an influential self-test, which indicates whether you are predominantly an activist, a reflector, a theorist, or a pragmatist. We have already discussed this in detail and, if you had completed all the activities you will have decided which learning style suits you best.

Activity 11 **(20 minutes)**

Aim:

To encourage you to think about available development opportunities and resources.

Instructions:

Select one interpersonal skill which you have identified as a development need. Brainstorm a list of options for accessing or creating learning activities designed to improve your skills in this area.

Do not evaluate or place any limitations on the options you put forward at this stage: try to think freely and creatively. Write down all your suggestions as they emerge on a large sheet of paper: allow ideas to prompt other ideas.

Once you feel that the 'flow' of suggestions has stopped, move to evaluation. Consider the possibilities of each method. How would it work? What resources would it require? What benefits and drawbacks would it present?

Identify which learning style or styles (Activist, Pragmatist, Theorist, Reflector) each method would best suit in identifying options.

9 LEARNING FROM OTHERS

9.1 Development methods

Development methods vary and their use will often depend on resources, timescale and individual learning styles of participants. Some of the most popular development methods are:

CDs/videos/podcasts – these are portable, inexpensive and could be useful if information needs to be quickly absorbed. CDs are quite often used on foreign language training programmes.

Case studies – are sometimes used on training programmes or in isolation on individualised training programmes. The 'scenario' approach can help to reinforce learning, especially if case studies from within the workplace are used.

Coaching – the features of coaching are that it is objective, short-term, time limited, goal specific, action and performance orientated, personally tailored and involves feedback

Computer based training – many companies offer interactive training which is delivered via a computer. This kind of training tends to be highly specific and ensures that participants receive consistent input. With many packages users progress at their own pace and can 'backtrack' to check or correct their understanding.

Mentoring – a mentor could be someone from within the organisation who offers support and guidance to another person. They are more experienced that the trainee and meet regularly to offer help,

'Sitting with Nellie' – is a simple method of development which involves sitting alongside someone more experienced or watching them perform a task. It is useful if the development does not require too much learning or intellectual 'engagement' with a task.

Training courses – vary in quality and careful selection is needed to make them effective. For example, questions should be asked at the outset about content, aims and objectives and experience of trainers. Training can be external or in-house if a specially tailored programme is required or if several participants need the same type of training.

Tutorials – include guidance to proceed through learning some technique or procedure, e.g., a tutorial on using a computer software package. There are an increasing number of online tutorials (tutorials available on diskette, CD-ROM, over the Internet, etc.).

Peer-based methods – includes formats where peers focus on helping each other learn, e.g., by exchanging ongoing feedback, questions, supportive challenges, materials, etc.

Networked learning – is a process of developing and maintaining connections with people and information, and communicating in such a way so as to support one another's learning. Networked learning can be practised in both formal and informal settings. In formal settings the learning achieved through networked communication is formally facilitated, assessed and/or recognised by an educational organisation. In an informal setting, individuals maintain a learning network for their own interests, for learning 'on-the-job', or for research purposes.

Formal learning – refers to learning through a programme of instruction in an educational institution, adult training centre or in the workplace, which is generally recognised in a qualification or a certificate. It is always organised and structured, and has learning objectives. From the learner's standpoint, it is always intentional: i.e. the learner's explicit objective is to gain knowledge, skills and/or competences.

Non-formal learning – refers to learning through a programme but it is not usually evaluated and does not lead to certification.

Informal learning – refers to learning resulting from daily work-related, family or leisure activities. It is never organised, has no set objective in terms of learning outcomes and is never intentional from the learner's standpoint. Often it is referred to as learning by experience or just as experience. The idea is that the simple fact of existing constantly exposes the individual to learning situations, at work, at home or during leisure time for instance. Examples of informal knowledge transfer include instant messaging, a spontaneous meeting on the Internet, a phone call to someone who has information you need, a live one-time-only sales meeting introducing a new product, a chat-room in real time, a chance meeting by the tea machine, a scheduled Web-based meeting with a real-time agenda, a techie walking you through a repair process, or a meeting with your assigned mentor or manager

Clive Shepherd (*E-learning in all its forms*) gives an overview of the three main facets of e-learning and how they can each be used across the spectrum of informal to formal learning.

	Formal	**Non-formal**	**Informal**
Online content	Self-study courses	Rapid e-learning content, podcasts, demos, presentations	User-generated content - whether text, images, videos, audio files, presentations etc
Live online learning	Virtual classroom sessions which are packaged as courses or which form part of formal, blended solutions	Webinars and other facilitated sessions	Web conferencing, instant messaging and similar tools for meetings initiated by learners themselves
Asynchronous online learning	Forums, wikis and blogs as part of formal online or blended courses	Forums and blogs to provide a means of supporting ongoing support	Forums, wikis, blogs and micro-blogging which allow ongoing communication, reflection and knowledge

10 EVALUATION OF PROGRESS

10.1 Evaluation and review

Whenever you carry out PDP it is important to evaluate and review your outcomes so that you can assess whether the development activity was successful and to measure the impact it has had on your work. At the end of the development activity you should ask yourself the following questions:

- What can I do better as a result of the development

- Have additional development needs been identified?
- How effective was the development method?
- Could I have gained more from the activity?
- Did the development meet my needs and achieve the objectives I set?
- How will I make use of the development?
- What next?

As part of your appraisal (or self-appraisal) you should be able to:

- introduce and explain the methods you used to collect information on your PDP and its effectiveness
- explain the practical ways you collected feedback
- explain how you analysed the information your collected
- explain how you used the results of your analysis to inform the further development of your PDP
- use your learning log for evidence

10.2 Personal development plan

PDP is a continuous cycle of:

- Self-assessment and evaluation
- Identification of needs and goals
- Planning a course of action to meet these needs and goals
- Carrying out your action plan and recording your achievements
- Reflecting on the outcomes and evaluating your progress, which should then reveal new needs and goals (Figure below)

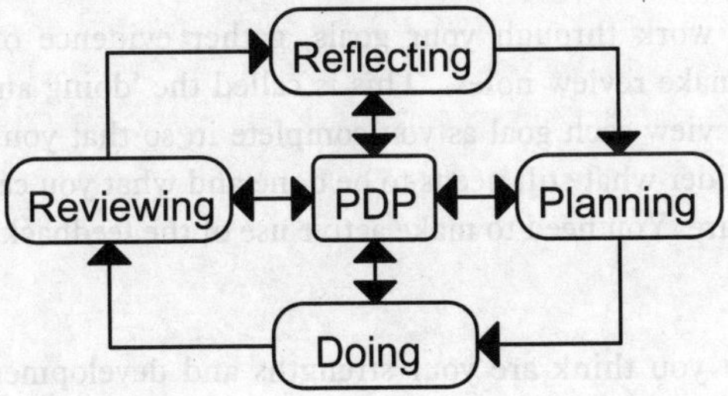

1. **Reflecting** - it is important to take time and reflect on where you are in your professional and personal development and to evaluate your progress towards meeting your objectives. Reflecting helps you to make sense of your experiences, thoughts, knowledge and ideas, to realise what is effective and how things could be improved, and to identify what to do in the future. You need to record your achievements and update your skills set. By revisiting these you can see how you have made progress and improved your skills. You need to identify goals that you can complete over the short, medium and long term. You should discuss your achievements and goals with your supervisor(s) and draw up a plan of action for

achieving the goals. This may mean setting new targets or re-setting those that need re-scheduling.

This reflective process is an attempt to identify the best way for you to learn new things and what obstacles you met that got in the way of you fully achieving your goals. Basically, if you did something during your learning that went well keep doing it, but if you did something that did not work think about how you could do it differently next time you identify a learning need.

The following questions will help you reflect on your learning style:

- Were your objectives easy to achieve and why?
- Were your objectives difficult to achieve and why?
- Which were the most valuable learning activities and why?
- Which were the least valuable learning activities and why?
- In what ways have you been able to apply your learning in practice?
- What benefits to your organisation do you feel have occurred as a result of your learning?

Use this section to record your thoughts about your next Development Plan. If you have not achieved your objectives what could you do differently? Did you discover something that highlighted another subject that you need to learn?

You can use these reflections when you start your next PDP cycle.

2. Planning - it is important to record the goals set. Take time to think about your expectations for each goal. This will help you when you come to review your goals. You need to ensure that you record your goals so that you can then record your achievements. Develop your action/research plan clearly. You may find that a GANTT chart helps with this. A GANTT chart can be produced in MS Word, MS Excel or the timeline of MS Outlook Tasks.

3. Doing - as you work through your goals, gather evidence of the new skills and achievements and make review notes. This is called the 'doing and reviewing' process. It is important to review each goal as you complete it, so that you can record what you have achieved, consider what still needs to be done and what you can do to improve your approach in the future. You need to make active use of the feedback you receive.

Using feedback

Make a list of what you think are your strengths and development opportunities (the politically correct term for weaknesses!)

Below that, list the feedback you have from other people about your strengths and development opportunities. The more honest and thorough you are, the more likely you are to succeed with your development plan.

Check if there any patterns or themes in the feedback. These will provide you with some clues about your focus areas.

Feedback Source	Strength	Development Need
e.g. from; partner boss trusted friend colleague(s)	List by each feedback source, the areas in which you have a strength. These will be the things you are 'good' at or the things you should 'continue' to do e.g. Attention to detail Subject matter expertise Creative	List by each feedback source, the areas in which you have a development need. These will be the things you could be 'better' at or the things you should 'start' doing. e.g. Active listening at home Presentation skills at work Being a role model for the kids

4. Reviewing - if you spend some time reviewing your goal after you have completed it, you should learn more about yourself and be in a position to enhance your personal, academic and career development. What did you expect to achieve? What did you achieve? What can you do to build on strengths or improve weaknesses? Why did you not achieve what you expected to? How can you overcome this in the future?

10.3 Reflective log

It is recommended that you carry out this reflective evaluation both during and at the end of any task or learning you might undertake. One way of encouraging reflective practice in your professional life is to keep a reflective diary or log.

Many of us keep diaries that list our business or social appointments. Some of us also keep 'to do' lists. A reflective log is like a personal diary or record in which we note not just what we have done or accomplished, and what we have learned but also reflect on our feelings. What did we find difficult? What should we do to resolve the situation? Often, a particular incident requires us to take a look at ourselves and our performance. Such critical incident analysis should be reported in the log or diary. However, when it comes to personal reflection, we should take care to include successes as well as difficulties so that we keep a balanced record of our achievement.

Reviewing our reflective diary can also provide useful information. By looking back on our experiences, we can reassess our goals. What have we accomplished? What should the next steps be? This leads us naturally back to revisit and update our professional profile and our action plan. And so the process continues....

At the end of the development activity you should ask yourself the following questions:

- What can I do better as a result of the development
- Have additional development needs been identified?
- How effective was the development method?
- Could I have gained more from the activity?
- Did the development meet my needs and achieve the objectives I set?
- How will I make use of the development?
- What next?

As part of your appraisal (or self-appraisal) you should be able to:

- introduce and explain the methods you used to collect information on your PDP and its effectiveness
- explain the practical ways you collected feedback
- explain how you analysed the information your collected
- explain how you used the results of your analysis to inform the further development of your PDP
- use your learning log for evidence

10.4 Reflective practice

Reflection involves:

- looking back at events and asking questions (retrospective reflection)
- looking forward (crystal ball gazing) and asking questions (Prospective reflection)

The outcomes of reflection can help inform learning and development needs.

Definition

> **Reflective practice** is the process of thinking about and critically analysing your actions with the objective of changing and improving occupational practice.

At some point in your life – whether at work or at home- you will have wondered why something happened, why you did something in a particular way and what might have happened if you had done it differently. If you are to become a reflective practitioner then you have to use that learning to increase your professional knowledge and skills to the benefit of many people. Therefore a portfolio acts as a tool for reflective thinking; it provides you with a structured format for documenting and reviewing your reflections on practice.

It is helpful to evaluate the success of your plan to help you to action plan in the future. Make sure your action steps are clear and practical rather than sketchy or vague.

Even if you do not have to submit your plan to a committee or manager, ask yourself the following questions:

- Does your plan reflect new learning and growth, not just time and effort?
- Are your goals clear?
- Have you used data to determine your goals?
- Does your plan reflect how your achievement will be enhanced?
- Does your plan include reflection on the outcomes and appropriate adjustment?
- Have you included methods of assessment?
- Have you identified evidence that you will gather?

10.5 Significant event analysis

Significant event analysis is a method of retrospective reflection which involves learning from mistakes. Those things that went well are highlighted together with those that went badly. Feasible areas for improvement are identified and an action plan drawn up. The key features of success of significant event analysis are that:

- something positive comes out of a negative event (i.e. a mistake)
- it should be a positive experience and should result in some improvement in practice
- that it focuses on improvement and development - not blame

Reflecting on your day-to-day practice enables you to analyse why and how you do things and to consider whether other approaches might benefit you more. Effective reflection requires you to be open-minded and to examine, question and assess your own practice so as to develop your skills and knowledge. You should:

- listen openly to the ideas of others
- reflect on your own work and on the work of those around you
- consider and implement ways to develop your practice

There are three stages to the reflection process:

1 think about your experience, understanding and ideas

2 reflect on what you have learnt from this experience

3 identify how this reflection will deliver outcomes and better practice, and how these will be applied.

Listening to others can provide you with vital information to assist you in reflecting upon your own practice. You should aim to listen carefully to feedback and not become defensive or take the feedback personally. The key focus is to improve practice.

As a reflective practitioner, you would then make time to carefully consider the situation and response after the event, and question your actions by asking the following questions.

- What action did I take that worked, and why?
- What action did I take that did not work, and why?
- What could I have done differently, and how will I ensure that I do this next time a similar situation arises?

Chapter roundup

- This area of the Unit is geared specifically to you as an individual and provides an opportunity to think seriously about your current situation and future plans.
- The process of self-managed learning can be regarded as an ongoing process throughout your studies and career.
- *Pedler, Burgoyne and Boydell* identify balanced learning skills as one of the meta qualities which allow managers to develop and deploy all the other skills, behaviour and resources they require for effective performance!
- Every manager needs clear images of his or her personal characteristics in order to perform effectively. This chapter gives you guidance on how to evaluate your self awareness.
- A personal skills audit requires you to identify, review and assess your own performance of management skills. The Edexcel guidelines specifically state you must evaluate your personal effectiveness in such areas as self management, leadership and interpersonal skills.
- A personal development plan is a clear development action plan for an individual which incorporates a wide set of developmental opportunities, including formal training, against SMART criteria.
- Portfolios can act as development tools to assist with your career development and enable you to identify and develop a route map to achieve your goals. The portfolio provides a record of interactions and events which you have observed and participated in, and of your development in relevant skills and competences.

Quick quiz

1 What resources are available for building up a good self-appraisal?

2 What is a personal development plan?

3 List some formal and informal learning methods and media.

4 What resource considerations should you make when evaluating self-development options?

5 What criteria do the Edexcel guidelines say your personal development plan can include?

6 What methods should you use to evaluate your progress?

7 What are the three stages of the reflection process?

8 What would you find out from a significant event analysis? is a method of retrospective reflection which involves learning from mistakes. Those things that went well are highlighted together with those that went badly.

Answers to quick quiz

1 Your list could include: Appraisal reports; potential assessments; role play, team participation, games and case studies; assessment centres; developing a personal portfolio; carrying out an individual SWOT analysis.

2 A clear development action plan for an individual which incorporates a wide set of developmental opportunities.

3 Your list could include: specialist education from dedicated centres; coaches; analysing own experience; on the job learning including rotations, secondments and deputisation; off-the-job learning including courses, simulations; knowledge acquisition (lectures, presentations etc); home study programmes in a variety of media including print, TV, audio, PC and Internet.

4 What resources are needed and how readily are they acquired?

Who is available to support you, and how?

What timeframe does each option require and how does this fit in with your schedules and other commitments?

5 Your list should include:

Career and personal development
Current performance
Future needs
Aims, objectives and targets
Review dates
Achievement dates
Learning programme/activities
Action plans

You should ensure that: your progress is on schedule (and amend if necessary); your planned activity is meeting your stated objectives; you have clearly identified the measures you will be using for evaluating your progress; you have clearly identified who can help you assess your performance and on what basis; you have built in review dates on a regular basis or at critical stages in your programme.

7 There are three stages to the reflection process:

- think about your experience, understanding and ideas
- reflect on what you have learnt from this experience
- identify how this reflection will deliver outcomes and better practice, and how these will be applied.

8 Significant event analysis is a method of retrospective reflection which involves learning from mistakes. Those things that went well are highlighted together with those that went badly.

Answers to activities

1 This will be completely specific to you.

2 This will be completely specific to you.

3 This will set out your own quantified objectives.

4

1 **Time management**. Fewer managers mean more responsibility for those in the business. Time management is essential to avoid stress and to get everything done.

2 **Prioritisation** is an integral part of time management. In marketing, managers may have to prioritise markets or customers and need to understand the process and criteria by which priorities can be established. At BPP we have to prioritise our work according to when each range of books is to be published, which depends on such external factors as the exam timetables of the various examining bodies.

3 **Delegation** is essential:

(a) in ensuring that tactical details of activities are attended to;

(b) to give younger managers and staff experience and chance to develop their skills;

(c) to act as a motivator.

4 **Communication**. The essence of the manager's job is communicating, both sending messages and listening to them. It must be done professionally both inside and outside the organisation.

5 **Negotiation** with clients and staff is a key aspect of bringing buyers and sellers, employees and the organisation together in a way which satisfies everyone's needs.

6 **Leadership**. The business manager is often a figurehead and must share the organisation's vision in order to communicate it effectively to others. Managers are in the business of leading the business down the path of customer orientation.

7 **Motivation**. Management roles can be very isolated and motivation has to be clear and effective to get the best out of those working at the customer interface.

8 **Team building**. Management is about coordination. Satisfying customers has to be a team effort. Managers have to be able to build teams even when they have no line authority, for example teams with advertising agencies and distributors as well as with operations and distribution.

5 This exercise does not take into account all your goals, nor all the interpersonal skills that may be relevant in achieving them. It may or may not reflect your own sense of priorities, or those suggested to you by a supervisor or mentor. That's fine: take only what you can use.

It may be harder to state the development 'needs' represented by your strengths than by your limitations. As our examples show, however, there may be a need to:

- recognise a 'down side' to your strengths and preferences: 'patience' may helpfully enable you to avoid interrupting people when listening, but it may prevent you from interrupting or redirecting a speaker when you need to;
- increase your flexibility, so that you can choose the most effective behaviour in a given situation, rather than relying on your strengths: being assertive rather than patient, or being patient but directive, as the need arises;
- increase the scope or level of your competence in your strength: to be patient in more difficult situations, for example.

The mix of urgency, importance and leverage in your ranking may highlight some development needs which are urgent, important *and* cost-effective to attempt. This is a great place to start! If your top priorities are all urgent and important, but relatively low on cost-effectiveness, you may not want to tackle them all at once in your initial development planning. Select a manageable mix of urgent/important *and* cost-effective changes to work on.

6 Here is a suggestion as to how you could have classified the skills.

Self-management	*Leadership*	*Interpersonal*
Time management	Delegation	Communication
Prioritisation	Motivation	Negotiation
	Leadership	
	Team building	

Did you find yourself wanting to allocate some of the skills to more than one category? Time management, for example, can relate to the management of your own time (hence a self-management skill), but also the management of other people's time, so also qualifying as a leadership skill. Communication and negotiation are also skills that can be classified as leadership skills as well as pure interpersonal skills. The purpose of this activity is to show you that in the context of management skills not everything can be classified in terms of black and white.

7 This will be completely specific to you.

8 There is no 'answer' to this activity – other than to attempt it. You may find that the requirement to write a PDJ entry makes you more observant of antecedent events, behaviours, thoughts and feelings. Don't neglect the 'Implications' section: although you may not be in a position to complete it immediately. Many people find the experience of writing a journal so helpful that they continue indefinitely, applying the observe-describe-reflect model to other areas of their work and life.

9 This will be completely specific to you

10 There is no answer to this activity.

11 You might usefully repeat this exercise on your other development needs as you identify them. You might also like to try the exercise with one or more other people, if you get the opportunity. A brainstorming group is very effective in generating options, and perhaps offering access to resources and contacts as well.

Part B

Working With and Leading People

Chapter 5 :
RECRUITMENT, SELECTION AND RETENTION PROCEDURES

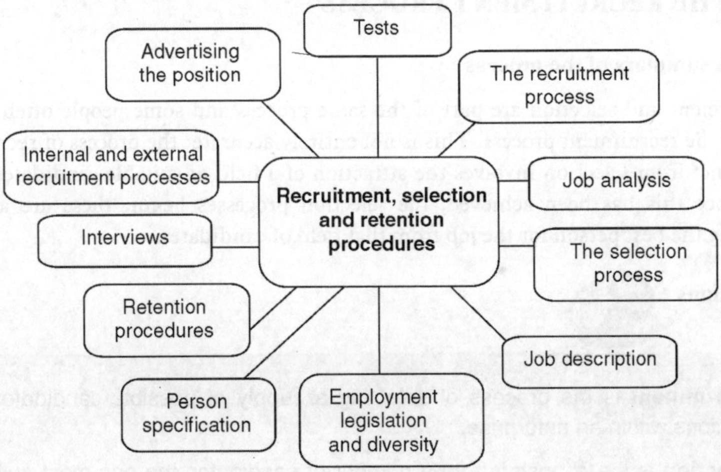

Introduction

The outcome of this chapter is for you to be able to implement recruitment, selection and retention procedures. The overall aim of the recruitment and selection process in an organisation is to obtain the quantity and quality of employees to fulfil the objectives of the organisation.

The process can be broken down into three main stages.

- Defining requirements, including the preparation of job descriptions, job specifications and personnel specifications
- Attracting potential employees, including the evaluation and use of various methods of reaching sources of applicants
- Selecting the appropriate person for the job

Once a person is recruited, it is management's responsibility to ensure that the individual is retained. A retention strategy will ensure the employee's needs are satisfied and means are found to keep him or her motivated towards achieving the organisation's goals.

The recruitment and selection process is covered by legislation that relates to equal opportunities and discrimination. However, most organisations will go beyond the requirements of equal opportunity and discrimination regulations and will encourage diversity in terms of sex, race, culture, age, religion, disability, sexual orientation and ethnicity.

Your objectives

After completing this chapter you should be able to:

(a) prepare documentation to select and recruit a new member of staff

(b) assess the impact of legal, regulatory and ethical considerations to the recruitment and selection process

(c) take part in the selection process evaluate own contribution to the selection process

1 THE RECRUITMENT PROCESS

1.1 A summary of the process

Recruitment and selection are part of the same process and some people often refer to both as the recruitment process. This is not entirely accurate; the process of recruitment as distinct from selection involves the attraction of a field of suitable candidates for the job. Once this has been achieved, the selection processes begin; these are aimed at selecting the best person for the job from that field of candidates.

Definitions

> **Recruitment** is the process of selecting a supply of possible candidates for positions within an enterprise.
>
> **Selection** is the choosing from a number of candidates the one most suitable for a specified position.

The recruitment process involves:

(a) Detailed human resource (HR) planning defines what resources the organisation needs to meet its objectives.

(b) The sources of labour should be forecast. Internal and external sources, and media for reaching both, will be considered.

(c) Job analysis produces two outputs.

  (i) A job description: a statement of the component tasks, duties, objectives and standards

  (ii) A person specification: a reworking of the job specification in terms of the kind of person needed to perform the job.

(d) Recruitment as such begins with the identification of vacancies, from the requirements of the HR plan or by a job requisition from a department, branch or office that has a vacancy.

(e) Preparation and publication of advertising information will have three aims.

  (i) Attract the attention and interest of potentially suitable candidates

  (ii) Give a favourable (but accurate) impression of the job and the organisation

(iii) Equip those interested to make an attractive and relevant application (how and to whom to apply, desired skills, qualifications and so on)

(f) Recruitment merges into selection at the stage of processing applications and short-listing applicants for interview

(g) Interviewing and selecting the best person for the job

(h) Notifying applicants of the results of the selection process is the final stage of the combined recruitment and selection process.

1.2 Recruitment policy

Detailed procedures for recruitment should only be devised and implemented within the context of a coherent **policy**, or code of conduct. A typical recruitment policy might deal with:

- Internal advertisement of vacancies
- Efficient and courteous processing of applications
- Fair and accurate provision of information to potential recruits
- Selection of candidates on the basis of suitability, without discrimination

1.3 The Recruitment Code

The Institute of Personnel and Development has issued a Recruitment Code.

The IPD Recruitment Code

1 Job advertisements should state clearly the form of reply desired, in particular whether this should be a formal application form or by curriculum vitae. Preferences should also be stated if handwritten replies are required.

2 An acknowledgement of reply should be made promptly to each applicant by the employing organisation or its agent. If it is likely to take some time before acknowledgements are made, this should be made clear in the advertisement.

3 Applicants should be informed of the progress of the selection procedures, what there will be (eg group selection, aptitude tests, etc), the steps and time involved and the policy regarding expenses.

4 Detailed personal information (eg religion, medical history, place of birth, family background, etc) should not be called for unless it is relevant to the selection process.

5 Before applying for references, potential employers must secure applicant's permission.

6 Applications must be treated as confidential.

7 The code also recommends certain courtesies and obligations on the part of the applicants.

Detailed **procedures** should be devised in order to make recruitment activity systematic and consistent throughout the organisation (especially where it is decentralised in the hands of line managers). Apart from the manpower resourcing requirements which need to be effectively and efficiently met, there is a **marketing** aspect to recruitment, as one 'interface' between the organisation and the outside world: applicants who feel they have been unfairly treated, or recruits who leave because they feel they have been misled, do not enhance the organisation's reputation in the labour market or the world at large.

1.4 Creating equal opportunities in recruitment

In order to encourage diversity and social inclusion it is essential to develop robust processes that allow those from all backgrounds to succeed. It may be necessary to hold open days and 'drop in' recruitment events and re-design application forms, or even discard forms altogether. A key opportunity is to go into target areas or communities rather than expecting potential applicants to seek the organisation out. In this way the organisation can genuinely encourage a broader staff base.

Activity 1 **(30 minutes)**

Find out, if you do not already know, what are the recruitment and selection procedures in your organisation, and who is responsible for each stage. The procedures manual should set this out, or you may need to ask someone in the personnel department.

Get hold of and examine some of the documentation your organisation uses. We show specimens in this chapter, but practice and terminology varies, so your own 'house style' will be invaluable. Compare your organisation's documentation with our example.

2 JOB ANALYSIS

The management of the organisation needs to analyse the sort of work needed to be done.

Definition

Job analysis is:

'the process of collecting, analysing and setting out information about the content of jobs in order to provide the basis for a job description and data for recruitment, training, job evaluation and performance management. Job analysis concentrates on what job holders are expected to do.' (*Armstrong*)

The definition shows why job analysis is important – the firm has to know what people are doing in order to recruit effectively.

2.1 Information that might be obtained from a job analysis.

Information	Comments
Purpose of the job	This might seem obvious. Someone being recruited to the accounts department will be expected to process or provide financial data. But this has to be set in the context of the organisation as a whole.

Information	Comments
Content of the job	The tasks you are expected to do. If the purpose of the job is to ensure, for example, that people get paid on time, the tasks involved include many activities related to payroll.
Accountabilities	These are the results for which you are responsible. In practice they might be phrased in the same way as a description of a task.
Performance criteria	These are the criteria which measure how good you are at the job. For a payroll technician, performance criteria includes task-related matters such as the timeliness and accuracy of your work – which are easily assessed.
Responsibility	This denotes the importance of the job. For example, a person running a department and taking decisions involving large amounts of money is more responsible than someone who only does what he or she is told. Similarly, someone might have a lot of discretion in determining what he or she will do or how he or she spends the day, whereas other people's tasks might be programmed in some detail according to a predictable routine.
Organisational factors	Who does the jobholder report to directly (line manager) or on grounds of functional authority?
Developmental factors	Relating to the job, such as likely promotion paths, if any, career prospects and so forth. Some jobs are 'dead-end' if they lead nowhere.
Environmental factors	Working conditions, security and safety issues, equipment etc.

2.2 Carrying out a job analysis

A job analysis has to be done systematically – that is why it is called an **analysis** – as the purpose is to obtain facts about the job. Therefore the job analysis involves the use of a number of different techniques to gather the data. The stages should be:

Step 1 Obtain documentary information, for main tasks and so on.

Step 2 Ask managers about more general aspects such as the job's purpose, the main activities, the responsibilities involved and the relationships with others.

Step 3 Ask the job holders similar questions about their jobs – perceptions might differ.

Step 4 Watch people at work – but they may not like it, and they may think you are engaged on a time and motion study.

2.3 Techniques of job analysis

Interviews establish basic facts about the job, from the job holder's point of view. You'll need to get hold of two sorts of information.

(a) **Basic facts** about the job, such as the job title, the jobholder's manager or team leader, people reporting to the jobholder, the main tasks or duties, official targets or performance standards.

(b) More **subjective issues**, which are harder to test which are still important, such as:

- The amount of supervision a person receives
- How much freedom a person has to take decisions
- How hard the job is
- The skills/qualifications you need to carry out the job
- How the job fits in elsewhere with the company
- How work is allocated
- Decision-making authority

This information should always be checked for accuracy.

2.4 Advantages and disadvantages of interviewing

Advantages	Disadvantages
Flexibility	Time consuming
Interactive	Hard to analyse
Easy to organise and carry out	Interviewee might feel on the defensive and might not be entirely frank
New or follow-on questions can be asked in the light of information received	
Reveals other organisational problems	

Interviewing procedures will be covered in greater detail later in this chapter.

Other techniques include:

(a) **Questionnaires**

Questionnaires are sometimes used in job analysis. Their success depends on the willingness of people to complete them accurately.

- They gather purely factual information
- They can cover large numbers of staff
- They provide a structure to the process of information gathering

(b) **Checklists and inventories**

A checklist would contain a list of activities and the job holder would have to note down how important these are in the job.

Activity description	Time spent on activity	Importance of activity
Processes sales invoices	Less than 10%	Unimportant
	10% to 20%	Not very important
	20-30%	Important
	...and so on	Very important

(c) **Observation**

People are watched doing the job. This is easy enough for jobs which can be easily observed or which are physical, but is harder for knowledge-based work. But observation is quite common in assessing performance – trainee school teachers are observed in the classroom.

(d) **Self-description**

Jobholders are asked to prepare their own job descriptions and to analyse their own jobs. This is quite difficult to do, because people often find it hard to stand back from what they are doing.

(e) **Diaries and logs**

People keep records of what they do over a period of time, and these can be used by the analyst to develop job descriptions. You may come across something like this in your working life, if, say, you have to keep a timesheet covering work for a particular client, or if it is part of your training record.

Which method should you use?

It depends. Any job analysis exercise might involve a variety of methods: Questionnaires or checklists save time. Interviews give a better idea of the detail. Self-description shows how people perceive their jobs, which may be very different from how managers perceive their jobs. Diaries and logs are useful for management jobs, in which a lot is going on.

It is not always easy to carry out a job analysis, especially for managers and supervisors. The case example below shows how job analysis techniques can be adapted

CASE EXAMPLE

People Management, 6 March 1997, described **workset**, a job analysis system developed by *Belbin*. Workset uses colour coding to classify work and working time into seven types.

1	Blue: tasks the job holder carries out in a prescribed manner to an approved standard
2	Yellow: individual responsibility to meet an objective (results, not means)
3	Green: tasks that vary according to the reactions and needs of others
4	Orange: shared rather than individual responsibility for meeting an objective
5	Grey: work incidental to the job, not relevant to the four core categories
6	White: new or creative undertaking outside normal duties
7	Pink: demands the presence of the job holder but leads to no useful results

The manager gives an outline of the proportion of time which the manager expects the jobholder to spend on each 'colour' of work. The job holder then briefs the manager on what has actually been done. This highlights differences: between managers' and job-holders' perceptions of jobs; between the perceptions of different jobholders in the same nominal position, who had widely different ideas as to what they were supposed to do.

Important issues arise when there is a gap in perception. Underperformance in different kinds of work can be identified, and people can be steered to the sort of work which suits them best.

Activity 2 **(10 minutes)**

Analyse your own working time according to the Workset classification above. Do the results surprise you?

2.5 Competences

A more recent approach to job design is the development and outlining of competences.

Definition

A person's **competence** is 'a capacity that leads to behaviour that meets the job demands within the parameters of the organisational environment and that, in turn, brings about desired results', (*Boyzatis*). Some take this further and suggest that a competence embodies the ability to transfer skills and knowledge to new situations within the occupational area.

2.6 Different sorts of competences.

(a) **Behavioural/personal** competences: underlying personal characteristics people bring to work (eg interpersonal skills); personal characteristics and behaviour for successful performance, for example, 'ability to relate well to others'. Most jobs require people to be good communicators.

(b) **Work-based/occupational competences** refer to 'expectations of workplace performance and the outputs and standards people in specific roles are expected to obtain'. They cover what people have to do to achieve the results of the job. For example, a competence of a certified accountant includes 'produce financial and other statements and report to management'.

(c) **Generic competences** can apply to all people in an occupation.

Many lists of competences confuse the following.

- Areas of **work** at which people are competent
- Underlying aspects of behaviour

2.7 Examples of competences for managers.

Competence area	Competence
Intellectual	• Strategic perspective • Analytical judgement • Planning and organising
Interpersonal	• Managing staff • Persuasiveness • Assertiveness and decisiveness • Interpersonal sensitivity • Oral communication
Adaptability	
Results	• Initiative • Motivation to achievement • Business sense

These competences can be elaborated by identifying **positive** and **negative** indicators.

3 JOB DESCRIPTION

The job analysis is used to develop the job description.

Definition

> **Job description**. A job description sets out the purpose of a job, where it fits in the organisation structure, the context within which the job-holder functions and the principal accountability of job holders and the main tasks they have to carry out.

3.1 Purpose of job description

Purpose	Comment
Organisational	The job description defines the job's place in the organisational structure
Recruitment	The job description provides information for identifying the sort of person needed (person specification)
Legal	The job description provides the basis for a contract of employment
Performance	Performance objectives can be set around the job description

3.2 Contents of a job description

(a) **Job title** (eg assistant financial controller). This indicates the function/ department in which the job is performed, and the level of job within that function.

(b) **Reporting to** (eg the assistant financial controller reports to the financial controller), in other words the person's immediate boss. (No other relationships are suggested here.)

(c) **Subordinates** directly reporting to the job holders.

(d) **Overall purpose** of the job, distinguishing it from other jobs.

(e) **Principal accountabilities or main tasks**

(i) Group the main activities into a number of broad areas.

(ii) Define each activity as a statement of accountability: what the job holder is expected to achieve (eg **tests** new system to ensure they meet agreed systems specifications).

(f) The current fashion for multi-skilled teams means that **flexibility** is some times expected.

Here are two examples of job descriptions.

JOB DESCRIPTION

1 *Job title:* Baking Furnace Labourer.

2 *Department:* 'B' Baking.

3 *Date:* 20 November 20X0.

4 *Prepared by:* H Crust, baking furnace manager.

5 *Responsible to:* baking furnace chargehand.

6 *Age range:* 20-40.

7 *Supervises work of:* N/A.

8 *Has regular cooperative contract with:* Slinger/Crane driver.

9 *Main duties/responsibilities:* Stacking formed electrodes in furnace, packing for stability. Subsequently unloads baked electrodes and prepares furnace for next load.

10 *Working conditions:* stacking is heavy work and requires some manipulation of 100lb (45kg) electrodes. Unloading is hot (35°–40°C) and very dusty.

11 *Employment conditions:*

Wages £7.20 ph + group bonus (average earnings £357.46 pw).

Hours: Continuous rotating three-shift working days, six days on, two days off. NB must remain on shift until relieved.

Trade Union: National Union of Bread Bakers, optional.

MIDWEST BANK PLC

1 *Job title:* Clerk (Grade 2).

2 *Branch:* All branches and administrative offices.

3 *Job summary:* To provide clerical support to activities within the bank.

4 *Job content:* Typical duties will include:

(a) Cashier's duties
(b) Processing of branch clearing
(c) Processing of standing orders
(d) Support to branch management.

5 *Reporting structure*

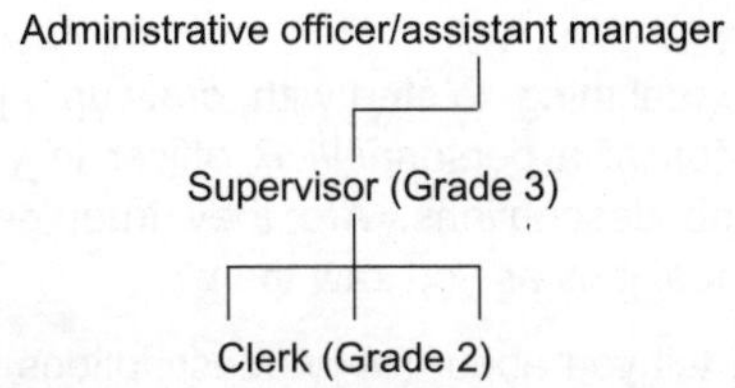

6 *Experience/education:* experience not required, minimum three GCSEs or equivalent.

7 *Training to be provided:* initial on-the-job training plus regular formal courses and training.

8 *Hours:* 38 hours per week.

9 *Objectives and appraisal:* Annual appraisal in line with objectives above.

10 *Salary:* refer to separate standard salary structure.

Job description prepared by: Head office personnel department.

Activity 3 **(20 minutes)**

Studying has placed you in a role in which you have to perform a fairly consistent set of duties, in fairly consistent conditions, within a structure that requires you to interact with other people, both superiors and peers (and possibly subordinates). Draw up a job description for yourself.

3.3 Alternatives to job descriptions

Detailed job descriptions are perhaps only suited for jobs where the work is largely repetitive and therefore performed by low-grade employees: once the element of **judgement** comes into a job description it becomes a straitjacket. Many difficulties arise where people adhere strictly to the contents of the job description, rather than responding flexibly to task or organisational requirements.

Perhaps job descriptions should be written in terms of the **outputs and performance levels** expected. Some firms are moving towards **accountability profiles** in which outputs and performance are identified explicitly.

Armstrong suggests a crucial difference between:

(a) A job – a group of tasks.

(b) A role. A part played by people in meeting their objectives by working competently and flexibly within the context of the organisation's objectives, structures and processes.

A **role definition** is wider than a job description. It is less concerned with the details of the job content, but how they interpret the job, and how they perceive them.

Activity 4 **(30 minutes)**

Without looking at the real thing, to start with, draw up a job description for your own job and for the job of a personnel/HR officer in your organisation. Now look at the official job descriptions. Are they true, detailed and up-to-date compared with the actual jobs as you saw them?

If not, what does this tell you about (a) job descriptions and (b) perceptions of the personnel/HR function?

4 PERSON SPECIFICATION

Definition

'A **person specification**, also known as a job or personnel specification, sets out the education, qualifications, training, experience personal attributes and competences a job holder requires to perform her or his job satisfactorily.'

(*Armstrong*)

The job description outlines the job: the person specification describes the person needed to do the job. For example, a position of secretary or personal assistant normally requires the holder to have word processing skills.

4.1 Traditional approaches to the person specification

The **Seven-Point Plan** put forward by *Professor Rodger* in 1951 draws the selector's attention to seven points about the candidate.

- **Physical attributes** (such as neat appearance, ability to speak clearly)
- **Attainment** (including educational qualifications)
- **General intelligence**
- **Special aptitudes** (such as neat work, speed and accuracy)
- **Interests** (practical and social)
- **Disposition** (or manner: friendly, helpful and so on)
- Background **circumstances**

4.2 Problems with the Seven-Point Plan.

(a) Physical attributes or disposition might include a person's demeanour. **Eye contact** is considered a sign of honesty and frankness in some cultures, but a sign of disrespect in others.

(b) **General intelligence** is not something that can be measured easily. A criticism of IQ tests is that test scores tell you that you are good at doing IQ tests – and not much else.

(c) **Attainment**: educational qualifications – no attention is paid to the circumstances in which these were obtained.

The plan does not identify a person's **potential**, or suggest how it can be aligned precisely to the organisation's requirements.

4.3 Five-Point Pattern

Munro-Fraser's Five-Point Pattern is one alternative.

- **Impact on others**: physical attributes, speech, manner
- **Acquired knowledge** and qualifications
- **Innate abilities**: ability to learn, mental agility
- **Motivation**: What sort of goals does the individual set, how much effort goes into achieving them, how successful.
- **Adjustment**: emotional stability, tolerance of slips.

4.4 New approaches: competences

The two methods described above have been in use for many years. More recruiters are using **competences** (see paragraph 2.5) in designing the person specification.

4.5 Preparing the specification

Each feature in the person specification should be classified as:

(a) **Essential.** For instance, honesty in a cashier is essential while a special aptitude for conceptual thought is not.

(b) **Desirable.** For instance, a reasonably pleasant manner should ensure satisfactory standards in a person dealing with the public.

(c) **Contra-indicated.** Some features are actively disadvantageous, such as an inability to work in a team when acting as project leader.

PERSON SPECIFICATION: Customer Accounts Manager

	ESSENTIAL	DESIRABLE	CONTRA-INDICATED
Physical attributes	Clear speech Well-groomed Good health	Age 25-40	Age under 25 Chronic ill-health and absence
Attainments	2 'A' levels GCSE Maths and English Thorough knowledge of retail environment	Degree (any discipline) Marketing training 2 years' experience in supervisory post	No experience of supervision or retail environment
Intelligence	High verbal intelligence		
Aptitudes	Facility with numbers Attention to detail and accuracy Social skills for customer relations	Analytical abilities (problem-solving) Understanding of systems and IT	No mathematical ability Low tolerance of technology

Interests	Social: team activity		Time-consuming hobbies 'Solo' interests only
Disposition	Team player Persuasive Tolerance of pressure and change	Initiative	Anti-social Low tolerance of responsibility
Circumstances	Able to work late, take work home	Located in area of office	

Activity 5 **(30 minutes)**

Turn your job description for Activity 3 in this chapter into a corresponding Personnel Specification, using the 'essential; desirable; contra-indicated' framework, and either the Seven-Point Plan or Five-Point Pattern. If you did not do Activity 3, do it now! (You might like to consider into which section of your personnel specification 'laziness' would fall....)

5 INTERNAL AND EXTERNAL RECRUITMENT PROCESSES

5.1 Recruit or promote?

Apart from the preliminary decision as to whether the job needs filling and the determination of the job description and personnel specification, a recruitment policy will outline the factors to be considered when deciding whether to recruit someone from outside to fill a vacancy *or* to promote or transfer someone from within the existing workforce.

Some of the factors to be considered in this decision are as follows.

(a) **Availability in the current staff** of the skills and attributes required to fill the vacancy. If the lead time to develop current staff to 'fit' the vacancy is too long, there may be no immediate alternative to external recruitment.

(b) **Availability in the external labour pool** of the skills and attributes required. Where there are skill shortages, it may be necessary to develop them within the organisation.

5.2 Internal recruitment

Internal recruitment occurs when a vacant position is filled by one of the existing employees. It generally applies to those jobs where there is some kind of career structure, as in the case of management or administrative staff. If a policy of internal recruitment is to be pursued the following advantages and disadvantages should be noted:

Advantages	Disadvantages
• Quick and inexpensive and no induction necessary • Career progression – internal promotion is evidence of the organisation's willingness to develop people's careers • Reduces the risk of employing the wrong person – selection can be made on the basis of known data • Will be familiar with the culture, structures, systems and procedures, objectives and other people in the organisation. This gives a head start for performance in the new position • No need to replace an internal post • Can act as a source of motivation and may be good for the general morale of the workforce (and avoid resentments)	• Limited number of applicants • External candidates might be better • Creates another vacancy • Could be difficulties if promoting someone to a job of supervising ex-workmates. • No suitable candidate • May create ill feeling among those not selected

5.3 External recruitment

External recruitment occurs when an organisation seeks to bring in someone from outside the organisation to fill a vacancy. In general its advantages and disadvantages are opposite to those of internal recruitment, but the following specific points should be noted.

Advantages	Disadvantages
• Wider pool of labour – may be necessary to restore manning levels, depleted by employee wastage and internal promotion policies • May be more suitable especially if an organisation is seeking specific skills and expertise not available internally • Can inject new blood into an enterprise. External recruits bring new ideas and different approaches to the job, gleaned from their experience working in other organisations • No need to replace an internal post	• Can be a long and expensive process and induction is still necessary • Increased risk of employing the wrong person • May block promotion for internal candidates • May create dissatisfaction among existing employees

5.4 Finding and attracting suitable candidates

There are a number of ways for organisations to find and attract suitable candidates but whatever method is chosen, it should deter people who do not meet the requirements without discouraging those who have much to offer but do not quite match the job specification. The objectives are to attract candidates of the right quality in the right number.

(a) As we have already noted, **internal promotion** is the cheapest way to recruit, and can help to motivate and keep existing employees. Using training and development programmes can also prepare employees for promotion. If internal recruitment is proposed, methods of finding and attracting candidates include a form of direct invitation where assessments are made of employees, and on the basis of these, management decide who will be offered a promotion opportunity. Some firms, however, allow employees to compete for vacancies by advertising internally, either on their website, through newsletters or by using notice boards; normal selection procedures then follow. Even where external recruitment is the main policy it does not prevent an existing employee from applying.

(b) **Nomination of existing employees** – some companies rely on recommendations from their existing staff and occasionally offer incentive schemes for successful introductions.

(c) **Casual applications** can be kept on file – sometimes applicants will write to the company on-spec, saving the time and money involved in a full-scale recruitment campaign.

(d) **Adverts** to attract candidates can be placed in appropriate publications eg, national newspapers, specialist trade magazines or local newspapers.

(e) The cheapest way to advertise is on a **website**. But this may be inefficient if a site does not attract enough visitors.

(f) **Recruitment consultants** – assist clients in selecting the best staff to fill particular vacancies. They tend to specialise in separate market sectors such as clerical and secretarial, accounting or computing.

(g) **Hiring temporary staff** can be a good way to get to know employees before offering them permanent positions.

(h) The **government employment services** – the unemployed register presents firms with a reservoir of potential employees categorised according to skill and pre-selected according to suitability.

(i) Building **relationships with local schools, colleges** and **universities** can attract promising candidates for trainee positions.

6 ADVERTISING THE POSITION

The object of recruitment advertising is to attract suitable candidates and deter unsuitable candidates.

6.1 Content of the advertisement

An advert should be:

(a) **Concise,** but comprehensive enough to be an accurate description of the job, its rewards and requirements.

(b) **Attractive** to the maximum number of the right people.

(c) **Positive and honest** about the organisation. Disappointed expectations will be a prime source of dissatisfaction when an applicant actually comes into contact with the organisation.

(d) **Relevant and appropriate to the job and the applicant**. Skills, qualifications and special aptitudes required should be prominently set out, together with special features of the job that might attract – or indeed deter – applicants, such as shiftwork or extensive travel.

The advertisement, based on information set out in the job description, job and person specifications and recruitment procedures, should contain information about:

(a) The **organisation**: its main business and location, at least.

(b) The **job**: title, main duties and responsibilities and special features.

(c) **Conditions:** special factors affecting the job.

(d) **Qualifications and experience** (required, and preferred); other attributes, aptitudes and/or knowledge required.

(e) **Rewards**: salary, benefits, opportunities for training, career development, and so on.

(f) **Application process**: how to apply, to whom, and by what date.

It should encourage a degree of **self-selection,** so that the target population begins to narrow itself down. The information contained in the advertisement should deter unsuitable applicants as well as encourage potentially suitable ones.

6.2 Factors influencing the choice of advertising medium

(a) **The type of organisation.** A factory is likely to advertise a vacancy for an unskilled worker in a different way to a company advertising for a member of the Institute of Personnel and Development for an HRM position.

(b) **The type of job**. Managerial jobs may merit national advertisement, whereas semi-skilled jobs may only warrant local coverage, depending on the supply of suitable candidates in the local area. Specific skills may be most appropriately reached through trade, technical or professional journals, such as those for accountants or computer programmers.

(c) **The cost of advertising.** It is more expensive to advertise in a national newspaper than on local radio, and more expensive to advertise on local radio than in a local newspaper etc.

(d) The **readership and circulation** (type and number of readers/listeners) of the medium, and its suitability for the number and type of people the organisation wants to reach.

(e) The **frequency** with which the organisation wants to advertise the job vacancy, and the duration of the recruitment process.

6.3 Media for recruitment advertising

(a) **In-house magazine, notice-boards,** e-mail or its 'intranet'. An organisation might invite applications from employees who would like a transfer or a promotion to the particular vacancy advertised.

(b) **Professional and specialist newspapers or magazines,** such as *Accountancy Age, Marketing Week* or *Computing.*

(c) **National newspapers** are used for senior management jobs or vacancies for skilled workers, where potential applicants will not necessarily be found through local advertising.

(d) **Local newspapers** would be suitable for jobs where applicants are sought from the local area.

(e) **Local radio, television and cinema.** These are becoming increasingly popular, especially for large-scale campaigns for large numbers of vacancies.

(f) **Job centres**. Vacancies for unskilled work (rather than skilled work or management jobs) are advertised through local job centres, although in theory any type of job can be advertised here.

(g) **School and university careers offices.** Ideally, the manager responsible for recruitment in an area should try to maintain a close liaison with careers officers. Some large organisations organise special meetings or **careers fairs** in universities and colleges (the so-called 'milk round'), as a kind of showcase for the organisation and the careers it offers.

(h) The **Internet**. Any personal computer user may access the network, independently or via an Internet service provider such as CompuServe.

Activity 6 **(20 minutes)**

What do you think of this advertisement? How can you improve it?

Dealing with individuals demands a certain... ...um...

You've heard the old line...
'You don't have to be mad to work here, but it helps'. It's like that at AOK, but in the nicest possible way. We believe that our Personnel Department should operate for the benefit of our staff, and not that staff should conform to statistical profiles. It doesn't make for an easy life, but dealing with people as individuals,

We're committed to an enlightened personnel philosophy. We firmly believe that our staff are our most important asset, and we go a long way both to attract the highest quality of people, and to retain them.

AOK is a company with a difference. We're a highly progressive, international organisation, one of the world's leading manufacturers in the medical electronics field.

...Character

As an expanding company, we now need another experienced Personnel Generalist to join us at our UK headquarters in Reigate, Surrey.

Essentially we're looking for an individual, a chameleon character who will assume an influential role in recruitment, employee relations, salary administration, compensation and benefits, or whatever the situation demands. The flexibility to interchange with various functions is vital. Within your designated area, you'll experience a large degree of independence. You'll be strong in personality, probably already experienced in personnel management in a small company. Whatever your background you'll certainly be someone who likes to help people help themselves and who is happy to get involved with people at all levels within the organisation.

Obviously, in a fast growing company with a positive emphasis on effective personnel work, your prospects for promotion are excellent. Salaries are highly attractive and benefits are, of course, comprehensive.

So if you're the kind of personnel individual who enjoys personal contact, problem-solving, and will thrive on the high pace of a progressive, international organisation, such as AOK, get in touch with us by writing or telephoning, quoting ref: 451/BPD, to AOK House, Reigate, Surrey.

7 THE SELECTION PROCESS

7.1 Procedure

Selection is the process that leads to a decision being made as to whether an individual is offered and takes up employment with an organisation. It is really a two–way process, not only is the firm selecting the individual but invariably the individual is making decisions as to the suitability of the job offered, the terms of employment and the organisation.

The stages include the following.

Step 1 Deal with responses to job advertisements. This might involve sending **application forms** to candidates. Not all firms bother with these, however, preferring to review CVs.

Step 2 Assess each application or CV against **key criteria** in the job advertisement and specification. Critical factors may include age, qualifications, experience or whatever.

Step 3 **Sort applications** into 'possible', 'unsuitable' and 'marginal'.

'Possibles' will then be more closely scrutinised, and a shortlist for interview drawn up. Ideally, this should be done by both the personnel specialist and the prospective manager of the successful candidate.

Step 4 **Invite candidates for interviews.**

Step 5 Reinforce interviews with **selection testing,** if suitable.

Step 6 Review un-interviewed 'possibles', and 'marginals', and put potential future candidates on hold, or in reserve.

Step 7 Send standard letters to unsuccessful applicants, and inform them simply that they have not been successful. Reserves will be sent a holding letter: 'We will keep your details on file, and should any suitable vacancy arise in future...'.

Step 8 Make a provisional offer to the recruit.

7.2 Selection methods

Attracting a wide choice of applicants will be of little use unless there is a way of measuring how people differ eg, in intelligence, attitudes, social skills, physical characteristics, experience etc and extending this to a prediction of performance in the workplace.

Successful selection means matching the organisation's and the applicant's requirements through the exchange of information.

The organisation provides applicants with an objective description of the company and the job, while the applicants provide information about their capabilities.

A number of techniques can reveal this information. Selecting is choosing from among the applicants the one that meets the position requirements. Methods of selection include the following:

- Application forms
- CVs and covering letters
- Shortlists
- Interviews
- Tests
- References
- Medical examinations
- Group selection methods
- Situational tests
- Assessment centres.

The selection process starts with the sifting and sorting of paper details – the application forms and submitted CVs. Once the shortlist is drawn up, the next stage is to determine the best methods of further assessment. The selection interview is probably the most popular of these methods, although other techniques – assessment centres, psychometric testing and ability testing – will all be considered.

We will discuss interviews and tests after briefly examining the other methods identified.

7.3 Application forms

The **application form** usually seeks information about the applicant on several fronts, namely:

(a) Personal details of address, age, family background, nationality
(b) Education and experience history
(c) Present employment terms and experience
(d) Social and leisure interests.

The application form should be regarded by the applicant as an opportunity to qualify for the interview. It usually includes a general section enabling the applicant to express career ambitions, personal preferences, etc, in his or her own words. This can be an important section in gauging an applicant's ability to express himself/herself in writing and perhaps even aspects of motivation, ambition and character.

As well as obtaining all the essential information about the applicant, the purposes of the application form are:

- To eliminate totally unsuitable candidates
- To act as a useful preliminary to selection interviews. Basic information can be gained which would otherwise take up valuable interview time. Some interviewers use the form as the framework for the interview itself; it can be a particularly useful guide for inexperienced interviewers. It forms the nucleus of the personal record of individual employees.

Activity 7 **(10 minutes)**

Suggest four possible design faults in job application forms. You may be able to draw on your own personal experience.

7.4 CVs and covering letters

A CV or 'Curriculum Vitae' will provide prospective employers with a summary of the applicant's relevant life experiences and skills to date. It is essentially a record of his or her personal, educational and work details, which emphasises the experience, knowledge and skills relevant to the type of job vacancy. The purpose of the CV is to generate enough interest for the employer to want to take the application further.

A CV should be divided under suitable headings and sub headings:

Curriculum Vitae

Sample headings

1. Name
2. Date of birth
3. Address
4. Telephone number
5. Education and training
6. Qualifications
7. Other relevant achievements
8. Interests
9. References

The key part of the CV is the career history, so the sections that go before should not be too long e.g. when dealing with training, only the most important and relevant training courses should be listed. If necessary others may be included under 'other relevant achievements

Many job adverts ask for a CV and a covering letter. A good covering letter introduces the author to the reader and stimulates interest in the attached CV and is essential when applying speculatively to an advertised position. Also, if there are further points that need to be mentioned in addition to an application form, it may be appropriate to attach a brief covering letter.

7.5 References

References are used by most employers as a key part of their selection process, but mainly to verify facts about the candidate rather than as an aid to decision-making. The reference check is usually the last stage in the selection process and referees should be contacted only after the applicant has given permission. Good referees are almost certain to know more about the applicant than the selector and it would be foolish not to seek their advice or treat the reference check as a mere formality.

A reference should contain two types of information.

(a) Straightforward **factual information.** This confirms the nature of the applicant's previous job(s), period of employment, pay, and circumstances of leaving.

(b) **Opinions** about the applicant's personality and other attributes. These should obviously be treated with some caution. Allowances should be made for prejudice (favourable or unfavourable), charity (withholding detrimental remarks), and possibly fear of being actionable for libel (although references are privileged, as long as they are factually correct and devoid of malice).

As well as the applicant's suitability for employment, the reference may provide information on strengths and weaknesses, training needs and potential for future development.

Written references save time, especially if a standardised letter or form has been pre-prepared. A simple letter inviting the previous employer to reply with the basic information and judgements required may suffice. A standard form to be completed by the referee may be more acceptable, and might pose a set of simple questions about:

- Job title
- Main duties and responsibilities
- Period of employment
- Pay/salary
- Attendance record

If a judgement of character and suitability is desired, it might be most tellingly formulated as the question: 'Would you re-employ this individual? (If not, why not?).'

Telephone references may be timesaving if standard reference letters or forms are not available. They may also elicit a more honest opinion than a carefully prepared written statement. For this reason, a telephone call may also be made to check or confirm a poor or grudging reference, which the recruiter suspects may be prejudiced.

7.6 Shortlists

Shortlisting applicants is undertaken by comparing information provided about the applicants against the essential and desirable characteristics listed in the person specification. This information comes from application forms, CVs, references and testimonials; university, college or school reports; service discharge documents; and possibly a medical report. They can be sorted into 'probable', 'possible' and 'rejected' or some similar set of headings. The aim is to find about six candidates who meet most of the essential requirements and some of the desirable ones.

Six is considered 'ideal' as they can all be interviewed during a single working day and compared with one another while impressions are still fresh in the interviewers' minds. More than six 'probables' allows more stringent standards to be implemented to reduce the numbers. Less than six means sorting through the 'possibles' to select enough to make up the numbers.

After short-listing, selected applicants are referred to as 'candidates'. They are placed on a shortlist and generally invited to interviews.

7.7 Group selection methods

Group selection methods might be used by an organisation as the final stage of a selection process as a more 'natural' and in-depth appraisal of candidates. Group assessments tend to be used for posts requiring leadership, communication or team-working skills: advertising agencies often use the method for selecting account executives, for example.

They consist of a series of tests, interviews and group situations over a period of two days, involving a small number of candidates for a job. After an introductory session to make the candidates feel at home, they will be given one or two tests, one or two individual interviews, and several group situations in which the candidates are invited to discuss problems together and arrive at solutions as a management team.

A variety of tools and techniques are used in group selection, including:

(a) **Group role-play exercises,** in which they can explore (and hopefully display) interpersonal skills and/or work through simulated managerial tasks

(b) **Case studies**, where candidates' analytical and problem-solving abilities are tested in working through described situations/problems, as well as their interpersonal skills, in taking part in (or leading) group discussion of the case study

These group sessions might be thought useful because of the following reasons.

(a) They give the organisation's selectors a longer opportunity to study the candidates.

(b) They reveal more than application forms, interviews and tests alone about the ability of candidates to persuade others, negotiate with others, and explain ideas to others and also to investigate problems efficiently. These are typically management skills.

(c) They reveal more about how the candidate's personality and attributes will affect the work team and his own performance.

7.8 Work sampling

Work sampling is a technique used for two purposes.

(a) It is used to discover the proportions of total time devoted to the various components of a job. It is also known as job sampling. Data obtained from work sampling can be used to establish allowances applicable to a job, to determine machine utilisation, and to provide the criteria for production standards. Although the same information can be obtained by time-study procedures, work sampling usually provides the information faster and at less cost.

(b) It is also used to describe a performance test designed to be a miniature replica of behaviour required on-the-job, which attempts to measure how well an employee will perform in the particular occupation. Such tests are considered a more precise device for measuring particular occupational abilities than simple motor skills or verbal ability tests.

7.9 Assessment centres

The assessment centre is really a combination of many forms of selection, but at present its use is confined more to the selection of employees for promotion. Groups of around six to ten candidates are brought together for one to three days of intensive assessment. They are presented, individually and as a group, with a variety of exercises, tests of ability, personality assessments, interviews, work samples, team problem-solving and written tasks. As well as being multi-method, other characteristics of assessment centres are that they use several assessors and they assess several dimensions of performance required in the higher-level positions.

Traditionally, the main purpose of assessment centres has been to contribute to management decisions about people, usually the assessment of management skills and potential as a basis for promotion decisions. Assessment centres are better at predicting future performance than are judgements made by unskilled managers, and it is the combination of techniques which contributes to their apparent superiority over other approaches.

8 INTERVIEWS

Most firms use the selection interview as their main source for decision-making.

8.1 Purpose of the interview

(a) Finding the best person for the job, by giving the organisation a chance to assess applicants (and particularly their interpersonal communication skills) directly.

(b) Making sure that applicants understand the job, what the career prospects are and have suitable information about the company.

(c) Giving the best possible impression of the organisation – after all, the candidate may have other offers elsewhere.

(d) Making all applicants feel that they have been given **fair treatment** in the interview, whether they get the job or not.

8.2 Conducting selection interviews: matters to be kept in mind

(a) The **impression** of the organisation given by the interview arrangements.

(b) The **psychological effects** of the location of the interview and seating arrangements.

(c) The **manner and tone** of the interviewers.

(d) Getting the candidates to talk freely (by asking open questions) and honestly (by asking probing questions), in accordance with the organisation's need for **information.**

(e) The **opportunity for the candidate to learn** about the job and organisation.

(f) The control of **bias** or hasty judgement by the interviewer.

8.3 Preparation for the interview

Welcoming the candidate. Candidates should be given:

(a) Clear instructions about the date, time and location – perhaps with a map.
(b) The name of a person to contact.
(c) A place to wait (with cloakroom facilities), perhaps with tea or coffee.

The interview room

(a) The interview is where the organisation 'sells' itself and the candidate aims to give a good impression. The layout of the room should be carefully designed. Being 'interrogated' by two people from the other side of a desk may be completely unsuitable.

(b) Some interviews are deliberately tough, to see how a candidate performs under pressure.

The agenda. The agenda and questions will be based on:

(a) The job description and what abilities are required of the jobholder.

(b) The personnel specification. The interviewer must be able to judge whether the applicant matches up to the personal qualities required from the jobholder.

(c) The application form or the applicant's CV: the qualities the applicant claims to possess.

8.4 Conduct of the interview

Questions should be paced and put carefully. The interviewer should not be trying to confuse the candidate, plunging immediately into demanding questions or picking on isolated points; neither, however, should s(he) allow the interviewee to digress or gloss over important points. The interviewer must retain control over the information-gathering process.

Type of question	Comment
Open questions	('Who...? What...? Where...? When...? Why....?) These force candidates to put together their own responses in complete sentences. This encourages them to talk, keeps the interview flowing, and is most revealing ('Why do you want to be a marketing assistant?')
Probing questions	Similar to open questions, these aim to discover the deeper significance of the candidate's answers, especially if they are initially dubious, uninformative, too short, or too vague. ('But what was it about marketing that **particularly** appealed to you?')
Closed questions	Invite only 'yes' or 'no' answers: ('Did you...?, 'Have you...?'). These elicit an answer **only** to the question asked. This may be useful where there are small points to be established ('Did you pass your exam?'), but they do not encourage the same degree of revelation as an open question, and may only give part of the picture. (Did candidate pass their exam first time, or with top grades, for example.) Candidates cannot express their personality, or interact with the interviewer on a deeper level. They make it easier for candidates to conceal things ('You never asked me...'). They make the interviewer work very hard.
Multiple questions	Two or more questions are asked at once. ('Tell me about your last job? How did your knowledge of accountancy help you there, and do you think you are up-to-date or will you need to spend time studying?'). This encourages the candidate to talk at some length, without straying too far from the point. It might also test the candidate's ability to listen, and to handle large

Type of question	Comment
	amount of information.
Problem-solving questions	Present the candidate with a situation and ask him/her to explain how he/she would deal with it. ('How would you motivate your staff to do a task that they did not want to do?'). Such questions are used to establish whether the candidate will be able to deal with the sort of problems that are likely to arise in the job.
Leading questions	Encourage the candidate to give a certain reply. ('We are looking for somebody who likes detailed figure work. How much do you enjoy dealing with numbers?' or 'Don't you agree that...?' 'Surely...?). The danger with this type of question is that the candidate will give the answer that he thinks the interviewer wants to hear.

Activity 8 **(10 minutes)**

Identify the type of question used in the following examples, and discuss the opportunities and constraints they offer the interviewee who must answer them.

(a) 'So, you're interested in a Business Studies degree, are you, Jo?'

(b) 'Surely you're interested in Business Studies, Jo?'

(c) 'How about a really useful qualification like a Business Studies degree, Jo? Would you consider that?'

(d) 'Why are you interested in a Business Studies degree, Jo?

(e) 'Why particularly Business Studies, Jo?'

8.5 Evaluating the response

(a) The interviewer must **listen carefully** to the responses and evaluate them so as to judge what the **candidate** is:

(i) **Wanting** to say
(ii) **Trying not** to say
(iii) **Saying, but does not mean, or is lying about**
(iv) **Having difficulty saying**

(b) In addition, the interviewer will have to be aware when he/she is hearing:

(i) Something he/she needs to know

(ii) Something he/she **doesn't** need to know

(iii) Only what he/she **expects** to hear

(iv) Inadequately – when his or her own attitudes, perhaps prejudices, are getting in the way of an objective response to the candidate

Candidates should be given the opportunity to ask questions. The choice of questions might well have some influence on how the interviewers assess a candidate's interest in and understanding of the job. Moreover, there is information that the candidate will need to know about the organisation, the job, and indeed the interview process.

8.6 Types of interview

Individual or **one-to-one interviews**. These are the **most common** selection method.

(a) **Advantages**

  (i) **Direct** face-to-face communication.

  (ii) **Rapport** between the candidate and the interviewer: each has to give attention solely to the other, and there is potentially a relaxed atmosphere, if the interviewer is willing to establish an informal style.

(b) The **disadvantage** of a one-to-one interview is the scope it allows for a biased or superficial decision.

  (i) The **candidate** may be able to **disguise** lack of knowledge in a specialist area of which the interviewer knows little.

  (ii) The **interviewer's** perception may be selective or **distorted**, and this lack of objectivity may go unnoticed and unchecked.

  (iii) The greater opportunity for personal rapport with the candidate may cause a **weakening of the interviewer's objective judgement**.

Panel interviews are designed to overcome such disadvantages. A panel may consist of two or three people who together interview a single candidate: most commonly, an HR specialist and the departmental manager who will have responsibility for the successful candidate. This saves the firm time and enables better assessment.

Large formal panels, or **selection boards**, may also be convened where there are a number of individuals or groups with an interest in the selection.

(a) **Advantage**. A number of people see candidates, and share information about them at a single meeting: similarly, they can compare their assessments on the spot, without a subsequent effort at liaison and communication.

(b) **Drawbacks**

  (i) Questions tend to be more varied, and more random, since there is **no single guiding force** behind the interview strategy. The candidate may have trouble switching from one topic to another so quickly, especially if questions are not led up to, and not clearly put – as may happen if they are unplanned. Candidate are also seldom allowed to expand their answers and so may not be able to do justice to themselves.

  (ii) If there is a **dominating member** of the board, the interview may have greater continuity – but that individual may also influence the judgements of other members.

  (iii) Some candidates may not perform well in a formal, artificial situation such as the board interview, and may find such a situation extremely stressful.

  (iv) Research shows that **board members rarely agree** with each other in their judgements about candidates.

8.7 The limitations of interviews

Interviews are criticised because **they fail to provide accurate predictions** of how a person will perform in the job, partly because of the nature of interviews, partly because of the errors of judgement by interviewers.

Problem	Comment
Scope	• An interview is **too brief** to 'get to know' candidates in the kind of depth required to make an accurate prediction of work performance. • An interview is an **artificial situation**: candidates may be on their best behaviour or, conversely, so nervous that they do not do themselves justice. Neither situation reflects what the person is really like.
The halo effect	A tendency for people to make an initial **general judgement** about a person based on a **single obvious attribute**, such as being neatly dressed or well-spoken. This single attribute will colour later perceptions, and might make an interviewer mark the person up or down on every other factor in their assessments.
Contagious bias	The interviewer changes the behaviour of the applicant by suggestion. The applicant might be led by the wording of questions or non-verbal cues from the interviewer, and change what (s)he is doing or saying in response.
Stereotyping	Stereotyping groups people together who are assumed to share certain characteristics (women, say, or vegetarians), then attributes certain traits to the group as a whole (emotional, socialist etc). It then (illogically) assumes that each individual member of the supposed group will possess that trait.
Incorrect assessment	Qualitative factors such as motivation, honesty or integrity are very difficult assess in an interview.
Logical error	An interviewer might decide that a young candidate who has held two or three jobs in the past for only a short time will be unlikely to last long in any job. (Not necessarily so.)
Inexperienced interviewers	• Inability to evaluate information about a candidate properly • Failure to compare a candidate against the requirements for a job or a personnel specification • Bad planning of the interview • Failure to take control of the direction and length of the interview • A tendency either to act as an inquisitor and make candidates feel uneasy or to let candidates run away with the interview • A reluctance to probe into fact and challenge statements where necessary

While some interviewers may be experts for the human resources function, it is usually thought desirable to include **line managers** in the interview team. They cannot be full-time interviewers, obviously: they have their other work to do. No matter how much training they are given in the interview techniques, they will lack continuous experience, and probably not give interviewing as much thought or interest as they should.

9 TESTS

In some job selection procedures, an interview is supplemented by some form of **selection test**. Tests must be:

(a) **Sensitive** enough to discriminate between different candidates.

(b) **Standardised** on a representative sample of the population, so that a person's results can be interpreted meaningfully.

(c) **Reliable**: in that the test should measure the same thing whenever and to whomever it is applied.

(d) **Valid**: it measures what it is supposed to measure.

9.1 Types of tests

The science of measuring mental capacities and processes is called 'psychometrics'; hence the term **psychometric testing**. Types of test commonly used in practice are:

- Intelligence tests
- Aptitude tests
- Personality tests
- Proficiency tests

Intelligence tests

Tests of **general intellectual ability** typically test memory, ability to think quickly and logically, and problem-solving skills.

(a) Most people have experience of IQ tests and the like, and few would dispute their validity as good measure of **general** intellectual capacity.

(b) However, there is no agreed definition of intelligence.

Aptitude tests

Aptitude tests are designed to **measure** and predict an individual's potential for performing a job or learning new skills.

- **Reasoning**: verbal, numerical and abstract
- **Spatio-visual ability**: practical intelligence, non-verbal ability and creative ability
- **Perceptual speed and accuracy**: clerical ability
- **'Manual' ability**: mechanical, manual, musical and athletic

Personality tests

Personality tests may measure a variety of characteristics, such as an applicant's skill in dealing with other people, his ambition and motivation or his emotional stability.

CASE EXAMPLE

Probably the best known example is the 16PF, originally developed by *Cattell* in 1950.

The 16PF comprises sixteen scales, each of which measure a factor that influences the way a person behaves.

The factors are functionally different underlying personality characteristics, and each is associated with not just one single piece of behaviour but rather is the source of a relatively broad range of behaviours. For this reason the factors themselves are referred to as source traits and the behaviours associated with them are called surface traits.

The advantage of measuring source traits, as the 16PF does, is that you end up with a much richer understanding of the person because you are not just describing what can be seen but also the characteristics underlying what can be seen.

The 16PF analyses how a person is likely to behave generally including, for example, contribution likely to be made to particular work contexts, aspects of the work environment to which the person is likely to more or less suited, and how best to manage the person.

The validity of such tests has been much debated, but is seems that some have been shown by research to be valid predictors of job performance, so long as they are used **properly.**

Proficiency tests

Proficiency tests are perhaps the most closely related to an assessor's objectives, because they **measure ability to do the work involved**. An applicant for an audio typist's job, for example, might be given a dictation tape and asked to type it.

9.2 Trends in the use of tests

(a) Continuing enthusiasm for personality tests.

(b) The continuing influence of cognitive ability intelligence tests.

(c) A focus on certain popular themes – sales ability or aptitude, customer orientation, motivation, teamworking and organisational culture are mentioned.

(d) The growing diversity of test producers and sources (meaning more choice, but also more poor quality measures).

(e) Expanded packages of tests, including tapes, computer disks, workbooks and so on.

(f) A growing focus on fairness: the most recent edition of the 16PF test, for example, has been scrutinised by expert psychologists to exclude certain types of content that might lead to bias.

9.3 Limitations of testing

(a) There is not always a direct relationship between ability in the test and ability in the job: the job situation is very different from artificial test conditions.

(b) The **interpretation of test results is a skilled task**, for which training and experience is essential. It is also highly subjective (particularly in the case of personality tests), which belies the apparent scientific nature of the approach.

(c) Additional difficulties are experienced with particular kinds of test. For example:

   (i) An aptitude test measuring arithmetical ability would need to be constantly revised or its content might become known to later applicants.

   (ii) Personality tests can often give misleading results because applicants seem able to guess which answers will be looked at most favourably.

   (iii) It is difficult to design intelligence tests which give a fair chance to people from different cultures and social groups and which test the **kind** of intelligence that the organisation wants from its employees: the ability to **score highly in IQ** tests does not necessarily correlate with desirable traits such as mature **judgement** or **creativity**, merely mental ability.

   (iv) Most tests are subject to coaching and practice effects.

(d) **It is difficult to exclude bias from tests**. Many tests (including personality tests) are tackled less successfully by women than by men, or by some candidates born overseas than by indigenous applicants because of the particular aspect chosen for testing.

9.4 Impact of legal considerations to the recruitment and selection process

It is unlawful to discriminate during the recruitment and selection process on the grounds of gender, marital status, race, colour, nationality, ethnic or national origins, disability, sexual orientation, perceived sexual orientation, religion, belief or non-belief or age. Employees involved in the recruitment and selection process must be aware of the legislation aimed at preventing discrimination against job applicants and potential employees, and ensure that employees are selected solely on the basis of merit.

If a successful claim is made against the organisation under relevant discrimination legislation there is no limit to the financial damages that could be awarded, which could include damages for the hurt feelings of the applicant and the loss of the chance of the job. Damages may also be increased if the employer's behaviour was insulting or malicious. In Employment Tribunal cases individuals have been awarded between £25,000 and £250,000 compensation where sex or race discrimination has been proven and individual employees may be liable for the payment of such compensation.

10 EMPLOYMENT LEGISLATION AND DIVERSITY

10.1 Employment

After the selection process, the formal offer of employment is made and (hopefully) acknowledged.

The Employment Protection (Consolidation) Act 1978 defines the terms of a contract of employment. The express terms are specifically stated in the contract, which must provide the names of the parties concerned, the date of the commencement of the job, its title, terms of payment, working hours, holiday, sick pay and pension entitlements, notice of termination of employment, discipline and grievance procedures.

A medical examination may be required. This ensures the person is physically suited to the job and safeguards the organisation from the engagement of anyone who suffers from infectious diseases and strictly forms part of the selection process.

10.2 Equal opportunities and discrimination legislation

'Equal opportunities' is a generic term describing the belief that there should be an equal chance for all workers to apply and be selected for jobs, to be trained and promoted in employment and to have that employment terminated fairly. Employers should only discriminate according to ability, experience and potential. All employment decisions should be based solely on a person's ability to do the job in question; no consideration should be taken of a person's sex, age, racial origin, disability or marital status.

Discrimination against various groups in an organisation has been made unlawful and legislation, which relates to equal opportunities and discrimination, includes the following.

(a) The *Equal Pay Act 1970* – this Act is intended to prevent discrimination between men and women with regards to the terms and conditions of employment. It aims to ensure that where men and women are employed in like work or work of an equivalent nature, they will receive the same terms and conditions of employment.

(b) The *Sex Discrimination Act 1975* – renders it unlawful to make any form of discrimination in employment affairs because of marital status or sex. The Act applies to offers of employment, dismissal and opportunities for promotion, transfer, training and other benefits. It applies especially to the selection process as it offers protection to both sexes against unfair treatment on appointment. Note that there are two kinds of discrimination, direct and indirect.

Direct discrimination – occurs when someone is treated less favourably than someone of the opposite sex – perhaps by being banned from applying for a job because of being a woman. This type is not difficult to discover.

Indirect discrimination – in this case, an employer may relate a condition to an applicant for a job that does not actually seem relevant to it, but which suggests that only one sex would be acceptable. An example of this may be advertising so that only men are encouraged to apply.

(c) The *Disability Discrimination Act 1995* – Provides for disabled people not to be discriminated against in a variety of circumstances including employment.

(d) The *Race Relations Act 1976* – discrimination is expressed in terms of 'racial grounds' and 'racial groups' and relate to colour, race, nationality or other ethnic or national origins. The term ethnic has been held to be much wider than race. The Race Relations Act uses a broadly similar approach to that of the Sex Discrimination Act and uses the same categorisations of direct and indirect discrimination and victimisation.

(e) The *Rehabilitation of Offenders Act 1974* – provides that a conviction, other than one involving imprisonment for more than 30 months, may become erased if the offender commits no further serious offences during the rehabilitation period, which varies according to the age of the person convicted and the length of the sentence imposed.

10.3 Formulating an effective equal opportunities policy

A number of employers label themselves as equal opportunity employers, establishing their own particular kind of equal opportunity policy. While some protection is afforded by employment legislation, the majority of everyday cases must rely on good practice to prevail.

The main areas where good practice can be demonstrated are:

- **Job analysis** – person specifications must not be more favourable to men or women.
- **Advertisements and documentation** – must not discriminate on sex or marital status grounds. This means that job titles must be sexless eg 'salesman' becomes 'sales person'.
- **Employee interviewing and selection** – questions must not be asked at interviews which discriminate by implication eg asking a woman whether or not she intends to have children.

Some employers have begun to address the underlying problems of equal opportunities, with further measures such as the following.

(a) Putting equal opportunities high on the agenda by appointing Equal Opportunities Managers who report directly to the Personnel/HR Director.

(b) Flexible hours or part-time work, term-time or annual hours contracts (to allow for school holidays) to help women to combine careers with family responsibilities. Terms and conditions, however, must not be less favourable.

(c) Career-break or return-to-work schemes for women.

(d) Fast-tracking school-leavers, as well as graduates, and posting managerial vacancies internally, giving more opportunities for movement up the ladder for groups (typically women and minorities) currently at lower levels of the organisation.

(e) Training for women-returners or women in management to help women to manage their career potential. Assertiveness training may also be offered as part of such an initiative.

(f) Awareness training for managers, to encourage them to think about equal opportunity policy.

(g) The provision of workplace nurseries for working mothers.

(h) Positive action to encourage job and training applications from minority groups.

(i) Alteration of premises to accommodate wheelchair users, blind or partially sighted workers and so on.

10.4 Diversity and equal opportunities

Definition

> **Diversity**: 'all the ways in which we are different and similar along an infinite number of lines.'

Diversity refers to a broad range of characteristics including: gender, age, race, disability, cultural background, sexual orientation, education, religious belief, class and family responsibilities. Four distinct dimensions characterise the many facets of differences and similarities of diverse employees. These four dimensions are as follows.

(a) **Personality dimensions**: The unique characteristics of each individual that directly impact communication with others, which may include, patient or impatient, doer or thinker, assertive or non-assertive, listener or talker, flexible or inflexible, rational or emotional.

(b) **Internal dimensions**: Diversity characteristics that for the most part are not within a person's control, but shape expectations, assumptions and opportunities such as, age, gender, ethnicity, race, physical ability and sexual orientation.

(c) **External dimensions**: Social factors and life experiences that are more under a person's control and also exert a significant impact on behaviour and attitude. Examples of these include religion, marital status, parental status, educational background, income, appearance, geographic location, and work experience.

(d) **Organisational dimensions**: Characteristics of a person's experience within an organisation that impact assumptions, expectations, and opportunities. This may include functional level or classification, management status, department/division/unit and work group, union affiliation, work location, seniority, work content or field.

From the employer's point of view, an organisation's workforce is **representative** when it reflects or exceeds the demographic composition of the external work force. A representative work force reflects or exceeds the current proportions of women, visible minorities and persons with disabilities in each occupation as are known to be available in the external work force and from which the employer may reasonably be expected to draw.

A representative work force is a good indication that an employer is not limiting access to the skills and talents of workers by discriminating on the basis of sex, race, colour or disability. A non-representative work force signals the need for evaluation and action, so that whatever is blocking or discouraging certain groups from employment and advancement may be corrected.

Some organisations set themselves goals on the representation of certain groups eg, there is an under-representation of certain ethnic groups within the police force. To address this type of problem, a **diversity assessment** will show how an organisation's systems may provide support or may act as a barrier to diversity.

Diversity assessment

A diversity assessment is a structured process to gather information about the experience of current employees and, if desired, former employees using employee focus groups, personal interviews with senior managers, and telephone interviews with employees who have left the organisation.

The three general approaches for implementing diversity in an organisation are:

(a) **Affirmative action**: an approach with a goal to gain representation and upward mobility for ethnic minorities and women. It is focused on special efforts for targeted groups who are under-utilised.

(b) **Valuing diversity**: an approach with a goal to improve the quality of relationships between people. It is focused on understanding the cultural similarities and differences within an organisation. There is strong research evidence (*Meredith Belbin's* 1981 studies on team effectiveness) to support the view that groups that have a diverse mix of experiences, skills, knowledge and working approaches are generally more creative and productive than groups with a more uniform profile. Diversity is therefore a valuable organisational asset, and needs to be perceived as such.

(c) **Managing diversity**: an approach with a goal to improve the full use of all human resources in the organisation. The process is focused on creating a diversity friendly management system. It opens up the whole system to change and questions the policies and practices of the organisation in light of the current diverse environment.

Managing diversity

Managing diversity is a strategic decision and commitment is more than adherence to legal responsibilities – it means creating an environment which values and uses the contributions of people with different backgrounds, experiences and perspectives. It is a value that needs to be taken on by all levels of staff and translated into a working culture.

The equal opportunities approach is often seen as trying to 'right a wrong' for certain groups and create a level playing field. Those working within a diversity framework, on the other hand, embrace different employees or customers as individuals and not members of a disadvantaged social group, and see difference as potentially a resource. It introduces equity.

Equality and equity

Definition

> **Equality** = sameness. When we treat people equally we ignore differences.
>
> **Equity** = fairness. When we treat people equitably we recognise differences.

Equity relates to the fairness of outcomes and of the procedures used to determine the outcomes.

Barriers to managing diversity

The two things that might get in the way of this are:

1. **Intentional discrimination** (attitudes) eg, sexism, racism, ageism, nationalism, nepotism, favouritism and protectionism
2. **Systemic discrimination** (behaviours) eg, seniority systems, referral systems, old boys/new girls networks, unnecessary language barriers, non-*bona fide* job requirements, limited advertising, unfair communications systems and non recognition of qualifications

A 'managing diversity' orientation implies the need to be proactive in managing the needs of a diverse workforce in areas (beyond the requirements of equal opportunity and discrimination regulations) such as:

- Tolerance of individual differences
- Communicating effectively with (and motivating) ethnically diverse work forces
- Managing workers with increasingly diverse family structures and responsibilities
- Managing the adjustments to be made by an increasingly aged work force
- Managing increasingly diverse career aspirations/patterns and ways of organising working life (including flexible working)
- Confronting issues of literacy, numeracy and differences in qualifications in an international work force
- Managing cooperative working in ethnically diverse teams.

As the workforce becomes more diverse, organisations need to create cultures in which all employees can develop their potential and flourish. Recognising 'individuality' is not only the right thing to do, but it can have a measurable impact on productivity and its profitability.

The 'business case' approach is shown in the figure below.

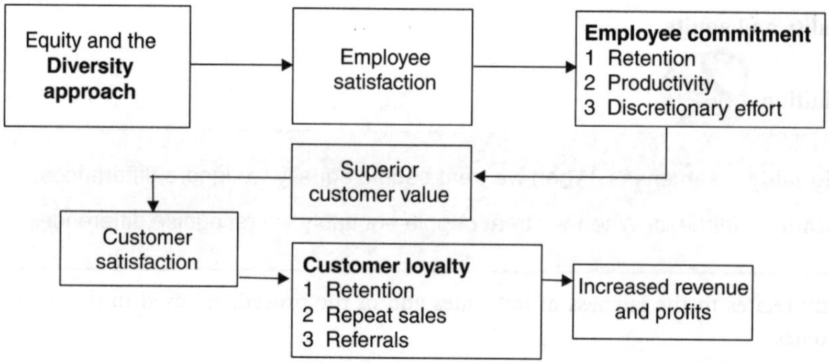

Figure 5.1: Business case for managing diversity

Benefits to the business of managing diversity

Management believe that the benefits will be:

(a) A more positive working environment. By respecting difference, individuals are made to feel more valued and consequently employee loyalty and productivity is increased, and staff turnover decreased.

(b) A contribution to raising the profile of the organisation in the community. A more diverse workforce better reflects the diversity of the customer base.

Encouraging the employment of diverse individuals can help to provide a working environment that can negate the destructive effects of direct and indirect discrimination, victimisation and harassment. A positive culture can be created where individual differences are welcomed and supported and a deeper level of understanding of the nature of diversity permeates the entire organisation.

10.5 Behaving ethically

By adopting a diversity approach the organisation's stakeholders perceive it as behaving 'ethically'. Within the organisation ethics might also be called morality, since it reflects the general expectations of any person in any society, acting in any capacity. It covers the principles we try to instil in our children, and expect of one another without needing to articulate the expectation or formalise it in any way. It includes:

- Concern for the well being of others
- Respect for the autonomy of others
- Trustworthiness and honesty
- Willing compliance with the law (with the exception of civil disobedience)
- Basic justice; being fair
- Refusing to take unfair advantage
- Benevolence: doing good
- Preventing harm

Managing ethics in the workplace involves identifying and prioritising values to guide behaviour in the organisation, and establishing associated policies and procedures to ensure they are carried out. One might call this 'values management'.

11 RETENTION PROCEDURES

11.1 Monitoring the HRM plan

Monitoring is a crucial component of the HRM plan. It is here that an employer can determine whether goals are being attained and problems resolved. Evaluation of the HRM plan can indicate levels of success, and indicate where further planning is needed to achieve the overall goals of the organisation.

Mission statements often talk about the success of the business, but as a part of the recruitment and retention strategy, companies should also include a well-conceived succession plan for employees. Retention issues are vital to the success of any organisation. Companies devote tremendous resources to recruiting good people, but they must be just as diligent about retaining them. To do this, effective retention strategies must be created that are based on a combination of all workplace conditions, such as issues of health and safety, employee treatment, motivating employees through recognition and rewards and enhancing employee loyalty. An organisation earns loyalty by creating a positive working environment that is stimulating and emphasises an employee's personal growth. Succession planning aims to establish the identity of individuals who will step in and take over key positions as and when the need arises.

Other areas included in a retention strategy are:

(a) **Analysis of wastage statistics**. This will establish where wastage is taking place, as it is unlikely to be the same throughout the firm and more likely to be concentrated in certain jobs, locations or departments.

(b) **Exit interviewing**. The reasons why staff are leaving may be established by conducting exit interviews so that any organisational problems or failings can be dealt with.

(c) **Remuneration package**. The package needs to be regularly reviewed to ensure it is flexible (adjusted to employee needs) and competitive.

(d) **Career and development policies**. Employees need career prospects and career development to sustain their motivation.

(e) **Job redesign programmes**. These are motivating as they make work more varied and therefore interesting.

(f) **Grievance handling**. Effective and efficient procedures (informal and formal) for dealing with grievances are required.

(g) **Equal opportunity policies**. Special policies may need to be developed and monitored for particular groups of staff such as women and those from ethnic minorities.

11.2 Health, safety and welfare

Because of concern by successive governments to avoid exploitation and discrimination, human resource management is perhaps more subject to legislation than any other aspect of corporate management.

In 1972, a Royal Commission on Safety and Health at Work reported that unnecessarily large numbers of days were being lost each year through industrial accidents, injuries and diseases, because of the 'attitudes, capabilities and performance of people and the efficiency of the organisational systems within which they work'. Since then, major legislation has been brought into effect in the UK, most notably:

(a) Health and Safety at Work Act 1974;

(b) The regulations introduced in January 1993 implementing EU directives on Health and Safety.

Some of the most important regulations are as follows.

- Reporting of Injuries, Diseases and Dangerous Occurrences Regulations (RIDDOR) 1995
- The Health and Safety (First Aid) Regulations 1981
- The Noise at Work Regulations 1989
- The Control of Substances Hazardous to Health Regulations 1994
- The Manual Handling Operations Regulations 1992
- The Workplace (Health, Safety and Welfare) Regulations 1992
- The Provision and Use of Work Equipment Regulations 1992
- The Health and Safety (Display Screen Equipment) Regulations 1992
- The Management of Health and Safety at Work Regulations 1992
- The Personal Protective Equipment at Work Regulations 1992

We will not be covering their provisions in detail here. Just be aware that the framework for personnel policy in the area of health and safety is extensive and detailed!

In the UK, the Health and Safety at Work Act 1974 provides for the introduction of a system of approved codes of practice, prepared in consultation with industry. Thus an employee, whatever his/her employment, should find that his/her work is covered by an appropriate code of practice.

Employers also have specific duties under the 1974 Act.

(a) All systems (work practices) must be safe.

(b) The work environment must be safe and healthy (well-lit, warm, ventilated and hygienic).

(c) All plant and equipment must be kept up to the necessary standard (with guards on machines and so on).

In addition, information, instruction, training and supervision should be directed towards safe working practices. Employers must consult with safety representatives appointed by a recognised trade union, and appoint a safety committee to monitor safety policy, if asked to do so. Safety policy and measures should be clearly communicated in writing to all staff.

The employee also has a duty:

1 To take reasonable care of himself/herself and others,

2 To allow the employer to carry out his or her duties (including enforcing safety rules), and

3 Not to interfere intentionally or recklessly with any machinery or equipment.

Under the Workplace (Health, Safety and Welfare) Regulations 1992 employers have additional general duties including:

- A written risk assessment of all work hazards
- Controls to reduce risks – with new or revised safety policies as required
- Informing employees (including temps) about health and safety
- Training in safety matters

These Regulations deal with matters such as machinery, temperature and ventilation, lighting, washroom facilities, doors and gates, fire and first aid that have been statutory requirements for many years in the UK under legislation such as the Offices, Shops and Railway Premises Act 1963. These are now expected and accepted by employees and employers and the modern role of welfare in organisations is less easy to define.

In its widest context, welfare, as the concern for people as individuals, can be seen in most personnel management policies, in selection interviewing, counselling, appraisal schemes and so on. In a narrow context, welfare can be viewed as a set of provisions that have a great deal of overlap with fringe benefits. These provisions have been identified by *Thomason* as canteen and recreational facilities, information services such as legal aid, the provision of houses, nurseries, transport and the like, further education provision and medical services. For example, because of the increased attention to equal opportunities and also the need to recruit more women returnees to the workforce, many organisations are improving their childcare arrangements. *Thomason* feels that such provisions may enable people to work better within the normal functioning of the enterprise and may have an effect on such factors as recruitment, loyalty and length of service.

11.3 Health and Safety Policy

An organisation's health and safety policy will include some or all of the following courses of action.

(a) **Job descriptions**, which stress health and safety aspect of the job.

(b) The **design of work systems** to reduce health and safety hazards; using engineering design to build in safety controls.

(c) **Creating patterns of work** to reduce accidents directly, eg the introduction of rest pauses, or indirectly, eg by reducing stress by introducing flexitime, job enrichment and so on.

(d) The **training of employees** – identifying what employees must know concerning health and safety and then devising the most appropriate method of instruction.

(e) **Formal procedures** are set up by most organisations. They range from employing a safety officer and a medical officer, to establishing disciplinary procedures to deal with rule breaking.

(f) **Accident prevention** by carrying out an analysis of accidents.

(g) **Participative management** in an attempt to involve the workforce in the question of health and safety. Involvement has been institutionalised in the Health and Safety at Work Act by the introduction of safety representatives. In some industries, such as mining, there is an obvious commitment on the part of employees toward a shared objective of safe working. In other firms, involving the workforce in safety matters is a problem that no amount of committees or publicity has yet solved. The problem may lie in an attitude generated by management who may see safety work as having a low status.

(h) **Employee counselling** has met with some success, particularly in reducing stress, an area of a great deal of current concern and research.

11.4 Motivating employees through recognition and rewards

Understanding what motivates people is necessary at all levels of management. On a basic level (according to *Maslow*) people need to be fed and to walk around without holes in their shoes. However, feeding people's minds, helping them to realise their potential, making them feel that their jobs are worth doing and they are contributing to the good of the whole organisation are just as important.

Motivation is frequently based on reward. Many writers describe rewards as having basically two dimensions – intrinsic and extrinsic.

Extrinsic rewards are those forms of reward that are outside the control of the individual and at the disposal of others; sometimes the individual's superior but more often the organisation itself. Extrinsic rewards can be 'seen' and are akin to *Herzberg's* hygiene (or maintenance) factors. Because extrinsic rewards are obvious and can be 'seen,' not only by the individual concerned but also by others, lack of attention can lead to job dissatisfaction and motivation problems. These rewards include salaries and conditions, incentive arrangements, share schemes, pension provision, sickness and holiday pay, family leave, parking, open access to learning and development opportunities, insurance and wider facilities such as crèches.

Intrinsic rewards are to a great extent within the control of the individual. They include feelings of personal satisfaction, a sense of achievement, status, recognition, the opportunities for advancement, responsibility and pride in the work. This form of reward forms part of *Maslow's* higher order thinking on motivation and is also often seen as akin to *Herzberg's* motivators (or 'satisfiers'); ie, those factors directly concerned with the satisfaction gained from the job itself.

While it is true that higher salaries offered by other organisations may be a threat to employee retention efforts, research shows that traditional pay programmes are ineffective for motivating high-performing, committed employees. Compensation has become a right – an expected reward for simply coming to work. Companies will lose their most valued employees if they fail to offer them the intangible intrinsic rewards that money cannot buy. Studies have found that recognition for a job well done is the top motivator of individual performance.

In fact, study after study has shown that what tends to stimulate and encourage top performance, growth and loyalty is praise and recognition. Employees want to:

- Feel they are making a contribution
- Have a manager who tells them when they do a good job
- Have the respect of peers and colleagues
- Be involved and informed about what's going on in the organisation
- Have interesting, challenging work.

Another key part of any retention strategy should include adopting flexible work arrangements. This addresses many work/life and childcare issues. Progressive companies are realising that restructuring full-time work to include alternative work options, such as flexitime, a compressed work week, and telecommuting, can be beneficial to both the employee and the employer.

Retaining employees today is harder than ever. Skilled workers are, and will continue to be, the most important asset of any organisation. Managers must realise this and must create a culture that fosters a sense of trust, loyalty, and commitment. Employees must know that if they work hard and are loyal they will be appreciated and valued.

11.5 Succession planning

Management and employee succession planning are both important issues. In an environment of rapid social and technical change, where knowledge, expertise and skill requirements are constantly changing, succession planning should be a fundamental part of the overall corporate plan. Unless dealing with a retirement or other planned departure, it is difficult, if not impossible, for a company to know exactly when it will encounter an employee loss. The departure can occur at any location or time, but will ultimately produce the same result: a void that the company must fill in order to successfully continue operations. Although it is not feasible to plan for every possible scenario, and particularly for the loss of several key leaders at the same time, it is entirely realistic to map out a chain of command and understand who will assume control if and when a key employee is lost.

Succession plans establish the identity of the individual who will step in and assume the role of a departed CEO, executive, project manager, or other key employee, allowing companies to make the transition and continue performing.

The planning process starts with:

(a) An **assessment of current staff resources**, analysed by departments, identifying the types of jobs at each level (job description) and the number and quality of staff in those jobs (staff appraisal).

(b) A **forecast of the staffing requirements**, by grades and skills, should then be agreed within the corporate plan (both the short- and long-term needs) to highlight any surplus staff as well as shortages.

(c) In the case of a **mismatch** between job specification and existing employees, every opportunity should be made to provide retraining or to undertake staff development. Again, the personnel appraisal records should indicate staff who have been willing or who are keen to widen or change their skills.

(d) Where there are **shortages,** recruitment programmes should be agreed. Vacancies should be identified and using the job description and job specification, recruitment and selection of appropriate staff should be carried out. The plan may require that training should then be provided for new recruits, as they will be unlikely to have the specific job knowledge required. In such cases, recruitment would be geared to the selection of people with the necessary ability and aptitude.

Management succession planning will probably entail compiling for each post, a list of perhaps three potential successors; and for each person (at least from a certain level upwards) a list of possible development moves. These lists then form the basis for long-term plans and development moves.

Succession planning is a difficult task. While the process must seek to achieve the organisation's goals and objectives, it must also take into account the aspirations of individuals and try to achieve a realistic fit between the person and the job.

Glaxo Wellcome's succession planning process is based on retaining 'star' employees as well as ensuring that key positions are filled. In addition to identifying critical positions and any gaps in the corporate structure, Glaxo seeks to develop – and thereby retain – employees with extraordinary skills and/or performance. The company also emphasises female and minority employees as part of its commitment to diversity.

Chapter roundup

- Effective recruitment practices ensure that a firm has enough people with the right skills.
- Most recruitment practices aim to fit the person to the job by identifying the needs of the job and finding a person who satisfies them.
- The recruitment process involves personnel specialists and 'line' managers, sometimes with the help of recruitment consultants.
- First the overall needs of the organisation have been identified in the recruitment process.
- To account for each individual position a job analysis is prepared, which identifies through various investigative techniques, the content of the job.
- A job description is developed from the job analysis. The job description outlines the tasks of the job and its place within the organisation.
- A person specification identifies the characteristics of a person who will be recruited to do the job identified in the job description.
- The person specification can be used to develop the job advertisement. The Seven-Point Plan and Five-Point Pattern are examples.
- In recent years, recruiters have been using 'competences' as a means to select candidates. A competence is a person's capacity to behave in a particular way, for example to fulfil the requirements of a job, or to motivate people. Work-based competences directly relate to the job (eg the ability to prepare a trial balance); behavioural competences relate to underlying issues of personality.
- The process of selection begins when the recruiter receives details of candidates interested in the job, in response, for example, to a job advert, or possibly enquiries made to a recruitment consultant.
- Many firms require candidates to fill out an application form. This is standardised and the firm can ask for specific information about work experience and qualifications, as well as other personal data. Some firms do not bother with an application form, being happy to accept CVs with a covering letter.

Chapter rounded (continued)

- Most firms use interviews, on a one-to-one basis, using a variety of open and closed questions. The interviewer should avoid bias in assessing the candidate.
- Selection tests can be used before or after interviews. Intelligence tests measure the candidate's general intellectual ability, and personality tests identify the type of person. Other tests are more specific to the job (eg proficiency tests).
- Interviews are unreliable as predictors of actual job performance for many posts, but they are traditional and convenient. A combination of interviews with other methods may be used.
- Current legislation that applies to recruitment and selection includes laws on equal pay, sex discrimination, the employment of disabled people, race relations and the rehabilitation of offenders.
- Motivation theories suggest that individuals have needs that must be satisfied. There are a number of different theories. Satisfaction theories are based on the assumption that a 'satisfied' worker will work harder. Extrinsic theories believe that individuals will work harder to obtain a desired reward, eg more money and intrinsic theories argue that effective performance is its own reward.
- As the workforce becomes more diverse in terms of gender, race, culture, age, religion, disability, sexual orientation and ethnicity, organisations need to create cultures in which all employees can develop their potential and flourish. Not only is this the 'right' thing to do, but also how an organisation manages diversity will have a measurable impact on productivity, retention and its profitability.
- Having gone to the trouble of employing suitable people, organisations must strive to retain them within the workforce. Retention strategies must be created that are based on a combination of all workplace conditions, such as issues of health and safety, employee treatment, motivating employees through recognition and rewards and enhancing employee loyalty.
- Succession planning aims to establish the identity of individuals who will step in and take over key positions as and when the need arises.

Quick quiz

1. What, in brief, are the stages of the recruitment and selection process?
2. Briefly summarise job analysis.
3. What is a currently fashionable approach to drawing up jobs analysis, job descriptions etc?
4. List the components of the Five-Point Pattern.
5. What are the characteristics of a good job advertisement?
6. What should application forms achieve?
7. What factors should be taken into account in an organisation's interview strategy?
8. Why are open questions useful?
9. Why do interviews fail to predict performance accurately?
10. List the desirable features of selection tests
11. What are the provisions of the Sex Discrimination Act 1975?

Answers to quick quiz

1 Identifying/defining requirements; attracting potential employees; selecting candidates.

2 **Job analysis**. The process of examining a 'job' to identify the component parts and the circumstances in which it is performed.

3 The use of competences – work based and behavioural.

4 Impact on others; acquired knowledge and qualifications; innate abilities; motivation; adjustment.

5 Concise; reaches the right people; gives a good impression; relevant to the job, identifying skills required etc.

6 They should give enough information to identify suitable candidates and weed out no-hopers, by asking specific questions and by getting the candidate to volunteer information.

7 In brief, giving the right impression of the organisation and obtaining a rounded, relevant assessment of the candidate.

8 They allow the candidate to volunteer more, and open avenues for further questions.

9 Brevity and artificiality of interview situation combined with the bias and inexperience of interviewers.

10 Sensitive; standardised; reliable; valid.

11 Sex Discrimination Act 1975 renders it unlawful to make any form of discrimination in employment affairs because of marital status or sex.

Answers to activities

1 Large organisations tend to have standard procedures. In order to ensure a standard process, you might have seen a specialist from the personnel/HR department only. Smaller organisations cannot afford such specialists so you might have been interviewed by your immediate boss – but perhaps someone else might also have interviewed you (your boss's boss) to check you out.

2–5 Your own research. Keep this documentation; it might be helpful in your Professional Development studies for Unit 13.

6 (a) Goods points about the advertisement and points for improvement

(i) It is attractively designed in terms of page layout.

(ii) The tone of the headline and much of the body copy is informal, colloquial and even friendly. It starts with a joke, implying that the company has a sense of humour.

(iii) The written style is fluent and attractive.

(iv) It appears to offer quite a lot of information about the culture of the company – how it feels about personnel issues, where it's going etc – as well as about the job vacancy.

Improvements that could be made

Job advertisements carry certain 'responsibilities': they are a form of pre-selection, and as such should be not be just attractive and persuasive, but accurate and complete enough to give a realistic and relevant picture of the post and the organisation.

(i) There is too much copy. Readers may not have the patience to read through so much (rather wordy) prose, particularly since the same phrases are repeated ('progressive international organisation', for example), or look rather familiar in any case ('in the nicest possible ways', 'our staff are our most important asset', 'a company with a difference' etc) and there is very little 'hard' information contained in the ad.

(ii) There are many words and expressions which sound good, and seem to imply good things, but are in fact empty of substance, and commit the organisation to nothing. They are usually the 'stock' expressions like 'committed to an enlightened personnel philosophy': what does that actually mean?

(iii) There are confusing contradictions, eg between the requirements for flexibility, 'interchange with various functions', do 'whatever the situation demands' etc and the more cautious 'within your designated area ...'.

(iv) The copywriters are in places too 'clever' for their own good. The first three lines, for example, could backfire quite badly if a reader failed to catch the next line, or simply didn't appreciate the self-deprecating tone.

(v) The advertisement does not give enough 'hard' information to make effective response likely – and then fails to do its job of facilitating response at all! Despite the invitation to telephone, no number is given. No named corespondent is cited, merely a reference number – despite the claimed emphasis on people as people, not numbers.

(b) **What is learnt about AOK**

The advertisement claims to say quite a lot about AOK, its culture, its people-centredness, its expansion and progressive outlook, flexibility, sense of humour etc. Such claims should always be taken with a pinch of salt. We may, however, infer some things about the company.

(i) It has a strong cultural 'flavour', and believes in 'selling' that culture quite hard. It likes, for example, telling people what it is 'committed to', what it 'firmly believes' etc.

(ii) It tends to stress its good points and opportunities: it certainly sees itself (even allowing for advertising hyperbole) as go-ahead, successful and expanding, flexible, people-oriented.

(iii) It is possibly not as deeply people-oriented as it tries to project. The areas of involvement for the Personnel Department enumerated, for example, seem rather limited and administrative: there is no suggestion of a wider strategic role for personnel, such as would indicate that 'people issues' really do affect management outlook.

7 (a) Boxes too small to contain the information asked for.

(b) Forms which are (or look) so lengthy or complicated that a prospective applicant either completes them perfunctorily or gives up (and applies to another employer instead).

(c) Illegal (eg discriminatory) or offensive questions.

(d) Lack of clarity as to what (and how much) information is required.

8 (a) Closed. (The only answer is 'yes' or 'no', unless Jo is prepared to expand on it, at his or her own initiative.)

(b) Leading. (Even if Jo was interested, (s)he should get the message that 'yes' would not be what the interviewer wanted, or expected, to hear.)

(c) Leading closed multiple! ('Really useful' leads Jo to think that the 'correct' answer will be 'yes': There is not much opportunity for any other answer, without expanding on it unasked.)

(d) Open. (Jo has to explain, in his or her own words.)

(e) Probing. (If Jo's answer has been unconvincing, short or vague, this question forces a more specific answer.)

Chapter 6 :
LEADERSHIP

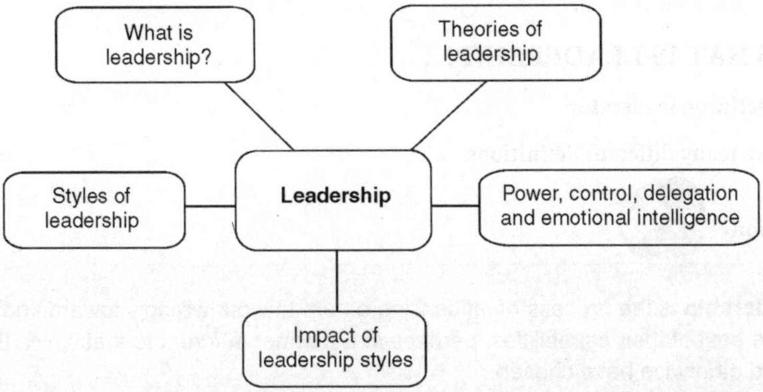

Introduction

The outcome of this chapter is for you to be able to evaluate the styles and impact of leadership. There are many ways of looking at leadership, and many interpretations of its meaning. Essentially it is a relationship through which one person influences the behaviour or actions of other people. Leadership is related to motivation, communication and delegation, as well as the activities of groups.

This chapter describes and comments on a number of the theoretical and practical aspects of leadership. A review of the main leadership theories is followed by a discussion on the alternative leadership styles available to a person in a management or supervisory position.

Much research has been undertaken in an attempt to understand what motivates individual employees at work and how managers can improve it.

The motivational strategy that is decided on will depend on the beliefs held and the culture that prevails in the organisation. *Maslow's* theory holds that human needs form a hierarchy ranging from the lowest-order needs (physiological needs) to the highest order need – self-actualisation. According to *Herzberg's* two-factor theory, there are two sets of motivating factors. *Vroom's* expectancy theory suggests that people are motivated to reach a goal if they think the goal is worthwhile and can see that the activities will help them achieve the goal. *McGregor* argues that the style of management adopted is a function of the manager's attitudes towards people and assumptions about human nature and behaviour.

Your objectives

After completing this chapter you should be able to:

(a) explain the skills and attributes needed for leadership

(b) explain the difference between leadership and management

(c) compare leadership styles for different situations

(d) explain ways to motivate staff to achieve objectives

1 WHAT IS LEADERSHIP?

1.1 Defining leadership

There are many different definitions.

Definition

> **Leadership** is the process of influencing others to work willingly towards goals, to the best of their capabilities, perhaps in a manner different to that which they would otherwise have chosen.

Buchanan and Huczynski define a leader as 'someone who exercises influence over other people'. Leadership is seen as 'a social process in which one individual influences the behaviour of others without the use or threat of violence'.

The essence of leadership is followership. In other words it is the willingness of people to follow that makes a person a leader (*Koontz, O'Donnell, Weihrich*).

Most definitions of leadership reflect the assumptions that it is a relationship through which one person influences the behaviour or actions of other people in an organisational context. It is a dynamic two-way process of leading and following that can affect both individual and organisational performance. For example, a leader can influence the interpretation of events, the choice of objectives and strategies, the organisation of work activities, the motivation of people to achieve the objectives, the maintenance of cooperative relationships, the development of skills and confidence by members and the enlistment of support and cooperation from people outside the group or organisation.

1.2 Differences between leadership and management

In the words of Peter Drucker and Warren Bennis, leadership is 'doing the right things'; management is 'doing things right'.

In other words, leadership – doing the right things – is deciding the best course of action to take. What are the things we should be doing to get us to where we want to go? What direction or course of action should we take? Where do we want to be in the end?

The act of management then follows the act of leadership. Once the best course of direction has been decided, management - doing things right - looks at the objectives established by leadership and works out the best way to get there. Generally speaking, leadership deals with the interpersonal aspects of a manager's job, whereas planning, organising and controlling deal with the administrative aspects. Leadership deals with change, inspiration, motivation and influence. Management deals more with carrying out the organisation's goals and maintaining equilibrium. Leaders command respect not just because of their pre-existing management capabilities, but also because of their overall presence, their assertiveness, their confidence and their ability to drive forward new ideas and make things happen.

John Kotter (The Leadership Factor, 1988) has made one of the most detailed and helpful distinctions between leadership and management, and in so doing has further described both. According to *Kotter*, management involves the following activities.

(i) **Planning and budgeting** – target-setting, establishing procedures for reaching the targets, and allocating the resources necessary to meet the plans.

(ii) **Organising and staffing** – designing the organisation structure, hiring the right people and establishing incentives.

(iii) **Controlling and problem-solving** – monitoring results against the plan, identifying problems, producing solutions and implementing them.

Everything here is concerned with logic, structure, analysis and control. If done well, it produces predictable results on time. Leadership requires a different set of actions and, indeed, a completely different mindset.

(i) Creating a sense of direction – usually borne out of dissatisfaction with the *status quo.* Out of this challenge a vision for something different is created.

(ii) Communicating the vision – which must meet the realised or unconscious needs of other people and the leader must work to give it credibility.

(iii) Energising, inspiring and motivating – in order to stimulate others to translate the vision into achievement.

All of these activities involve dealing with people rather than things.

Activity 1 **(10 minutes)**

Suppose you were in a cinema and smelt smoke. How would you categorise the following possible actions on your part? Your options are behavioural contagion, management and leadership.

(a) You rush to the door screaming 'Fire' and everyone follows you.

(b) You rush to the door, switch on the lights, hit the fire alarm, and, grabbing a fire extinguisher, start looking for the source of the fire. People start moving towards the exits when they hear the fire alarm.

(c) You rush to the door, switch on the lights, shout for people not to panic but to move towards the exits (which they do) and ask for help to locate the fire and get the fire extinguishers (which you get).

(d) You do any or all of the above, but nobody takes any notice.

1.3 Why should managers be leaders?

Whether or not we make the distinction between management and leadership, attempts to define what makes leadership 'special' have suggested some key points about the benefits effective leadership can bring and why it is valuable.

(a) Leaders energise and support **change,** which is essential for survival in highly competitive and fast-changing business environments. By setting visionary goals, encouraging contribution from teams, leaders create environments that:

   (i) Seek out new information and ideas
   (ii) Allow challenges to existing procedures and ways of thinking
   (iii) Invite innovation and creativity in finding better ways to achieve goals
   (iv) Support and empower people to cope with the turbulence.

(b) Leaders secure **commitment,** mobilising the ideas, experience and motivation of employees – which contributes to innovation and improved quality and customer service. This is all the more essential in a competitive, customer-focused, knowledge- based business environment

(c) Leaders set **direction,** helping teams and organisations to understand their purpose, goals and value to the organisation. This facilitates team-working and empowerment (allowing discretion and creativity about how to achieve the desired outcomes) without loss of coordination or direction

(d) Leaders support, challenge and develop **people,** maximising their contribution to the organisation. Leaders use an influence-based facilitate-empower style rather than a command-control style, and this is better suited to the expectations of empowered teams and the need for information sharing in modern business environments.

Activity 2 **(10 minutes)**

Reflect on your own experience of working under the direction of others. Identify the 'best' leader you have ever 'followed'. (You may need to think about non-work leaders such as a sports coach or school teacher.) Think about how this person behaved and interacted with you and others.

What qualities make you identify this person as a 'great leader', from your point of view as a follower?

2 THEORIES OF LEADERSHIP

2.1 Different approaches

Theories of leadership can be classified as follows:

- **Trait** – based on analysing the *personality characteristics* or preferences of successful leaders.
- **Activity based** – based on analysing what designated leaders actually do, and how they do it.

- **Contingency** – based on the belief that there is no 'one best way' of leading, but that effective leaders adapt their behaviour to the specific and changing variables in the leadership context: the nature of the task, the personalities of team members, the organisation culture and so on.
- **Style** – based on the view that leadership is an interpersonal process whereby different leader behaviours influence people in different ways. More or less effective patterns of behaviour (or 'styles') can therefore be adopted.

Yukl (1989) identified four approaches for studying leadership. The 'power influence approach' attempts to understand leadership effectiveness in terms of the amount and type of power possessed by the leader. This approach would examine how power is acquired, lost, and maintained. The 'behaviour approach' looks at the actual tasks performed by leaders. This involves evaluating daily activities and behavioural characteristics of leaders. The 'trait approach' looks at the personal attributes of leaders, such as energy, intuition, creativity, persuasiveness, and foresight. The 'situational approach' examines leadership in terms of its relationships with environmental factors, such as superiors, subordinates, and peers. This approach is often referred to as contingency theory because the role of the leader is contingent on the situation.

2.2 Trait theories of leadership

Early theories suggested that there are certain qualities, personality characteristics or 'traits' that make a good leader. These might be aggressiveness, self-assurance, intelligence, initiative, a drive for achievement or power, appearance, interpersonal skills, administrative ability, imagination, a certain upbringing and education, the 'helicopter factor' (ie the ability to rise above a situation and analyse it objectively) etc.

This approach has much in common with the 'great man' theory of history, which states that great men set the great events of history in motion. Thus, those who display leadership in one situation would probably be the leader in any other situation. They are leaders because of some unique and inherent set of traits that set them apart from normal people. Lists of leadership qualities were compiled that included:

- Physical traits, such as drive, energy, appearance and height
- Personality traits, such as adaptability, enthusiasm and self-confidence and
- Social traits, such as cooperation, tact, courtesy and administrative ability

Trait theory, although superficially attractive, is now largely discredited, in favour of other theories.

2.3 A contingency approach to leadership

A contingency approach to leadership is one that argues that the ability of a manager to lead and to influence his work group will vary according to:

(a) The leader's personality, character and preferred style of operating.

(b) The subordinates: their individual and collective personalities, and their preference for a particular style of leadership.

(c) The task: If the tasks of a work group are simple, few in number and repetitive, the best style of leadership will be different from a situation in which tasks are varied and difficult.

(d) The context

(i) The position of power held by the leader in the organisation and the group. A person with power is better able to choose a personal style and leadership, select subordinates and re-define the task of the work group

(ii) Organisational norms and the structure and technology of the organisation. No manager can act in a manner which is contrary to the customs and standards of the organisation.

For each of the three factors, a spectrum can be drawn ranging from 'tight' to 'flexible'. *Handy* argues that the most effective style of leadership in any particular situation is one which brings the first three factors – a leader, subordinates and task – into a 'best fit'.

The spectrum

	Tight	**Flexible**
The leader	Preference for autocratic style, high estimation of his own capabilities and a low estimation of his subordinates. Dislikes uncertainty	Preference for democratic style with confidence in his subordinates, dislikes stress, accepts reasonable risk and uncertainty
The subordinates	Low opinion of own abilities; do not like uncertainty in their work and like to be ordered. They regard their work as trivial; past experience in work leads to acceptance of orders, cultural factors lean them towards autocratic/dictatorial leaders	High opinion of own abilities; likes challenging important work; prepared to accept uncertainty and longer time scales for results; cultural factors favour independence.
The task	Job requires no initiative – it is routine, repetitive or has a certain outcome. It has a short time scale for completion. Trivial tasks	Important tasks with a longer time scale. It can involve problem-solving or decision-making and complex work

A best fit occurs when all factors are on the same level in the spectrum. In practice, there is likely to be a misfit. Confronted with a lack of fit, the leader must decide which factor(s) should be changed to bring all three into line. In the short-term, the easiest is to change the leadership style. There are often long-term benefits to be achieved from re-defining the task (eg job enlargement) or from developing the work group.

Activity 3 **(20 minutes)**

List four ways in which an organisation, by dealing with 'environmental constraints' can help its managers to adopt an appropriate management style.

3 STYLES OF LEADERSHIP

Leaders accept responsibility for the outcomes of the groups they lead. While leaders have to exercise authority, the way in which this is done (the *style* of leadership) might vary. It is generally accepted that a leader's style of leading can affect the motivation, efficiency and effectiveness of the leader's followers.

There are various classifications of leadership style. Although the labels and definitions of styles vary, style models are often talking about the same thing: a continuum of behaviours from:

- Wholly task-focused, directive leadership behaviours (representing high leader control) at one extreme, and
- Wholly people-focused, supportive/relational leadership behaviours (representing high subordinate discretion) at the other

3.1 Styles of leadership

Huneryager and Heckman identified four different styles of leadership:

(a) **Dictatorial style** – where the leader forces subordinates to work by threatening punishment and penalties.

(b) **Autocratic style** – where decision-making is centralised in the hands of the leader, who does not encourage participation by subordinates. Many of the most successful businesses have been led to success by autocrats who are paternalistic leaders, offering consideration and respect to the workforce, but retaining full rights in decision-making. This is typified by the Quaker companies in the early years of this century (eg, Cadbury, Rowntree, Reckitt and Colman). Such a style is frequently found today in professional firms. Often they find it hard to delegate, to bring on successors, to stand down at the right moment, to switch off and go home, and to appreciate the views of others.

(c) **Democratic style** – where decision-making is decentralised, and shared by subordinates in participative group action. It is important not to allow a preference for democratic social systems to blind managers into favouring democratic management styles in all situations. Businesses can stand (and often need) firmer, more single-minded management than nation states would generally find healthy. Those who lead using the democratic approach suffer from being unable to move as quickly as competitor businesses led by autocrats and from people in the ranks not being clear as to exactly which direction they should be pulling in.

(d) **Laissez-faire style** – where subordinates are given little or no direction at all, and are allowed to establish their own objectives and make all their own decisions.

As we shall see from various studies a considerate style of leadership is frequently found to be the most effective and leads to greater job satisfaction, though task centred styles are often associated with high employee performance and, on occasions, with employee satisfaction as well.

3.2 A continuum of leadership styles

Tannenbaum and Schmidt proposed a continuum of behaviours (and associated styles), which reflected the balance of control exercised in a situation by the leader and the team.

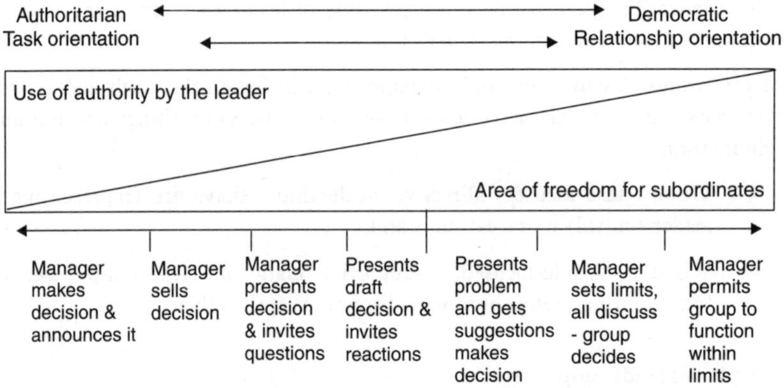

Figure 6.1: Tannenbaum and Schmidt's continuum of leadership styles

The continuum suggests a range of styles between authorisation and democratic without any suggestion that any one style is right or wrong. *Tannenbaum and Schmidt's* continuum recognises that the appropriate style depends upon:

- The leader (personality, values, natural style etc)
- The subordinates (their knowledge, experience, attitude etc)
- The situation (such forces as the organisation's culture, time pressures, levels of authority and responsibility etc)

3.3 Ashridge Management College

A further development of the continuum was published by the Ashridge Management College in 1966. Basically, they suggest four distinct management styles.

(a) **Tells** – the autocratic dictator. The manager makes all the decisions, and issues instructions, which must be obeyed without question. Communication is downward with no feedback until after the event. The strengths are that quick decisions can be made when speed is required and it is the most efficient type of leadership for highly programmed routine work. The weaknesses are that it does not encourage the subordinates to give their opinions when these might be useful and communications between the manager and subordinate will be one-way and the manager will not know until afterwards whether the orders have been properly understood

(b) **Sells** – the persuader. The manager still makes all the decisions, but believes that subordinates have to be motivated to accept them in order to carry them out properly. The strengths are that employees are made aware of the reasons for decisions. Selling decisions to staff might make them more committed. Staff will have a better idea of what to do when unforeseen events arise in their work because the manager will have explained his intentions. The weaknesses are that communications are still largely one-way. Subordinates might not accept the decisions and it does not encourage initiative and commitment from subordinates.

(c) **Consults** – partial involvement. The manager confers with subordinates and takes their views into account, but has the final say. Ashridge points out that this must be an honest approach not an attempt to hoodwink staff where the manager has no intention of changing a predetermined decision. The benefits are that employees are involved in decisions before they are made. This encourages motivation through greater interest and involvement. An agreed consensus of opinion can be reached and for some decisions consensus can be an advantage rather than a weak compromise. The weaknesses are that it might take much longer to reach decisions and subordinates might be too inexperienced to formulate mature opinions and give practical advice. Consultation can too easily turn into a façade concealing, basically, a sells style.

(d) **Joins** – the democrat. Leader and followers make the decision on the basis of consensus. It is clearly most effective where all members within the group have knowledge and experience to contribute so that an evenly balanced informed discussion can lead to the best decision. It can provide high motivation and commitment from employees. It shares the other advantages of the consultative style (especially where subordinates have expert power). The problems are that the authority of the manager might be undermined. Decision-making might become a very long process, and clear decisions might be difficult to reach and subordinates might lack enough experience.

The Ashridge studies came to the following conclusions.

(a) In an ideal world, subordinates preferred the 'consults' style of leadership.

(b) People led by a 'consults' manager had the most favourable attitude to their work.

(c) Most subordinates feel they are being led by a 'tells' or 'sells' manager.

(d) In practice, **consistency** was far more important to subordinates than any particular style. The least favourable attitudes were found amongst subordinates who were unable to perceive any consistent style of leadership in their superiors.

Activity 4 **(20 minutes)**

Suggest an appropriate style of management for each of the following situations. Think about your reasons for choosing each style in terms of the results you are trying to achieve, the need to secure commitment from others, and potential difficulties with both.

(a) Due to outside factors, the personnel budget has been reduced for your department and one-quarter of your staff must be made redundant. Records of each employee's performance are available.

(b) There is a recurring administrative problem which is minor, but irritating to every one in your department. Several solutions have been tried in the past, but without success. You think you have a remedy, which will work, but unknown problems may arise, depending on the decisions made.

(c) A decision needs to be made about working hours. The organisation wishes to stagger arrival and departure times in order to relieve traffic congestion. Each department can make its own decisions. It doesn't really matter what the times are, so long as department members conform to them.

(d) Even though they are experienced, members in your department don't seem to want to take on responsibility. Their attitude seems to be: 'You are paid to manage, we are paid to work: you make the decisions.' Now a decision has come up which will personally affect every person in your department.

3.4 *Rensis Likert*

Likert (*New patterns of Management*) also described a range of four management styles or 'systems'.

System 1: **Exploitative authoritative**. The leader has no confidence or trust in his subordinates, imposes decisions, never delegates, motivates by threat, has little communication with subordinates and does not encourage teamwork.

System 2: **Benevolent authoritative**. The leader has only superficial trust in subordinates, imposes decisions, never delegates, motivates by reward and, though sometimes involving others in problem solving, is basically paternalistic.

System 3: **Participative**. The leader has some confidence in subordinates, listens to them but controls decision making, motivates by reward and a level of involvement, and will use the ideas and suggestions of subordinates constructively.

System 4: **Democratic**. The leader has complete confidence in subordinates who are allowed to make decisions for themselves. Motivation is by reward for achieving goals set by participation, and there is a substantial amount of sharing of ideas, opinions and cooperation.

Likert recognised that each style is relevant in some situations; for example, in a crisis, a System 1 approach is usually required. Alternatively when introducing a new system of work, System 4 would be most effective. His research shows that effective managers are those who adopt either a System 3 or a System 4 leadership style. Both are seen as being based on trust and paying attention to the needs of both the organisation and employees.

3.5 *Blake and Mouton's* Managerial Grid

Robert Blake and Jane Mouton carried out research (The Ohio State Leadership Studies) into managerial behaviour and observed two basic dimensions of leadership: concern for **production** (or task performance) and **concern for people**.

Along each of these two dimensions, managers could be located at any point on a **continuum** from very low to very high concern. *Blake and Mouton* observed that the two concerns did not seem to correlate, positively or negatively: a high concern in one dimension, for example, did not seem to imply a high or low concern in the other dimension. Individual managers could therefore reflect various permutations of task/people concern.

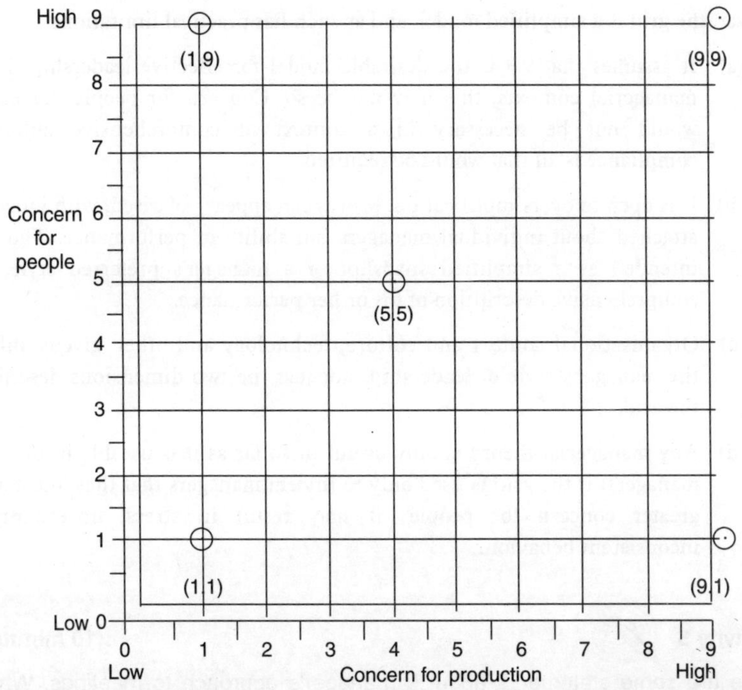

Figure 6.2: Blake and Mouton's managerial grid

The extreme cases shown on the grid are:

(a) 1.1 **impoverished**: the manager is lazy, showing little interest in either staff or work.

(b) 1.9 **country club**: the manager is attentive to staff needs and has developed satisfying relationships. However, there is little attention paid to achieving results.

(c) 9.1 **task management**: almost total concentration on achieving results. People's needs are virtually ignored.

(d) 5.5 **middle of the road** or the **dampened pendulum**: adequate performance through balancing the necessity to get out work while maintaining morale of people at a satisfactory level.

(e) 9.9 **team**: high performance manager who achieves high work accomplishment through 'leading' committed people who identify themselves with the organisational aims.

The managerial grid was intended as an appraisal and management development tool. It recognises that a balance is required between concern for task and concern for people, and that a high degree of both is possible (and highly effective) at the same time.

The grid thus offers a number of useful insights for the identification of management training and development needs. It shows in an easily assimilated form where the behaviour and assumptions of a manager may exhibit a lack of balance between the dimensions and/or a low degree of concern in either dimension or both. It may also be used in team member selection, so that a 1.9 team leader is balance by a 9.1 co-leader, for example.

However, the grid is a simplified model, and as such has practical limitations.

(a) It assumes that 9.9 is the desirable model for effective leadership. In some managerial contexts, this may not be so. Concern for people, for example, would not be necessary in a context of comprehensive automation: compliance is all that would be required.

(b) It is open to oversimplification. Scores can appear polarised, with judgements attached about individual managers' suitability or performance. The grid is intended as a simplified snapshot of a manager's preferred style, not a comprehensive description of his or her performance.

(c) Organisational context and culture, technology and other 'givens' influence the manager's style of leadership, not just the two dimensions described by the grid.

(d) Any managerial theory is only useful in so far as it is useable in practice by managers: if the grid is used only to inform managers that they 'must acquire greater concern for people', it may result in stress, uncertainty and inconsistent behaviour.

Activity 5 **(10 minutes)**

Here are some statements about a manager's approach to meetings. Which position on *Blake's* Grid do you think each might represent?

(a) I attend because it is expected. I either go along with the majority position or avoid expressing my views

(b) I try to come up with good ideas and push for a decision as soon as I can get a majority behind me. I don't mind stepping on people if it helps a sound decision

(c) I like to be able to support what my boss wants and to recognise the merits of individual effort. When conflict arises I do a good job of restoring harmony.

4 POWER, CONTROL, DELEGATION AND EMOTIONAL INTELLIGENCE

4.1 Power

Organisations feature a large number of different activities to be coordinated, and large numbers of people whose **cooperation and support** is necessary for the manager to get anything done. As you have probably noticed if you have worked for any length of time, organisations rarely run as clockwork, and all depend on the directed energy of those within them.

Definition

Power is the **ability** to get things done.

A manager without power, of whatever kind, cannot do his/her job properly, and this applies to leaders too. Power is not something a person has in isolation: it is exercised over other individuals or groups. Neither is it the exclusive preserve of managers.

Leadership and power are closely linked. People tend to follow those who are powerful. And because others follow, the person with power leads.

But leaders have power for different reasons. Some are powerful because they alone have the ability to increase your pay or give you a bonus. Others are powerful because they can assign you tasks that you are not fond of or dismiss you. Yet, while leaders of this type have formal, official power, their teams are unlikely to be enthusiastic about their approach to leadership, if these are all they rely on.

On the more positive side, leaders may have power because they are experts in their fields, or because their team members admire them. People with these types of power do not necessarily have formal leadership roles, but they influence others effectively because of their skills and personal qualities. And when a leadership position opens up, they will probably be the first to be considered for promotion.

4.2 French and Raven's five forms of power

One of the most notable studies on power was conducted by social psychologists John French and Bertram Raven in 1959. They identified five bases of power:

(a) **Legitimate** - this comes from the belief that a person has the right to make demands, and expect compliance and obedience from others. A president, prime minister, monarch and CEO has power. People holding these formal, official positions - or job titles - typically have power. Social hierarchies, cultural norms, and organisational structure all provide the basis for legitimate power. However, relying on legitimate power as your only way to influence others is not enough. To be a leader, you may not need legitimate power at all.

(b) **Reward** - this results from one person's ability to compensate another for compliance. People in power are often able to give out rewards. Raises, promotions, desirable assignments, training opportunities, and even simple compliments are all examples of rewards. The problem with this basis of power is that you may not have as much control over rewards as you need. Supervisors probably do not have complete control over salary increases, and managers often cannot control promotions all by themselves. And even a CEO needs permission from the board of directors for some actions. So when you use up available rewards, or the rewards do not have enough perceived value to others, your power weakens.

(c) **Expert** - this is based on a person's superior skill and knowledge. When you have knowledge and skills that enable you to understand a situation, suggest solutions, use solid judgement, and generally outperform others, people will probably listen to you. When you demonstrate expertise, people tend to trust you and respect what you say. As a subject matter expert, your ideas will have more value, and others will look to you for leadership in that area. This is one of the best ways to improve your leadership skills.

(d) **Referent** - this is sometimes thought of as charisma, charm, admiration, or appeal. Referent power comes from one person liking and respecting another, and strongly identifying with that person in some way. Celebrities have referent power, which is why they can influence everything from what people buy to whom they elect to office. In a workplace, a person with charm often makes everyone feel good, so he or she tends to have a lot of influence. Relying on referent power alone is not a good strategy for a leader who wants longevity and respect. When combined with other sources of power, however, it can help you achieve great success.

(e) **Coercive** - this comes from the belief that a person can punish others for non-compliance. Threats and punishment are common tools of coercion. Implying or threatening that someone will be fired, demoted, denied privileges, or given undesirable assignments are examples of using coercive power. While your position may give you the capability to coerce others, it does not automatically mean that you have the will or the justification to do so. As a last resort, you may sometimes need to punish people. However, extensive use of coercive power is rarely appropriate in an organisational setting.

If you are aware of these sources of power, you can.

- Understand why you are influenced by someone, and decide whether you want to accept the base of power being used.
- Recognise your own sources of power.
- Build your leadership skills by using and developing your own sources of power, appropriately, and for best effect.

4.2 Influence

Influence denotes any 'changes in behaviour of a person or group due to anticipation of the response of others'.

The term influence is often used in conjunction with other terms such as power and/or authority. In some cases, they are considered as mutually exclusive concepts, with influence covering those ways of influencing behaviour that cannot be termed power or authority. A range of ways to influence behaviour is outlined below.

(a) **Emulation** – although it requires no direct contact between individuals, it is a powerful influence on behaviour. People often pick out certain behaviour patterns and strive to equal or surpass them. In organisations, participants are aware of the behavioural patterns of co-workers and various executives. Certain individuals become 'models' with their behaviour patterns being adopted by others, hoping to attain similar success.

(b) **Suggestion** – is an explicit attempt to influence behaviour by presenting an idea or advocating a particular course of action. Typically this mode is used when several alternative behaviour patterns for individuals or groups are acceptable and the person influencing is merely suggesting a preferred pattern. If this tolerance for different behaviour were not present, the influencer would use some other mode such as persuasion or even coercion.

(c) **Persuasion** – implies urging and the use of some inducement in order to evoke the desired response. It involves more pressure than a mere suggestion but falls short of the type of force implied by the term coercion.

(d) **Coercion** – involves forcible constraint, which may include physical pressure (arm-twisting). In organisations, salaries and / or promotions can be used to constrain or influence behaviour. In many cases the threat of dismissal is also a powerful influencer.

More recently, the interest in corporate culture also recognises the importance of people identifying with their employer. One of the reasons this is important is that it makes conflict less likely, and therefore power in the traditional sense becomes less important. It is less necessary to exercise tight control over employees, and there is more scope for delegation.

Some, however, have argued that this is really power use in a more subtle form. Managers, by manipulating an organisation's culture are effectively influencing people's attitudes and beliefs, in the same way that politicians might use 'propaganda' to influence people. Managers are clearly much more able to achieve this than anyone else in the organisation. In so doing they may be able to get people to do the same things they could by using more overt power – the 'carrot and stick approach,' – but without any overt conflict. So, the ability to influence people in this way could be seen as a very effective form of power, even though it does not fit easily into the standard definition.

4.3 Authority

If an organisation is to function as a cooperative system of individuals, some people must have authority or power over others. Authority and power flow downwards through the formal organisation.

It is also important to know *Weber's* contribution to our understanding of authority. *Weber* identified three forms of authority.

(a) Traditional
(b) Charismatic
(c) Rational/legal

Traditional and charismatic authority are vested in particular individuals. Rational/legal authority is vested in an office (or the person occupying it for the time being). Traditional authority is vested in someone by virtue of tradition and custom. The most obvious examples are royalty. They are considered to be able to give orders (and have them obeyed) purely by virtue of their 'station in life', and not as a result of any abilities they might have. Charismatic authority is vested in someone by virtue of his or her personality. A religious leader, for example, might generate strong feelings of loyalty and commitment among his or her followers.

Where someone has authority, however, it is clearly a particularly useful form of power since you can expect your orders to be carried out without the implicit bargaining that is involved in the dependency model. Nevertheless, there are limits even to authority. If people make demands that are seen as unreasonable, this will eventually undermine their authority. If people give subordinates reason to believe they are not in fact well qualified for the job, their authority will be undermined. Authority is rarely, if ever, granted unconditionally.

4.4 Emotional intelligence

In a world of work where people are increasingly accepted to be the competitive edge, any idea that seems to offer the possibility of enabling them to work together more cooperatively and productively is likely to raise a great deal of interest. Writers on emotional intelligence have based their approaches very much around competencies.

Definition

> Emotional intelligence can be defined as "achieving one's goals through the ability to manage one's own feelings and emotions, being sensitive to and able to influence other key people and being able to balance one's motives and drives with conscientious and ethical behaviour.'

Higgs and Dulewicz from Henley Management College identified seven elements of emotional intelligence in their book *'Making sense of emotional intelligence'*:

1. self-awareness: being aware of one's feelings and managing them;
2. emotional resilience: being able to maintain one's performance when under pressure; balances task needs with individual and team needs;
3. motivation: having the drive and energy to attain challenging goals or targets;
4. inter-personal sensitivity: showing sensitivity and empathy towards others; builds awareness and achieves 'buy-in' to decisions;
5. influence: influencing and persuading others to accept one's views or proposals; provides rationale for change;
6. intuitiveness: making decisions using reason and intuition when appropriate;
7. conscientiousness: being consistent in one's words and actions, and behaving according to prevailing ethical standards.

These elements are broken down into the following three areas:

- **Drivers**: motivation and decisiveness, traits that energise people and drive them towards achieving goals.
- **Constrainers**: conscientiousness, integrity and emotional resilience, factors that control and curb the excesses of the drivers.
- **Enablers**: sensitivity, influence and self-awareness, traits that facilitate performance and help individuals to succeed.

While intelligence quotient (IQ) purely measures cognitive capacity, emotional intelligence is argued to involve emotional centres based in a different part of the brain working in harmony with the intellectual centres. People with good levels of emotional intelligence are said to be more able to manage and harness their emotions. They are also better able to understand other people's emotions, to communicate with them, relate to them and influence them.

Supporters of the concept claim that emotionally intelligent managers are (for example) better at resolving workplace conflict and are better negotiators and better leaders. All writers agree that emotional intelligence is not a substitute for IQ and technical and professional abilities. Managers need to be professionally competent first.

Higgs and Dulewicz argue that their components of emotional intelligence divide into two categories. The first category is those that people can clearly learn through established learning methods, such as personal development strategies like sensitivity, influence and self-awareness. The second category relates to the more enduring elements of an individual's personality that are more difficult to learn, like motivation, emotional resilience and conscientiousness. For this category, the development approach should consist of training strategies that exploit each individual's characteristics to the full and on developing 'coping strategies' that minimise the impact of potential limitations.

4.5 Control

Control is the general ability to direct and organise the efforts of the workforce. Different types of control have been identified.

(a) **Simple control** – refers to control by straightforward direct supervision.

(b) **Technical control** – refers to control that is imposed by the technology used in a factory. For example, the pace at which people must work on a production line is determined in part by the speed at which the line runs. The use of power here is more subtle, but is nevertheless clearly in the hands of the managers that control the technology.

(c) **Bureaucratic control** – refers to control by means of formal rules and regulations. Bureaucratic organisations typically have large books of rules that specify things like hours of work, entitlement to time off under various circumstances (eg annual leave, compassionate leave, maternity leave, etc.), grievance procedures, and so on). There are also rules or 'standard operating procedures' that people must follow in the course of their work. This form of control involves a still more subtle form of power. One might almost think of the rules as having a sort of authority, legitimated by people's understanding about the way in which the rules were derived – typically assumed to be some sort of 'rational' process. Further legitimacy might be obtained by the involvement of employee representatives in writing the rules.

The exercise of control is also an expression of leadership style and systems of management. The style of managerial leadership is a function of the manager's attitudes towards people and assumptions about human nature and behaviour eg, *McGregor's* Theory X and Theory Y.

***McGregor's* Theory X and Theory Y**

Douglas McGregor, defined two opposing images of human nature, which he called **Theory X** and **Theory Y** and suggested that the style of supervision or management adopted would depend on the view taken as to how subordinates behave.

He proposed an authoritarian–democratic approach to management style. His **Theory X** manager – the **authoritarian** – is tough and supports tight controls with punishment/reward systems. The contrasting style is that of the **Theory Y** manager – the **democrat** – who is benevolent, participative and a believer of self-controls.

The central principle of Theory X is that people have an inherent hatred of work, and as such must be cajoled, coerced (*Etzioni*), directed, threatened and even punished if corporate objectives are to be achieved. In many instances people prefer to be directed, wish to avoid responsibility, and prefer security rather than satisfying ambition. Blake's grid would show managers having a high score on the 'concern for production' axis.

The basis of Theory Y is that people do not hate work and find it a natural function. They are motivated on their own initiative and will strive for *Maslow's* self-actualisation. There is some support for Theory Y. If the right conditions can be developed for employees to work and satisfy their personal ambitions within their work, then high levels of motivation and productivity can be achieved. Theory Y is about creating a climate whereby people will motivate themselves. Blake's grid would show managers will have a high score on the 'concern for people' axis.

4.6 Delegation

Leadership is the art of getting someone else to do something you want done because he/she wants to do it. This is delegation of authority and it refers to the successful transfer of authority to someone else.

We begin our discussion of delegation with an investigation into the nature of authority.

Definition

Authority is the *right* of a person to ask someone else to do something and expect it to be done. Authority is thus another word for 'position power'.

Managerial authority consists of:

(a) **Making decisions within the scope of authority** given to the position. For example, a supervisor's authority is limited to his/her team and with certain limits. For items of expenditure more than a certain amount, the supervisor may have to go to someone else higher up the hierarchy.

(b) **Assigning tasks** to subordinates, and expecting satisfactory performance of these tasks.

Activity 6 **(15 minutes)**

What types of authority and power are being exercised in the following case?

Marcus is an accountant supervising a team of eight technicians. He has to submit bank reconciliation statements every week to the chief accountant. However, the company runs four different bank accounts and Marcus gets a team member, Dave, to do it for him.

Marcus asks Isabella to deal with the purchase ledger – the company obtains supplies from all over the world, and Isabella, having worked once for an international bank, is familiar with letters of credit and other documentation involved with overseas trade. Isabella has recently told Marcus that Maphia Ltd, a supplier, should not be paid because of problems with the import documentation, even though Marcus has promised Maphia to pay them.

Marcus is getting increasingly annoyed with Sandra, the departmental PA, who seems to be leaving Marcus's typing until last, although she says she has piles of other work to do. 'Like reading the newspaper,' thinks Marcus, who is considering pulling rank by giving her an oral warning.

Definition

> **Line authority** is the authority a manager has over a subordinate, arising from their respective positions in the organisation hierarchy. In other words, if you have line authority you an exercise position power over someone immediately below you.

There are other forms of authority which individuals (or departments) may exercise in the organisation.

Definition

> **Staff authority** is the influence wielded when an expert gives specialist **advice** to another manager or department, even if there is no direct line authority. (An example might be the influence of legal advice from the legal department, or advice on budgetary constraints from the accounts department.)

Definition

> **Functional authority** is staff authority which has been built into the structure and policies of the organisation, for example where a specialist department lays down *procedures* and *rules* for other departments to follow within the area of its expertise. (The Personnel/HR department, for example, may impose certain recruitment and selection procedures on other departments.)

Definition

> **Delegation** of authority is when a superior gives to a subordinate part of his or her own authority to make decisions.

Note that delegation can only occur if the superior initially possesses the authority to delegate; a subordinate cannot be given organisational authority to make decisions unless it would otherwise be the superior's right to make those decisions personally.

Managers and leaders must delegate some authority because:

(a) There are **physical and mental limitations** to the work load of any individual or group in authority.

(b) Managers and leaders are free to **concentrate on the aspects of the work** (such as planning), which only they are competent (and paid) to do.

(c) The **increasing size and complexity** of some organisations calls for specialisation, both managerial and technical.

However, by delegating authority to assistants, the supervisor takes on the extra tasks of:

- **Monitoring their performance**
- **Coordinating** the efforts of different assistants.

The process of delegation is as follows.

Step 1 **Specify the expected performance** levels of the assistant, keeping in mind the assistant's level of expertise.

Step 2 **Formally assign tasks** to the assistant, who should formally agree to do them.

Step 3 **Allocate resources and authority** to the assistant to enable him or her to carry out the delegated tasks at the expected level of performance.

Step 4 **Maintain contact** with the assistant to review the progress made and to make constructive criticism. **Feedback** is essential for control, and also as part of the learning process.

Remember that ultimate **accountability** for the task remains with the leader: if it is not well done it is at least partly the fault of poor delegation, and it is still the leader's responsibility to get it re-done.

Disadvantages of delegation

Of course there are problems with delegation.

Many managers and leaders are **reluctant to delegate** and attempt to do many routine matters themselves in addition to their more important duties.

(a) **Low confidence and trust** in the abilities of their staff: the suspicion that 'if you want it done well, you have to do it yourself'.

(b) The burden of **accountability for the mistakes of subordinates**, aggravated by (a) above.

(c) A **desire to 'stay in touch**' with the department or team – both in terms of workload and staff – particularly if the manager does not feel 'at home' in a management role.

(d) **Feeling threatened.** An unwillingness to admit that assistants have developed to the extent that they could perform some of the leader's duties. The leader may feel threatened by this sense of 'redundancy'.

(e) **Poor control and communication systems** in the organisation, so that the manager feels he has to do everything himself, if he is to retain real control and responsibility for a task, and if he wants to know what is going on.

(f) An **organisational culture** that has failed to reward or recognise effective delegation, so that the manager may not realise that delegation is positively regarded (rather than as shirking responsibility).

(g) **Lack of understanding** of what delegation involves – not giving assistants total control, or making the manager himself redundant.

To overcome the reluctance of manager to delegate:

(a) **Train the subordinates** so that they are capable of handling delegated authority in a responsible way. If assistants are of the right 'quality', supervisors will be prepared to trust them more.

(b) Have a system of **open communications,** in which the leader and assistants freely interchange ideas and information. If the assistant is given all the information needed to do the job, and if the supervisor is aware of what the assistant is doing:

(i) The assistant will make better-informed decisions.

(ii) The supervisor will not panic because he does not know what is going on.

(c) **Ensure that a system of control is established**. If responsibility and accountability are monitored at all levels of the management hierarchy, the dangers of relinquishing authority and control to assistants are significantly lessened.

5 IMPACT OF LEADERSHIP STYLES

5.1 Style and effectiveness

Much has been written on the subject of what constitutes good leadership but it is probably most true to say that the effectiveness of leaders is best measured by looking at the impact they have on the performance of those they lead. Excellent leadership can deliver results from an organisation well above what could reasonably be predicted, while at the same time morale among employees is high; conversely, poor leadership often results in under performing businesses, unhappy employees and highly defensive organisational behaviours.

Rensis Likert's research showed that **effective managers** display each of the four characteristics below, in relation to leadership skills. Such managers:

(a) **Expect high levels of performance** from subordinates, other departments and themselves.

(b) **Are employee-centred.** They spend time getting to know their workers and develop a situation of trust whereby their employees feel able to bring their problems to them. Such managers face unpleasant facts in a constructive manner and help their staff to do the same.

(c) **Do not practise close supervision.** The truly effective manager knows performance levels that can be expected from each individual and has helped them to define their own targets. The manager judges results and does not closely supervise the actions of subordinates.

(d) **Operate the participative style of management as a natural style.** If a job problem arises they do not impose a favoured solution. Instead, they pose the problem and ask the staff member involved to find the best solution. Having then agreed their solution the participative manager would assist his staff in implementing it.

5.2 Organisational climate and culture

Organisational climate is directly related to the leadership and management style of the leader, based on the values, attributes, skills, and actions, as well as the priorities of the leader. The ethical climate then is the 'feel of the organisation' about the activities that have ethical content or those aspects of the work environment that constitute ethical behaviour. The ethical climate is the feel about whether we do things right; or the feel of whether we behave the way we ought to behave. The behaviour (character) of the leader is the most important factor that impacts the climate.

On the other hand, culture is a long-term, complex phenomenon. Culture represents the shared expectations and self-image of the organisation. The mature values that create 'tradition' or the 'way we do things here.' Things are done differently in every organisation. The collective vision and common folklore that define the institution are a reflection of culture. Individual leaders cannot easily create or change culture because culture is a part of the organisation. Culture influences the characteristics of the climate by its effect on the actions and thought processes of the leader. But, everything a leader does will affect the climate of the organisation. It also influences the decision-making processes, the styles of management and what everyone determines as success.

Research published in the March–April 2000 *Harvard Business Review* (*Goleman*, 'Leadership that gets results') investigated how each of six distinctive leadership styles correlated with specific components of an organisation's culture.

These cultural components are:

- **Flexibility** – employees' ability to innovate without excessive rules and regulations
- **Responsibility** – how responsible employees feel towards the organisation
- **Standards** – the level of standards expected in the organisation
- **Rewards** – the accuracy of performance feedback and rewards
- **Clarity** – how clear employees are about the mission, vision and core values
- **Commitment** – employees' commitment to a common purpose

Daniel Goleman suggests that effective leaders choose from six distinctive leadership styles.

(i) **Coercive** (Do what I tell you) – this describes a leader that demands immediate compliance. This style can destroy an organisational culture and should only be used with extreme caution. It is useful in an emergency, and may work in a crisis or as a last resort with a problem employee. This leadership style has the most negative impact on the overall organisational culture.

(ii) **Pacesetting** (Do as I do, now) – describes a leader who sets extremely high standards for performance. This style can also destroy a good culture and only works with a highly motivated and competent team who are able to 'read' the leader's mind. Others will feel overwhelmed and give up because they cannot see themselves reaching unrealistic standards. This style also has a negative impact on the overall organisational culture, especially on rewards and commitment.

(iii) **Coaching** (Try this) – describes a leader who is focused on developing people for the future. These leaders are good at delegating, and are willing to put up with short-term failures, provided they lead to long-term development. This style works best when wanting to help employees improve their performance or develop their long-term strengths and has a positive impact on the overall organisational culture.

(iv) **Democratic** (What do you think?) – describes a leader who achieves consensus thorough participation. This style builds trust, respect and commitment, and works best when wanting to receive input or get employees to 'buy-in' or achieve consensus. If handled correctly, this style has a positive impact on the overall organisational culture.

(v) **Affiliative** (People come first) – this describes a leader who is interested in creating harmony and building emotional bonds with employees. This style works best when motivating employees, building team harmony, improving communication, increasing morale or repairing broken trust and has a positive impact on the overall organisational culture. Because this style has virtually no downside, it is often described as the best overall approach.

(vi) **Authoritative** (Come with me) – describes a visionary leader who gives people lots of scope to innovate and take calculated risks, provided that they move in the direction of the stated vision. This style works best when change requires a new vision or when employees are looking for a new direction but fails when employees are more knowledgeable or experienced than the leader, or if the authoritative style becomes overbearing. Provided that it is used subtly, this style has the most positive impact on the overall organisational culture.

Activity 7 **(15 minutes)**

In your career so far, you might have worked for a number of managers. Jot down the following features of each situation on a scale of 1 to 5 for comparative purposes.

(a) The degree to which you had autonomy over your own work.

(b) The degree to which you were consulted on decisions that affected you.

(c) The degree to which your advice was sought about decisions affecting your section.

If you worked for managers who had different approaches to these issues, do you think these approaches influenced your effectiveness? What score to questions (a), (b) and (c) would you give your ideal boss? and your current boss?

5.3 Leadership and vision

Leadership is a dynamic process in a group (or team), where one individual influences the others to contribute voluntarily to the achievement of group tasks in a given situation. The role of the leader is to direct the group towards their goals.

Leadership starts with having a vision of the future, then developing a plan to achieve it.

In the literature concerning leadership, vision has a variety of definitions, all of which include a mental image or picture, a future orientation, and aspects of direction or goal. Vision provides guidance to an organisation by articulating what it wishes to attain. By providing a picture, vision not only describes an organisation's direction or goal, but also the means of accomplishing it. It has a compelling aspect that serves to inspire, motivate, and engage people. It answers the questions: Who is involved? What do they plan to accomplish? Why are they doing this? Vision therefore does more than provide a picture of a desired future; it encourages people to work, to strive for its attainment.

Given a clear vision and a strategy the leader can empower people to achieve the goals. Empowerment means giving employees control of the decision-making process and allowing them to be independent of the leader.

5.4 Empowerment

Empowerment and delegation are related.

Definition

> **Empowerment** is the current term for making workers (and particularly work teams) responsible for achieving, and even setting, work targets, with the freedom to make decisions about how they are to be achieved.

Empowerment goes in hand in hand with:

(a) **Delayering** or a cut in the number of levels (and managers) in the chain of command, since responsibility previously held by middle managers is, in effect, being given to operational workers.

(b) **Flexibility**, since giving responsibility to the people closest to the products and customers encourages responsiveness – and cutting out layers of communication, decision-making and reporting speeds up the process.

(c) **New technology**, since there are more 'knowledge workers'. Such people need less supervision, being better able to identify and control the means to clearly understood ends. Better information systems also remove the mystique and power of managers as possessors of knowledge and information in the organisation.

According to *Max Hand*, the main reason for empowerment is the people lower down the organisation possess the knowledge of what is going wrong with a process but lack the authority to make changes. Those further up the structure have the authority to make changes, but lack the profound knowledge required to identify the right solutions. The only solution is to change the culture of the organisation so that everyone can become involved in the process of improvement and work together to make the changes.'

The change in organisation structure and culture as a result of empowerment can be shown below.

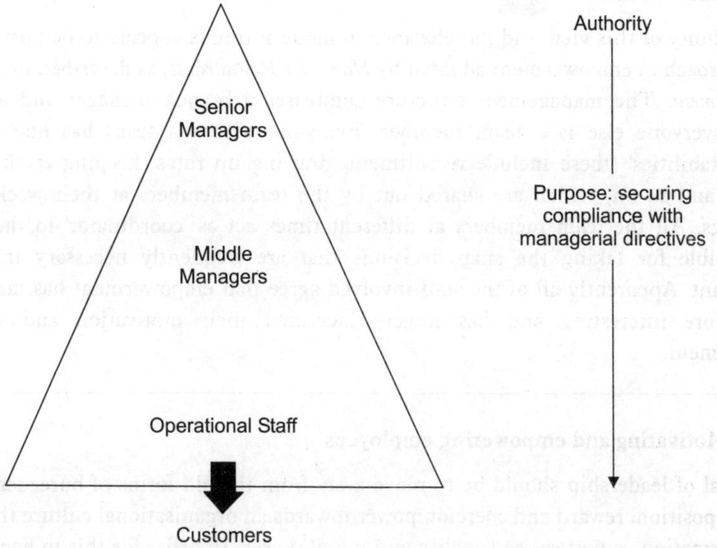

Traditional hierarchical structure: fulfilling management requirements

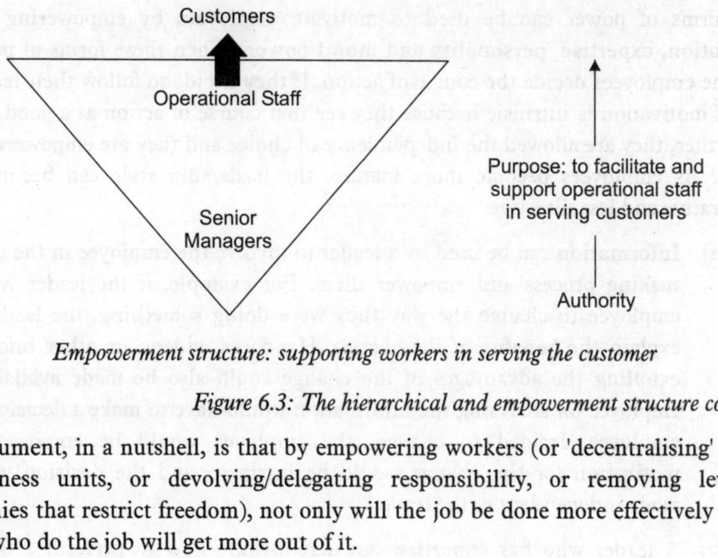

Empowerment structure: supporting workers in serving the customer

Figure 6.3: The hierarchical and empowerment structure compared

The argument, in a nutshell, is that by empowering workers (or 'decentralising' control of business units, or devolving/delegating responsibility, or removing levels in hierarchies that restrict freedom), not only will the job be done more effectively but the people who do the job will get more out of it.

CASE EXAMPLE

The validity of this view and its relevance to modern trends appears to be borne out by the approach to empowerment adopted by *Harvester Restaurants*, as described in *Personnel Management*. The management structure comprises a branch manager and a 'coach', while everyone else is a team member. Everyone within a team has one or more 'accountabilities' (these include recruitment, drawing up rotas, keeping track of sales targets and so on) which are shared out by the team members at their weekly team meetings. All the team members at different times act as 'coordinator' to the person responsible for taking the snap decisions that are frequently necessary in a busy restaurant. Apparently all of the staff involved agree that empowerment has made their jobs more interesting and has hugely increased their motivation and sense of involvement.

5.5 Motivating and empowering employees

The goal of leadership should be to move away from the old forms of bureaucracy that rely on position, reward and coercion power towards an organisational culture that relies on information, expertise, personality and moral power. In order for this to happen, the leader has to be less controlling.

Four forms of power can be used to motivate employees by empowering them – **information, expertise, personality** and **moral power**. When these forms of power are used, the employees decide the course of action. If they decide to follow their leader, the form of motivation is intrinsic because they see that course of action as a good thing to do. Further, they are allowed the independence of choice and they are empowered in the process. As employees become more mature, the leadership style can become more collaborative and less directive.

(a) **Information** can be used by a leader to involve the employee in the decision-making process and empower them. For example, if the leader wants the employee to change the way they were doing something, the leader could explain the benefits of the change. Handouts, videos, or other information extolling the advantages of the change could also be made available. The employee on analysing the information would have to make a decision. If the employee decided to change, the employee would be empowered, the motivation for the change would be intrinsic, and the decision would be made independent of the leader.

(b) A leader who has **expertise** can demonstrate how to perform a task. The employee who watches the demonstration decides whether they are able to perform that task. Competence or expertise is the root of power and leaders without competence cannot maintain power. However, a leader cannot be expert in all things. Consequently, he or she must use the expertise of others to motivate employees to change. For example, if a new technique will benefit an organisation, the leader needs to send key employees to another place where that technique is being successfully used. The employees observe the new process and decide whether it is beneficial and if it will work in their organisation. Employees who are exposed to this form of power frequently choose to imitate what they have observed. It is their choice, the motivation is intrinsic, they are independent of the person with the expertise, and they have been empowered.

(c) A leader who has **personality** or referent power is described as a person who is generally liked and admired by others because of it. When a leader uses this form of power it usually comes in the form of a request (verbal) or a signal (non-verbal). The subordinate hears the request or sees the signal and changes their behaviour to comply with the leader's wishes. The change in behaviour is done willingly, is intrinsically motivated, and the employee remains independent of the leader. The employee has made a conscious decision to grant the leader's wishes.

(d) A leader who has **moral power** has communicated a shared set of values and obligations which lay out the right thing to do for the good of employees, the organisation, the stakeholders and possibly the community as a whole. These values may be set out as a mission statement or vision, possibly arrived at through discussion with followers and explained through procedures, rules and regulations. This type of power requires the least maintenance as following the standards laid down becomes a matter for the individual's conscience and will be enforced through personal values, peer pressure and organisational culture.

5.6 Leadership and change

Change can be classified into two categories – planned and unplanned.

- **Planned change** – is a deliberate and conscious effort designed to meet forthcoming input changes that can be seen or predicted. For example, changes in the buying patterns or customer requirements.
- **Unplanned change** – is thrust upon the organisation by environmental events beyond its control. For example, changes in the bank rate, sudden changes in the value of a currency, unexpected scarcity of a raw material or a serious fire.

The role of the leader is to anticipate the need for change, create an atmosphere of acceptance of change and manage the stages of introduction and implementation. He or she can expect resistance to change since all major changes threaten somebody's security or somebody's status.

One of the most important factors in the successful implementation of organisational change is the style of managerial behaviour. In certain situations, and with certain members of staff, it may be necessary for leaders to make use of hierarchical authority and attempt to impose change through a coercive, autocratic style of behaviour. In most cases, however, the introduction of change is more likely to be effective with a participative style of behaviour. If staff are kept informed of proposals, are encouraged to adopt a positive attitude and have personal involvement in the implementation of the change, there is a greater likelihood of their acceptance of the change.

Chapter roundup

- Leadership is the process of influencing others to work willingly towards the achievement of organisational goals.
- There are many different definitions of leadership. Key themes (which are also used to distinguish leadership from management) include interpersonal influence, securing willing commitment to shared goals, creating direction and energy and an orientation to change.
- There are three basic schools of leadership theory: trait theories, style theories and contingency theories.
- Leadership styles are clusters of leadership behaviour that are used in different ways in different situations. While there are many different classifications of style, they mainly relate to the extent to which the leader is focused primarily on task/performance (directive behaviour) or relationships/people (supportive behaviour).
- Leaders need to adapt their style to the needs of the team and the situation. This is the basis of contingency approaches such as Handy's best 'fit' model.
- Power is the ability to get things done. There are many types of power in organisations: position or legitimate power, expert power, personal power, resource power and negative power.
- Emotional intelligence means achieving one's goals through the ability to manage one's own feelings and emotions, being sensitive to and able to influence other key people and being able to balance one's motives and drives with conscientious and ethical behaviour.
- Authority is the right to take certain decisions within boundaries.
- Empowerment means giving employees control of the decision-making process and allowing them to be independent of the leader.

Quick quiz

1. How do people become leaders in a group or situation?
2. What type of task makes tight control a suitable style?
3. What is the difference between a 'sells' and 'consults' style of management?
4. What factors in the environment influence the choice of a tight or loose style?
5. What might be the disadvantages of a 'tells' style of management?
6. Why is consistency of management style important, and why might this be a problem?
7. Do teams need to have a leader? Would they be as effective without one?
8. What is the most effective style suggested by *Blake and Mouton's* managerial grid; why is it so effective in theory? Why might it not be effective in practice?
9. What is the difference between power and authority?
10. What is expert power?

Answers to quick quiz

1 Through different forms of influence such a vision, inspiration and motivation.

2 Those which lack initiative, are routine, trivial or have a short time scale.

3 'Sells' – the manager still makes all decisions but explains them to subordinates to get them to carry them out willingly. 'Consults' – the manager confers with subordinates, takes their views and feelings into account, but retains the right to make the final decision.

4 The position of power held by the leader, organisational norms, structure and technology, the variety of tasks and subordinates.

5 'Telling' is one-way, there is no feedback. It does not encourage contributions or initiative.

6 Inconsistency results in subordinates feeling unsure and distrusting the manager.

7 Someone has to ensure the objective is achieved, make decisions and share out resources. If everyone on the team is equally able and willing to do these things (unlikely in practice) a good information system is probably all that is needed, not a leader.

8 It is effective if there is sufficient time and resources to attend fully to people needs, if the manager is good at dealing with people and if the people respond. It is ineffective when a task has to be completed in a certain way or by a certain deadline even if people don't like it.

9 Authority is the right to do something; power is the ability to do it.

10 Power based on the acknowledgement of expertise.

Answers to activities

1 Categorisation of different behaviour on smelling smoke in a cinema is as follows.

(a) Behavioural contagion: people are simply copying you, without any conscious intention to lead on your part.

(b) Management. You are dealing with logistics: planning and organising. You are not, however, concerned with influencing the people: they simply respond to the situation.

(c) Leadership. You intend to mobilise others in pursuit of your aims, and you succeed in doing so.

(d) Whatever it is, it isn't leadership – because you have gained no followers.

2 This will depend on your own observations and opinions.

3 The environment can be improved for leaders if senior management ensure that:

(a) Managers are given a clear role and the power (over resources and information) to back it up

(b) Organisational norms can be broken without fear of punishment: the organisation culture is adaptive and managers can change things if required

(c) The organisational structure is not rigid and inflexible: managers can redesign task and team arrangements

(d) Team members are selected or developed so that they are, as far as possible, of the same 'type' in terms of their attitudes to work and supervision

(e) Labour turnover is reduced as far as possible (by having acceptable work conditions and terms, for example) so that the team does not constantly have to adjust to new members or leaders.

4 Styles of management suggested in the situations described, using the tells-sells-consults-joins model.

(a) You may have to 'tell' here: nobody is going to like the idea and, since each person will have his or her own interests at heart, you are unlikely to reach consensus. You could attempt to 'sell', if you can see a positive side to the change in particular cases: opportunities for retraining, say.

(b) You could 'consult' here: explain your remedy to staff and see whether they can suggest potential problems. They may be in a position to offer solutions – and since the problem affects them too, they should be committed to solving it.

(c) We prefer a 'joins' style here, since the team's acceptance of the decision is more important than the details of the decision itself.

(d) We would go for 'consult' despite the staff's apparent reluctance to participate. They may prefer you to 'tell' – but may resist decisions they disagree with anyway. Perhaps their reluctance is to do with lack of confidence – or lack of trust that you will take their input seriously, in which case, persistent use of a 'consults' style may encourage them. You could use a 'sells' approach initially, to get them used to a less authoritarian style than they seem to expect.

5 *Blake's* Grid positioning of the given managerial approaches are:

(a) 1.1: low task, low people
(b) 9.1: High task, low people
(c) 1.9: high people, low task

6 Marcus exercises position power because he has the right, given to him by the chief accountant, to get his staff, such as Dave, to do bank reconciliations. Dave does not do bank recs because of Marcus's personality or expertise, but because of the simple fact that Marcus is his boss. Marcus also exercises position power by getting Isabella to do the purchase ledger. However, Isabella exercises expert power because she knows more about import/export documentation than Marcus. She does not have the authority to stop the payment to Maphia, and Marcus can ignore what she says, but that would be a bad decision. Sandra is exercising negative power as far as Marcus is concerned, although she is claiming, perhaps, to exercise resource power – her time is a scarce resource. No-one appears to be exercising physical power as such, although Marcus's use of the disciplinary procedures would be a type of coercive power.

7 This will depend on your own experience.

Chapter 7 :

BUILD WINNING TEAMS

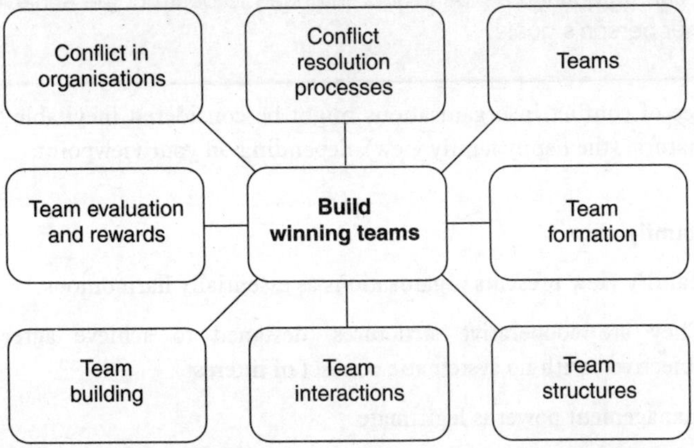

Introduction

The outcome of this chapter is for you to be able to develop an understanding of how to build winning teams. We begin by looking at the existence of conflict in organisations from different viewpoints and discuss the causes and outcomes of it. Management responses to the handling of conflict range from denial to encouraging cooperation. The win-win model identifies three ways to approach conflict resolution.

Teams have been described as collections of people who must rely on group collaboration if each member is to experience the optimum of success. We identify the mix of knowledge, skills and experience necessary for a team to fulfil its functions. The process known as team building or team maintenance has become an important element in helping work groups to function more effectively and we will be looking at some of the skills and methods used in the process.

Your objectives

After completing this chapter you should be able to:

(a) assess the benefits of teamworking for an organisation

(b) demonstrate working in a team as a leader and member towards specific goals, dealing with any conflict or difficult situations

(c) review the effectiveness of the team in achieving the goals

1 CONFLICT IN ORGANISATIONS

1.1 Differing perspectives

Definition

> **Conflict** can be defined as 'behaviour intended to obstruct the achievement of some other person's goals.

The existence of conflict in organisations might be considered inevitable (the conflict view) or unnatural (the happy family view), depending on your viewpoint.

The happy family view

The happy family view presents organisations as essentially harmonious

- They are cooperative structures, designed to achieve agreed common objectives, with no systematic conflict of interest
- Management power is legitimate
- Conflicts are exceptional and arise from aberrant incidents, such as misunderstandings, clashes of personality and external influences

This kind of view is reasonably common in managerial literature, which attempts to come up with training and motivational techniques for dealing with conflicts that arise in what are seen as potentially 'conflict-free' organisations. Conflict is thus blamed on bad management, lack of leadership, poor communication, or 'bloody-mindedness' on the part of individuals or interest groups that impinge on the organisation. The theory is that a strong culture, good two-way communication, cooperation and motivational leadership will eliminate conflict. Cooperation is assumed to be desirable and achievable.

The conflict view

The conflict view in contrast, sees organisations as arenas for conflict on individual and group levels. Members battle for limited resources, status, rewards and professional values. Organisational politics involve constant struggles for control, and choices of structure, technology and organisational goals are part of this process. Individual and organisational interests will not always coincide.

Organisations may be seen as political coalitions of individuals and groups that have their own interests. Management has to create a workable structure for collaboration, taking into account the objectives of all the stakeholders in the organisation. A mutual survival strategy, involving the control of conflict through compromise, can be made acceptable in varying degrees to all concerned.

Activity 1 **(15 minutes)**

How accurate is the 'happy family' perspective when applied to your own organisation, or to any organisation with which you are sufficiently familiar?

To what extent would you subscribe to the claim that the 'happy family' view is publicised by managers within their own organisations, not so much as an accurate description of reality, but rather because adoption of the 'happy family' perspective itself helps to reduce the level of articulated conflict?

The 'evolutionary' view

This view regards conflict as a means of **maintaining the status quo**, as a useful basis for **evolutionary change.**

- **Conflict** keeps the organisation **sensitive to the need to change**, while reinforcing its essential framework of control.
- The **legitimate pursuit of competing interests** can balance and preserve social and organisational arrangements.

The constructive conflict view

This '**constructive conflict**' view may perhaps be the most useful for managers and administrators of organisations, as it neither:

(a) Attempts to dodge the issues of conflict, which is an observable fact of life in most organisations; nor

(b) Seeks to pull down existing organisational structures altogether.

Conflict can be highly desirable. Conflict is constructive, when its effect is to:

- Introduce different **solutions** to problems
- **Define power relationships** more clearly
- Encourage **creativity**, the testing of ideas
- **Focus attention** on individual contributions
- **Bring emotions** out into the open
- **Release hostile feelings** that have been, or may be, repressed otherwise

Conflict can also be destructive. It may:

- **Distract attention** from the task
- **Polarise** views and 'dislocate' the group
- Subvert **objectives** in favour of secondary goals
- Encourage **defensive** or 'spoiling' behaviour
- Force the group to **disintegrate**
- Stimulate emotional, **win-lose conflicts**, ie hostility

1.2 Conflict between groups

Conflicts of interest may exist throughout the organisation – or even for a single individual. There may be conflicts of interest between local management of a branch or subsidiary and the organisation as a whole.

- Sales and production departments in a manufacturing firm (over scheduling, product variation)
- Trade unions and management.

Interest groups such as trade unions tend to wield greater power in conflict situations than their members as individuals. Trade Unions are organisations whose purpose it is to promote their members' interests. (Strike action has to be preceded by a ballot.)

Activity 2 **(10 minutes)**

What other examples of 'conflicts of interest' can you identify within an organisation? Having selected some instances, can you detect any common patterns in such conflicts?

CASE EXAMPLE

Conflict can also operate **within** groups.

In an experiment reported by *Deutsch* (1949), psychology students were given puzzles and human relation problems to work at in discussion groups. Some groups ('cooperative' ones) were told that the grade each individual got at the end of the course would depend on the performance of his group. Other groups ('competitive' ones) were told that each student would receive a grade according to his own contributions.

No significant differences were found between the two kinds of group in the amount of interest and involvement in the tasks, or in the amount of learning. But the cooperative groups, compared with the competitive ones, had greater productivity per unit time, better quality of product and discussion, greater coordination of effort and sub-division of activity, more diversity in amount of contribution per member, more attentiveness to fellow members and more friendliness during discussion.

1.3 Conflict and competition

Sherif and Sherif conducted a number of experiments into groups and competing groups.

(a) People tend to identify with a group.

(b) New members of a group quickly learn the norms and attitudes of the others, no matter whether these are 'positive' or 'negative', friendly or hostile.

(c) When a group competes, this is what happens to it **within the group**.

(i) Members close ranks, and submerge their differences; loyalty and conformity are demanded.

(ii) The 'climate' changes from informal and sociable to work and task-oriented; individual needs are subordinated to achievement.

(iii) Leadership moves from democratic to autocratic, with the group's acceptance.

(iv) The group tends to become more structured and organised.

(v) The opposing group begins to be perceived as 'the enemy'.

(vi) Perception is distorted, presenting an idealised picture of 'us' and a negative stereotype of 'them'.

(vii) Communication between groups decreases.

In a 'win-lose' situation, where competition is not perceived to result in benefits for both sides.

(a) The **winning** group will:

(i) Retain its cohesion
(ii) Relax into a complacent, playful state
(iii) Return to group maintenance and concern for members' needs
(iv) Be confirmed in its group 'self-concept' with little re-evaluation

(b) The **losing** group might behave as follows.

(i) Deny defeat if possible, or place the blame on the arbitrator, or the system

(ii) Lose its cohesion and splinter into conflict, as 'blame' is apportioned.

(iii) Be keyed-up, fighting mad.

(iv) Turn towards work-orientation to regroup, rather than members' needs or group maintenance.

(v) Tend to learn by re-evaluating its perceptions of itself and the other group. It is more likely to become a cohesive and effective unit once the 'defeat' has been accepted.

Members of a group will act in unison if the group's existence or patterns of behaviour are threatened from outside. Cohesion is naturally assumed to be the result of positive factors such as communication, agreement and mutual trust – but in the face of a 'common enemy' (competition, crisis or emergency) cohesion and productivity benefit.

Activity 3 **(10 minutes)**

How applicable are *Sherifs'* 1965 research findings to the cause, symptoms and treatment of conflict in a modern organisation? In what ways, if at all, could *Sherifs'* findings be used as a means of improving employee performance within an organisation?

1.4 Causes of conflict

(a) **Differences in the objectives** of different groups or individuals.

(b) **Scarcity of resources.**

(c) **Interdependence of two departments** on a task. They have to work together but may do so ineffectively.

(d) **Disputes about the boundaries of authority.**

(i) The technostructure may attempt to encroach on the roles or 'territory' of line managers and usurp some of their authority.

(ii) One department might start '**empire building**' and try to take over the work previously done by another department.

(e) **Personal differences,** as regards goals, attitudes and feelings, are also bound to crop up. This is especially true in **differentiated organisations,** where people employed in the different sub-units are very different.

1.5 Symptoms of conflict

- Poor communications, in all 'directions'
- Interpersonal friction
- Inter-group rivalry and jealousy
- Low morale and frustration
- Widespread use of arbitration, appeals to higher authority, and inflexible attitudes

1.6 The tactics of conflict

(a) **Withholding information** from one another

(b) **Distorting information.** This will enable the group or manager presenting the information to get their own way more easily.

(c) **Empire building.** A group (especially a specialist group such as research) which considers its influence to be neglected might seek to impose rules, procedures, restrictions or official requirements on other groups, in order to bolster up their own importance.

(d) **Informal organisation.** A manager might seek to by-pass formal channels of communication and decision-making by establishing informal contacts and friendships with people in a position of importance.

(e) **Fault-finding** in the work of other departments: department X might duplicate the work of department Y – hoping to prove department Y 'wrong' – and then report the fact to senior management.

2 CONFLICT RESOLUTION PROCESSES

2.1 Management responses to the handling of conflict

Not all of these are effective.

Response	Comment
Denial/ withdrawal	'Sweeping it under the carpet'. If the conflict is very trivial, it may indeed blow over without an issue being made of it, but if the causes are not identified, the conflict may grow to unmanageable proportions.

Response	Comment
Suppression	'Smoothing over', to preserve working relationships despite minor conflicts. As *Hunt* remarks, however: 'Some cracks cannot be papered over'.
Dominance	The application of power or influence to settle the conflict. The disadvantage of this is that it creates all the lingering resentment and hostility of 'win-lose' situations.
Compromise	Bargaining, negotiating, conciliating. To some extent, this will be inevitable in any organisation made up of different individuals. However, individuals tend to exaggerate their positions to allow for compromise, and compromise itself is seen to weaken the value of the decision, perhaps reducing commitment. **Negotiation** is: 'a process of interaction by which two or more parties who consider they need to be jointly involved in an outcome, but who initially have different objectives seek by the use of argument and persuasion to resolve their differences in order to achieve a mutually acceptable solution'.
Integration/ collaboration	Emphasis must be put on the task, individuals must accept the need to modify their views for its sake, and group effort must be seen to be superior to individual effort.
Encourage cooperative behaviour	Joint problem-solving team, goals set for all teams/departments to follow.

Activity 4 **(25 minutes)**

In the light of the above consider how conflict could arise, what form it would take and how it might be resolved in the following situations.

(a) Two managers who share a secretary have documents to be typed.

(b) One worker finds out that another worker who does the same job as he does is paid a higher wage.

(c) A company's electricians find out that a group of engineers have been receiving training in electrical work.

(d) Department A stops for lunch at 12.30 while Department B stops at 1 o'clock. Occasionally the canteen runs out of puddings for Department B workers.

(e) The Northern Region and Southern Region sales teams are continually trying to better each others results, and the capacity of production to cope with the increase in sales is becoming overstretched.

2.2 The win-win model

One useful model of conflict resolution is the **win-win model**. This states that there are three basic ways in which a conflict or disagreement can be worked out.

Method	Frequency	Explanation
Win-lose	This is quite common.	**One party gets what (s)he wants at the expense of the other party**: for example, Department A gets the new photocopier, while Department B keeps the old one (since there were insufficient resources to buy two new ones). However well-justified such a solution is (Department A needed the facilities on the new photocopier more than Department B), there is often lingering resentment on the part of the 'losing' party, which may begin to damage work relations.
Lose-lose	This sounds like a senseless outcome, but actually **compromise** comes into this category. It is thus very common.	**Neither party gets what (s)he really wanted**: for example, since Department A and B cannot both have a new photocopier, it is decided that neither department should have one. However 'logical' such a solution is, there is often resentment and dissatisfaction on *both* sides. (Personal arguments where neither party gives ground and both end up storming off or not talking are also lose-lose: the parties may not have lost the argument, but they lose the relationship …) Even positive compromises only result in half-satisfied needs.
Win-win	This may not be common, but working towards it often brings out the best solution.	**Both parties get as close as possible to what they really want.** How can this be achieved?

It is critical to the **win-win approach** to discover **what both parties really want** – as opposed to:

- What they think they want (because they have not considered any other options)
- What they think they can get away with
- What they think they need in order to avoid an outcome they fear

For example, Department B may want the new photocopier because they have never found out how to use all the features (which do the same things) on the old photocopier; because they just want to have the same equipment as Department A; or because they fear that if they do not have the new photocopier, their work will be slower and less professionally presented, and they may be reprimanded (or worse) by management.

The important questions in working towards win-win are:

- What do you want this for?
- What do you think will happen if you don't get it?

These questions get to the heart of what people really need and want.

In our photocopier example, Department A says it needs the new photocopier to make colour copies (which the old copier does not do), while Department B says it needs the new copier to make clearer copies (because the copies on the old machine are a bit blurred). Now there are **options to explore**. It may be that the old copier just needs fixing, in order for Department B to get what it really wants. Department A will still end up getting the new copier – but Department B has in the process been consulted and had its needs met.

EXAMPLE: THE WIN-WIN APPROACH

Two men are fighting over an orange. There is only one orange, and both men want it.

(a) If one man gets the orange and the other does not, this is a **win-lose** solution.

(b) If they cut the orange in half and share it (or agree that neither will have the orange), this is a **lose-lose** solution – despite the compromise.

(c) If they talk about what they each need the orange for, and one says 'I want to make orange juice' and the other says 'I want the skin of the orange to make candied peel', there are further options to explore (like peeling the orange) and the potential for both men to get exactly what they want. This is a **win-win** approach.

Win-win is not always possible: It is **working towards it** that counts. The result can be mutual respect and cooperation, enhanced communication, more creative problem-solving and – at best – **satisfied needs all round.**

Activity 5 **(30 minutes)**

Suggest a (i) win-lose, (ii) compromise and (iii) win-win solution in the following scenarios.

(a) Two of your team members are arguing over who gets the desk by the window: they both want it.

(b) You and a colleague both need access to the same file at the same time. You both need it to compile reports for your managers, for the following morning. It is now 3.00pm, and each of you will need it for two hours to do the work.

(c) Manager A is insisting on buying new computers for her department before the budgetary period ends. Manager B cannot understand why – since the old computers are quite adequate – and will moreover be severely inconvenienced by such a move, since her own systems will have to be upgraded as well, in order to remain compatible with department A. (The two departments constantly share data files.) Manager B protests, and conflict erupts.

3 TEAMS

3.1 Teams and teamwork

Definition

> A **team** is a 'small number of people with *complementary skills* who are committed to a *common* purpose, performance goals and approach, for which they hold themselves *mutually accountable'*. (*Katzenbach & Smith*)

The dictionary defines **teamwork** as the joint action of a group of people in which the individual interests of group members become secondary to achieving the goals of the group.

The essential difference between a team and a group lies in the fact that a group works together without a common purpose – a team working together is a unified whole, a selection of individuals working towards the same goal. It cannot be said that a number of people brought together by work are a team, and even a group of people who share a common interest will not necessarily achieve anything by discussing it together. Teamwork starts when a group of individuals have a **common goal** and work together to achieve it, regardless of personal preference or personality. It means taking an objective view for the greater good of the team.

The basic work units of organisations have traditionally been specialised hierarchical departments. Team working can break down 'departmental barriers', provide developmental challenges, free-up management, or improve customer service. Teams allow work to be shared among a number of individuals, so that it gets done faster and with a greater range of skills and information than by individuals working alone.

A team may be called together temporarily, to achieve specific task objectives (project team), or may be more or less permanent, with responsibilities for a particular product, product group or stage of the production process (a product or process team).

There are two basic approaches to the organisation of teamwork:

(a) **Multi-disciplinary teams** – bring together individuals with different skills and specialisms so that their skills, experience and knowledge can be pooled or exchanged. They:

   (i) increase workers' awareness of their overall objectives and targets

   (ii) aid coordination and communication across functional boundaries

   (iii) help to generate new ideas and solutions to problems, since the team has access to more perspectives and 'pieces of the jigsaw'.

(b) **Multi-skilled teams** – bring together a number of individuals who can perform any of the group's tasks. These tasks can then be shared out in a more flexible way between group members, according to who is available and best placed to do a given job at the time it is required.

   Multi-skilling is the cornerstone of team empowerment, since it cuts across the barriers of job descriptions and demarcations to enable teams to respond flexibly to changing demands.

3.2 Self-managed teams

Self-managed teams are the most highly developed form of team working. They are permanent structures in which team members collaboratively decide all the major issues affecting their work: work processes and schedules, task allocation, the selection and development of team members, the distribution of rewards and the management of group processes (problem-solving, conflict management, internal discipline and so on). The team leader is a member of the team, acting in the role of coach and facilitator: leadership roles may be shared or rotated as appropriate.

Self-managed teamworking is said to have advantages in:

- Saving managerial costs
- Gains in quality and productivity, by harnessing the commitment of those who perform the work
- Encouraging individual initiative and responsibility, enhancing organisational responsiveness (particularly in front-line customer-facing units)
- Gains in efficiency, through multi-skilling, the involvement of fewer functions in decision-making and coordinating work, and (often) the streamlining of working methods by groups.

3.3 Applications of team working

Normally, teams will consist of people from the same employer, but sometimes there may be teams from different employers: examples are design project teams in construction, which bring together architects and engineers from different firms, or teams which include customers or suppliers.

The collaborative nature of teams makes them particularly effective for **increasing communication,** generating new ideas and evaluating ideas from different viewpoints. Common applications of teamworking therefore include the following.

- **Problem-solving or brainstorming groups**: generating creative ideas for problem solving and innovation. Small groups of people are invited to contribute ideas, without any initial evaluation or censorship: this freedom encourages people to 'bounce' ideas off each other and build on each other's ideas, creating more innovative ideas than would otherwise be possible.
- **Quality and service circles**: drawing people together from different disciplines to share ideas about quality and service issues. This has been a popular technique in involving employees at different levels of the organisation in quality assurance, as part of a Total Quality Management (TQM) orientation. Such discussions are said to result not only in specific suggestions for quality improvements, but to a greater awareness and discussion of performance issues in the organisation, and to higher morale in employees. Similar options include **health and safety circles** and other groups that meet regular to discuss matters of concern.
- **Project teams**: set up to handle particular tasks or projects. This enables a range of cross-functional expertise to collaborate on a project, creating a 'horizontal' organisation. In the case of account teams, dedicated to particular customers or clients (eg advertising agency accounts), this offers the customer

a more satisfying 'horizontal' experience of the organisation than having to be constantly transferred between departments.

- **Representative groups**: set up to discuss and put forward the views of interest groups in the organisation. An employee representative team (a works council, the local branch of a trade union or staff association, say) might consult and negotiate with management, for example, representing the views and interests of employees. This is often an important channel of upward communication, so that management can benefit from 'grass roots' knowledge of issues at the front line of the organisation.
- **Briefing groups**: allowing information and instructions to be presented to a number of people together.

3.4 Benefits of team working

Organisations have introduced team working for the following reasons, among others:

- to improve productivity
- to improve quality of products or services
- to improve customer focus
- to speed the spread of ideas
- to respond to opportunities and threats and to fast-changing environments
- to increase employee motivation
- to introduce multi-skilling and employee flexibility.

There can be benefits for employees too. The most commonly-quoted outcomes are greater job satisfaction and motivation, and improved learning. But the introduction of team working needs skilful management and resources devoted to it, or initiatives may fail.

Activity 6 **(10 minutes)**

What functions do teams perform in your own organisation? List a number of different teams of which you are aware (or perhaps a member). What is their function – and why is this function most effectively performed by a team (as opposed to individuals working on their own)?

4 TEAM FORMATION

4.1 Establishing objectives

Every team must have something to work on that supports the goals of the organisation, its stakeholders, customers, suppliers and employees. Unfortunately, most teams are established without clear and actionable objectives. Therefore it should come as no surprise that research shows that nearly nine out of every ten teams fail to achieve the desired results.

So before the first team is formed, someone must provide very specific answers to the following questions:

- What is the team empowered to do? Is it going to accomplish a specific task, make a recommendation or actually manage itself? Has the organisation defined the team's authority to make recommendations and to implement its plan? Is there a defined review process so both the team and the organisation are consistently aligned in direction and purpose?

- Will it solve a problem, complete a project, meet an objective, make a consensus decision, redesign a process or manage a particular aspect of the business? At the same time, do team members clearly understand their boundaries?
- How far may members go in pursuit of solutions? Are limitations (i.e. monetary and time resources) defined at the beginning of the project before the team experiences barriers and rework?
- What indices and indicators will the team track to measure and verify its results?
- What resources, support, coordination, training, coaching and tools will the team need to gain its objectives and achieve the desired results?
- How will the team and the organisation know when the team has completed its mission?
- How will they know if and when the team should be disbanded, reformulated or continue on with new challenges?

4.2 Team formation – *Tuckman*

Developing the characteristics outlined above is the first stage of building an effective and enjoyable team. There are many theories on how teams form and, while each theory has unique characteristics, most agree on two things. First, that there are predictable stages every team goes through on its way to becoming a highly productive, efficient team. And second, that leaders and group members who are aware of these stages can improve the quality of their team's interactions during each stage. *Tuckman*, identified four stages of team development: Forming, Storming, Norming, and Performing. It describes the interaction between team members in two-dimensions: task and relations.

The **Forming** stage – involves the introduction of team members, either at the initiation of the team, or as members are introduced subsequently. Members are likely to be influenced by the expectations and desires they bring with them, and will be keen to understand how the group will operate. They will be wary about introducing new ideas. The objectives being pursued may as yet be unclear and a leader may not yet have emerged. This is a stage of transition from a group of individuals to a team. As team members grow more confident, the team are likely to enter the next stage.

The **Storming** phase – frequently involves more or less open conflict between team members who will have different opinions as to how the team should operate. There may be changes agreed in the original objectives, procedures and norms established for the group. If the team is developing successfully this may be a fruitful phase as more realistic targets are set and trust between the group members increases. The best teams will understand the conflict, actively listen to each other, and navigate an agreed way forwards. Other teams may disintegrate as they bolster their own opinions to weather the storms of the group. As the team emerges with an agreed method of operating, it enters the next stage.

The **Norming** phase – a period of settling down: there will be agreements about work sharing, individual requirements and expectations of output. Norms and procedures may evolve which enable methodical working to be introduced and maintained. During this phase, team members are able to reconcile their own opinions with the greater needs of the team. Cooperation and collaboration replace the conflict and mistrust of the previous phase.

Finally the team reaches the final phase,

The **Performing** phase – emphasis is now on reaching the team goals, rather than working on team process. The team sets to work to execute its task. The difficulties of growth and development no longer hinder the group's objectives. Relationships are settled, and team members are likely to build loyalty towards each other. The team is able to manage more complex tasks, and cope with greater change.

Teams have a finite life. They form for a specific purpose and must disband once their mission is complete. Consequently there is a fifth and final stage, sometimes called **Adjourning**. Achieving closure, acknowledging the end of a project and moving on is a vital part of the lifecycle of every team.

4.3 Moving through the phases

The action steps for moving through team development:

Forming to storming

- Build a shared purpose/mission and continuously clarify team outcomes.
- Create a sense of urgency and rationale for the purpose/mission.
- Select members based on resource and skill needs.
- Invest time getting to know each member's skills, experience and personal goals.
- Bring individuals together to work on common tasks.
- Define recognition and rewards, both individual and team-based.
- Work on personal commitment by linking personal goals to team roles.

Storming to norming

- Build a common understanding by periodically communicating the team's purpose/mission.
- Acknowledge times when the team is struggling and take time to discuss ways to move toward 'Norming'.
- Set out to achieve a few performance goals and tasks.
- Encourage members to express their differing opinions, ideas, and feelings by asking open-ended questions.
- Make connections between divergent perspectives; acknowledge where there are differences.
- Build a set of operating agreements (rules for team behaviour).
- Raise issues, confront deviations from commitments, and allow conflict to occur.

Norming to performing

- Develop shared leadership based on expertise and development needs.
- Translate common purpose and team expectations into performance goals that are specified and measurable.
- Build consensus on overarching goals and approaches.
- Formally give and receive feedback within the team.
- Maintain focus on external relationships: commitments, requirements, feedback, and competitive realities.
- Celebrate successes, share rewards, recognise team and individual achievements.
- Continue to evaluate team against performance goals.

Activity 7 **(10 minutes)**

Read the following descriptions of team behaviour and decide to **which** category they **belong** (forming, storming, norming, performing, dorming).

(a) Two of the group arguing as to whose idea is best
(b) Progress becomes static
(c) Desired outputs being achieved
(d) Shy member of group not participating
(e) Activities being allocated

4.4 *Woodcock*

An alternative model was developed by *Woodcock*, who classified teams into four categories showing different stages of development.

Category	Comment
Undeveloped	The team-leader takes most decisions. People are not quite sure what the objectives should be. Personal interaction is based on hiding feelings.
Experimenting	The group turns in on itself, with people raising and facing key issues.
Consolidating	The task and its objectives become clear, people begin to get along with each other on a personal level, and people begin to agree on procedures
Mature	Working methods are methodical, people are open with their feelings leadership style is contributory and the group recognises its responsibilities to the rest of the organisation

4.5 *Adair's* action-centred leadership

Professor Adair's action-centred or situational model sees the leadership process in a context made up of three interrelated variables – task needs, the individual needs of team members and the needs of the team as a whole.

(a) The total situation dictates the relative priority that must be given to each of the three sets of needs

(b) Effective leadership is identifying and acting on that priority.

The diagram below shows the overlap of the task, team and individual needs, and indicates some measure of interrelation between these factors.

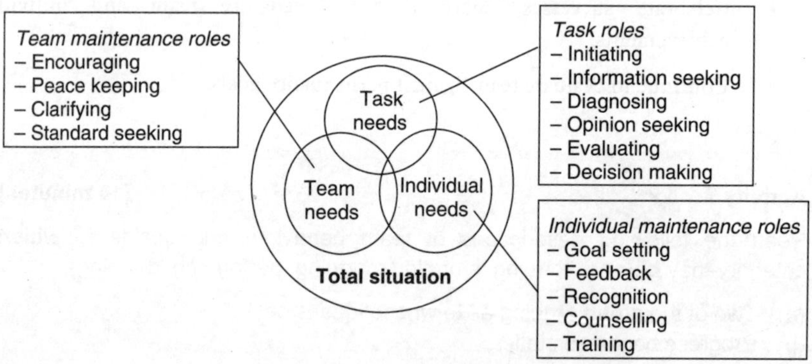

Figure 7.1: Adair's situational model of leadership

Adair's model of leadership is more a question of appropriate behaviour than of personality or of being in the right place at the right time. His model stresses that effective leadership lies in what the leader does to meet the needs of task, team and individuals. This takes the model nearer the contingency approaches of modern theorists, whose concern is with a variety of factors – task, people and situation – all having a bearing on leadership and leadership styles.

4.6 Effective and successful teams

Effective and successful **teams are** characterised by:

Size and composition – ideally a team should have seven to nine people and no delegates. You do not want people who have to take the team's ideas back to someone else to get authorisation. In the best teams, no one hesitates to act out of a fear that what they are about to do is not in their area of responsibility. Good team players take action.

Diversity – **members must have adequate levels of complementary skills.** A team should be made up of people who have different opinions about things, people who approach their work in different ways, intuitive thinkers as well as logical thinkers. Diversity (of skills and opinions) is one of the keys to a successful team.

Shared culture – to have a successful team, you must have a shared organisational culture. People from different parts of a company will, in all likelihood, have disparate styles, expectations, and reward systems. A shared organisational culture will mitigate the differences.

Well-defined goals – **the team must have a specific goal or goals** and have a well-defined purpose or vision of what the team will accomplish. The team's mission and mode of operation must be clearly defined and every team member has to understand it. That includes an understanding of the project's purpose, the strategy for getting the work accomplished, the ultimate goal, the benefits people will receive if the goal is met, the measurement system that's going to be used, and how differences of opinion (conflicts) are going to be handled.

Positive attitude and cooperative spirit – in successful teams all team members are positive thinkers. A team cannot function with excuse-driven, 'no-can-do' members on board. Team members need to be fiercely independent, and at the same time, intensely collaborative. They constantly ask questions and challenge ideas to achieve results as part of an open and positive feedback process.

Mutual respect and accountability – successful teams have three things in common:

(a) mutual respect among team members – team members know each other's individual strengths and preferences as well as working styles;

(b) a **sense of mutual accountability;** ***and***

(c) a common vision about where the team is going.

Each member of the team must know that he or she can influence the team's agenda. When there exists a feeling of trust among team members and open and honest communication is encouraged the team has an even better chance of success. Team members are confident in each other ability – there is mutual trust and support. Unfortunately, there is going to be contention in any team, but team members have to respect one another and appreciate each other's contribution.

5 TEAM STRUCTURES

5.1 Flexible structures

The structures that most organisations adopt are line organisations, project organisations or matrix organisations.

- A line organisation is based on a hierarchy of managers responsible for ongoing operations supported by staff organisations, which exist to serve the goals of the line. Companies that produce products typically have a line organisation structure

- Staff functions are those, which need to serve all the lines, such as human resources and accounting. In a for-profit company, line managers will be responsible for the bottom line profitability of their line of business.

- In service-based businesses such as architecture or design, the project organisation is more common. In such a business, a senior manager will be responsible for one or more projects and the staff on those projects will report directly to the project manager. Each project manager then has responsibility for personnel development as well as for project delivery.

- Due to the rapidly changing environment and the need for effective coordination in very complex situations, most large corporate projects today operate in a matrix environment. In this setting the leader needs to be sensitive to a larger array of political arenas than in a project or line structure. In a matrix structure, the project manager may have little written authority, but needs to rely primarily on personal relationships and 'personal power.' The diagram below gives an indication of how the matrix structure works.

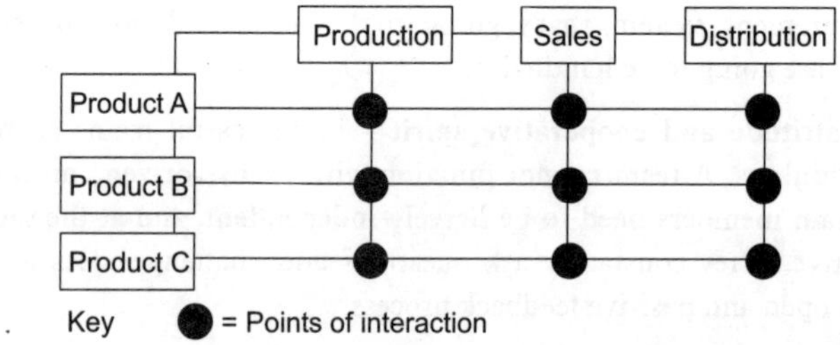

Figure 7.1: Matrix structure

It shows that the team working on Product C would be responsible not only to the head of that product, but also to the heads of the production, sales and distribution departments.

Within a team you will find a mixture of different people with different assignments – but that does not necessarily require a specific structure. For each issue or process someone needs to be the recognised leader; someone has to believe it is his or her responsibility to drive an issue otherwise it may become forgotten. There will also be a sub-set of people most appropriate to make contributions. It could mean that a leader for one issue might be a contributor for another.

The team structure that develops (either formally or informally) will be flexible such that the right people work together for any given topic.

5.2 Linking pin

Rensis Likert proposed that the structure of an organisation should be formed around effective work groups rather than around individuals. He devised an overlapping structure that involved a linking pin process in which the leader/superior member of one team/group was a subordinate member of the team/group above – see diagram below of a project organisation:

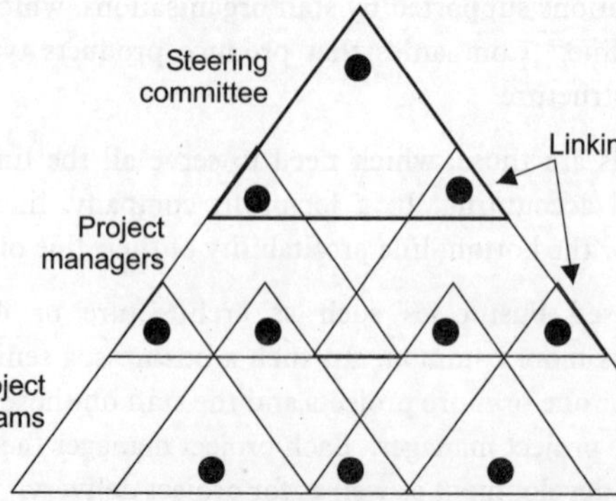

Figure 7.2: Project organisation

Likert argued that this type of structure improved communications, increased cooperation, more team commitment and faster decision-making.

5.3 Working culture

The working culture of an organisation is determined by the following elements:

- Labour force (e.g. size, characteristics).
- Work organisation (e.g. functions, structures).
- Working environment (e.g. safety, health issues).
- Employment conditions (e.g. salary, training).
- Labour relations (e.g. union membership, sector organisation).

The key elements of the labour force include:

- Numbers employed
- Social characteristics (diversity)
- Contractual status (type of contracts)
- Recruitment sources

From its mix of personnel, policies and environment, every organisation represents a unique working culture, which will affect the way it performs.

The working culture of most British organisations – whether service sector, public sector or manufacturing – has yet to move beyond the traditional highly controlled, 'head down', 'assembly line' model, characterised by measurable targets and a rigid chain of command.

Teamwork has become an important part of the working culture and many businesses now look at teamwork skills when evaluating a person for employment. Most companies realise that teamwork is important because either the product is sufficiently complex that it requires a team with multiple skills to produce, and/or a better product will result when a team approach is taken.

5.4 Diversity issues within teams

Diversity can be defined as the presence of differences among members of a social unit. It is an increasingly important factor in organisational life as organisations worldwide become more diverse. *Jackson et al* (1995) differentiate between two sources of diversity – readily detectable attributes and underlying attributes.

- **Readily detectable attributes** are those, which can be easily recognised in a person such as age, gender, or national/ethnic origin.
- **Underlying attributes** represent personal characteristics, which are not so easily identifiable, such as cultural beliefs, personality characteristics, or knowledge level.

Frequently, critics of diversity initiatives charge that such initiatives operate as an outgrowth of a 'politically correct' environment. They contend that organisations have diversity initiatives just because they are the 'right thing to do'. It has become increasingly apparent, however, that appropriate management of a diverse workforce is critical for organisations that seek to improve and maintain their competitive advantage. Focusing on diversity and looking for more ways to be a truly inclusive organisation – one that makes full use of the contributions of all employees – is not just a nice idea; it is good business sense that yields greater productivity and competitive advantage.

Teams with members from varied backgrounds can bring different perspectives, ideas and solutions, as well as devise new products and services, challenge accepted views and generate a dynamic synergy.

Winning team players are aware of and appreciate diversity in their team member's individual styles, perspective, and opinions. A team that does not appreciate and value diversity among its team members defeats the purpose of a team. At their best, winning teams bring together players with diverse talents, experience, and perspective to accomplish results that no one team member could accomplish on their own. Teams that lack diversity in breadth of skills, experience, and point of view are poorly prepared to solve complex problems or succeed at challenging tasks that, by their nature, require diversity

5.5 Anti-discriminatory practice

Everyone is unique. Working practices and behaviours that discriminate, stereotype or label people are limiting and impact negatively on group levels of motivation. A team that can acknowledge and appreciate difference is strong. There is no simple short cut to integrating the values of equality and diversity into an organisation's culture. There can be commitment across the top team and a superb set of policies but, in the end, many elements of the working culture are actually determined at team level. That means everyone has a part to play in developing an inclusive (rather than exclusive) culture.

Team leaders should:

- Promote a flexible approach to work.
- Use team meetings to discuss equalities issues including the development, progress and monitoring of the operational team equality action plan.
- Support their team, and the individuals in it, to feel comfortable in raising equalities issues in meetings and performance reviews.
- Include a discussion and review of equalities targets and equalities issues, including any training and development needs, in the team meetings.
- Act promptly, confidentially, sympathetically and appropriately to informal or formal complaints by individuals in the team concerning discrimination, victimisation or harassment.
- Promote opportunities for their team and themselves to receive training, support and development opportunities on equalities issues.

6 TEAM INTERACTIONS

6.1 Belbin's Team Role Theory

Belbin researched business game teams and drew up a widely used framework for understanding roles within work groups. He identifies nine team roles.

Role and description	Team-role contribution	Allowable weaknesses
1 **Plant** – creative, imaginative, unorthodox	Solves difficult problems	Ignores details, too preoccupied to communicate effectively
2 **Resource investigator** – extrovert, enthusiastic, communicative	Explores opportunities, develops contacts	Over-optimistic, loses interest once initial enthusiasm has passed
3 **Coordinator** – mature, confident, a good chairperson	Clarifies goals, promotes decision-making, delegates well	Can be seen as manipulative, delegates personal work
4 **Shaper** – challenging, dynamic, thrives on pressure	Has the drive and courage to overcome obstacles	Can provoke others, hurts people's feelings
5 **Monitor evaluator** – sober, strategic and discerning	Sees all options, judges accurately	Lacks drive and ability to inspire others, overly critical
6 **Team worker** – mild, cooperative, perceptive and diplomatic	Listens, builds, averts friction, calms the waters	Indecisive in crunch situations, can be easily influenced
7 **Implementer** – reliable, disciplined, conservative and efficient	Turns ideas into practical actions	Somewhat inflexible, slow to respond to new possibilities
8 **Completer** – anxious, painstaking, conscientious	Searches out errors and omissions, delivers on time	Inclined to worry unduly, reluctant to delegate, can be a nitpicker
9 **Specialist** – single-minded, self-starting, dedicated	Provides knowledge and skills in rare supply	Contributes only on a narrow front, dwells on technicalities, overlooks the 'big picture'

These team roles are not fixed within any given individual. Team members can occupy more than one role, or switch to 'backup' roles if required: hence, there is no requirement for every team to have nine members. However, since role preferences are based on personality, it should be recognised that individuals:

- will be naturally inclined towards some roles more than other
- will tend to adopt one or two team roles more or less consistently
- are likely to be more successful in some roles than in others

The nine roles are complementary, and *Belbin* suggested that an ideal team should represent a mix or balance of all of them. If managers know employees' team role preferences, they can strategically select, 'cast' and develop team members to fulfil the required roles.

Belbin insists that a sharp distinction needs to be made between:

(a) **Team role** ('a tendency to behave, contribute and interrelate with others at work in certain distinctive ways'), and

(b) **Functional role** ('the job demands that a person has been engaged to meet by supplying the requisite technical skills and operational knowledge')

Activity 8 **(10 minutes)**

The following phrases and slogans project certain team roles: identify which. (Examples drawn from *Belbin*, 1993)

(a) The small print is always worth reading.
(b) Let's get down to the task in hand.
(c) In this job you never stop learning.
(d) Without continuous innovation, there is no survival.
(e) Surely we can exploit that?
(f) When the going gets tough, the tough get going.
(g) I was very interested in your point of view.
(h) Has anyone else got anything to add to this?
(i) Decisions should not be based purely on enthusiasm.

6.2 Dynamics within teams

In order to evaluate and manage team dynamics, it may be helpful for the team leader to:

(a) Assess who (if anybody) is performing each of *Belbin's* team roles. Who is the team's plant, coordinator, monitor-evaluator and so on? There should be a mix of people performing task and team maintenance roles.

(b) Analyse the frequency and type of individual members' contributions to group discussions and interactions.

(i) Identify which members of the team habitually make the most contributions, and which the least (eg by taking a count of contributions from each member, during a sample ten to fifteen minutes of group discussion).

(ii) If the same people tend to dominate discussion whatever) is discussed (ie regardless of relevant expertise), the team has a problem in its communication process.

Additional factors influencing team dynamics include team members' attitudes – excitement and enthusiasm are valuable commodities and can be encouraged through praise and appreciation. Praise where it is due costs very little. Being overly critical and cynical towards other's work can lead to a dulling of the critical faculty by blocking one's openness to alternative ideas, reducing the will to experiment. The team should be always looking for ideas that are fresh, fun and effective. Having found such ideas, studying and copying the methods of their realisation can lead to the development of new ones.

Good communications between team members and with employees inside and outside the organisation are also important for success. Acknowledging and talking through problems can be helpful in lifting mind-blocks, even with team members who do not specialise in the same area. Sometimes a suggestion from a completely different direction can be just what is needed in reengaging one's creative thought processes.

Neil Rackham and Terry Morgan have developed a helpful categorisation of the types of contribution people can make to team discussion and decision-making

Category	Behaviour	Example
Proposing	Putting forward suggestions, new concepts or courses of action	'Why don't we look at a flexi-time system?'
Building	Extending or developing someone else's proposal.	'Yes. We could have a daily or weekly hours allowance, apart from a core period in the middle of the day'.
Supporting	Supporting another person or his/her proposal.	'Yes, I agree, flexi-time would be worth looking at'
Seeking information	Asking for more facts, opinions or clarification.	'What exactly do you mean by flexi-time?'
Giving information	Offering facts, opinions or clarification.	'There's a helpful outline of flexi-time in this article.'
Disagreeing	Offering criticism or alternative factors or opinions, which contradict a person's proposals or opinions.	'I don't think we can take the risk of not having any staff here at certain periods of the day'.
Attacking	Attempting to undermine another person or their position: more emotive than disagreeing.	'In fact, I don't think you've thought this through at all.'
Defending	Arguing for one's own point of view.	'Actually, I've given this a lot of thought, and I think it makes sense.'
Blocking/ difficulty stating	Putting obstacles in the way of a proposal, without offering any alternatives.	'What if the other teams get jealous? It would only cause conflict.'
Open behaviour	Risking ridicule and loss of status by being honest about feelings and opinions.	'I think some of us are afraid that flexi-time will show up how little work they really do in a day.'
Shutting-out behaviour	Interrupting or overriding others; taking over.	'Nonsense. Let's move onto something else – we've had enough of this discussion.'
Bringing-in behaviour	Involving another member; encouraging contribution	'Actually, I'd like to hear what Fred has to say. Go on, Fred.'
Testing understanding	Checking whether points have been understood.	'So flexi-time could work over a day or a week; have I got that right?'

Category	Behaviour	Example
Summarising	Drawing together or summing up previous discussion.	'We've now heard two sides to the flexi-time issue: on the one hand, flexibility; on the other side possible risk. Now ...'

Each type of behaviour may be appropriate in the right situation at the right time. A team may be low on some types of contribution – and it may be up to the team leader to encourage, or deliberately adopt, desirable behaviours (such as bringing-in, supporting or seeking information) in order to provide balance.

6.3 Politics of working relationships

An important aspect of management studies is politics in the work place. By this we mean political behaviour rather than preference for one party rather than another. Political behaviour is broadly concerned with competition, conflict, rivalry, influence and power relationships in organisations. Organisations are political systems in the sense that they are composed of individuals and groups who have their own interests, priorities and goals: there is competition for finite resources, power and influence; there are cliques, alliances, pressure groups and blocking groups, centred around values, opinions and objectives which may be opposed by others. Managers are constantly involved in compromise, reconciling or controlling differences, and settling for 'reality' rather than 'ideal'.

Political behaviour is based around the notion of coalitions and the assumption that individuals and groups can succeed together where they might fail alone. Various coalitions will seek to protect their interests and positions of authority.

Office politics, when viewed as a negative influence, can reduce organisational productivity, create a lack of trust, undermine staff morale, exclude key people from the decision-making processes and increase internal conflict that leads to a drain of its talent pool.

The workplace politicians are characterised with animal stereotypes based on the model devised by management development experts *Simon Baddeley* and *Dr Kim James*.

The donkey	Unprincipled and unethical, they are useless at interpersonal skills but like to stay close to authority figures within the firm. They make judgments based on feelings rather than knowledge of the organisation's procedures or bureaucracy.
The fox	Unsurprisingly in the cunning and clever category, they are quick to exploit weaknesses in their allies and opponents alike. In human terms fox-like behaviour is demonstrated through being interested in power and in fraternising with powerful people. These individuals may seem unprincipled, self-driven, typically seen as unethical and they have trouble showing their feelings.
The sheep	They are the innocents. Loyal yet politically clueless, they do not put themselves about to build networks in the organisation. Sheep act with integrity, sticking to ethical, corporate and professional rules.
The owl	Politically astute, wise owls can cope with being disliked, are non-defensive, use coalitions but are aware of other people's concerns.

If office politics are a fact of life, individuals who want to reach the upper echelons must master the scheming. The recommended strategies for surviving and thriving in a political landscape are as follows.

Agenda setting	Politically, agendas combine a vision for change with a strategy for achieving that vision. Effective leaders develop this agenda from a sense of what they want and what they are prepared to trade off against something more desirable in the longer-term. In setting an agenda, effective politicians recognise the concerns of major stakeholders.
Mapping the political terrain	Office politics work within the informal system and there are no route maps to what is a changing and hazardous territory. So before entering, determine the channels of communication to find the best ways to hear and be heard. Then identify the main players with political influence, not always the most senior people but those who have their ear and thus maximise the chances of your ideas being adopted.
Coalition building	A memo to your superior can be effective, but is often a sign of impotence and betrays a lack of political sophistication. The rules of engagement dictate that no strategy will work without a power base and line managers face a power gap. Moving up the food chain brings more authority but it also brings more dependence because success hinges on the efforts of a diverse group of people.
Bargaining and negotiation	Horse-trading among different interest groups presents the toughest challenge to many managers. The principled search for an agreement beneficial to all parties rests on separating the people from the problem. The trick is to focus on interests not positions.
Building a power base	Managers should build up elements of their power base by being sensitive to what others consider legitimate behaviour in acquiring and using power. Politically astute managers will develop an intuitive understanding of various types of power and methods of influence which bolster their authority.
Selling your ideas	As a manager you need friends and allies to get things done. To promote change or innovation get preliminary agreement from those most affected. Make them your cheer-leaders and build your resource base on the way to securing the necessary approvals from higher management.

A good team will experience heightened creativity in each other's company, compared to that which is achievable individually. But sometimes there is conflict between team members, resulting in work taking a back seat to relationships and office politics. This, in turn, leads to the marginalisation of certain members of the team and the accompanying elevation of others to positions of power. This can only cause unrest as raised expectations followed by disappointment and demotivation will result from the breakdown of communications within the team.

7 TEAM BUILDING

7.1 Issues involved in team building

Woodcock suggests that to achieve a successful team, the following nine aspects of its functioning and performance must have taken place.

(a) Clear objectives and agreed goals
(b) Openness and confrontation
(c) Support and trust
(d) Cooperation and conflict
(e) Sound procedures
(f) Appropriate leadership
(g) Regular reviews
(h) Individual development
(i) Sound inter-group relations

Definition

> **Team-building** may be described as a systematic attempt to develop the processes of collaborative functioning within a team (such as communication, problem-solving, decision-making and conflict resolution) in such a way as to help the team to overcome any barriers to effective pursuit of its shared goals.

In its simplest terms, the stages involved in team building are to:

- clarify the team goals
- identify those issues which inhibit the team from reaching their goals
- address those issues, remove the inhibitors and enable the goals to be achieved

There are three main issues involved in team building.

1 **Team identity:** get people to see themselves as part of the group. A manager might seek to reinforce the **sense of identity** of the group.

- **Name** – staff at McDonald's restaurants are known as the Crew
- **Badge or uniform** – this often applies to service industries, but it is unlikely that it would be applied within an organisation
- Expressing the team's **self-image**: teams often develop their own jargon, especially for new projects
- Building a team **mythology** – in other words, stories from the past ('classic mistakes' as well as successes)
- **A separate space**: it might help if team members work together in the same or adjacent offices, but this is not always possible

2 **Team solidarity**: implies cohesion and loyalty inside the team. A team leader might be interested in:

- Expressing solidarity
- Encouraging interpersonal relationships – although the purpose of these is to ensure that work does get done
- Dealing with conflict by getting it out into the open; disagreements should be expressed and then resolved
- Controlling competition – the team leader needs to treat each member of the team fairly and to be seen to do so; favouritism undermines solidarity
- Encouraging some competition with other groups if appropriate. For example, sales teams might be offered a prize for the highest monthly orders; London Underground runs best-kept station competitions

Getting commitment to the team's shared objectives may involve a range of leader activity.

3 **Shared objectives**: encourage the team to commit itself to shared work objectives and to cooperate willingly and effectively in achieving them.

7.2 *Belbin* – putting the team together

Meredith Belbin, one of the most influential modern writers on teams, identifies a number of basic steps in the early stages of team building.

(a) Articulating the purpose and terms of reference of the team: setting clear and meaningful goals

(b) Selecting team membership and 'casting' team members in appropriate roles

(c) Deciding the 'style' in which the team will operate: whether through meetings, independent working, working in pairs – or whatever suits the members

Team members may be pre-selected as representatives of specific functions/departments or interest groups. Members may be selected on the basis of:

(a) The skills, knowledge and expertise required by the task

(b) Power or influence in the wider organisation, required to champion the team's interests or to mobilise resources

(c) The skills required for task processes: skills in stimulating discussion, skills in checking and attending to detail, skills in implementation and follow-through

(d) The skills required for teamworking: skills in discussion, conflict resolution and so on

Belbin suggested that process roles – the ways people contribute to discussion, decision-making and teamworking – are at least as important as functional roles: whether a person is an accounting, marketing or technical expert.

7.3 Team spirit

The most important and fundamental aspect of teambuilding is developing and fostering a **team spirit**. It increases the chances of successful performance and winning but what is team spirit?

- It is a combination of **respect, trust, interconnectedness** and **enjoyment** amongst a group of individuals who work towards agreed common goals. These qualities are essential to success, for every individual must feel needed, valued, respected and wanted if he or she is to contribute fully to the group.
- It is a feeling of **loyalty** that the members of a group have toward others in the group.
- It is a group of people who **pull together**. Team members begin to envision what they can create together, begin to sense the possibilities for developing breakthrough solutions or delivering unparalleled service. Here they realise they can accomplish far more collectively than separately.
- It is the **desire** to work as a team. It helps the team as a whole develop a sense of solidarity and single-minded purpose, while empowering individual team members to assume responsibility for the goals, roles, competencies and resources needed to realise their shared vision.
- **Selflessness** (acting with less concern for yourself than for the success of the joint activity). Remember it's working together with commitment, allegiance, loyalty, dedication, (intellectually or emotionally) to a course of action.

7.4 Building blocks

Woodcock adopts a practical approach to team building. He argues that to build an effective team you must first identify the blockages to team building then decide on the building blocks to be used. He then discusses the general issues to be taken into account and outlines an action plan for implementation.

Identifying the best building blocks to use to overcome the blockages is a very important stage in team building. Inappropriate and misjudged team building activities can lead to a misuse of time, a waste of money and other resources, a lowering in morale because of the wasted effort and an increase in cynicism from the members.

The factors that lead to blockages in effectiveness and the building blocks used to overcome them are as follows.

Blockages	Building block
Inappropriate leadership	The leader can adopt a suitable leadership style
Insufficient mix of member skills and personalities	Ensure team members are suitably qualified. If necessary, get members to adopt another role than they would normally
Unconstructive climate	Strive to achieve an atmosphere of cooperation
An absence of clear and agreed goals and objectives	The team has been brought together for a purpose so this can be clarified and developed into sub-objectives which are agreed

Blockages	Building block
Poor achievement	Performance is improved in a climate of trust and learning
Ineffective work methods	Develop sensible procedures for performing the team's tasks
Lack of communication – people afraid to challenge key issues	Develop a climate so that people can speak their minds constructively
Individual development needs not addressed	Individuals are given opportunities to grow or develop within the team
Low creativity	Techniques such as brainstorming can improve creativity. Much depends on how new ideas are treated
Poor and unconstructive interpersonal relationships	Some people will never get on or have much in common but they can still work together effectively. Induction exercises might be required to break the ice
Non-existent or inadequate review and control of performance	The performance of the team can be reviewed at regular intervals

7.5 Team building tools

Once the difficulties or blockages have been identified, team building can be greatly accelerated by the use of special team-building events, activities, and exercises to help group members change individual behaviour to improve team performance. A range of techniques can be employed, including participation, empowerment, leadership development, outward-bound courses, team building games, team building exercises, team building activities and team building adventures and the use of formal processes, which evaluate the performance of teams and team members as a basis for feedback and for improvement.

(a) **Participation** is the first step in the process of involving team members in the company's decision-making processes. Instead of planning everything from the top level of the organisation, a participative leader would invite the team members to contribute their ideas to the process so that everyone will feel as though they have contributed and that their voice has been heard.

(b) **Empowerment** goes much further. It allows team members to have the discretion to make decisions that are relevant to their own sphere of operations, without the need to refer to a higher level of management.

(c) **Adventure courses** – with all the participants being involved in quite physical tasks with a need for the group members to help each other. There are less physical versions, like building bridges in competitive groups. Whatever the format, a debriefing stage is an essential part of the exercise. 'How did we perform as a team?' or 'Where did we go wrong?' are the key kinds of question to consider.

(d) **Team volunteering** – is also an effective team-building tool. Teams connect with their community, develop new working skills and make a difference to people's lives. Examples include decorating classrooms, planting trees, taking disabled people for outings or visiting old people to have a chat.

7.6 Delegation and empowerment

Delegation is different from empowerment. Delegation is entrusting a task to a team while still retaining all the decision making control. Empowerment, however, requires that a certain amount of responsibility and decision making capability is vested in the team. Assigning responsibility implies confidence in the team and confidence in its ability to take certain decisions on its own. It gives the team the independence to formulate an action plan and then implement that plan.

It is not always possible to empower staff as sometimes the nature of the job might be such that the leader has to be in effective control and will be responsible for any chain of events that occurs. However there are many situations when as a leader you can learn to empower rather than delegate. Empowerment is a much more effective method of leading people as the people you are leading have an opportunity to discover their strengths and weaknesses. It also allows you in a leadership position to assess the ability of the people you are leading and to see how you could maximise their individual potential.

When you empower the people that you are leading they will be able to take ownership of what they are task to do. They will be more motivated to achieve the targets you set them on. Unlike delegation, when you empower you will not have to be constantly present to ensure that the job gets done.

Empowered teams can bring benefits in the following ways.

- Empowered product marketing teams are able to come up with ideas that help create better products and services in line with customer expectations.
- Empowered sales teams are better at achieving their targets and forming long-term partnerships with clients.
- Empowered teams in the services sector can help to bring about greater customer satisfaction and retention levels. For example, where a customer services team is not empowered to handle complaints, they have to be polite but buy time when faced with an irate customer so they can refer back to their supervisor and work out a solution. In contrast to the customer services team that is empowered to handle complaints in a particular manner which, when faced with an irate customer, may be empowered to use small promotional methods like discounts, offers or schemes to resolve the matter efficiently. The benefits to the company can be enormous since customer retention is likely to go up.

Lack of empowerment can be a functional glass ceiling and it can prove to be a stumbling block especially for teams that front organisations in customer services or client relations.

Lack of empowerment can also slow down the work flow because the decision making is vested higher up the hierarchy. A certain amount of authority and decision making leeway helps improve work efficiency and also ensures that a team takes pride in its existence.

7.7 Coaching and mentoring

Coaching may be described as bringing out the best in a person; improving a person's skills. **Mentoring** is a relationship with an experienced organisation member who can share, guide and provide feedback.

When you empower a person you have automatically been promoted to the role of a mentor. The mentor's role is different from the coach in the sense that you are required to understand the way in which your mentee thinks and functions. You are then required to enhance their ability by showing them how what they are doing can be done better. Being a mentor requires patience, perseverance and faith in the person or persons you are mentoring. You need to show to that you are approachable and someone who is critical without being overbearing.

The coaching relationship is more specific in terms of the objectives. The components of successful coaching include:

- first hand experience and understanding of achievement in the workplace at a high level;
- performer-empowering attitudes and assumptions;
- strong rapport creation and maintenance skills;
- excellent listening skills; and
- sophisticated questioning skills.

Activity 9 **(20 minutes)**

Why might the following be effective as team-building exercises?

(a) Sending a project team (involved in the design of electronic systems for racing cars) on a recreational day out karting.

(b) Sending two sales teams on a day out playing 'War Games', each being an opposing combat team trying to capture the other's flag, armed with paint guns

(c) Sending a project team on a conference at a venue away from work, with a brief to review the past year and come up with a vision for the next year

These are actually commonly used techniques. If you are interested, you might locate an activity centre or company near you that offers outdoor pursuits, war games or corporate entertainment and ask them about team-building exercises and the effect they have on people.

8 TEAM SUPPORT, EVALUATION AND REWARDS

8.1 Supporting teams

Organisations succeed because of teams – people working together to accomplish common objectives. In most organisations, however, the process of establishing teams and managing their accomplishment of projects and tasks is haphazard at best. One of the main reasons teams fail to function at their best is that there are no systems to support best team practices. Many of the problems teams have, such as poor communication, personality conflicts, weak accountability, missed deadlines, cost overruns and so on can be diminished or eliminated by implementing improved team practices.

A supportive environment, which is genuinely interested in the results the team is going to produce, can energise a team to perform beyond anyone's expectations. A hostile environment can doom a team to failure no matter how good the people are in it. However, a supportive environment is more than just interest in the team – it is a whole culture that values teams and is characterised by informal teams forming and disbanding in response to the needs of the organisation.

8.2 Supervising teams

Proper supervision, neither too loose nor too tight, also contributes to team success. Team leaders need to be involved enough to know what the teams needs and to provide it. But they must never meddle in the team's functioning. Leaders have four primary roles in a team environment:

- to resolve conflicts that cannot be resolved by the team
- to give direction and functional expertise to the team and to members needing help
- to find the needed resources
- to judge the performance of the team and its individual members

8.3 Establish a way to monitor progress

For all teamwork, it is important to create a method for tracking how well the team is moving towards its objectives. A measurement system can be used on a regular basis to review progress, identify opportunities for improvement and learn from mistakes.

Metrics and measurements may be viewed as a time consuming activity with no real benefit, however this is just what is required in order to create and sustain high performance teamwork. Teams must know if what they are doing is effective and if they are on track to meet their goals. If they are not on track they need to know this and more importantly, they need to know why they are not on track so that they can modify their performance, get back on track and achieve their goals.

8.4 Evaluating teams

The task of the team leader is to build a 'successful' or an 'effective' team. The criteria for team effectiveness include:

- **Task performance**: fulfilment of task and organisational goals. Effectiveness is the degree to which goals are accomplished and efficiency is the use of resources in attaining goals
- **Team functioning**: constructive maintenance of team working, managing the demands of team dynamics, roles and processes
- **Team member satisfaction**: fulfilment of individual development and relationship needs

In most cases effectiveness and efficiency are related. The team could be effective in accomplishing its goals but it may not be efficient in its use of machinery or human resources. In circumstances where there is some physical or countable task, the measurement is relatively straightforward and there are certain elements that can be used to evaluate the team's performance, these include:

- The quantity of work performed
- The quality of work performed *and*
- The association of work performed with time allowed

Given the type of work done by teams, there may be no obvious objective measures, such as sales figures, number of complaints or components made per hour, available for assessing their performance. Therefore, some form of subjective measure is required. There are various ways of judging the performance of teams in the absence of objective measures. One way is to observe and rate the team's behaviour on some set of agreed criteria. Another is to interview all who may have a view about the team and its performance. A third is to administer a pre-prepared questionnaire to team members and their managers. Some researchers have used senior management as judges of a team's performance as well as, and sometimes instead of, team members' own judgements.

Concerns about working as a member of a team often revolve around issues of assessment – people fear they will receive a lower evaluation as a member of a team than they would if they worked alone. Or, there is the fear that other team members will not carry their share of the work, yet receive the same amount of credit as the harder-working members of the team.

Credit for work in a team project may be based on:

(a) A **single evaluation** provided to the group – all individuals would receive the same amount of credit for the work in a team regardless of their actual contributions.

(b) **Evaluations of individual team members** – each individual team member would receive an individual score, which may be the same or different than the credit given to their team mates

(c) A **combined assessment** using both group and individual assessment scores to determine the final credit given each team member – this matches the needs for individual accountability as well as evaluation of teams for reaching a group goal(s).

8.5 Rewarding effective teams

Organisations may try to encourage effective team performance by designing reward systems that recognise team, rather than individual success. Indeed, individual performance rewards may act against team cooperation performance because:

(a) They emphasise individual rather than team performance

(b) They encourage team leaders to think of team members only as individuals rather than relating to them as a team

For **team rewards** to be effective, the team must have certain characteristics.

- Distinct roles, targets and performance measures
- Significant autonomy and thus influence over performance
- Maturity and stability
- Cooperation
- Interdependence of team members

Reward schemes that focus on team (or organisation) performance include:

(a) **Profit sharing** schemes, based on a pool of cash related to profit

(b) **Gainsharing** schemes, using a formula related to a suitable performance indicator, such as added value. Improvements in the performance indicator must be perceived to be within the employees' control, otherwise there will be no incentive to perform

(c) **Employee share option** schemes, giving staff the right to acquire shares in the employing company at an attractive price

Chapter roundup

- Conflict can be viewed as inevitable owing to the class system; a continuation of organisation politics by other means; something to be welcomed as it avoids complacency; something resulting from poor management, or something that should be avoided at all costs.
- Conflict can be constructive, if it introduces new information into a problem, if it defines a problem, or if it encourages creativity. It can be destructive if it distracts attention from the task or inhibits communication.
- Causes of conflict include operative goal incompatibility, differentiation, interdependence, resource scarcity, power, uncertainty and rewards.
- Conflict can be managed by separating the conflicting parties, restricting communication or imposing a solution, a number of techniques are available actively to promote cooperative behaviour.
- Teams have a 'sense of identity' that a random crowd of individuals does not possess.
- A team is more than a group. It has joint objectives and accountability and may be set up by the organisation under the supervision or coaching of a team leader, although self-managed teams are growing in popularity.
- Teamworking may be used for: organising work; controlling activities; generating ideas; decision-making; pooling knowledge.
- The effectiveness of the leader is dependent upon meeting three areas of need within the work group: the need to achieve the common task, the need for team maintenance and the individual needs of team/group members.
- Multidisciplinary teams contain people from different departments, pooling the skills of specialists.
- Multi-skilled teams contain people who themselves have more than one skill.
- Ideally team members should perform a balanced mix of roles. *Belbin* suggests coordinator, shaper, plant, monitor-evaluator, resource-investigator, implementer, team-worker, finisher and specialist.
- Team members make different types of contribution (eg proposing, defending, blocking)
- A team develops in stages: forming, storming, norming, performing (*Tuckman*) and adjourning.
- Team development can be facilitated by active team building measures to support team identity, solidarity and commitment to shared objectives.

Quick quiz

1 What are the features of the 'happy family' view of the organisation?

2 Give an alternative to the happy family view

3 When can conflict be constructive?

4 What happens when two groups are put in competition with each other?

5 What are the possible outcomes of conflict, according to the 'win-win' model?

6 What causes conflict?

7 What is a team?

8 List *Belbin's* nine roles for a well-rounded team?

9 Who described the stages of group development?

(a) *Woodcock*
(b) *Belbin*
(c) *Tuckman*
(d) *Rackham and Morgan*

10 List the teambuilding issues identified by *Woodcock*.

11 List six of *Rackham and Morgan's* categories of contribution to group discussion.

Answers to quick quiz

1 Organisations are cooperative and harmonious. Conflict arises when something goes wrong.

2 Conflict is inevitable, being in the very nature of the organisation. Conflict can be constructive.

3 It can introduce solutions, define power relations, bring emotions, hostile or otherwise, out into the open.

4 They become more cohesive internally and more achievement-oriented.

5 Win-lose, lose-lose, win-win.

6 Different objectives, scarcity of responses, personal differences, interdependence of departments.

7 A small number of people with complementary skills who are committed to a common purpose, performance goals and approach for which they hold themselves basically accountable.

8 Coordinator, shaper, plant, monitor-evaluator, resource-investigator, implementer, teams worker, finisher, specialist.

9 (c): *Tuckman*. You should be able to identify the team-relevant theories of *Woodcock and Belbin* as well.

10 Leaders, Members. Climate. Objectives. Achievement. Work methods. Communications. Individuals, Creativity. Interpersonal communications. Review and control.

11 Proposing, building, supporting, seeking information, giving information, disagreeing.

Answers to activities

1 The 'happy family' perspective rarely fits most organisations, even those pursuing a common ideological goal, like a political party. Such organisations regularly face conflict (eg the Conservatives' divisions over Europe), if only about how to attain their goals. Cynics argue that managers promote the 'happy family' view to suppress conflict. Asda at one time referred to all its staff as 'colleagues'.

2 Conflicts occur anywhere in an organisation. Individuals, groups, departments or subsidiaries compete for scarce (financial/human/physical) resources.

3 *Sherifs'* work applies to conflict in organisations. To improve employee performance, win-lose conflict can be turned towards competitors, who become 'the enemy'.

4 (a) Both might need work done at the same time. Compromise and coordinated planning can help them manage their secretary's time.

(b) Differential pay might result in conflict with management – even an accusation of discrimination. There may be good reasons for the difference (eg length of service). To prevent conflict such information should be kept confidential. Where it is public, it should be seen to be not arbitrary.

(c) The electricians are worried about their jobs, and may take industrial action. Yet if the engineers' training is unrelated to the electricians' work, management can allay fears by giving information. The electricians cannot be given a veto over management decisions: a 'win-lose' situation is inevitable, but both sides can negotiate.

(d) The kitchen should plan its meals better – or people from both departments can be asked in advance whether they want puddings.

(e) Competition between sales regions is healthy as it increases sales. The conflict lies between sales regions and the production department. In the long-term, an increase in production capacity is the only solution. Where this is to be possible, proper coordination methods should be instituted.

5 (a) (i) Win-lose: one team member gets the window desk, and the other does not. (Result: broken relationships within the team.)

(ii) Compromise: the team members get the window desk on alternate days or weeks. (Result: half satisfied needs.)

(iii) Win-win: what do they want the window desk for? One may want the view, the other better lighting conditions. This offers options to be explored: how else could the lighting be improved, so that both team members get what they really want? (Result: at least, the positive intention to respect everyone's wishes equally, with benefits for team communications and creative problem-solving.)

(b) (i) Win-lose: one of you gets the file and the other doesn't.

(ii) Compromise: one of you gets the file now, and the other gets it later (although this has an element of win-lose, since the other has to work late or take it home).

(ii) Win-win: you photocopy the file and both take it, or one of you consults his or her boss and gets an extension of the deadline (since getting the job done in time is the real aim – not just getting the file). These kinds of solutions are more likely to emerge if the parties believe they can both get what they want.

(c) (i) Win-lose: Manager A gets the computers, and Manager B has to upgrade her systems.

(ii) Compromise: Manager A will get some new computers, but keep the same old ones for continued data-sharing with Department B. Department B will also need to get some new computers, as a back-up measure.

(ii) Win-win: what does Manager A want the computers for, or to avoid? Quite possibly, she needs to use up her budget allocation for buying equipment before the end of the budgetary period: if not, she fears she will lose that budget allocation. Now, that may not be the case, or there may be other equipment that could be more usefully purchased – in which case, there is no losing party.

6 Your own observation: remember, these will be useful examples to use, if asked in an assessment.

7 Categorising the behaviour of group members in the situations described results in the following: (a) storming, (b) dorming, (c) performing, (d) forming, (e) norming.

8 Completer/finisher
Implementer
Specialist
Plant
Resource investigator
Shaper
Teamworker
Coordinator
Monitor evaluator

9
- Recreation helps the team to build informal relationships: in this case, the chosen activity also reminds them of their tasks, and may make them feel special, as part of the motor racing industry, by giving them a taste of what the end user of their product does.
- A team challenge purses the group to consider its strengths and weaknesses, to find it's natural leader. This exercise creates and 'us' and 'them' challenge: perceiving the rival team as the enemy heightens the solidarity of the group.
- This exercise encourages the group the raise problems and conflicts freely, away from the normal environment of work and also encourages brainstorming and the expression of team members' dreams for what the team can achieve in the future.

Chapter 8 :

DEVELOPMENT NEEDS, LEARNING STYLES AND PROCESSES

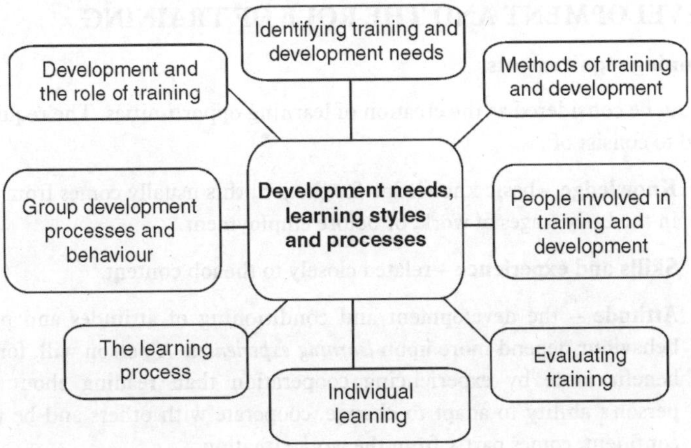

Introduction

Human resource development is the process by which the knowledge, skills and attitudes of employees are enhanced to the benefit of the organisation, the individual and the group. Development is the growth or realisation of a person's ability through conscious or unconscious learning. Training is a planned process to modify attitude, knowledge, skill or behaviour through learning experiences to achieve effective performance in an activity or range of activities.

The different types of learning theory we will be looking at in this chapter include the behaviourist and the cognitive approaches. Learning theory highlights the importance of feedback in sustaining and improving performance.

The term lifelong learning recognises that learning is not confined to childhood or the classroom, but takes place throughout life and in a range of situations. Learning can no longer be divided into a place and time to acquire knowledge (school) and a place and time to apply the knowledge acquired (the workplace). Instead, learning can be seen as something that takes place on an on-going basis from our daily interactions with others and with the world around us

Your objectives

After completing this chapter you should be able to:

(a) Identify training and development needs

(b) Discuss the methods of development and training

(c) Identify the people involved in training and development

(d) Evaluate training

(e) Outline the learning process

(f) Review development needs and activities and evaluate the effectiveness of activities

(g) Understand how groups develop

(h) Explain the factors involved in planning the monitoring and assessment of work performance

1 DEVELOPMENT AND THE ROLE OF TRAINING

1.1 Training requirements

Training can be considered as the creation of learning opportunities. The required needs can be said to consist of:

- **Knowledge** – basic knowledge for the job; this usually comes from education in the early stages of work, or before employment.
- **Skills and experience** – related closely to the job content.
- **Attitude** – the development and conditioning of attitudes and patterns of behaviour depend more upon *learning experiences*. A person will, for example, benefit more by experiencing cooperation than reading about it, and a person's ability to adapt to change, cooperate with others and be more self-confident, comes partly from the work situation.

People learn better when they see the *relevance* of what they are learning in relation to their own jobs. They should be given opportunities to try out their ideas in a situation as near as possible to real life conditions and practices. Therefore, training that is relevant and provides persons or groups with an opportunity to use the ideas learnt will be preferred.

Effective learning can take place according to *Bass and Vaughan* (1966) when the following four requirements exist.

- **Drive** – the motivation of the individual who must accept and be committed to the need for training.
- **Stimulus** – the signal received and interpreted by a trainee.
- **Response** – the behaviour resulting from a stimulus. This can be developed through training.
- **Reinforcement** – information that the learner receives giving an indication of progress – ideally as soon as possible to enable more effective learning to occur.

It is important to distinguish between the terminology used when discussing training and development.

Education. Instruction in knowledge and skills to enable people to be prepared for various roles in society. Its focus is broadly-based for the needs of the individual and to a lesser extent the needs of society.

Training. The acquisition of knowledge and skills for the purposes of an occupation or task. Its focus is much more narrowly-based than education or development, and is job or task-oriented.

Development. Concerned more with changes in attitude, behaviour and employee potential than with immediate skill. It relates more to *career* development than *job* development. It is a learning activity concentrating on the future needs of an organisation.

1.2 Factors affecting job performance

There are many factors affecting a person's performance at work, as shown in the diagram below. Training and development are the ways by which organisations seek to improve the performance of their staff and, it is hoped, of the organisation.

Figure 8.1: Factors affecting job performance

1.3 What is development?

Definition 

Development is 'the growth or realisation of a person's ability and potential through the provision of learning and educational experiences'.

Training is 'the planned and systematic modification of behaviour through learning events, programmes and instruction which enable individuals to achieve the level of knowledge, skills and competence to carry out their work effectively'. (*Armstrong, Handbook of Personnel Management Practice*)

1.4 Overall purpose of employee and management development

- **Ensure** the firm meets current and future performance objectives by
- **Continuous improvement** of the performance of individuals and teams, and
- **Maximising people's** potential for growth (and promotion).

1.5 Development activities

- Training, both on and off the job
- Career planning
- Job rotation
- Appraisal
- Other learning opportunities

Activity 1 **(10 minutes)**

Note down key experiences which have developed your capacity and confidence at work, and the skills you are able to bring to your employer (or indeed a new employer!).

Organisations often have a **training and development strategy**, based on the overall strategy for the business. We can list the following steps.

Step 1 Identify the skills and competences are needed by the **business plan**

Step 2 Draw up the **development strategy** to show how training and development activities will assist in meeting the targets of the corporate plan.

Step 3 **Implement** the training and development strategy.

The advantage of such an approach is that the training is:

- Relevant
- Problem-based (ie corrects a real lack of skills)
- Action-oriented
- Performance-related

1.6 Training and the organisation

Benefits for the organisation of training and development programmes

Benefit	Comment
Minimise the learning costs of obtaining the skills the organisation needs	Training supports the business strategy
Lower costs and **increased productivity,** thereby improving performance	Some people suggest that higher levels of training explain the higher productivity of German as opposed to many British manufacturers

Benefit	Comment
Fewer accidents, and better health and safety	EU health and safety directives require a certain level of training. Employees can take employers to court if accidents occur or if unhealthy work practices persist
Less need for detailed supervision	If people are trained they can get on with the job, and managers can concentrate on other things. Training is an aspect of **empowerment**
Flexibility	Training ensures that people have the **variety** of skills needed – multi-skilling is only possible if people are properly trained
Recruitment and succession planning	Training and development attracts new recruits and ensures that the organisation has a supply of suitable managerial and technical staff to take over when people retire
Change management	Training helps organisations manage change by letting people know why the change is happening and giving them the skills to cope with it
Corporate culture	(1) Training programmes can be used to build the corporate culture or to direct it in certain ways, by indicating that certain **values** are espoused. (2) Training programmes can **build relationships** between staff and managers in different areas of the business
Motivation	Training programmes can increase commitment to the organisation's goals

Training cannot do everything. Look at the wheel below paragraph 1.2 again. Training only really covers:

Aspect of performance	Areas covered
Individual	Education; Experience; possibly Personal Circumstances (if successful completion of training is accompanied by a higher salary)
Physical and job	Methods of work
Organisational and social	Type of training and supervision

In other words, **training cannot improve performance problems** arising out of:

- Bad management
- Poor job design
- Poor equipment, factory layout and work organisation
- Other characteristics of the employee (eg intelligence)
- Motivation – training gives a person the ability but not necessarily the willingness to improve
- Poor recruitment

Activity 2 **(10 minutes)**

Despite all the benefits to the organisation, many are still reluctant to train. What reasons can you give for this?

1.7 Training and the individual

For the individual employee, the benefits of training and development are more clear-cut, and few refuse it if it is offered.

Benefit	Comment
Enhances portfolio of **skills**	Even if not specifically related to the current job, training can be useful in other contexts, and the employee becomes more attractive to employers and more promotable
Psychological benefits	The trainee might feel reassured that he/she is of continuing value to the organisation
Social benefit	People's social needs can be met by training courses – they can also develop networks of contacts
The job	Training can help people do their job better, thereby increasing job satisfaction

2 IDENTIFYING TRAINING AND DEVELOPMENT NEEDS

2.1 The training process in outline

In order to ensure that training meets the real needs of the organisation, large firms adopt a planned approach to training. This has the following steps.

Step 1 Identify and define the **organisation's training needs**. It may be the case that recruitment might be a better solution to a problem than training.

Step 2 **Define the learning required** – in other words, specify the knowledge, skills or competences that have to be acquired. For technical training, this is not difficult: for example all finance department staff will have to become conversant with a new accounting system.

Step 3 **Define training objectives** – what must be learnt and what trainees must be able to do after the training exercise.

Step 4 **Plan training programmes** – training and development can be planned in a number of ways, employing a number of techniques, as we shall learn about in section 3. (Also, people have different approaches to learning, which have to be considered.) This covers:

- Who provides the training
- Where the training takes place
- Divisions of responsibilities between trainers, managers and the individual.

***Step* 5** Implement the training.

***Step* 6** Evaluate the training: has it been successful in achieving the learning objectives?

***Step* 7** Go back to Step 2 if more training is needed.

Activity 3 **(15 minutes)**

Draw up a training plan for introducing a new employee into your department. Repeat this exercise after you have completed this chapter to see if your chosen approach has changed.

2.2 Training needs analysis

Training needs analysis covers three issues.

Current state	Desired state
Organisation's current results	Desired results, standards
Existing knowledge and skill	Knowledge and skill needed
Individual performance	Required standards

The difference between the two columns is the **training gap**. Training programmes are designed to improve individual performance, thereby improving the performance of the organisation.

CASE EXAMPLE

Training for quality

The British Standards for Quality Systems (BS EN ISO 9000: formerly BS 5750) which many UK organisations are working towards (often at the request of customers, who perceive it to be a 'guarantee' that high standards of quality control are being achieved) includes training requirements. As the following extract shows, the Standard identifies training needs for those organisations registering for assessment, and also shows the importance of a systematic approach to ensure adequate control.

The training, both specific to perform assigned tasks and general to heighten quality awareness and to mould attitudes of all people in an organisation, is central to the achievement of quality.

The comprehensiveness of such training varies with the complexity of the organisation. The following steps should be taken:

1 Identifying the way tasks and operations influence quality in total

2 Identifying individuals' training needs against those required for satisfactory performance of the task

3 Planning and carrying out appropriate specific training

4 Planning and organising general quality awareness programmes

5 Recording training and achievement in an easily retrievable form so that records can be updated and gaps in training can be readily identified

BSI, 1990

Training surveys

Training surveys combine information from a variety of sources to discern what the training needs of the organisation actually are. These sources are:

(a) The **business strategy** at corporate level.

(b) **Appraisal and performance reviews** – the purpose of a performance management system is to improve performance, and training maybe recommended as a remedy.

(c) **Attitude surveys** from employees, asking them what training they think they need or would like.

(d) **Evaluation of existing training** programmes.

(e) **Job analysis** can be used. To identify training needs from the job analysis, the job analysis can pay attention to:

  (i) Reported difficulties people have in meeting the skills requirement of the job

  (ii) Existing performance weaknesses, of whatever kind, which could be remedied by training

  (iii) Future changes in the job.

  The job analysis can be used to generate a training specification covering the knowledge needed for the job, the skills required to achieve the result and attitudinal changes required.

2.3 Setting training objectives

The training manager will have to make an initial investigation into the problem of the gap between job or competence **requirements** and current performance of **competence**.

If training would improve work performance, training **objectives** can then be defined. They should be clear, specific and related to observable, measurable targets, ideally detailing:

- **Behaviour** – what the trainee should be able to do
- **Standard** – to what level of performance?
- **Environment** – under what conditions (so that the performance level is realistic)?

EXAMPLE: TRAINING OBJECTIVE

'At the end of the course the trainee should be able to describe ... or identify ... or distinguish x from y ... or calculate ... or assemble ...' and so on. It is insufficient to define the objectives of training as 'to give trainees a grounding in ...' or 'to encourage trainees in a better appreciation of ...': this offers no target achievement which can be measured.

Training objectives link the identification of training needs with the content, methods and technology of training. Some examples of translating training needs into learning objectives are given in *Personnel Management, A New Approach* by *D Torrington and L Hall.*

Training needs	**Learning objectives**
To know more about the Data Protection Act	The employee will be able to answer four out of every five queries about the Data Protection Act without having to search for details.
To establish a better rapport with customers	The employee will immediately attend to a customer unless already engaged with another customer. The employee will greet each customer using the customer's name where known. The employee will apologise to every customer who has had to wait to be attended to.
To assemble clocks more quickly	The employee will be able to assemble each clock correctly within thirty minutes.

Having identified training needs and objectives, the manager will have to decide on the best way to approach training: there are a number of types and techniques of training, which we will discuss below.

3 METHODS OF TRAINING AND DEVELOPMENT

3.1 Formal training

Formal training

(a) **Courses** may be run by the organisation's training department or may be provided by external suppliers.

(b) **Types of course**

(i) **Day release**: the employee works in the organisation and on one day per week attends a local college or training centre for theoretical learning.

(ii) **Distance learning, evening classes and correspondence courses,** which make demands on the individual's time outside work.

(iii) **Revision courses** for examinations of professional bodies.

(iv) **Block release** courses which may involve four weeks at a college or training centre followed by a period back at work.

(v) **Sandwich courses,** usually involve six months at college then six months at work, in rotation, for two or three years.

(vi) A **sponsored full-time course** at a university for one or two years.

(c) **Computer-based training** involves interactive training via PC. The typing program, Mavis Beacon, is a good example.

(d) **Techniques** used on the course might include lecturers, seminars, role play and simulation.

3.2 Disadvantages of formal training

(a) An individual will not benefit from formal training unless he or she **is motivated to learn.**

(b) If the **subject matter** of the training course does not **relate to an individual's job**, the learning will quickly be forgotten.

3.3 On the job training

Successful on the job training

(a) The assignments should have a **specific purpose** from which the trainee can learn and gain experience.

(b) The organisation must **tolerate any mistakes** which the trainee makes. Mistakes are an inevitable part of on the job learning.

(c) The work should **not be too complex.**

Methods of on the job training

(a) **Demonstration/instruction:** show the trainee how to do the job and let them get on with it. It should combine **telling** a person what to do and **showing** them how, using appropriate media. The trainee imitates the instructor, and asks questions.

(b) **Coaching:** the trainee is put under the guidance of an experienced employee who shows the trainee how to do the job.

(i) **Establish learning targets**. The areas to be learnt should be identified, and specific, realistic goals (eg completion dates, performance standards) stated by agreement with the trainee.

(ii) **Plan a systematic learning and development programme.** This will ensure regular progress, appropriate stages for consolidation and practice.

(iii) **Identify opportunities for broadening the trainee's knowledge and experience:** eg by involvement in new projects, placement on inter-departmental committees, suggesting new contacts, or simply extending the job, adding more tasks, greater responsibility etc.

(iv) **Take into account the strengths and limitations of the trainee** in learning, and take advantage of learning opportunities that suit the trainee's ability, preferred style and goals.

(v) **Exchange feedback**. The coach will want to know how the trainee sees his or her progress and future. He or she will also need performance information in order to monitor the trainee's progress, adjust the learning programme if necessary, identify further needs which may emerge and plan future development for the trainee.

(c) **Job rotation:** the trainee is given several jobs in succession, to gain experience of a wide range of activities. (Even experienced managers may rotate their jobs, to gain wider experience; this philosophy of job education is commonly applied in the Civil Service, where an employee may expect to move on to another job after a few years.)

(d) **Temporary promotion:** an individual is promoted into his/her superior's position while the superior is absent due to illness. This gives the individual a chance to experience the demands of a more senior position.

(e) **'Assistant to' positions:** a junior manager with good potential may be appointed as assistant to the managing director or another executive director. In this way, the individual gains experience of how the organisation is managed 'at the top'.

(f) **Action learning:** a group of managers are brought together to solve a real problem with the help of an 'advisor' who exposes the management process that actually happens.

(g) **Committees:** trainees might be included in the membership of committees, in order to obtain an understanding of inter-departmental relationships.

(h) **Project work:** work on a project with other people can expose the trainee to other parts of the organisation.

Activity 4 **(15 minutes)**

Suggest a suitable training method for each of the following situations.

(a) A worker is transferred onto a new machine and needs to learn its operation.

(b) An accounts clerk wishes to work towards becoming qualified with the relevant professional body.

(c) An organisation decides that its supervisors would benefit from ideas on participative management and democratic leadership.

(d) A new member of staff is about to join the organisation.

3.4 Induction training

On the first day, a manager or personnel/HR officer should welcome the new recruit. He/she should then introduce the new recruit to the person who will be their **immediate supervisor.**

The immediate supervisor should commence the **on-going process of induction**.

Step 1 Pinpoint the areas that the recruit will have to learn about in order to **start the job**. Some things (such as detailed technical knowledge) may be identified as areas for later study or training.

Step 2 Explain first of all the nature of the job, and the goals of each task, both of the recruit's job and of the department as a whole.

Step 3 Explain about hours of work, and stress the importance of time-keeping. If flexitime is operated, the supervisor should explain how it works.

Step 4 Explain the structure of the department: to whom the recruit will report, to whom he/she can go with complaints or queries and so on.

Step 5 Introduce the recruit to the people in the office. One particular colleague may be assigned to the recruit as a **mentor**, to keep an eye on them, answer routine queries, 'show them the ropes'.

Step 6 Plan and implement an appropriate **training programmes** for whatever technical or practical knowledge is required. Again, the programme should have a clear schedule and set of goals so that the recruit has a sense of purpose, and so that the programme can be efficiently organised to fit in with the activities of the department.

Step 7 Coach and/or train the recruit; and check regularly on their progress, as demonstrated by performance, as reported by the recruit's mentor, and as perceived by the recruit him or herself.

Note that induction is an **on-going process**, embracing mentoring, coaching, training, monitoring and so on. It is not just a first day affair! After three months, six months or one year the performance of a new recruit should be formally appraised and discussed with them. Indeed, when the process of induction has been finished, a recruit should continue to receive periodic appraisals, just like every other employee in the organisation.

Appraisal is covered in detail in Chapter 10.

Activity 5 **(30 minutes)**

'Joining an organisation with around 8,500 staff, based on two sites over a mile apart and in the throes of major restructuring, can be confusing for any recruit. This is the situation facing the 20 to 30 new employees recruited each month by the Guy's and St Thomas' Hospital Trust, which was formed by the merger of the two hospitals in April.

In a climate of change, new employees joining the NHS can be influenced by the negative attitudes of other staff who may oppose the current changes. So it has become increasingly important for the trust's management executive to get across their view of the future and to understand the feelings of confusion new staff may be experiencing.'

Personnel Management Plus, August 1993

See if you can design a **one day** induction programme for these new recruits, in the light of the above. The programme is to be available to **all** new recruits, from doctors and radiographers to accountants, catering and cleaning staff and secretaries.

4 PEOPLE INVOLVED IN TRAINING AND DEVELOPMENT

4.1 The trainee

Many people now believe that the ultimate responsibility for training and development lies, not with the employer, but with the **individual**. People should seek to develop their own skills, to improve their own careers rather than wait for the organisation to impose training upon them. Why? The current conventional wisdom is that:

(a) **Delayering** means there are fewer automatic promotion pathways; promotion was once a source of development but there might not be further promotions available.

(b) **Technological change** means that new skills are always needed, and people who can find new work will be learning new skills.

Activity 6 **(2 minutes)**

You are currently studying for a business qualification. Was this your own decision, or were you encouraged to do so by your employer? Do you think that this will have any impact on your training and development?

4.2 The human resources department or training department

The human resources department is ideally concerned with developing people. Some organisations have extensive development and career planning programmes. These shape the progression of individuals through the organisation, in accordance with the performance and potential of the individual and the needs of the organisation. Of course, only large organisations can afford to use this sort of approach.

The HR department also performs an **administrative** role by recording what training and development opportunities an individual might be given – in some firms, going on a training programme is an entitlement that the personnel department might have to enforce.

4.3 The supervisor and manager

Line managers and supervisors bear some of the responsibility for training and development within the organisation by identifying:

- The training needs of the department or section
- The current competences of the individuals within the department
- Opportunities for learning and development on the job
- When feedback is necessary

The **supervisor** may be required to organise training programmes for staff.

4.4 Mentoring

Definition

> **Mentoring** is the use of specially trained individuals to provide guidance and advice which will help develop the careers of those allocate to them. A person's line manager should not be his or her mentor.

Mentors can assist in:

- Drawing up personal development plans
- Advice with administrative problems people face in their new jobs
- Help in tackling projects, by pointing people in the right direction

Mentoring is covered in more depth in Chapter 10.

4.5 The training manager

The training manager is a member of staff appointed to arrange and sometimes run training. The training manager generally reports to the **human resources** or **personnel director,** but also needs a good relationship with line managers in the production and other departments where the training takes place.

4.6 Responsibilities of the training manager

Responsibility	Comment
Liaison	With HRM department and operating departments
Scheduling	Arranging training programmes at convenient times
Skills identifying	Discerning existing and future skills shortages
Programme design	Develop tailored training programmes
Feedback	The trainee, the department and the HR department

5 EVALUATING TRAINING

Definition

> **Validation of training** means observing the results of the course and measuring whether the training objectives have been achieved.
>
> **Evaluation of training** means comparing the actual costs of the scheme against the assessed benefits which are being obtained. If the costs exceed the benefits, the scheme will need to be redesigned or withdrawn.

Ways of validating and evaluating a training scheme

(a) **Trainees' reactions to the experience.** This form of monitoring is rather inexact, and it does not allow the training department to measure the results for comparison against the training objective.

(b) **Trainee learning:** measuring what the trainees have learned on the course by means of a test at the end of it.

(c) **Changes in job behaviour following training.** This is possible where the purpose of the course was to learn a particular skill.

(d) **Organisational change as a result of training:** finding out whether the training has affected the work or behaviour of **other** employees not on the course – seeing whether there has been a general change in attitudes arising from a new course in, say, computer terminal work. This form of monitoring would probably be reserved for senior managers in the training department.

(e) **Impact of training on organisational goals:** seeing whether the training scheme has contributed to the overall objectives of the organisation. This too is a form of monitoring reserved for senior management, and would perhaps be discussed at board level in the organisation. It is likely to be the main component of a cost-benefit analysis.

Activity 7 **(10 minutes)**

Outline why it is important to evaluate and validate a training programme and describe possible methods for achieving this.

6 THE LEARNING PROCESS

6.1 Learning theories

There are different schools of learning theory, which explain and describe how people learn.

(a) **Behaviourist psychology** concentrated on the relationship between **stimuli** (input through the senses) and **responses** to those stimuli. 'Learning' is the formation of **new** connections between stimulus and response, on the basis of **conditioning**. We modify our responses in future according to whether the results of our behaviour in the past have been good or bad. We are continually looking for ways to achieve more positive reinforcement, in terms of rewards, and avoid negative reinforcement, ie punishment.

The principles for learning underlying this approach include:

(i) The learner must be able to respond **actively**
(ii) **Frequency of repetition** of responses is important in acquiring skills
(iii) **Immediate feedback** of results is strongly motivating
(iv) Learning is helped when **objectives are clear**

(b) The **cognitive approach** argues that the human mind takes sensory information and imposes organisation and meaning on it: we interpret and rationalise. We use feedback information on the results of past behaviour to make **rational decisions** about whether to maintain successful behaviours or modify unsuccessful behaviours in future, according to our goals and our plans for reaching them. The principles for learning associated with cognitive theories are:

(i) Instruction should be **well organised** and be clearly structured – making it easier to learn and to remember.

(ii) The way a **problem is displayed** is important if learners are to understand it.

(iii) **Prior knowledge** is important – things must fit with what is already known

6.2 Effective training programmes

Whichever approach it is based on, learning theory offers certain useful propositions for the design of **effective training programmes**.

Proposition	Comment
The individual should be **motivated** to learn	The advantages of training should be made clear, according to the individual's motives – money, opportunity, valued skills or whatever.
There should be clear **objectives and standards** set, so that each task has some meaning	Each stage of learning should present a challenge, without overloading the trainee or making them lose confidence. Specific objectives and performance standards for each will help the trainee in the planning and control process that leads to learning, and providing targets against which performance will constantly be measured.
There should be timely, relevant **feedback** on performance and progress	This will usually be provided by the trainer, and should be concurrent – or certainly not long delayed. If progress reports or performance appraisals are given only at the year end, for example, there will be no opportunity for behaviour adjustment or learning in the meantime.
Positive and negative **reinforcement** should be judiciously used	Recognition and encouragement enhance an individual's confidence in their competence and progress: punishment for poor performance – especially without explanation and correction – discourages the learner and creates feelings of guilt, failure and hostility
Active **participation** is more telling than passive reception (because of its effect on the motivation to learn, concentration and recollection)	If a high degree of participation is impossible, practise and repetition can be used to reinforce receptivity. However, participation has the effect of encouraging 'ownership' of the process of learning and changing – committing the individual to it as their **own** goal, not just an imposed process.

6.3 Learning styles

The way in which people learn best will differ according to the type of person. That is, there are **learning styles** which suit different individuals. *Peter Honey and Alan Mumford* have drawn up a popular classification of four learning styles.

(a) **Theorists**

Seek to understand basic principles and to take an intellectual, 'hands-off' approach based on logical argument. They prefer training to be:

(i) Programmed and structured

(ii) Designed to allow time for analysis

(iii) Provided by teachers who share his/her preference for concepts and analysis

(b) **Reflectors**

(i) Observe phenomena, think about them and then choose how to act

(ii) Need to work at their own pace

(iii) Find learning difficult if forced into a hurried programme

(iv) Produce carefully thought-out conclusions after research and reflection

(v) Tend to be fairly slow, non-participative (unless to ask questions) and cautious

(c) **Activists**

(i) Deal with practical, active problems and do not have patience with theory

(ii) Require training based on hands-on experience

(iii) Excited by participation and pressure, such as new projects

(iv) Flexible and optimistic, but tend to rush without due preparation

(d) **Pragmatists**

(i) Only like to study if they can see its direct link to practical problems

(ii) Good at learning new techniques in on-the-job training

(iii) Aim is to implement action plans and/or do the task better

(iv) May discard good ideas which only require some development

Training programmes should ideally be designed to accommodate the preferences of all four styles. This can often be overlooked especially as the majority of training staff are activitists.

6.4 The learning cycle

Another useful model is the **experiential learning cycle** devised by *David Kolb*. Experiential learning involves **doing,** however, and puts the learners in an active problem-solving role: a form of **self-learning** which encourages the learners to formulate and commit themselves to their own learning objectives.

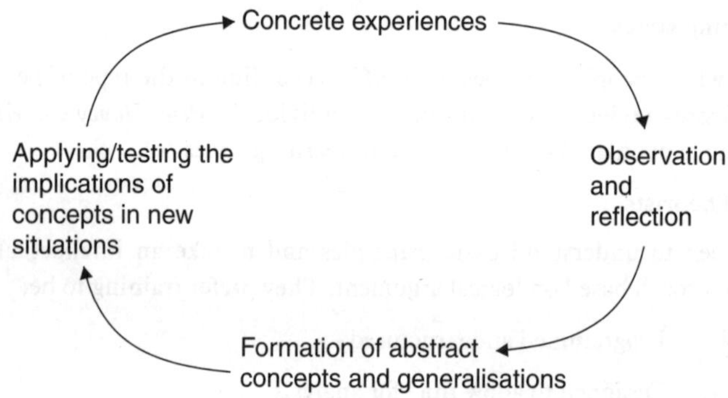

Figure 8.2: Kolb's experiential learning cycle

EXAMPLE

An employee interviews a customer for the first time (concrete experience). He observes his own performance and the dynamics of the situation (observation) and afterwards, having failed to convince the customer to buy his product, the employee analyses what he did right and wrong (reflection). He comes to the conclusion that he failed to listen to what the customer really wanted and feared, underneath his general reluctance: he realises that the key to communication is listening (abstraction/ generalisation). In his next interview he applies his strategy to the new set of circumstances (application/ testing). This provides him with a new experience with which to start the cycle over again.

Simplified, this 'learning by doing' approach involves:

Act → Analyse action → Understand principles → Apply principles

Activity 8 **(15 minutes)**

With reference to *Kolb's* learning cycle, think of a situation on your present course where you have been involved in a practical exercise or 'experiential learning'. Illustrate the stages of the learning cycle using your chosen example.

6.5 Barriers to learning

According to *Peter Senge*, there are seven sources of **learning disability** in organisations which prevent them from attaining their potential – which trap them into 'mediocrity', for example, when they could be achieving 'excellence'.

(a) **'I am my position'**. When asked what they do for a living, most people describe the tasks they perform, not the **purposes** they fulfil; thus they tend to see their responsibilities as limited to the boundaries of their position.

(b) **'The enemy is out there'**. If things go wrong it is all too easy to imagine that somebody else 'out there' was at fault.

(c) **The illusion of taking charge**. The individual decides to be more active in fighting the enemy out there, trying to destroy rather than to build.

(d) **The fixation on events**. Conversations in organisations are dominated by concern about events (last month's sales, who's just been promoted, the new product from our competitor), and this focus inevitably distracts us from seeing the longer-term patterns of change.

(e) **The parable of the boiled frog**. Failure to adapt to gradually building threats is pervasive. (If you place a frog in a pot of boiling water, it will immediately try to scramble out; but if you place the frog in room temperature water, he will stay put. If you heat the water gradually, the frog will do nothing until he boils: this is because 'the frog's internal apparatus for sensing threats to survival is geared to sudden changes in his environment, not to slow, gradual changes'.)

(f) **The delusion of learning from experience**. We learn best from experience, but we never experience the results of our most important and significant decisions. Indeed, we never know what the outcomes would have been had we done something else.

(g) **The myth of the management team**. All too often, the management 'team' is not a team at all, but is a collection of individuals competing for power and resources.

Activity 9 **(20 minutes)**

How far do *Senge's* seven learning disabilities apply to your own organisation, or to some other significant organisation with which you may be familiar?

For individuals, the barriers may be:

- 'A waste of time': people see no personal benefit from training
- Training programmes employ the wrong techniques for people's learning styles
- Unwillingness to change

6.6 Encouraging learning: what managers can do

Managers can try to **develop the learning organisation** learning organisation:

- Encourages continuous learning and knowledge generation at all levels
- Has the processes to move knowledge around the organisation
- Can transform knowledge into actual behaviour

Definition

Learning organisation is 'An organisation that facilitates the learning of all its members and continuously transforms itself'.

6.7 The building of the learning organisation

Characteristics	Comments
Systematic problem-solving	Problems should be tackled in a scientific way
Experimentation	Experimentation can generate new insights
Learn from experience	Knowledge from past failures can help avoid them in future
Learn from others	Customers and other firms can be a good source of ideas. Learning opportunities should be sought out
Knowledge transfer	Knowledge should be transferred throughout the organisation

7 INDIVIDUAL LEARNING

7.1 Lifelong learning

Increasingly, and especially in the professional sectors, it is becoming the responsibility of the individual to ensure that they take responsibility for their own development.

Definition

> **Lifelong learning** 'Learning activity undertaken throughout life, with the aim of improving knowledge, skills and competence within a personal and/or employer-related perspective.'

The idea that learning goes on throughout our lives and that learning opportunities are presented to us continuously has been formally reflected in the government's commitment to Lifelong Learning and its aim to develop that same commitment in organisations and individuals everywhere.

Pedler, Burgoyne and Boydell acknowledge the same concept in *The Learning Company*, McGraw-Hill (1991).

> 'Each of us is in a process of development as a person and as a worker. We can become aware of the process and, to some extent, direct ourselves towards desired ends – towards becoming the person and professional we want to be.'

From a professional point of view, your objective should be to ensure 'growth' during your career. This objective can obviously benefit your organisation as well as you. The growth should be triggered by a job that provides challenging, stretching goals. The clearer and more challenging the goals, the more effort you will exert, and the more likely it is that good performance will result. If you do a good job and receive positive feedback, you will feel successful (psychological success). These feelings will increase your feelings of confidence and self-esteem. This should lead to you becoming more involved in your work, which in turn leads to the setting of future stretching goals.

7.2 Encouraging lifelong learning

As we have noted, lifelong learning is key to both professional and personal growth. But, it also needs to be a way of life at your organisation.

Some examples of ways to create a workplace atmosphere that encourages learning include:

Instead of a 'to do' list, keep a 'to learn' list. Staff can be encouraged to jot down any learning needs they have. For example, do they want to know more about time management or negotiating? Would they like to learn more about quality improvement or ethical issues? They get added to the list, too.

Keep your eyes open! Staff could be encouraged to observe a co-worker whom they admire. A lot can be learned by watching, especially when observing people who are really good at what they do. Some of their excellent work habits may be adopted.

Practice what you learn. Knowledge by itself is great but it takes on real value when it is *applied*. Share with your staff how you put new knowledge to work for you on the job and suggest they try the same strategy.

Show others how it is done. A great way to learn is by teaching others. Ask staff to help train new employees. Or, each time you hold a meeting or give a presentation, ask a different member of staff to help lead the meeting.

Learn in groups. Suggest that your staff work together in groups of two or three. They can bounce ideas off each other and, as a result, learn more than they would by working on their own.

Think outside the box. When people stick to the exact same routine every day, they may go on 'autopilot' and stop learning. Encourage them to switch things around a bit-as long as it does not interfere with a colleague's or client's needs or rights.

Make learning a priority. The motivation to keep on learning has to come from within. Demonstrate that lifelong learning is a daily habit for you and the people you work with may decide to make it a priority in their lives, too.

8 GROUP DEVELOPMENT PROCESSES AND BEHAVIOUR

We all belong to groups. They can be social, casual, formal or informal. Social groups include families, friends, clubs, voluntary organisations, religious societies and some work-related groupings of people, such as a regular lunch-time card school. Some groups are work groups, which may be formally established as part of the organisation or informally created by those working together or sharing an interest. Formal groups include committees.

Definition

> **Group:** a collection of individuals with a common interest and who share a common identity. A group has a leader, a set of social norms and a reason for its existence. It may be informal or formally established and its existence may be permanent or temporary.

Groups may come together spontaneously or be formally established. However, they do not become teams until they have gone through the process of team formation.

8.1 Group formation

Organisations create formal groups (also referred to as official groups) automatically as departments and specialisms develop. Groups are also created to perform such tasks as exchanging ideas, sharing information, coordinating work and performing tasks that require the collective use of skills. The Board of Directors is a formal group; so are the Health and Safety Committee and the night shift operatives in machine shop four.

Informal (or unofficial) groups form at work because of:

(a) People's needs to socialise
(b) A need for self-help (for example, a baby sitting circle)
(c) A need for protection and collective action (for example, a union)

The aims of an informal group and the organisation may be different. It is important that organisations recognise the existence of informal groups and try to use them constructively, rather than making what are likely to be futile attempts to suppress them.

A group of people can be appointed to be a team, but a group has to go through the process of becoming a team before it can function as one. The composition of the group will affect its ability to become effective. Simply setting up a team does not make a group of people into a team, nor does it make it effective. Teams have to be formed with care.

8.2 Stages of group development

There are two dimensions – personal relations and task functions – that are central to the process of group development. This is illustrated in the figure below.

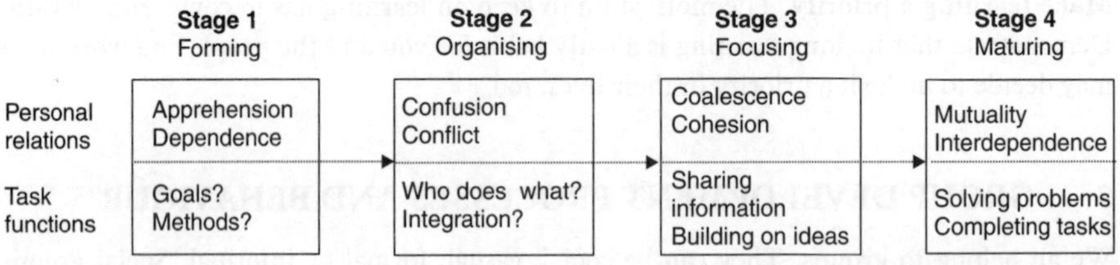

Figure 8.3: Stages of group development

As people progress through the stages towards becoming a group, personal relations evolve from apprehensive, tentative interactions and dependence on leaders or formal instructions through confusion and conflict (either overt or covert) to cohesiveness and ultimate interdependence. Obviously, some groups never reach the mature stage, which is the optimal use of human resources, even when tasks are accomplished reasonably well. Progress on task functions often parallels the development of personal relations, although one-to-one correlation is not necessary. The first stage involves understanding the task, group goals, and alternative means of achieving them. The organising stage means resolving issues/conflict such as leadership, authority-responsibility relationships, and methods of doing and coordinating the work. In stage three the group begins to share information and feelings and build on each other's ideas to get the job done. The mark of a mature group is its capacity to solve specific problems or to complete tasks, while at the same time improving its ability to do so. This calls for simultaneous attention to task accomplishment and group development.

8.3 Internal training and development methods for groups

Group training encourages participants to learn from each other through discussing issues, pooling experiences and critically examining opposite viewpoints. Instructors guide discussions rather than impart knowledge directly. They monitor trainee's understanding of what is going on, ask questions to clarify points and sometimes, but not always, prevent certain members from dominating the group. Some of the most popular methods follow.

(a) **The lecture method**: this is regarded as an economical way of giving a large amount of information to many people. Some people prefer listening to reading and good lecturers can help learning and assist understanding. Lectures are of little value if the aim of training is to change attitudes, or develop job or interpersonal skills.

(b) **Discussion methods**: discussion and participation are known ways of securing interest and commitment. Discussion methods in this respect are useful ways of shaping attitudes, encouraging motivation and securing understanding. Discussion methods can also underline the nature, and the difficulties of group problem-solving.

(c) **Case study method**: in this approach to training, learning occurs through participation in the definition, analysis and solution of the problem or problems. It demonstrates the nature of group problem-solving activity and usually underlines the view that there is no one best solution to a complex business problem. Casework creates interest and enthusiasm among members but, when they lack knowledge and experience, the exercise can fail.

(d) **Role playing**: this method requires trainees to project themselves into a simulated situation that is intended to represent some relevant reality, say, a confrontation between management and a trade union. The merit of role-playing is that it influences attitudes, develops interpersonal skills and heightens sensitivity to the views and feelings of others. However, it requires careful organising and giving tactful feedback is not easy unless the exercise is filmed in such a way that instant playback is possible.

(e) **Business games**: games simulate realistic situations, mergers, take-overs, etc in which groups compete with one another and where the effects of the decision taken by one group may affect others. The benefits are said to include development of an appreciation of the complex character of decision-taking, understanding of risk and the nature of teamwork. Although business games and case studies can be devised to correspond to real life situations, the classroom environment means that participants might not take them seriously.

(f) **T-group exercises** (the T stands for training) leave the group to their own devices. The trainer simply tells them to look after themselves and remains as an observer. The group itself has to decide what to do and, understandably, the members feel helpless at first and then they pool their experiences and help each other. They eventually form a cohesive group, appoint a leader and resolve any conflicts within the group. The advantages claimed for T-group exercises are that members recognise the need to learn from experience and from each other. They also observe how others react to offers of help. Since the group begins in a leaderless state and ends by appointing a leader, it demystifies the process of leader selection. They exercise interpersonal communication skills and learn to understand group dynamics.

Next we look at group behaviour.

8.4 Group behaviour

Groups establish norms or acceptable standards of behaviour. The things which the group has in common and which characterise it are group norms. All members of the group are expected to conform to these. Groups put pressure on members to conform, and those who wish to belong will do so. Failure to conform can lead to conflict with the rest of the group. In extreme cases an individual can be excluded from all desirable groups and forced to seek another job.

Rituals

Groups develop their own rituals, such as meeting in a certain place for coffee breaks, going to the same pub for lunch or meeting after work on Fridays. Individuals may tend to seek acceptance and pretend to conform to such norms as working late, while regularly making excuses to go on time. Similarly, a member may conceal non-adherence to norms by avoiding some aspects of the social activities of the group – having to catch a particular train or getting a lift can be used to avoid after-work drinking sessions.

Where bonus payments are related to group performance there is much stronger pressure on members to conform. Unauthorised breaks and failure to meet targets that affect the performance of the group as a whole are likely to attract strong pressure to conform.

EXAMPLE: GROUP RITUALS IN THE WORKPLACE

An ice cream factory had several lines for filling different flavours of ice cream into tubs, cartons, choc ices and ice lollies. Each filling line had a team, with a leader who allocated jobs – usually in strict rotation so as to avoid boredom. The elite team worked on choc ices. The lowest level in the pecking order was the team responsible for stacking incoming supplies of cartons and loading delivery trucks.

Each team had its special table in the canteen. The ice lolly team brought in cakes they made and shared them. The stackers and loaders took their breaks elsewhere. The choc ice team took their break at a different time from everyone else. Entry to that group was by invitation and seniority. Managers had learned that it was not a good idea to try to allocate new members to choc ices: there would be an astonishing rise in the number of choc ices incorrectly wrapped or partly coated. Teams organised their own informal breaks on a rota basis. Anyone overstaying would lose the next break as the team leader would not relieve them.

The factory paid bonuses to teams that exceeded monthly targets for filling cartons and tubs. There were strict quality controls which included a variation of not more than ½ per cent either side of the declared weight. Quality checks showing unacceptable variations in fill weight led to the conveyor being slowed down and consequent loss of bonuses. Individuals who persistently underfilled in an attempt to earn bonuses were banished to the menial jobs of fetching boxes of empty cartons and removing filled tubs to the cold store. These people would also miss out on rounds of drinks in the Friday pub session.

8.5 Group cohesiveness

Group cohesiveness develops over time as the group moves through the stages to maturity. It refers to the ability of a group to stick together. A strongly cohesive group can become exclusive, with entry being virtually impossible. Individuals find it much easier to join less cohesive groups and groups in the earlier stages of formation.

Factors which affect the development of group cohesiveness are:

(a) Similarity of work
(b) Physical proximity in the work place
(c) The work flow system and whether or not it gives continuing contact
(d) The structure of tasks – whether individualised or group
(e) Group size – smaller groups are more cohesive
(f) Threats from outside – where a group sees other groups as the enemy
(g) Prospects of rewards
(h) Leadership style of the manager
(i) Common social factors, such as race, social status and cultural origins

Next we look at the factors that affect the effectiveness of groups, and the features of effective and ineffective groups.

8.6 Group effectiveness

The personalities of group members and the traits they bring to the group play an important part in deciding its effectiveness. Personal goals also affect effectiveness. It is easy for groups, especially informal ones, to decide that a low level of productivity is the norm. Groups can be motivated to improve their performance. This requires:

(a) A clearly defined task
(b) Effective leadership
(c) Small group size
(d) Skills and abilities matched to the task
(e) Proximity at work, for example an open-plan office
(f) Rewards that are regarded as fair by the group

Factors for identifying effective work groups

A number of factors are involved in identifying effective and ineffective work groups. Some are quantifiable and others are qualitative.

Effective work group	Ineffective work group
Quantifiable factors	
(a) Low rate of labour turnover	(a) High rate of labour turnover
(b) Low accident rate	(b) High accident rate
(c) Low absenteeism	(c) High absenteeism
(d) High output and productivity	(d) Low output and productivity
(e) Good quality of output	(e) Poor quality of output
(f) Individual targets are achieved	(f) Individual targets are not achieved
(g) There are few stoppages and interruptions to work	(g) Time is lost owing to disagreements between supervisor and subordinates
Qualitative factors	
(a) There is a high commitment to the achievement of targets and organisational goals	(a) There is no understanding of organisational goals or the role of the group
(b) There is a clear understanding of the group's work	(b) There is a low commitment to targets
(c) There is a clear understanding of the role of each person within the group	(c) There is confusion and uncertainty about the role of each person within the group
(d) There is a free and open communication between members of the group and trust between members	(d) There is mistrust between group members and suspicion of the group's leader
(e) There is idea sharing	(e) There is little idea sharing
(f) The group is good at generating new ideas	(f) The group does not generate any good new ideas
(g) Group members try to help each other out by offering constructive criticisms and suggestions	(g) Group members make negative and hostile criticisms of each other's work
(h) There is group problem solving which gets to the root causes of the work problem	(h) Work problems are dealt with superficially, with attention paid to the symptoms but not the cause
(i) There is an active interest in work decisions	(i) Decisions about work are accepted passively
(j) Group members seek a united consensus of opinion	(j) Group members hold strongly opposed views
(k) The members of the group want to develop their abilities in their work	(k) Group members find work boring and do it reluctantly
(1) The group is sufficiently motivated to be able to carry on working in the absence of its leader	(1) The group needs its leader there to get work done

FOR DISCUSSION

Select a group you are involved in, for example a seminar or tutorial group, and analyse its effectiveness in terms of the features it shows from the above list. How valid are these factors in deciding whether or not a group is effective?

8.7 Relationships with other groups

A group's effectiveness is also affected by its relationships with other groups. Contact with other groups can bring power struggles, personal conflict between leaders, territorial disputes and distrust of motives. Relations in the work place often seem to parallel gang warfare in Los Angeles, where each group will go to any lengths to protect its turf.

Effectiveness can be improved and constructive competition encouraged by:

(a) Rewarding groups on the basis of their contribution to the organisation as a whole and their efforts to collaborate, rather than rewarding only individual group performance

(b) Encouraging staff to move across group boundaries so that understanding and cooperation are improved

(c) Avoiding putting groups into situations where one must emerge a winner and another a loser

(d) Encouraging communication between groups through committees, discussion groups, joint planning meetings and so on

Chapter roundup

- In order to achieve its goals, an organisation requires a skilled workforce. This is partly achieved by training.
- The main purpose of training and development is to raise competence and therefore performance standards. It is also concerned with personal development, helping and motivating employees to fulfil their potential.
- A thorough analysis of training needs should be carried out as part of a systematic approach to training, to ensure that training programmes meet organisational and individual requirements. Once training needs have been identified, they should be translated into training objectives.
- Individuals can incorporate training and development objectives into a personal development plan.
- There are a variety of training methods. These include:
  - Formal education and training
  - On-the-job training
  - Awareness-oriented training
- There are different schools of thought as to how people learn. Different people have different learning styles.
- Managers can design and manage the organisation to encourage learning.
- A SWOT analysis helps to identify your personal strengths and weaknesses and the opportunities and threats that affect your career opportunities and future prospects.
- Competences are the critical skills, knowledge and attitudes that you must have to perform effectively. They are expressed in visible, behavioural terms and reflect the skills, knowledge and attitude (the main components of any job), which must be demonstrated to an agreed standard and must contribute to the overall aims of the organisation.
- In your development plan you must establish targets that you are aiming for and remember that all good plans must be monitored and evaluated.
- Individuals find it much easier to join less cohesive groups and groups in the earlier stages of formation.
- Groups can be motivated to improve their performance using techniques such as clearly defined tasks, effective leadership, small groups sizes, proximity at work and fair rewards.

Quick quiz

1 List examples of development opportunities within organisations.

2 List how training can contribute to:

(a) Organisational effectiveness
(b) Individual effectiveness and motivation

3 According to ISO 9000, what are the main steps to be adopted in a systematic approach to training?

4 Define the term 'training need'.

5 How should training objectives be expressed?

6 What does learning theory tell us about the design of training programmes?

7 List the four learning styles put forward by *Honey and Mumford*.

8 List the four stages in *Kolb's* experiential learning cycle.

9 What is the supervisor's role in training?

10 What are the levels of training validation/evaluation?

Answers to quick quiz

1 Career planning, job rotation, deputising, on-the-job training, counselling, guidance, education and training.

2 (a) Increased efficiency and productivity; reduced costs, supervisory problems and accidents; improved quality, motivation and morale.

(b) Demonstrates individual value, enhances security, enhances skills portfolio, motivates, helps develop networks and contacts.

3 Identify how operations influence quality; identify individual training needs against performance requirements; plan and conduct training; plan and organise quality awareness programmes; record training and achievement.

4 The required level of competence minus the present level of competence.

5 Actively – 'after completing this chapter you should understand how to design and evaluate training programmes'.

6 The trainee should be motivated to learn, there should be clear objectives and timely feedback. Positive and negative reinforcement should be used carefully, to encourage active participation where possible.

7 Theorist, reflector, activist and pragmatist.

8 Concrete experience, observation/reflection, abstraction/generalisation, application/testing.

9 Identifying training needs of the department or section. Identifying the skills of the individual employee, and deficiencies in performance. Providing or supervising on-the-job training (eg coaching). Providing feedback on an individual's performance.

10 Reactions, learning, job behaviour, organisational change, ultimate impact.

Answers to activities

1 Few employers throw you in at the deep end – it is far too risky for them! Instead, you might have been given induction training to get acclimatised to the organisation, and you might have been introduced slowly to the job. Ideally, your employer would have planned a programme of tasks of steadily greater complexity and responsibility to allow you to grow into your role(s).

2 Cost: training can be costly. Ideally, it should be seen as an investment in the future or as something the firm has to do to maintain its position. In practice, many firms are reluctant to train because of poaching by other employers – their newly trained staff have skills which can be sold for more elsewhere. This got so bad that staff at one computer services firm were required to pay the firm £4,000 if they left (to go to another employer) within two years of a major training programme.

3 The answer to this activity will depend on your own personal situation and that of your employer. There is no 'right or wrong' answer.

4 Training methods for the various workers indicated are as follows.

(a) Worker on a new machine: on-the-job training, coaching.

(b) Accounts clerk working for professional qualification: external course – evening class or day-release.

(c) Supervisors wishing to benefit from participative management and democratic leadership: internal or external course. However, it is important that monitoring and evaluation takes place to ensure that the results of the course are subsequently applied in practice.

(d) New staff: induction training.

5 Here is the actual programme for new recruits (of all types) at Guy's and St Thomas' Hospital Trust, as published in *Personnel Management Plus*.

9.00	Welcome	
9.05	Introduction	*Ground rules and objectives for the day*
9.25	Presentation	*The history of Guy's and St Thomas' hospitals*
10.25	Presentation	*Talk on structure of the management team, trust board and executive*
10.45	Group exercise	*With chief executive Tim Matthews on patient care, funding, hospital processes and measuring the care provided*
12.20	Lunch	
1.15	Tour of Guy's	
2.30	Presentation	*Looking at trust with new eyes – suggestions for change*
2.50	Presentation	*Information on staff organisations*
3.10	Presentation	*Security issues, fire drills, health and safety (including handouts)*
3.30	Presentation	*Session on occupational health*
3.40	Presentation	*Local areas and staff benefits*
3.45	Tour of St Thomas'	
4.30	Presentation	*Facilities management and patient care*
4.45	Closing session	*Evaluation and finish*

Particularly important is the focus on patient care and the group exercises. 'Feedback from the participants shows that they enjoy the discussions and learn a lot more about their colleagues and the trust by participating rather than being talked at.'

6 This will depend on your own situation.

7 Validation of a new course is important to ensure that objectives have been achieved. Evaluation of it is more difficult, but at least as important because it identifies the value of the training programme to the organisation.

8 Which part of *Kolb's* cycle you have experienced will be individual to you. For example, you may have been involved in a group project where you contributed less than other group members. Here the cycle is as follows.

- Concrete experience (make a poor contribution to group project)
- Observation/reflection (note that you felt unsure about the subject matter of the group project from the outset)
- Abstraction/generalisation (conclude that your style is to keep quiet when unsure in order to avoid showing your ignorance)
- Application/testing (at the next available opportunity speak out if you don't understand something – you will probably not be alone!)

9 The answers to this activity will depend on your own personal situation and that of your employer. There is no 'right or wrong' answer which we can include here.

Chapter 9 :

PLANNING, WORK ORIENTATION AND JOB DESIGN

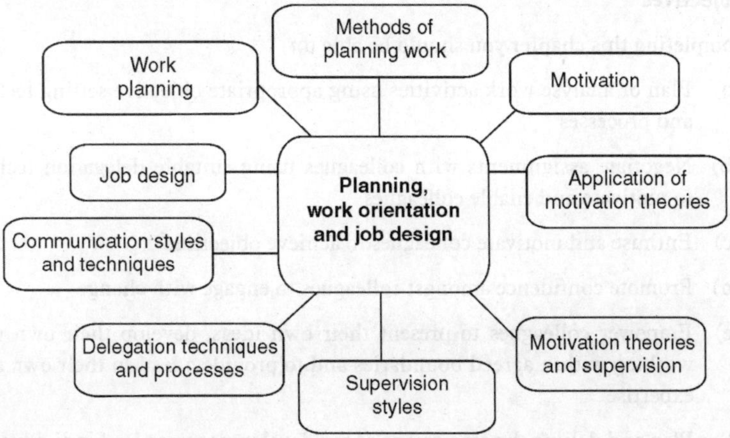

Introduction

Planning helps the organisation to define its purposes and activities. It enables performance standards to be set so that results can be compared with the standard to help managers to see how the organisation is progressing towards its goals.

Because organisations have goals they want to satisfy, they need to direct their activities by:

- Deciding what they want to achieve
- Deciding how and when to do it and who is to do it
- Checking that they do achieve what they want, by monitoring what has been achieved and comparing it with the plan
- Taking action to correct any deviation

Much research has been undertaken in an attempt to understand what motivates individual employees at work and how managers can improve it.

The motivational strategy that is decided on will depend on the beliefs held and the culture that prevails in the organisation. *Maslow's* theory holds that human needs form a hierarchy ranging from the lowest-order needs (physiological needs) to the highest order need – self-actualisation. According to *Herzberg's* two-factor theory, there are two sets of motivating factors. *Vroom's* expectancy theory suggests that people are motivated to reach a goal if they think the goal is worthwhile and can see that the activities will help them achieve the goal. Delegation is one of the main functions of effective management.

In essence, delegation is the process whereby a manager assigns part of his authority to a subordinate to fulfil those duties.

The DISC system describes behavioural styles using a combination of four basic tendencies; Dominance, Influence, Steadiness, and Compliance.

Supervisors can be seen as having a particular concern with the directing and guiding and performance activities of management. They are required to act in a fair and sensitive manner and to provide a pivotal role as both the link and buffer between the expectations of senior management and operatives.

Your objectives

After completing this chapter you should be able to:

(a) Plan or analyse work activities using appropriate objective setting techniques and processes

(b) Negotiate assignments with colleagues using suitable delegation techniques to motivate and enable colleagues

(c) Enthuse and motivate colleagues to achieve objectives

(d) Promote confidence amongst colleagues to engage with change

(e) Empower colleagues to present their own ideas, develop their own ways of working within agreed boundaries and to provide a lead in their own areas of expertise

(f) Plan and deliver the assessment of the development needs of individuals

1 WORK PLANNING

1.1 Planning for the achievement of objectives

Objectives represent the goals that direct the course of action taken by the organisation. Hence, they are a vital element within the planning process – representing as they do specific 'benchmarks' or points that indicate the direction the organisation is following – plus what it is to achieve and the time period involved. The objectives of the supervisor are the 4 Ms – to make the best use of:

- Machine capacity – this includes servicing and maintenance
- Manpower (Human resources) – this includes training
- Materials – including best type of ordering/delivery schedules
- Money – including cost reduction planning.

The setting of objectives is essential to the process of planning, since this activity:

- commits managers and their staff to the future plans and makes sure that they direct their efforts to those activities which will maximise results
- provides direction to the planning process at all organisational levels
- directs the organisational activities as a whole and provides coordination in pursuing established plans
- provides standards of performance allowing assessment of the organisational efficiency and effectiveness (the former relating to optimisation of resource-usage and the latter relating to attainment).

Individual objectives must be directed towards, or 'dovetailed' with organisational goals. Each managerial job must be focused on the success of the business as a whole, not just one part of it, so that the results can be measured in terms of his or her contribution. People must know what their targets of performance are.

Work objectives – at team level, they relate to the purpose of the team and the contribution it is expected to make to the goals of the department and the organisation. At individual level, they are related specifically to the job. They clarify what the individual is expected to do and they enable the performance of the individual to be measured.

Standing aims and objectives include qualitative aims – issues such as promptness and courtesy when dealing with customer requests – and quantified targets eg, for a sales team would be to ensure that all phone calls are picked up within three rings.

Output or improvement targets – have most of the features of SMART objectives. A sales person may be given a target of increasing the number of sales made in a particular district in a certain time. Many organisations have targets that involve the number of defects in goods produced, or seek to find ways of working more efficiently.

Development goals – deal with how an individual can improve his or her own performance and skills. These goals are set at the appraisal interview and are part of the performance management system.

1.2 Principles of planning work

The planning of work involves the allocation of time to the requirements of work to be done. This must be applied to the organisation as a whole, to individual departments and sections and to single employees. An important feature of the principles is the role of time. Planning must be geared to terms of time and the degree of flexibility built into planning will vary according to the length of time being planned for. The principles of planning will revolve around:

(a) the determination of the length of time the plans will be concerned with;
(b) planning by departments and groups of individuals;
(c) planning by individuals;
(d) the implementation of planning principles;
(e) the updating of and alterations to plans.

There are three time ranges that are normally involved in planning work – the long-term, the medium-term and the short-term. Different organisations will include different lengths of time under the same heading. For example, a length of five years might be considered long-term for an organisation producing footwear but short-term in, say, the aviation industry. It may well be that three years is short-term to an organisation but to a department within that organisation it may be medium-term. Indeed, to an individual employee it may be long-term.

Planning in the long-term involves forecasting and as such may be somewhat inaccurate and is, therefore, normally expressed only in general terms. Medium-term plans are likely to be less inaccurate and less forecasting is required. In the short-term forecasting will be fairly accurate and the plans made will probably be adhered to without alteration.

Within organisations departmental plans are devised to meet specific objectives, the origins of those objectives stemming directly from the goals, aims and objectives of the organisation as a whole. There are two aspects that should be considered here:

(a) the internal departmental/group planning via the determination of schedules etc;

(b) the coordination of the work of all the departments/groups within the organisation to ensure that the overall objectives of the organisation are attained.

1.3 Work planning

Work planning is the establishment of work methods and practices to ensure that predetermined objectives are efficiently met at all levels. It is necessary to ensure that work is carried out in accordance with the organisation's requirements and needs, whether those requirements are clearly defined or are merely implied. It necessitates planning and organising on the part of the organisation and the employee.

(a) Task sequencing or prioritisation – ie considering tasks in order of importance for the objective concerned

(b) Scheduling to timetabling tasks and allocating them to different individuals within appropriate time scales

(c) Establishing checks and controls to ensure that:

  (i) Priority deadlines are being met and work is not 'falling behind'
  (ii) Routine tasks are achieving their objectives

(d) Contingency plans: arrangements for what should be done if a major upset were to occur eg if the company's main computer were to break down

(e) Coordinating the efforts of individuals

(f) Reviewing and controlling performance

The overall aim encompassing each of the individual objectives outlined above is to instil method into work – by working methodically existing systems can be improved and new systems will be effective from the date of implementation.

Some jobs (eg assembly line worker), are entirely routine, and can be performed one step at a time, but for most people, some kind of planning and judgement will be required.

1.4 Assessing where resources are most usefully allocated

A manager or supervisor is responsible for allocating resources between **competing areas,** where total resources are limited and in **different ways** to achieve the same objective (eg to increase total profits, sell more, or cut costs etc).

ABC analysis (Pareto analysis) suggests that only a small proportion of items will be significant. For example a business might have 99 customers who each spend £10 per month and one customer who spends £100,000 per month. Pareto's Law assumes that, for sales, approximately 80% of sales volume is accounted for by 20% of the customers. This means that the manager will:

(a) Concentrate scarce resources on the crucial 20%.

(b) Devise policies and procedures for the remaining 80%, or delegate.

A piece of work will be **high priority** in the following cases.

- If it has to be completed by a certain time (ie a deadline)
- If other tasks depend on it
- If other people depend on it

Routine priorities or regular peak times (eg tax returns etc) can be **planned ahead of time,** and other tasks planned around them.

Non-routine priorities occur when **unexpected demands** are made. Thus planning of work should cover routine scheduled peaks and contingency plans for unscheduled peaks and emergencies.

1.5 Methodical working

The majority of organisations approach work planning methodically. Employees, however, often do not realise that if they do not plan their own individual and personal approach to work then the results desired by the organisation will not be achieved despite the efforts of the organisation.

There are distinct advantages to be gained from ensuring that tasks are tackled in some semblance of order, be it chronological or priority. Once a task has been commenced it should be completed as far as is practically possible. Efficiency is impaired by moving from one task to another.

Efficiency requires working systematically or methodically

(a) Ensure that **resources** are available, in sufficient supply and good condition

(b) Organise work in **batches** to save time spent in turning from one job to another

(c) Work to **plans,** schedules, checklists etc

(d) Taking advantage of work **patterns**

(e) Follow up tasks:

(i) Check on the progress of an operation
(ii) Checking the task is completed when the deadline is reached
(iii) Check payments are made when they fall due
(iv) Retrieve files relevant to future discussions, meetings, correspondence

It is important that routine in all aspects of the employee's work should be established:

- Important and difficult tasks should always be attempted when the employee is fresh, normally during the morning.
- Tasks, requests and instructions should be written down; memory often proves defective.
- The adage 'never put off until tomorrow what can be done today' should be put into action.
- Often there are tasks which need to be done daily. These tasks should indeed be carried out each day, preferably at the same time.
- The regular routine, once established, should be written down. This will enable the employee to use it as both a reminder and a checklist.

Additionally, if the employee is absent or leaves the organisation the written routine will enable a substitute or replacement to function more effectively.

Although emphasis has been placed above on the employee working methodically, the method employed by the organisation in devising, implementing and operating administrative systems and procedures is of equal importance.

1.6 Work allocation

Managers and supervisors divide duties and allocate them to available staff and machinery. Here are all the considerations.

(a) **General tasks**. Some tasks (eg filing, photo-copying) may not have the attention of a dedicated employee. Who will do the work, and will it interfere with their other duties?

(b) **Peak periods in some tasks may necessitate re-distribution of staff to cope** with the work load.

(c) **Status and staff attitudes** must be considered. Flexibility in reassigning people from one job to another or varying the work they do may be hampered by an employee's perception of his or her own status.

(d) Individual **temperaments** and abilities may differ.

(e) Planning should allow for **flexibility** in the event of an employee proving unfit for a task, or more able than his present tasks indicate.

(f) Efforts will have to be **coordinated** so that all those involved in a process (eg sales orders) work together as a team or a number of groups.

2 METHODS OF PLANNING WORK

2.1 Methods and systems

We should recognise and understand that different organisations and different individuals have individual characteristics, tastes, styles, preferences and objectives. These particular objectives may well be attained via different methods and systems. It is thus difficult to state categorically that all methods apply to all organisations. All that can be given are guidelines to the methods available. The following are probably the most common:

- checklists
- scheduling
- work programmes
- action sheets
- planning charts and boards

2.2 Checklists

A checklist is often used at individual level and is perhaps the simplest system, being essentially a list of items or activities. The preparation of a typical checklist would involve:

(a) the formulation of a list of activities and tasks to be performed within a given period;

(b) the identification of urgent or priority tasks;

(c) the maintenance of a continuous checklist with the addition of extra activities and tasks as and when required.

This system is obviously limited in its application because of its simplicity. It is suited to fairly mundane or routine tasks but it is these tasks that are often the very essence of the attainment of objectives. Typical uses of checklists would include:

- purchasing requirements;
- points to cover at an interview;
- points to cover at a meeting eg, an agenda;
- organising a conference or meeting.

2.3 Scheduling

Scheduling is where priorities and deadlines are planned and controlled. A schedule establishes a timetable for a logical sequence of tasks, leading up to completion date.

(a) All involved in a task must be given adequate **notice** of work schedules.

(b) The schedules themselves should allow a **realistic time allocation** for each task.

(c) Allowance will have to be made for **unexpected events.**

(d) A **deadline** is the *end* of the longest span of time which may be allotted to a task, ie the last acceptable date for completion. Failure to meet them has a 'knock-on' effect on other parts of the organisation, and on other tasks within an individual's duties. Diary entries may be made on appropriate days (eg: – 'Production completed?' 'Payment received?' 'Bring forward file x' 'One week left for revision').

A number of activities may have to be undertaken in sequence, with some depending on, or taking priority over others.

(a) **Activity scheduling** provides a list of necessary activities in the order in which they must be completed. You might use this to plan each day's work.

(b) **Time scheduling** adds to this the time scale for each activity, and is useful for setting deadlines for tasks. The time for each step is estimated; the total time for the task can then be calculated, allowing for some steps which may be undertaken simultaneously by different people or departments.

2.4 Work programmes and other aids to planning

From activity and time schedules, detailed **work programmes** can be designed for jobs which are carried out over a period of time. Some tasks will have to be started well before the deadline, others may be commenced immediately before, others will be done on the day itself. **Organising a meeting,** for example, may include:

Step 1 Booking accommodation two months before
Step 2 Retrieving relevant files one week before
Step 3 Preparing and circulating an agenda two to three days before

Step 4 Checking conference room layout the day before

Step 5 Taking minutes on the day

The same applies to stock ordering in advance of production (based on a schedule of known delivery times), preparing correspondence in advance of posting etc.

Once time scales are known and final deadlines set, it is possible to produce **job cards, route cards** and **action sheets**.

	Activity	*Days before*	*Date*	*Begun*	*Completed*
1	Request file	6	3.9		
2	Draft report	5	4.9		
3	Type report	3	6.9		
4	Approve report	1	8.9		
5	Signature	1	8.9		
6	Internal messenger	same day	9.9		

Longer-term schedules may be shown conveniently on charts, pegboards or year planners, holiday planners etc. These can be used to show lengths of time and the relationships between various tasks or timetabled events.

Activity 1 **(30 minutes)**

Choose a task or event that needs planning.

(a) Make a checklist

(b) Re-arrange items in order of priority and time sequence

(c) Estimate the time for each activity and schedule it, working back from a deadline

(d) Prepare an action sheet

(e) Draw a chart with columns for time units, and rows for activities

(f) Decide what items may have to be 'brought forward' later and how

3 MOTIVATION

3.1 Meaning of motivation

Definitions

Motivation is 'a decision-making process through which the individual chooses the desired outcomes and sets in motion the behaviour appropriate to acquiring them'. (*Buchanan and Huczynski*)

Motives: 'learned influences on human behaviour that lead us to pursue particular goals because they are socially valued'. (*Buchanan and Huczynski*)

In practice the words motives and motivation are commonly used in different contexts to mean the following.

(a) Goals or outcomes that have become desirable for a particular individual. We say that money, power or friendship are motives for doing something.

(b) The mental process of choosing desired outcomes, deciding how to go about them (and whether the likelihood of success warrants the amount of effort that will be necessary) and setting in motion the required behaviours.

(c) The social process by which other people motivate us to behave in the ways they wish. Motivation in this sense usually applies to the attempts of organisations to get workers to put in more effort.

From a manager's point of view motivation is the controlling of the work environment, rewards and sanctions in such a way as to encourage desired behaviours and performance from employees.

3.2 Organisational goals and motivation

An organisation has goals, which can only be achieved by the efforts of the people who work in the organisation. Individuals also have their own 'goals' in life and these are likely to be different from those of the organisation. Once recruited, the new employee might be subjected to a variety of techniques to enhance his or her performance at work and help the organisation achieve its goals. This means that the employee must be motivated.

You may be wondering why motivation is important. It could be argued that if a person is employed to do a job, he or she will do that job and no question of motivation arises. If the person does not want to do the work, he or she can resign. The point at issue, however, is the efficiency and effectiveness with which the job is done.

The claim is that if individuals can be 'motivated', they will perform better and more willingly – **above mere compliance** with rules and procedures. If their personal needs and goals are integrated with those of the team and organisation, individuals will work more efficiently (so that productivity will rise) or produce a better quality of work, or might contribute more of their creativity and initiative to the job.

There is on-going debate about exactly what motivation strategies can aim to achieve in the way of productivity, quality and other business benefits, but it has become widely accepted that **committed** employees add value to the organisation. This is particularly true in environments where initiative and flexibility are required of employees in order to satisfy customer demands and keep pace with environmental changes.

Job satisfaction is an even more ambiguous concept, although (as we will see) it is associated with motivation.

(a) It is difficult to prove that 'happy bees make more honey'.

(b) Job satisfaction is difficult to define: it means different things to different people, and over time – according to the individual's changing needs, goals and expectations.

On the other hand, low morale, dissatisfaction or de-motivation can cause direct and indirect performance problems, through effects such as:

(a) Higher than usual (or higher than acceptable) labour turnover

(b) Higher levels of absenteeism, and deterioration in time-keeping and discipline

(c) Reduction in upward communication, employee involvement (such as participation in suggestion schemes or quality circles)

(d) Higher incidence of employee disputes and grievances

(e) Restricted output quantity and/or quality (through lack of commitment or deliberate sabotage)

Activity 2 **(10 minutes)**

What factors in yourself or your job or organisation motivate you to:

- Turn up to work at all?
- Do an average day's work?
- 'Bust a gut' to do your best on a task, or for a boss or customer?

3.3 Rewards and incentives

Definitions

A **reward** is a token (monetary or otherwise) given to an individual or team in recognition of some contribution or success.

An **incentive** is the offer or promise of a reward for contribution or success, designed to motivate the individual or team to behave in such a way as to earn it

Not all the incentives that an organisation can offer its employees are directly related to **monetary** rewards. The satisfaction of **any** of the employee's wants or needs may be seen as a reward for past or incentive for future performance.

Different individuals have different goals, and get different things out of their working life: in other words they have different orientations to work. There are many reasons why a person works, or is motivated to work well.

(a) The **human relations** school of management theorists regarded **work relationships** as the main source of satisfaction and reward offered to the worker.

(b) Later writers suggested a range of 'higher-order' motivations, notably:

(i) **Job satisfaction,** interest and challenge in the job itself – rewarding work

(ii) **Participation** in decision-making – responsibility and involvement

(c) **Pay** has always occupied a rather ambiguous position, but since people need money to live, it will certainly be part of the reward package.

Rewards offered to the individual at work may be of two basic types.

(a) **Extrinsic rewards** are separate from (or external to) the job itself, and dependent on the decisions of others (that is, also external to the control of the workers themselves). Pay, benefits, cash and non-cash incentives and working conditions are examples of extrinsic rewards.

(b) **Intrinsic rewards** are those which arise from the performance of the work itself. They are therefore psychological rather than material and relate to the concept of job satisfaction. Intrinsic rewards include the satisfaction that comes from completing a piece of work, the status that certain jobs convey, and the feeling of achievement that comes from doing a difficult job well.

4 APPLICATION OF MOTIVATION THEORIES

4.1 Content and process theories

Many theories try to explain motivation and why and how people can be motivated. One classification is between content and process theories.

(a) **Content theories** ask the question: '**What** are the things that motivate people?' They assume that human beings have a set of needs or desired outcomes. *Maslow's* hierarchy theory and *Herzberg's* two-factor theory, both discussed below, are two of the most important approaches of this type.

(b) **Process theories** ask the question: '**How** can people be motivated?' They explore the process through which outcomes **become** desirable and are pursued by individuals. This approach assumes that people are able to select their goals and choose the paths towards them, by a conscious or unconscious process of calculation. Expectancy theory and *Handy's* 'motivation calculus' are theories of this type.

4.2 *Maslow's* hierarchy of needs

Maslow outlined five needs, as in the diagram below, and put forward certain propositions about the motivating power of each need.

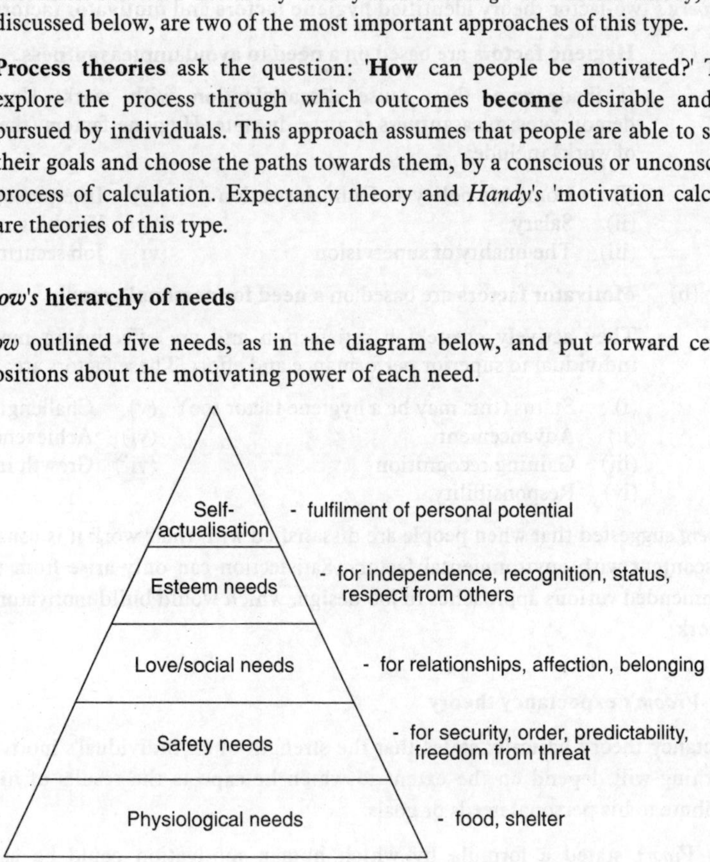

Figure 9.1: Maslow's hierarchy of needs

(a) Any individual's needs can be arranged in a '**hierarchy** of relative pre-potency'.

(b) Each level of need is **dominant until satisfied**; only then does the next level of need become a motivating factor.

(c) A need which has been satisfied no longer motivates an individual's behaviour. The need for self-actualisation can rarely be satisfied.

Activity 3 **(10 minutes)**

Decide which of *Maslow's* categories the following fit into.

(a) Receiving praise from your manager	(e) A pay increase
(b) A family party	(f) Joining a local drama group
(c) An artist forgetting to eat	(g) Being awarded the OBE
(d) A man washed up on a desert island	(h) Buying a house

4.3 *Herzberg's* two-factor theory

Herzberg's two-factor theory identified **hygiene factors** and **motivator factors.**

(a) **Hygiene factors** are based on a **need to avoid unpleasantness.**

If inadequate, they cause **dissatisfaction** with work. Unpleasantness demotivates: pleasantness is a steady state. Hygiene factors (the conditions of work) include:

(i)	Company policy and administration	(iv)	Interpersonal relations
(ii)	Salary	(v)	Working conditions
(iii)	The quality of supervision	(vi)	Job security

(b) **Motivator factors** are based on a **need for personal growth.**

They actively create job satisfaction and are effective in motivating an individual to superior performance and effort. These factors are:

(i)	Status (this may be a hygiene factor too)	(v)	Challenging work
(ii)	Advancement	(vi)	Achievement
(iii)	Gaining recognition	(vii)	Growth in the job
(iv)	Responsibility		

Herzberg suggested that when people are dissatisfied with their work it is usually because of discontent with environmental factors. Satisfaction can only arise from the job. He recommended various approaches to job design, which would build motivator factor into the work.

4.4 *Vroom's* expectancy theory

Expectancy theory basically states that the strength of an individual's motivation to do something will depend on the extent to which he expects the results of his efforts to contribute to his personal needs or goals.

Victor Vroom stated a formula by which human motivation could be assessed and measured. He suggested that the strength of an individual's motivation is the product of two factors.

(a) The strength of his preference for a certain outcome, *Vroom* called this **valence**: it can be represented as a positive or negative number, or zero – since outcomes may be desired, avoided or regarded with indifference.

(b) His expectation that the outcome will in fact result from a certain behaviour. *Vroom* called this 'subjective probability' or **expectancy**. As a probability, it may be represented by any number between 0 (no chance) and 1 (certainty).

In its simplest form, the expectancy equation may be stated as: $F = V \times E$

Where

F = the force or strength of the individual's motivation to behave in a particular way

V = valence: the strength of the individual preference for a given outcome or reward and

E = expectancy: the individual's perception that the behaviour will result in the outcome/ reward.

In this equation, the lower the values of either valence or expectancy, the less the motivation. An employee may have a high expectation that increased productivity will result in promotion (because of managerial promises, say), but if he is indifferent or negative towards the idea of promotion (because he dislikes responsibility), he will not be motivated to increase his productivity. Likewise, if promotion was very important to him -but he did not believe higher productivity would get him promoted (because he has been passed over before, perhaps), his motivation would also be low.

Activity 4 **(10 minutes)**

How might a manager use *Vroom's* expectancy theory to improve the motivation of team members?

4.5 *Handy's* motivation calculus

Charles Handy suggests that for any individual decision, there is a conscious or unconscious **motivation calculus** which is an assessment of three factors.

(a) The individual's own set of needs.

(b) The desired results – what the individual is expected to do in his job.

(c) 'E' factors (effort, energy, excitement in achieving desired results, enthusiasm, emotion, and expenditure).

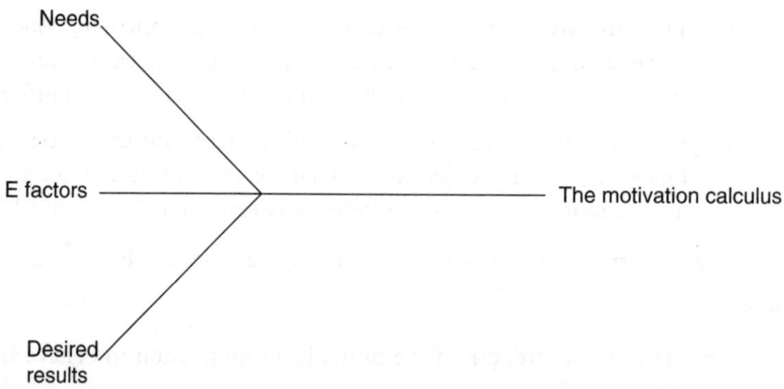

The **motivation decision** will depend on:

- The **strength of the individual's needs**
- The **expectancy** that expending 'E' will lead to a desired result
- How far the result will be **instrumental** in satisfying the individual's needs

Consequences for management

(a) **Intended results should be made clear,** so that the individual can complete the calculation by knowing **what is expected,** the **reward,** and **how much 'E'** it will take.

(b) Individuals are more committed to **specific goals** which they **have helped to set themselves.**

(c) **Feedback**. Without knowledge of **actual results,** there is no check that the 'E' expenditure was justified (and will be justified in future).

(d) If an individual is **rewarded** according to performance tied to standards (management by objectives), however, he or she may well set lower standards: the instrumentality part of the calculus (likelihood of success and reward) is greater if the standard is lower, so less expense of 'E' is indicated.

There are various ways of looking at motivation. *Handy* groups early motivation theories under three headings.

(a) **Satisfaction theories** are based on the assumption that a 'satisfied' worker will work harder (although there is little evidence to support the assumption). Satisfaction may reduce labour turnover and absenteeism, but will not necessarily increase individual productivity. Some theories hold that people work best within a compatible work group, or under a well-liked leader.

(b) **Incentive theories** are based on the assumption that individuals will work harder to obtain a desired reward, ie positive reinforcement, although most studies are concentrated on money as a motivator. *Handy* notes that incentive theories can work if:

(i) the individual perceives the increased reward to be worth the extra effort

(ii) the performance can be measured and clearly attributed to the individual

(iii) the individual wants that particular kind of reward

(iv) the increased performance will not become the new minimum standard

(c) **Intrinsic theories** are based on the belief that higher-order needs are more prevalent in modern man than we give him credit for. People will work hard in response to factors in the work itself – participation, responsibility etc – effective performance is its own reward

4.6 Managerial implications of process theories

Expectancy theory suggests that:

(a) **Intended results should be made clear,** so that the individual can complete the calculation by knowing what is expected, the reward, and how much effort it will take.

(b) Individuals are likely to be more committed to **specific goals,** which they **have** helped **to set themselves,** taking their needs and expectations into account.

(c) Immediate and on-going **feedback** should be given. Without knowledge of actual results, there is no check that 'E' expenditure was justified (or will be justified in the future).

(d) If an individual is **rewarded** according to performance tied to standards, he or she may well set lower standards: the expectancy part of the calculation (likelihood of success and reward) is greater if the standard is lower, so less expense of 'E' is indicated.

5 MOTIVATION THEORIES AND SUPERVISION

5.1 The job as a motivator

The job itself can be used as a motivator or it can be a cause if dissatisfaction. Many attempts to improve the motivation and job satisfaction of employees have concentrated on job design.

Definition

Job design is the incorporation of the tasks the organisation needs to be done into a job for one person.

There are five core job dimensions that are thought to contribute to job satisfaction:

(a) skill variety – or the extent to which a job involves the use of several different skills and talents;

(b) task identity – or the extent to which a job involves completing an entire piece of work from beginning to end;

(c) task significance – the task is perceived to have a role, purpose, meaning and value, or the degree of impact the job is believed to have on other people;

(d) autonomy – the opportunity to exercise discretion or self-management (in areas such as target setting and work methods) – or the extent to which the worker feels freedom and discretion to act in different ways in relation to the job

(e) feedback – the extent to which workers are provided with information on the results of their work.

Frederick Herzberg suggest three ways of improving job design to make jobs more interesting to the employee, and hopefully to improve performance: job enrichment, job enlargement and job rotation.

Job enrichment – is planned, deliberate action to build greater responsibility, breadth and challenge of work into a job. Job enrichment is similar to **empowerment.** Job enrichment represents a 'vertical' extension of the job into greater levels of responsibility, challenge and autonomy. A job may be enriched by:

- Giving the job-holder **decision-making tasks** of a higher order
- Giving the employee greater **freedom** to decide how the job should be done
- Encouraging employees **to participate** in the planning decisions of their superiors
- Giving the employee regular **feedback**

Job enlargement is the attempt to widen jobs by increasing the number of operations in which a jobholder is involved. It is a 'horizontal' extension of the job by increasing task variety and reducing task repetition.

(a) Tasks that span a larger part of the total production work should reduce boredom and add to task meaning, significance and variety.

(b) Enlarged jobs might be regarded as having higher status within the department, perhaps as stepping-stones towards promotion.

Job enlargement is, however, limited in its intrinsic rewards, as asking a worker to complete three separate tedious, unchallenging tasks is unlikely to be more motivating than asking him to perform just one tedious, unchallenging task.

Job rotation – is the planned transfer of staff from one job to another to increase task variety. It is a 'sequential' extension of the job. It is also sometimes seen as a form of training, where individuals gain wider experience by rotating as trainees in different positions.

It is generally admitted that the developmental value of job rotation is limited – but it can reduce the monotony of repetitive work.

5.2 What motivates people?

Many theorists over the years have attempted to define what motivates people at work – ie, what drives them to be productive and deliver what the organisation wants of them.

The concept of motivation describes the impetus to act with energy and purpose. We are all motivated to: eat, sleep, have fun, make love, and work. The challenge for management is to discover what motivates people at work to do what is necessary for the organisation to succeed. In the past, in the industrial-bureaucratic era of rigid hierarchy and electromechanical tools, management's task was to motivate employees to obey orders and perform set tasks. Today, in the age of service industries (and especially information age techno-service), managements' task is to motivate employees to take responsibility for: solving problems, responding to customer needs, cooperating with team members, and continuously improving products and services. In the industrial bureaucratic era, motivation for most workers was mostly compliance, showing up on time, and doing what they were told to do. In the techno-service era, this kind of compliance is not enough; another type of motivation becomes essential. The organisation requires people who are motivated, enabled, and empowered to achieve results by exercising judgement.

There are two kinds of motivation. One is extrinsic motivation, which has to do with control, getting people to do something they may not want to do. Extrinsic motivation is caused by positive or negative incentives - carrots and sticks. These are most effective when people are in need or afraid. Well-fed people do not jump for carrots, and self-confident people do not allow bosses to beat them. Intrinsic motivation, the second kind of motivation, results when internal drives and values are engaged at work.

When employees are asked to rank what they most value in their work, they choose a combination of extrinsic and intrinsic factors. Extrinsic factors include better pay and benefits, employment security, opportunity for advancement, and working conditions. Intrinsic factors include challenging work, enjoyable work, meaningful work and above all, opportunity to experience a sense of accomplishment. However, what is challenging, enjoyable, and rewarding depends on employees' individual values (and skills), which differ among people at work.

Sometimes the distinction between intrinsic and extrinsic becomes blurred. Pure intrinsic motivation implies that people would be motivated to work, even if they were not paid, as is the case when people play a game for fun. Pure extrinsic motivation implies that people would not be motivated to do something unless they were paid.

An increasing number of new generation self-developers take a job for the pay and benefits, but they are intrinsically motivated by other work such as artistic or volunteer activities. *Maccoby* compares the motivation of job enrichment with empowered teams – with its emphasis on skills development, problem-solving, continuous improvement, quality products, improved customer service, flexible response to change:

Job enrichment	Empowered teams
• aimed to reduce costs of high turnover and increase productivity	• aims to improve organisational flexibility and quality for competitive advantage
• aimed to increase autonomy improves work experience and job satisfaction	• increased autonomy improves skill, decision-making, adaptability and use of new technology
• had little impact on management	• involves redefinition of management function
• quick fix, applied to problem groups only	• can take time to change culture
• Personnel administration technique	• human resource management strategy

Maccoby argues that people coming into employment today have different needs from employees of the past. These are due to changes in, for example, the way people are educated (learning is more self-directed) and social relationships (people are less prepared to do as they are told). Therefore, according to *Maccoby*, work has to match workers' dominant values for them to be motivated.

5.3 Social Character Type Theory

Maccoby's theory of social character explores the dominant values that determine motivation, and allows us to differentiate five value types: the expert, helper, defender, innovator and self-developer.

Type	Dominant values	Description
Expert	Mastery, control, autonomy	You approach your work as an expert. Whatever your job, you want to provide high-quality work and to exercise your skill and competence
Helper	Caring for people, relatedness, sociability	You approach your work as a helper. You want to help people.
Defender	Dignity, power, self esteem, protection	You approach your work as a defender. You want to defend against those who do not respect the law, who do harm, or who undermine the values essential to a good organisation.
Innovator	Competition, glory, creating, experimenting	You approach your work as an innovator who knows how to play the game of business. You want to win by making the organisation more successful.
Self-developer	Balancing mastery and play, knowledge and fun	You approach your work as the means to a self-fulfilling life. You want your work to further your own development.

These value types cut across categories of gender, generation, and culture or ethnic group. They describe values that are shared by people everywhere. To understand what motivates ourselves and others, we must identify the dynamic values that determine our needs. Such an understanding leads the way to both organisational productivity and development of our individual potential at work.

Maccoby describes recent historical changes that require a rethinking of what motivates people at work.

(a) The first historical change is that the nature of work continues to shift from manufacturing to service. Over 70 percent of the workforce is now in the service sector.

(b) The second dramatic historical change that affects motivation is that people can no longer count on lifetime careers in a single company.

(c) A third transformation occurring in today's workplace is that the social character of the workforce continues to change from the traditional experts adapted to functional roles in the industrial bureaucracy to the new generation of self-developers who are better adapted to service in the age of information technology.

The new generation of today's self-developers have typically been raised in a family with dual wage earners who share work and child-rearing roles. At an early age, these self-developers learn they cannot always count on their parents to be around when needed. Today's children have to learn interpersonal skills to get along with one another in day care centres and nursery schools and to support each other in the absence of their parents. These childhood experiences form people for whom both self-reliance and teamwork feel natural. Sharing ideas and networking are easy for them. Knowing that they can't count on lifetime employment in an ever-changing market, they naturally put a premium on self-development in order to maintain their employability. This shift in family structure continues. During the 21st century, most employees in the U.S. and Western Europe, at least, will be self-developers, shaped by the combined forces of changing technology, education, and family life.

Maccoby describes this 'new generation's work needs. Theyare:

- Clear management commitments on responsibilities and rewards
- Opportunities for expression, challenge and development
- Increased business
- Understanding and development
- Teamwork combined with individual growth
- Fair and meaningful rewards
- Reasons, information, to be included, to know why

5.4 Costa & McCrae's Five-Factor Theory

Considerable research by Costa and McCrae and others supports the relationship between personality and job performance variables, training efficiency, academic performance, and motivation.

A personality trait is a stable disposition to behave in a certain way (e.g., honest, friendly, moody). Personality is used to explain the stability of a person's behaviour and how a person is distinct from other people. In general, it is believed that about 60% of our personality originates from genetic factors while about 40% originates from experiences in the environment. The Five Factor Theory of Personality or 'The Big Five' was developed by Robert McCrae and Paul Costa. A person's personality is a combination of these five traits (abbreviated as OCEAN) in various degrees.

(a) **O**penness to experience - people exhibit imaginative, curious, broadminded, intelligent behaviours

(b) **C**onscientiousness - people exhibit dependable, responsible, hardworking, achievement-oriented behaviours

(c) **E**xtraversion - people exhibit sociable, gregarious, assertive and talkative behaviours

(d) **A**greeableness - people exhibit courteous, flexible, good-natured, cooperative behaviours

(e) **N**euroticism or emotional stability - people exhibit anxious, depressed, angry, worried, insecure actions

By describing the individual's standing on each of the five factors, they can provide a comprehensive sketch that summarises the individual's emotional, interpersonal, experiential, attitudinal and motivational style.

The five broad traits, or domains, are represented by several subscales, termed facets.

- Openness to experience is made up of the facets: fantasy, aesthetics, Feelings, actions, ideas, and values.
- Conscientiousness is measured by the facets: competence, order, dutifulness, achievement-striving, self-discipline, and deliberation.
- Extraversion is measured by the facets: warmth, gregariousness, assertiveness, activity, excitement seeking, and positive emotions.
- The Agreeableness facets are: trust, straightforwardness, altruism, compliance, modesty, and tender-mMindedness.
- Neuroticism comprises facet scales measuring anxiety, anger, hostility, depression, self-consciousness, impulsiveness, and vulnerability.

The five factors are summarised in the following table:

Factor	Nature of Factor	Characteristics of High Scorers	Characteristics of Low Scorers
Openness	Toleration for and exploration of the unfamiliar	creative, artistic, curious, imaginative, nonconformist	conventional, down-to-earth, preserving the status quo
Conscientiousness	Degree of organisation, persistence, and motivation in goal-directed behaviour	organised, reliable, neat, ambitious.	unreliable, lazy, careless, negligent, spontaneous and often unprepared.
Extraversion	Capacity for joy, need for stimulation, interest in other people and external events	talkative, optimistic, sociable, affectionate	reserved, comfortable being alone, stays in the background
Agreeableness	One's orientation along a continuum from compassion to antagonism in thoughts, feelings, and actions	good-natured, trusting, helpful	rude, unco-operative, irritable, aggressive, competitive
Neuroticism	Emotional stability, proneness to distress, excessive cravings or urges, unrealistic ideas	worrying, insecure, high anxiety, easily tempted	calm, secure, relaxed, stable

What do the Big Five predict about our behaviour?

First, having a trait means reacting consistently to the same situation over time, for example, being agreeable or co-operative means consistently going along with reasonable requests, but does not mean always complying with others' wishes.

Second, to respond consistently in the same situation people must have a capacity to respond to situational cues, that is to have the trait to be responsive to situations. For example, if someone purchases a house in the woods, they might want that house because of its secluded location.

Third, behaving differently in a given situation does not mean there is inner inconsistency. For example, someone who likes to attend parties might not often do so because of a stronger desire to work.

Overall, traits are relatively poor predictors of single behavioural acts, but are better predictors of general trends of a person's behaviour. Looking at past behaviour of an individual may be the best predictor of future behaviour.

How might these factors relate to motivation?

Extraversion has an interpersonal component and is strongly related to positive affect such as being enthusiastic, energetic, interested and friendly. Research found that extraverts show less anxiety over negative feedback. They are highly motivated to seek social situations and to be dominant in those situations. Extraverts are motivated by change, variety in their lives, challenge, and are easily bored. They have more recently been seen as adaptive, ambitious and hardworking.

Agreeableness also has an interpersonal component. Agreeable individuals tend toward conformity in groups, toward modesty, toward not being demanding, and toward being sympathetic. These individuals might be motivated to helping others and to sociable behaviour in general. There may be a link between the motivational processes operating within individuals in regards to this trait, such that agreeable individuals strive for intimacy and solidarity in groups they belong to, which provides emotional rewards.

Conscientiousness is related to such things as achievement, perseverance, organisation and responsibility. Conscientious individuals are motivated toward achievement through social conformity.

Neuroticism tends to be viewed negatively and is associated with negative affect, being tense and nervous. A person could be neurotic and conscientious which may have negative health effects but may motivate an individual toward success in work situations.

Openness is associated with tolerance of ambiguity (which means when something is not clear), a capacity to absorb information, being focused and the ability to be aware of more feelings, thoughts and impulses simultaneously. The result is deeper more intense experiences. Open individuals are motivated to seek out the unfamiliar and to look for complexity.

5.5 Empowerment techniques

Empowerment is a feature of the new management model, based on managing resources and capabilities as opposed to the traditional method, based on managing assets.

Traditional model	New model
Built around assets	Built around capabilities
Directed at managing numbers with rationality and analysis	Focus on creating value with intuition and analysis
Most tasks simplified. One best way to work defined by management	Enriched work; employees engaged in multiple tasks and expanding their knowledge. All employees learning continually and contributing to enterprise learning

Traditional model	New model
Hierarchical with independent parts. Managers give orders; workers obey	The boundary-less organisation. Networked with interdependent parts. Participative management, self-managing work teams
Reactive	Responsive
Command and control	Empowered employees
Risk-averse blame culture	Encouraging radical ideas and risk-taking

There are different degrees of empowerment and leadership within organisations:

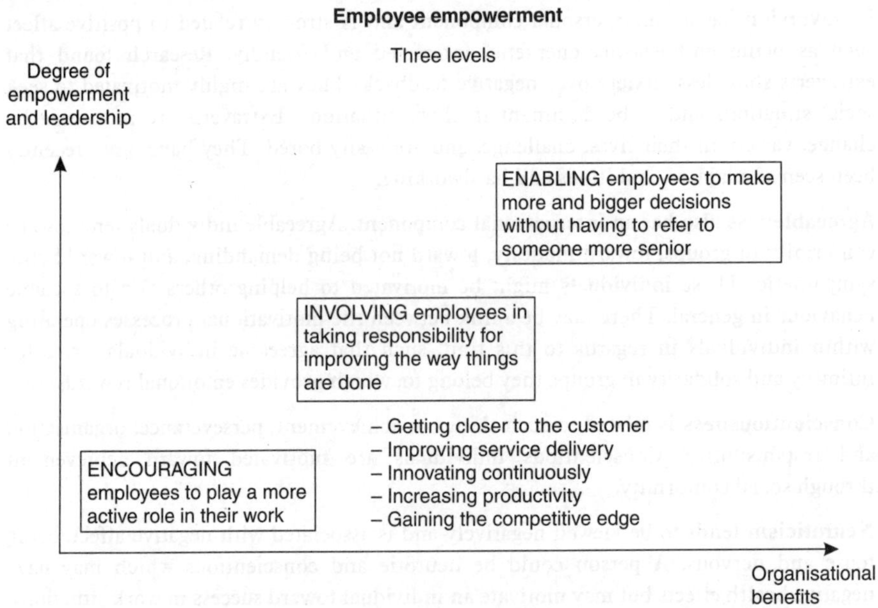

Figure 9.2: Degrees of empowerment and leadership within organisations

Bowen and Lawler (1992) describe three levels:

(a) **Suggestion involvement** – at a basic level staff may simply be able to contribute ideas and make suggestions but play no fundamental part in decision making and planning.

(b) **Job involvement** – at a higher-level, employees' jobs may be redesigned to enable autonomous or semi-autonomous team working. Teams may be responsible for decision-making and planning in their own area of work with management offering support rather than control.

(c) **High involvement** – at the highest level there may be a deliberate effort to enable 'vertical' teams which cut across hierarchical levels in the organisation, and there may be special provision for staff at all levels to be involved in strategic decision-making. There are different degrees of empowerment. *Bowen and Lawler* (1992) describe three levels:

Employee empowerment can be meaningful only if three basic ingredients exist:

(a) **Trust** – as well as believing in a person's capabilities, you must trust them to perform or get on with the job.

(b) **Competence** – there ought to be the mindset that individual employees can be expected to deliver to the best of their competence with the minimum of supervision.

(c) **Teamwork** – not all company problems can be solved by one person. The sheer rate of change and turbulence implies that as fresh problems and challenges appear, individuals are likely to group together in flexible teams without barriers of hierarchy or status, to solve the problems within the framework of the company's values and objectives. The company is bound together by these beliefs and values – by people that are committed to one another and to their common goals. Remember, TEAM stands for 'Together Everyone Achieves More'.

There are four ways to breed empowerment:

(a) The **enlisting of support from employees** in tackling immediate organisational issues – empowerment is achieved by involving people in the development of their own solutions to specific issues. This is done by expecting teams to not just propose ways forward or to hope that someone else will do something; but to actually solve the problem in their part of the organisation, according to the constraints within which they work and the resources they have.

(b) **Gaining the 'hearts and minds' of people** – empowerment is about winning both the hearts and minds of people so that they can take the opportunities made available to them for expanded responsibility. For example, at the management level, this could be achieved by sharing the vision and corporate values throughout the company.

(c) **Structural means** (organisational and work grouping) – an organisation that is empowered has a flat structure with the minimum number of management layers. Work should be organised around basic operations to form 'whole tasks'. The basic organisational unit should be the primary workgroup – with a designated leader. Each workgroup and its leader should, as far a possible, plan and organise its own work, and be fully able to evaluate its performance against agreed standards of excellence. Jobs are to be structured so that work-group members can personally plan, execute and evaluate at least one operation in the process. All workgroup members should have the opportunity to participate in the group's processes of planning, problem solving and evaluation

(d) The **style or behaviour of individual managers** – leaders, managers and supervisors empower their team members not by abdicating or giving up control, but by changing the way control is exercised. They learn to delegate more, and allow individuals and teams more scope to act, monitor and plan their own performance; and to account for their acts and judgement calls. But at the end of it all, they (the managers) still have the responsibility of providing guidance and support to their staff. These leaders also need to help the staff to develop the competencies and skills required to function effectively in an empowered environment.

Leaders, managers or supervisors can empower others by:

- articulating a clear vision and goals
- helping them to master challenges
- modelling the correct behaviour
- providing support
- arousing positive emotions
- providing good information
- providing necessary resources
- connecting to outcomes
- being fair, reliable, open, caring, and competent

Activity 5 **(10 minutes)**

Look back to Chapter 6 describing power and leadership and then outline the main differences between power and empowerment.

6 DELEGATION TECHNIQUES AND PROCESSES

6.1 Allocating work

Whatever its structure, the various operations of the organisation have to be distributed among its members. It is necessary to plan, organise, direct and control their activities. Delegation relates to the location of decision-making and, as we have already noted in an earlier chapter, one person cannot exercise all authority in making decisions as a firm grows. There is a limit to the number of persons that a manager can personally supervise. After this limit a manager must delegate authority to subordinates to make decisions.

The tasks delegated should be a mixture of different sorts of work – routine and non–routine, blended to suit the current circumstances and the subordinates' abilities and aspirations as well as those of their boss.

6.2 Delegation and empowerment

Delegation is the process of assigning tasks and granting sufficient authority for their accomplishment. The one to whom authority is delegated becomes accountable to the superior for doing the job, but the superior still remains responsible for getting the job done.

The idea of delegation is to make sure that responsibility and authority are equal for every job. When delegation is implemented correctly, people have the authority that they need to execute their responsibilities. However, assigning authority does not mean that someone has the ability, motivation and understanding necessary to perform.

In the new-generation adaptive organisation, delegation is replaced by empowerment, and responsibility by ownership. Authority and responsibilities are formal aspects of organising. They are based upon organisational properties and not individual capabilities. Empowerment and ownership are social aspects of organising. They are based on efficacy and initiative, and not just on roles and requirements. They belong to people.

6.3 Variations in the process of delegation

There are immense differences between the processes of delegation employed in different organisations; you can find one firm where delegation flows freely and informally and another where it is only reluctantly employed. However, there is one feature that is common to almost all variants and that is its direction. It is almost always downward.

There is no 'correct procedure' for delegation, and even if there were you would not become a good delegator by learning it. 'It is not what you do, it is the way that you do it.' Let us take as examples different ways of delegation.

- *By abdication* – at one extreme, it is not uncommon to leave everything to a junior, which is a very crude and usually ineffective method.
- *According to custom and practice* – in some organisations it is customary to have work done by the age-old system whereby precedent rules. This method scarcely sounds progressive but it is common enough in the bureaucracies both of the Civil Service and major companies.
- *By explanation* – this more progressive way involves the manager in 'briefing' his subordinate along the lines of how the task should be done, without explaining too much because that could verge on actually doing the job. This is one of those cases when explanation is wanted – not too little and not too much – a fine balance that requires the art of management.
- *By consultation* – prior consultation was once quite novel in manager/union relations and also between managers and subordinates, but nowadays prior consultation is considered to be important and very effective. Another thing that has been realised by some, though not admitted by all, is that the middle grades of worker are immensely powerful; by contributing or withholding their cooperation they make the success of their seniors by no means automatic.

At least managers should have the humility to admit that sometimes good ideas come from below: indeed, the point of view of the person nearest the scene of action is more likely to be relevant. Delegation can benefit greatly from this sort of person.

What is more effective, more profitable and more humane, is for jobs to be apportioned to willing rather than merely to consenting subordinates, whose advice is sought before the method of doing the work is finally laid down. Again, there must be balances because managers cannot afford to spend most of their lives in consultation and only a residual portion in action.

In planning delegation therefore, a manager/ supervisor must ensure that:

- He/she does not delegate so much as to totally overload a subordinate.
- The subordinate has reasonable skill and experience in the area concerned.
- Appropriate authority is delegated.
- He/she remembers to monitor and control.

- He/she is not simply 'passing the buck' or 'opting out'.
- All concerned know that the task has been delegated.
- He/she puts time aside for coaching and guiding.
- If delegation goes well then the person will expect a reward, eg upgrade job/more pay.
- Delegation can be temporary and may be varied to give a rounded experience.

6.4 The techniques of delegation

Delegation is not just handing off work you don't want to do. Other things to consider when delegating include:

- qualifications of subordinate
- necessity of employee commitment
- expansion of employee capabilities
- evidence of shared values and perspectives
- sufficient time for delegation

Effective delegation is like starting a new exercise programme. You know it will be the right thing to do and you will love the results, but it is tough to make a commitment and get started. A delegation model outlining the techniques of delegation is shown below.

- Assess your current workload by reviewing and/or writing a job description and creating a time budget for your typical week (ie, x % spent on meetings, e-mail, sales, billing, etc.)
- Decide which tasks on your time budget consume too much time and don't effectively support your job description. These are the tasks that should be delegated!
- Decide what tasks need to be done and determine which employee would benefit most from the learning experience. Although most employees don't have extra time to do more work, many would welcome an assignment that stretches them.
- Clearly describe the assignment and where it fits in the 'big picture' to the employee who will take responsibility for it. Giving the employee an understanding of why the task is so important and how it contributes to the company's goals will increase the employee's commitment and accountability.
- Jointly define the time, money, staff, training, and resources needed to accomplish the task. Doing this step together will clarify what is needed and show that you are working in partnership with your employee to help him or her succeed.
- Work together to outline initial ideas about how to proceed.
- Give the employee the appropriate level of authority to carry out the assignment.
- Both parties should come to an agreement about how success will be measured and how often. If the job is completed successfully, what would the result look like? Determining what constitutes success and how you will

measure it before you start any job allows everyone to understand the expectations.

- Provide feedback and support during the process and at its completion. Staying on top of the work, while not actually doing it is critical. Feedback allows course corrections. It's disheartening to get to the end of a failed project and know that better communication with your employee could have influenced its success.

6.5 Problems of delegation

Many managers and supervisors are reluctant to delegate and attempt to do many routine tasks themselves in addition to their more important duties. This may happen for the following reasons:

(a) **Low confidence and trust** in the abilities of their staff: the suspicion that 'if you want it done well, you have to do it yourself.'

(b) The burden of **accountability for the mistakes of subordinates.**

(c) A **desire to 'stay in touch'** with the department or team – both in terms of workload and staff- particularly if the manager does not feel 'at home' in a management role.

(d) **Feeling threatened.** An unwillingness to admit that assistants have developed to the extent that they could perform some of the supervisor's duties.

(e) **Poor control and communication systems** in the organisation, so that the manager feels he has to do everything himself, if he is to retain real control and responsibility for a task.

(f) An **organisational culture** that has failed to reward or recognise effective delegation, so that the manager may not feel that delegation is positively regarded.

(g) **Lack of understanding** of what delegation involves – not giving assistants total control, or making the manager himself redundant.

(h) **Lack of training** and development of managers in delegation skills and related areas.

6.6 Overcoming the reluctance of managers to delegate

(a) **Train the subordinates** so that they are capable of handling delegated authority in a responsible way. If assistants are of the right 'quality', supervisors will be prepared to trust them more.

(b) Have a system of **open communications,** in which the supervisor and assistants freely interchange ideas and information. If the assistant is given all the information needed to do the job, and if the supervisor is aware of what the assistant is doing:

(i) The assistant will make better-informed decisions.

(ii) The supervisor will not panic because he does not know what is going on.

(c) **Ensure that a system of control is established.** If responsibility and accountability are monitored at all levels of the management hierarchy, the dangers of relinquishing authority and control to assistants are significantly lessened.

6.7 Supervision styles

Effective delegation is best promoted by knowing how to delegate and how to overcome barriers to delegation.

How should a supervisor delegate?

The first thing to do is to prepare for delegation. It is essential to know what you want to delegate and to plan for it. Usually it is better to be precise about delegation and to decide that particular tasks will be delegated rather than responsibility for broad areas of work. Once you have made decisions on what is to be delegated then you can look around and select the individual who you think could, with your support and perhaps training, do the work that you intend to pass down. Of course, the failure to train and develop people for delegation is the most frequent cause of failure, so it really is important to consider what new skill, knowledge or experience the subordinate will need to do the delegated work.

The preparatory work done, the supervisor in delegating must brief the subordinate as to:

(a) precisely what is to be done;
(b) what results are required;
(c) the scale and scope of the authority that will accompany the delegation.

The supervisor must also communicate to all those who need to know what authority the person to whom work has been delegated now has.

There should be close control of delegated work, and the subordinate must know that the supervisor is prepared to help and give advice if this is required. Feedback is vital: a person in receipt of delegated work needs to know not only that he or she is doing the job properly, but also whether the job is being done well.

The people that are directly involved in doing the work are those that have the greatest knowledge of the process's inefficiencies and benefits. The supervisor will support these people by:

- soliciting their expertise and allowing them to take some operational decisions
- backing them up and helping them to become more efficient
- providing counselling and advice
- bringing the organisation's resources to bear on problems identified by the workforce

The climate of the organisation is a prime determinant of the effectiveness of delegation. If fear, distrust and uncertainty surround the process of delegation, people will become at best sceptical of the purpose and value of delegation and at worst cynical about and hostile to it.

The decision about when to delegate is also important:

(a) Is the acceptance of staff affected required for morale, relationships or ease of implementation of the decision?

(b) Is the **quality** of the decision most important? Many technical financial decisions may be of this type, and should be retained by the supervisor if he or she alone has the knowledge and experience to make them.

(c) Is the **expertise or experience** of assistants relevant or **necessary** to the task, and will it enhance the quality of the decision?

(d) Can **trust** be placed in the competence and reliability of the assistants?

(e) Does the **decision** require tact and confidentiality, or, on the other hand, maximum exposure and assimilation by employees?

Activity 6 **(20 minutes)**

You are the manager of an accounts section of your organisation and have stopped to talk to one of the clerks in the office to see what progress he is making. He complains bitterly that he is not learning anything. He gets only routine work to do and it is the same routine. He has not even been given the chance to swap jobs with someone else. You have picked up the same message from others in the office. You discuss the situation with Jean Howe the recently appointed supervisor. She appears to be very busy and harassed. When confronted with your observations she says that she is fed up with the job. She is worked off her feet, comes early, goes late, takes work home and gets criticised behind her back by incompetent clerks.

What has gone wrong?

7 COMMUNICATION STYLES AND TECHNIQUES

7.1 Applied leadership techniques

Knowing how to adapt the way you work with others, how you communicate, provide information and learning, how you identify and agree tasks, are the main factors enabling successfully managing and motivating others - and yourself.

In terms of motivating others you cannot 'impose' motivation on another person. You can inspire them perhaps, which lasts as long as you can sustain the inspiration, but sustainable motivation must come from within the person. A good manager and leader will enable and provide the situation, environment and opportunities necessary for people to be motivated - in pursuit of goals and development and achievements that are truly meaningful to the individual. This implies that you need to discover, and at times help the other person to discover what truly motivates them to achieve their own unique potential. Being able to explain personality and to guide people towards resources that will help them understand more about themselves is all part of the process. Help others to help you understand what they need - for work and for whole life development, and you will have an important key to motivating, helping and working with people.

Each of the different theories and models of personality and human motivation is a different perspective on the hugely complex area of personality, motivation and behaviour. It follows that for any complex subject, the more perspectives you have, then the better your overall understanding will be.

7.2 The DISC Personality System

It is the leader's responsibility to connect with team members in a way that engages them and pulls them forward. To do this, the leader needs to know each of his or her team members' natural behavioural style (how they intrinsically operate) and their adapted behavioural style (how they respond to the demands of various environments) and how they prefer to communicate.

DISC was developed by William Marston in 1928 as a model for explaining normal behaviour. Research has shown that behavioural characteristics can be grouped together in four major divisions called personality styles. People with similar personality profiles styles tend to exhibit specific behavioural characteristics common to that profile. All people share these four styles in varying degrees of intensity. The DISC system describes behavioural styles using a combination of four basic tendencies; Dominance, Influence, Steadiness, and Compliance.

'D' - Active/Task -oriented
Dominating,
Directing, Demanding,
Determined, Decisive, Doing.

'I' - Active/People -oriented
Inspiring,
Influencing, Inducing,
Impressing, Interactive,
Interested in people.

'C' - Passive/Task -oriented
Cautious,
Competent, Calculating,
Compliant, Careful,
Contemplative.

'S' - Passive/People -oriented
Steady,
Stable, Shy,
Security-oriented,
Servant, Submissive,
Specialist.

D stands for dominance; it measures how you handle or respond to problems or challenges. High *D* individuals bring vision and execution to an organisation. They are very task-oriented and are great at executing and implementing. Under extreme pressure a High *D* tends to come across as arrogant, cocky, abrupt, and self-focused, with a default emotion of anger.

I stands for influence; it describes how you deal with people and contacts. *I* types are highly relational. Usually they are the life and soul of the party, great influencers, and terrific salespeople. Under stress they can be too trusting, overly effusive, and charismatic to a fault, with a default emotion of optimism.

S is for steadiness; it describes how you handle pace and consistency. *S* types are wonderful supporters. They are calm and consistent, and they don't like fast-paced change. They are also very relational and are great to have on a team. Under pressure they hold a grudge and become slow to act, with a default emotion of stoicism.

C is for compliance; it measures how you deal with processes and constraints. The *C* type is very task-oriented and greatly values detail and accuracy. They want to make sure everything follows policy and procedure. Under pressure, they become bound by procedures and lean on their supervisor, with a default emotion of fear.

Everyone is a combination of these four DISC characteristics. Some people are high or low on a particular segment; some are in the middle. There is no right or wrong combination. But how you score on the DISC profile greatly impacts how you interact with people, handle problems, and look at life.

Activity 7 **(10 minutes)**

The DISC Personality Test will help you to find out which 'quadrant' you are in; whether you are a D (dominant), I (influential), S (steady) or C (conscientious) person.

There are 15 sets of adjectives below. For each set of 4 adjectives, choose the adjective that best describes you. At the end of the test, count the number of ticks you have in one row and add them together.

1	Strong-willed	Persuasive	Kind	Humble
2	Independent	Sociable	Pleasant	Cooperative
3	Bold	Lively	Loyal	Passive
4	Competitive	Cheerful	Obliging	Open-minded
5	Daring	Humorous	Calm	Precise
6	Pioneering	Trusting	Lenient	Tolerant
7	Persistent	Entertaining	Obedient	Neat
8	Energetic	Sociable	Lenient	Peaceful
9	Risk Taker	Good-mixer	Patient	Precise
10	Determined	Energetic	Self-controlled	Systematic
11	Aggressive	Charismatic	Good-natured	Careful
12	Restless	Talkative	Controlled	Conventional
13	Decisive	Popular	Neighbourly	Organised
14	Adventurous	Friendly	Moderate	Receptive
15	Brave	Inspiring	Submissive	Shy

7.3 How is DISC used?

Understand the DISC type. Then play to the person's preferences and overall type.

With Dominant people

- Build respect to avoid conflict
- Focus on facts and ideas rather than the people
- Have evidence to support your

With Influential people

- Be social and friendly, building the relationship
- Listen to them talk about their ideas
- Help them find ways to translate the

arguments • Be quick, focused, and to the point • Ask 'what' not 'how' • Talk about how problems will hinder accomplishments • Show them how they can succeed	talk into useful action • Don't spend much time on the details • Motivate them to follow through to complete tasks • Recognise their accomplishments
With Conscientious people • Warn them in time and generally avoid surprises • Be prepared. Don't ad-lib • Be logical, accurate and use clear data • Show how things fit into the bigger picture • Be specific in disagreement and focus on the facts • Be patient, persistent and diplomatic	**With Steady people** • Be genuinely interested in them • Create a human working environment for them • Give them time to adjust to change • Clearly define goals for them and provide ongoing support • Recognise and appreciate their achievements • Avoid hurry and pressure • Present new ideas carefully

DISC work styles

Work styles can be illustrated as follows:

A 'D' person is direct and tends to take charge of situations, is very productive, finding no need to waste time on relationships or talking	An 'I' person accomplishes tasks through influencing others by persuasion and enjoys developing relationships with many people. This person has a difficult time staying focused on tasks for any length of time.
A 'C' person is cautious in his/her approach to work and has a great need to do things 'right.' This person works from lists and gathers all the facts before proceeding.	An 'S' person is a steady worker, quiet, and unobtrusive.

DISC communication styles

Each person has a different style of communicating:

A 'D' person speaks in a forceful voice. S/he tells even when asking a question. This person can be blunt and wants the bottom line.	An 'I' person accomplishes tasks through influencing others by persuasion and enjoys developing relationships with many people. This person has a difficult time staying focused on tasks for any length of time.

A 'C' person is cautious in his/her approach to work and has a great need to do things 'right.' This person works from lists and gathers all the facts before proceeding.	An 'S' person is a steady worker, quiet, and unobtrusive.

DISC motivation styles

Each person will be motivated by different methods.

A 'D' person will need: • New, non-routine challenging tasks and activities • Power and authority to take risks and make decisions • Freedom from controls, supervision, and details • Freedom from routine and mundane tasks • Changing environments in which to work and play • Personal evaluation based on results, not methods	An 'I' person will need: • Practical procedures • Flattery, praise, popularity, and acceptance • A friendly environment with few conflicts and arguments • Freedom from controls, details, rules and regulations • A forum to express ideas • Group activities in professional and social environments • Other people available to handle details
A 'C' person will need: • Standards of high quality • Limited social interaction • Specialised or technical tasks • Logical organisation of information • Tasks and projects that can be followed through to completion • Practical work procedures and routines. • Few conflicts and arguments • Instructions and reassurance that they are doing what is expected of them	An 'S' person will need: • Recognition for loyalty and dependability • Safety and security • No sudden changes in procedure or lifestyle • Activities that can be started and finished. • Practical procedures and systems • Stability and predictability • Tasks that can be completed at one time • Few conflicts and arguments • A team atmosphere

DISC personal growth areas

For 'D's:	For 'I's:
Strive to be an 'active' listener. Be attentive to other team members' ideas until everyone reaches a consensus. Be less controlling and domineering. Develop a greater appreciation for the opinions, feelings, and desires of others. Put more energy into personal relationships. Show your support for other team members. Take time to explain the 'whys' of your statements and proposals. Be friendlier and more approachable.	Weigh the pros and cons before making a decision; be less impulsive and more results oriented. Exercise control over your actions, words, and emotions. Focus more on details and facts. Remember to slow down your pace for other team members. Talk less; listen more. Consider and evaluate ideas from other team members. Concentrate on following through with tasks.
For 'C's	**For 'S's**
Concentrate on doing the right things, not just doing things right. Be less critical of others' ideas and methods. Respond more quickly to accomplish team goals. Strive to build relationships with other team members. Be more decisive. Focus less on facts and more on people. Take risks along with other team members.	Be more open to change. Be more direct in your interactions. Focus on overall goals of the team rather than specific procedures. Deal with confrontation constructively. Develop more flexibility. Increase pace to accomplish goals. Show more initiative. Work at expressing thoughts, opinions, and feelings.

DISC leadership/supervision styles

Leadership/supervision requires a determination to understand and direct the employee. An effective leader/supervisor coaches his/her employee. S/he works with the employee to improve performance and complete the job in the most productive way.

Once you understand the DISC personality style of your employee, you are ready to implement a plan of action. Each one requires a different style. There are four leadership/supervisory approaches that must be taken into consideration:

1 **Supporting approach**

Lead a 'D' person by giving compliments on results and ability to lead others. Speak briefly and directly. Offer challenges and show how to win and give options for ways to accomplish goals.

Lead an 'I' person by helping with details. Give enthusiastic compliments in front of others and allow opportunities and time for interaction. Let him/her talk about feelings and ideas.

Lead an 'S' person by asking informally about concerns. Notice and give friendly, informal, sincere compliments on strengths such as being a reliable team member, completing the task, being good with co-workers and clients, creating friendly relationships, listening, etc.

Lead a 'C' person by providing opportunities to use facts, logic and analysis to get quality results. Create opportunities for others to see him/her as an expert in his/her field. Speak with precise, factual, formal statements complimenting on work well done.

2 **Motivating approach**

Lead the 'D' by helping to eliminate problems that are slowing or stopping the desired results. Ask for solutions to problems in a positive way.

Lead the 'I' person by showing how to get approval from others by improving job performance.

Lead the 'S' person by creating a step-by-step plan of action for new situations and setting time limits. Coach in areas in which s/he is uncomfortable.

Lead the 'C' person by helping him/her work on problem-solving techniques focusing on faster responses.

3 **Directing approach**

Lead a 'D' person by showing how to be productive in the fastest, simplest, most practical way. Be firm. Explain in a direct way how you want the task done, outlining boundaries clearly.

Lead an 'I' person by giving as few details as possible, speaking in a descriptive, fast paced manner. Get clear and specific feedback for complete understanding of how s/he will do the task.

Lead an 'S' person by walking through the process in a step-by-step procedure. Train one-on-one and submit all instructions in writing. Give feedback in an informal, relaxed manner on a regular, consistent basis.

Lead a 'C' person by speaking with precise, factual, formal statements and tell this employee the level of perfection required. Ask for feedback on important information and give time to process and to perfect the information

4 **Empowering approach**

Lead the 'D' person by allowing control over the job as long as you approve of the results. Offer opportunities to supervise others. Allow control over the task as long as the results are approved by you. Set clear boundaries of authority but allow freedom within those boundaries.

Lead the 'I' person by giving freedom to complete the job after you are sure your expectations are understood, including the deadline date, setting dates to monitor whether or not the task is on schedule and giving opportunities and time to talk to other people.

Lead the 'S' person by putting your expected results in writing, informing him/her of available resources, and checking in on a regular basis to answer any questions.

Lead the 'C' person by creating a clear description of results and quality expected and by explaining the positive impact on the team due to his/her task completion.

8 SUPERVISION STYLES

8.1 What is your supervision style?

Rarely does someone's style reflect a 'true' type as listed below, and may depend on the type of people you are supervising. However, it is helpful to know what style you use frequently, and to understand ways in which your style both helps and impedes your ability to be an effective leader.

1. **Authoritarian supervision** is based on the belief that members require continuous attention because they are often undependable or immature - basically, because people will attempt to work as little as possible unless someone monitors them carefully. Because members cannot be trusted to fulfil their tasks, the supervisor must check on them frequently. The supervisor is ultimately responsible for members' performance. Consequently, close observation is an essential part of the supervisor's responsibilities.
2. **Laissez faire supervision** is based on the desire to allow members the freedom to use their talents and skills in accomplishing job responsibilities. This philosophy of practice is often articulated as, 'Hire good people and then get out of their way.' As a result, members view supervision as an admission to failure; that is, as something to submit to when they encounter a situation they are unable to handle on their own.
3. **Companionable supervision** is based principally on a friendship-like relationship. Above all else, supervisors seek to be liked and to create harmonious relationships among members; they concentrate on being buddies with the staff they supervise and avoid confronting members about poor job performance or mistakes in judgement as long as possible.
4. **Synergistic supervision** is a cooperative effort between the supervisor and members that allows to effect of the joint effort to be greater than the sum of their individual contributions. Supervision in this approach has a dual focus: accomplishment of the organisation's goal and support of the staff in the accomplishment of their personal and professional development goals. This approach to supervision emphasises the identification of potential problems early; the supervisor and member then jointly develop strategies to prevent or ameliorate problem situations. Supervision is dedicated to assisting all members to enhance their knowledge and skills, which can lead to advancement within the organisation and profession.

8.2 Supervisor's role in communications and working culture

A supervisor plays a vital role in communication. He or she works not only as a receiver or sender but also as a facilitator. To make a communication system effective the supervisor needs to work as a developer as well as a maintenance person.

As a sender, the individual should be seen as:

- sharing, not telling
- trying to relate to other people, not to control them

- seeking truth rather than convincing others
- judging his or her own contribution by the feedback obtained from others rather than personal judgement
- looking for agreement and any disagreement and seeking the meaning the other person intends in the areas of difference
- seeking to be empathetic
- trying to eliminate from his behaviour actions that threaten

As a receiver the individual should:

- Try to help the sender clarify his or her meaning
- seek understanding
- identify what is not being said as much as he or she tries to understand what is being said

The supervisor's role in improving communications include the following measures:

- Encourage, facilitate and reward communication. Status and functional barriers can be minimised by improving opportunities for formal and informal networking and feedback.
- Give training and guidance in communication skills, including consideration of recipients, listening and giving feedback.
- Minimise the potential for misunderstanding. Make people aware of the difficulties arising from differences in culture and perception, and teach them to consider others' viewpoints. Solving the problems created by diversity involves:
  - treating people first and foremost as individuals
  - acknowledging the special circumstances or particular context that may lead to exclusion for some groups of people
  - working to change that situation
  - developing a workforce within which people are valued for the contribution they make

  While the main responsibility for eliminating discrimination and providing equal opportunity is that of the employer, individual employees at all levels have responsibilities too. They must not discriminate or knowingly aid their employer to do so.
- Adapt technology, systems and procedures to facilitate communication: making it more effective (clear mobile phone reception), faster (laptops for e-mailing instructions), more consistent (regularly reporting routines) and more efficient (reporting by exception).
- Manage conflict and politics in the organisation, so that no basic unwillingness exists between units.
- Establish rules, regulations and codes of practice and disciplinary procedures for non-conformance. Any successful organised activity requires that everyone concerned understands what behaviour is expected and is able and

willing to behave in the required way. It is management's job to show that rules are necessary and to convince its employees that the observation of rules is not only a condition of employment but also a process that benefits everyone. If the employee understands the requirements of his or her own job, has the requisite skill and knowledge to perform, is convinced of its usefulness to related jobs and to the overall purposes of the organisation, he or she should be suitably disposed to organisational discipline. Provided penalties for poor performance are coupled with competent and fair supervision then employees' tolerance for discipline is unlikely to diminish.

- Establish communication channels and mechanisms in all directions: regular staff or briefing meetings, house journal or intranet and quality circles. Upward communication should particularly be encouraged using mechanisms such as inter-unit meetings, suggestion schemes, 'open door' access to managers and regular performance management feedback sessions.

The communication style of the manager/supervisor can also affect the working culture of the organisation. The term working culture can include employment characteristics such as working conditions, cooperation schemes, work-control, workload, degree of specialisation, ethical issues, etc. In many successful companies, leaders/supervisors serve as role models, set the standards for performance, communicate the regulations and codes of practice expected, motivate and discipline employees, make the company special and are a symbol to the external environment. The working culture created by leaders can result in many functions being carried out in quite different ways.

9 JOB DESIGN

9.1 Factors affecting job design

Job design is the set of tasks and activities that are grouped together to define a particular job. A number of core job dimensions can be used to characterize any job. Each of these core job dimensions can significantly affect the satisfaction and performance of the individual who occupies the job.

Jobs are designed to get productivity and employee satisfaction.

Job design is the process of:

- deciding the contents of the job
- deciding methods to carry out the job
- deciding the relationship that exists in the organisation.

Job design is affected by organisational, environmental and behavioural factors. A properly designed job will make it more productive and satisfying .If a job fails on this count, it must be redesigned based on the feedback. The various factors affecting job design include:

- Organisational factors e.g., characteristics of task, work flow, ergonomics and work practices.
- Environmental factors e.g. employees' abilities and availability.
- Behavioural factors e.g., feedback, autonomy, use of abilities and variety.

9.2 Work methods

Work methods and practices are influenced by:

- the job that needs to be done - its purpose, manner, order and deadline
- the law - making sure the job is done in a safe and secure manner in accordance with the regulations and codes of practice
- the culture of the organisation - the 'way we do things round here' based on the organisation and work group's values

The work methods chosen should bring together the above to ensure jobs gets done in the right order and in the best way possible in accordance with legal requirements and the organisation's procedures. There should be no duplication or part cover of the work and efforts should be harnessed to a common goal.

Work practices – are set ways of performing work .These methods may arise from tradition or the collective wishes of employees. Work practices used to be determined by time and motion study using repeated observations to establish the standard time needed to complete the given job. A newer technique called the Maynard Operating Sequence Technique (MOST) uses statistics of average workers working at an average rate. MOST is the best, most scientific way to develop standard work that can be reliably used to determine labour requirements and job performance expectations.

Work systems – changing work practices and the impact of technology influence working values. Not only does technology dictate the method and pace of work, which reduces personal discretionary power, but also changes the mix of skills required by the organisation. Working culture changes from a 'craft skill' perspective to one of 'machine-feeder and machine-minder'. The decision-making environment becomes more 'programmable'. Also a change in technology may involve a company recruiting 'new blood' or 'buying-in' services, and as a result new and different values are introduced into the organisation, which may have a marked effect on the values of individuals and internal coalitions.

9.3 Working culture and practices

Company culture - individual and group values and behaviour will be influenced by the way that individuals view the organisation so that the values of people working in a small family business with tight central planning and control will be different from a large, decentralised and bureaucratic organisation, even though both are operating in the same industry.

Social and cultural expectations - not very long ago securing a job was the primary consideration. The worker was prepared to work on any job and under any working conditions. Now, it is not the same. Literacy, knowledge and awareness of workers have improved considerably as have their expectations from the job. Hence, jobs are designed to meet the expectations of workers.

When designing jobs for international operations, designs are almost certain to neglect national and cultural differences .Hours of work, holidays, rest breaks, religious beliefs, management styles and worker sophistication and attitudes are just some of the predictable differences that can affect the design of jobs across international borders. Failure to consider these social expectations can create social dissatisfaction, low motivation, hard to fill job openings and a low quality of work life, especially, when foreign nationals are involved in the home country or overseas.

Decision-making system - the success of any company policy will often depend upon the extent that the people involved have participated in its formulation. In many cases individuals and groups will contribute enthusiastically towards company policy because of their involvement, even though it may penalise them. But in other situations where policy is imposed without consultation or participation, conflict is the likely outcome.

The company's financial and market position - the use of power by individuals and groups will be influenced by the company's financial and market positions. For example people see a clear distinction between boom and recession, growth and decline, and investment and lack of it. As a result the attitudes and values of people tend to change, often quite conspicuously, as the environment changes. Policy changes in one organisation that faces a highly competitive and volatile market might be more acceptable than if the same policy was proposed in a company that enjoys competitive strengths and has a big order book.

9.4 Workplace diversity

The term 'workplace diversity' refers to differences between people who work for a particular company. This can comprise race, ethnicity, gender, disability, education, background and much more besides and it deals with how people perceive themselves and others, how each and every one of them can fulfil their potential and how every person working in the same organisation can work together to reap the benefits of the variety of skills that each person possesses in working towards a common goal.

Many companies have woken up to the fact that customers come from all kinds of different backgrounds and realise that by having a diverse work force it becomes easier to gain a better understanding of the different types of people in society in general. This is invaluable when devising and implementing marketing strategies.

Companies have also realised that in broadening their recruitment process to positively encourage people of all backgrounds to apply for jobs, they increase their chances of getting the right person for the job and do not miss out on skills and talent, which they might otherwise have done if they had adopted a more narrow-minded approach to recruitment.

Businesses also realise that a diverse workforce presents a much deeper 'pool' of experience and ideas, which they can tap into. And, in the global economy we all work in these days, having a diverse workforce is very beneficial especially when trying to foster business relations with people from overseas.

Perhaps most importantly, companies know of the increased awareness of employee rights with regard to legislation relating to discrimination and equality and, therefore, they must ensure that their workplace adopts an equal opportunity policy for all their workers.

Chapter roundup

- Work objectives clarify what the individual is expected to do and they enable the performance of the individual to be measured.
- Work planning is the establishment of work methods and practices to ensure that predetermined objectives are efficiently met at all levels. It is necessary to ensure that work is carried out in accordance with the organisation's requirements and needs
- Supervisors often have to plan the use of resources in their section and schedule activities to ensure that work is done on time, to standard and to budget.
- Scheduling is where priorities and deadlines are planned and controlled. A schedule establishes a timetable for a logical sequence of tasks, leading up to a completion date.
- Motivation is the controlling of the work environment, rewards and sanctions in such a way as to encourage desired behaviours and performance from employees.
- Various means have been suggested or improving job satisfaction but there is little evidence that a satisfied worker actually works harder.
- Pay is the most important of the hygiene factors, but it is ambiguous in its effect on motivation.
- Process theories of motivation do not tell managers what to offer employees in order to motivate them but help managers to understand the dynamics of employees' decisions about what rewards are worth going for.
- Content theories of motivation suggest that each person has a package of needs: the best way to motivate an employee is to find out what his/her needs are and offer him/her rewards that will satisfy those needs.
  - *Abraham Maslow* identified a hierarchy of needs which an individual will be motivated to satisfy, progressing towards higher order satisfactions, such as self-actualisation.
  - *Frederick Herzberg* identified two basic need systems: the need to avoid unpleasantness and the need for personal growth. He suggested factors which could be offered by organisations to satisfy both types of need: 'hygiene' and 'motivator' factors respectively.
- Rewards offered to the individual at work may be of two basic types.
  - Extrinsic rewards are separate from (or external to) the job itself, and dependent on the decisions of others
  - Intrinsic rewards are those which arise from the performance of the work itself.
- Ways in which managers can improve employees' motivation range from encouraging employees to accept responsibility to careful design of jobs (including job enrichment, job enlargement and job rotation) to increasingly sophisticated and performance-related pay and incentive schemes.

- Maccoby's theory of social character explores the dominant values that determine motivation, and allows us to differentiate five value types: the expert, helper, defender, innovator and self-developer
- According to the Five-Factor Model (FFM), developed by Costa and McCrae, there are five broad categories at the top of the personality trait hierarchy: neuroticism-emotional stability, extraversion, openness to experience, agreeableness, and conscientiousness
- Empowerment' is the term given to organisational arrangements that allow employees more autonomy, discretion and unsupervised decision-making responsibility.
- The DISC Profile is a non-judgemental tool for understanding how to improve communication skills by determining communication styles and techniques
- Delegation is the process of assigning tasks and granting sufficient authority for their accomplishment.

Quick quiz

1 List some planning and scheduling aids.

2 List the five categories in *Maslow's* Hierarchy of Needs.

3 List three ways in which an organisation can offer motivational satisfaction.

4 What is the difference between a reward and an incentive?

5 According to *Herzberg*, leadership style is a motivator factor. True or false?

6 'People will work harder and harder to earn more and more pay.' Do you agree? Why (or why not)?

7 A 'horizontal' extension of the job to increase task variety is called:

   A Job evaluation
   B Job enrichment
   C Job enlargement
   D Job rotation

8 List the stages in the process of delegation.

9 List some problems in delegation.

10 Is consultation the same as negotiation? If not, explain the difference.

Answers to quick quiz

1 The following are probably the most common:
- checklists
- scheduling
- work programmes
- action sheets
- planning charts and boards.

2 Physiological, safety, love/social, esteem, self-actualisation.

3 Relationships, belonging, challenge, achievement, progress, security, money.

4 A reward is given for some contribution or success. An incentive is an offer or reward.

5 False: it is a hygiene factor.

6 See Paragraph 3.3.

7 C. Make sure you can define all the other terms as well.

8 Specify performance levels; formally assign task; allocate resources and authority; back off; give feedback.

9 Low trust, low competence, fear, worry about accountability.

10 Consultation is not the same as negotiation. Negotiation implies acceptance by both parties that agreement between them is required before a decision is taken. Consultation implies a willingness to listen to the views of another while reserving the right to take the final decision, with or without agreement on both sides.

Answers to activities

1 The answer will depend on the activity you have chosen.

2 This will depend on your own situation.

3 *Maslow's* categories for the listed circumstances are as follows:

(a) Esteem needs
(b) Social needs
(c) Self-actualisation needs
(d) He will have physiological needs
(e) Safety needs initially; esteem needs above a certain income level
(f) Social needs or self-actualisation needs
(g) Esteem needs
(h) Safety needs or esteem needs

4 Expectancy theory has various practical applications.

(a) Motivation can be measured and responses to incentives (to an extent) predicted, using attitude surveys or interviews in which team members are invited to state valence and expectancy..

(b) Managers need to fulfil their promises of rewards – otherwise expectancy will be lowered next time.

(c) Managers need to give some thought to the value of incentives and rewards to individual employees -otherwise valence will be low.

(Some organisations offer a 'cafeteria' system of rewards and benefits, allowing employees to select those that they value.)

(d) Managers need to give employees clear information on expected results, offered rewards and progress -via on-going feedback – in order for them to make motivational calculations.

5

Power	Empowerment
• External source	• Internal source
• Ultimately, few people have it	• Ultimately, everyone can have it
• The capacity to have others do what you want	• The capacity to have others do what they want
• To get more implies taking it away from someone else	• To get more does not affect what others have
• Leads to competition	• Leads to cooperation

6 The problem appears to be that the new supervisor is taking too much of the department's work on to herself. While she is overworked, her subordinates are apparently not being stretched and as a result motivation and morale amongst them are poor. The supervisor herself is unhappy with the position and there is a danger that declining job satisfaction will lead to inefficiencies and eventually staff resignations.

There could be a number of causes contributing to the problem.

(a) Jean Howe may have been badly selected, ie she may not have the ability required for a supervisory job.

(b) Alternatively she may just be unaware of what is involved in a supervisor's role. She may not have realised that much of the task consists of managing subordinates; she is not required to shoulder all the detailed technical work herself.

(c) There may be personality problems involved. Jean Howe regards her clerks as incompetent and this attitude may arise simply form an inability to get on with them socially. (Another possibility is that her staff actually are incompetent.)

(d) The supervisor does much of the department's work herself. This may be because she does not understand the kind of tasks which can be delegated and the way in which delegation of authority can improve the motivation and job satisfaction of subordinates.

As manager you have already gone some way towards identifying the actual causes of the problem. You have spoken to some of the subordinates concerned and also to the supervisor. You could supplement this by a review of personnel records relating to Jean Howe to discover how her career has progressed so far and what training she had received (if any) in the duties of a supervisor. You may then be in a position to determine which of the possible causes of the problems are operating in this case.

7 The results of the DISC Personality Test will tell you the various degrees of each personality trait you are.

If you have most of your ticks in the first column, then you are a D (dominant) person.

D (Dominant) - people are generally direct, positive and straightforward and like to be in charge, do things fast and want immediate results for their efforts. They are determined, independent people who like to solve problems and face challenges.

People who belong to this category are probably the sales superstars and the kind of strong, entrepreneurial leaders. They are people you want to have around in your organisation. They are very results oriented and you can except to see things getting done efficiently. However, they have very low patience and you must continually engage them to keep them in the organisation.

They will stay with you to the extent that they feel that following you helps them to achieve their personal goals for their life. Also, they might be cause for some conflicts between people because they are more task-oriented and they would probably step on some toes along the way. Be careful about putting two Ds in the same team, conflict will always arise from two strong-headed individuals.

If you have most of your ticks in the second column, you are an I (influential) person.

I (Influential) people are very people-oriented. They are friendly outgoing, sociable and they often are around friends. They define themselves by their relationships and they thrive on social contact. They can get along well with most people because they are generally interested in people.

These people are important in an organisation because they bring the human touch. They can make new recruits feel welcome and give them a sense of belonging. However, these people are generally not very good at doing tasks well; they are generally less meticulous and would miss out certain details in their work. Learn to use these people accordingly because while they may not perform certain tasks well, they are essential to building a relationship-based organisation.

If you have most of your ticks in the third column, you are an S (steady) person.

S (Steady) individuals generally thrive supporting a D (dominant) leader and doing the work behind the scenes. These people are loyal, have good self-control, often good listeners and tend to want to avoid disagreements and conflicts.

They are good in an organisation because you need people who can be supportive and loyal. Not everyone can be the one to receive the honour, not everyone can be the head of a team or an organisation, but the S (steady) individuals are usually happy where they are. That's why S (steady) people are absolutely essential for any team to work.

S (steady) personalities generally work well in support roles like managerial roles or as assistants to heads of departments.

If you have most of your ticks in the fourth column, you are a C (conscientious) person.

C (Conscientious) people are very useful in any organisation; they are precise, very systematic people who need a lot of information when performing a project. They are like the S (steady) people in that they would choose to avoid conflict and tend to be more accommodating to others.

When you are planning something in your organisation, you need conscientious people to be around to check you. Sometimes they are able to see things that you can't, and have foresight about particular events or scenarios that might arise and make provision for them.

Chapter 10 : PERFORMANCE MONITORING AND ASSESSMENT

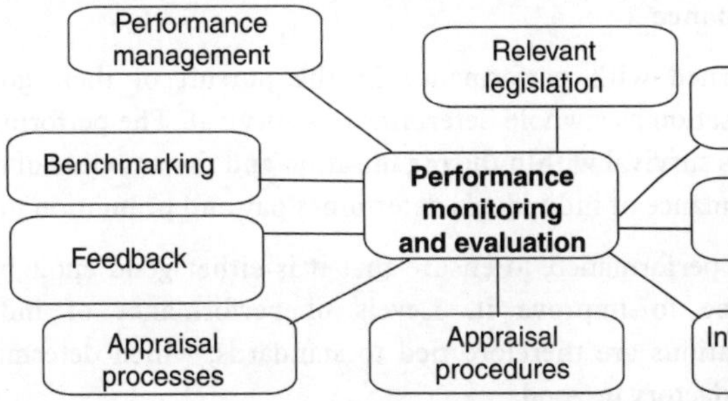

Introduction

The performance management process provides an opportunity for the employee and performance manager to discuss development goals and jointly create a plan for achieving those goals. Development plans should contribute to organisational goals and the professional growth of the employee. Achieving the overall goal requires several ongoing activities, including identification and prioritisation of desired results, establishing means to measure progress toward those results, setting standards for assessing how well results were achieved, tracking and measuring progress toward results, exchanging ongoing feedback among those participants working to achieve results, periodically reviewing progress, reinforcing activities that achieve results and intervening to improve progress where needed. Note that results themselves are also measures. Feedback is given and assistance with corrective actions is required where the performance does not match the standard set. The appraisal interview is the vehicle for giving feedback to the employee through which they can find out about their strengths and weaknesses and discuss what steps to take to improve future performance. As such it is a crucial part of the appraisal process.

Your objectives

After completing this chapter you should be able to:

(a) Plan or analyse work activities using appropriate objective setting techniques and processes

(b) Review development needs and activities and evaluate the effectiveness of activities

(c) Use suitable methods, with clearly defined and relevant criteria and objectives, to assess the performance of colleagues

(d) Identify factors affecting the quality of performance and use these to provide clear and constructive feedback on performance to colleagues

(e) Incorporate results of assessments into personal development plans and other organisational procedures for dealing with performance issues

(f) Evaluate the success of the assessment process

1 PERFORMANCE MANAGEMENT

1.1 Controlled performance

Organisations are concerned with performance in the pursuit of their goals. The performance of an organisation as a whole determines its survival. The performance of a department determines its survival within the organisation and the amounts of resources allocated to it. The performance of individuals determines pay and promotion prospects.

It is necessary to control performance, to ensure that it is either good enough, or that something is being done to improve it. Levels of performance of individuals, departments and organisations are therefore tied to standards, which determine what counts as inadequate, satisfactory or good.

Control involves setting standards, measuring performance against standards, taking decisions about the extent to which performance is satisfactory, and taking appropriate action to correct deviations from standards, shown in the figure below.

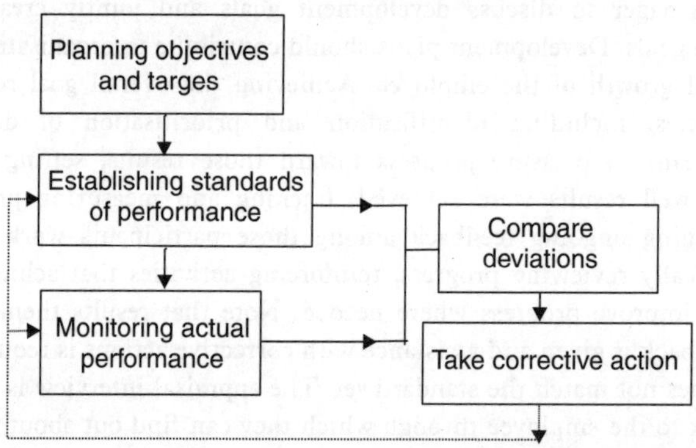

Figure 10.1: Controlling performance

The need for controlled performance leads to a deliberate and ordered allocation of functions, or division of labour, between organisation members. The activities and interactions of members are also intentionally programmed and structured. Admission to membership of organisations is controlled and the price of failure to perform to standard is usually loss of membership.

1.2 Features of performance management

Definition

> **Performance management** is: a means of getting better results by managing performance within an agreed framework of goals, standards and competence requirements. It is a process to establish a shared understanding about what is to be achieved, and an approach to managing and developing people.

This definition highlights key features of performance management.

Aspect	Comment
Agreed framework of goals, standards and competence requirements	The manager and the employee agree about a standard of performance, goals and the skills needed.
Performance management is a process	Managing people's performance is an on-going activity, involving continual monitoring, discussion and adjustment.
Shared understanding	The goals of the individual, unit and organisation as a whole need to be integrated: everyone needs to be 'on the same page' of the business plan.
Approach to managing and developing people	Managing performance is not just about plans, systems or resources: it is an **interpersonal** process of influencing, empowering, giving feedback and problem-solving.
Achievement	The aim is to enable people to realise their potential and maximise their contribution to the organisation's success.

Other features of performance management described by *Armstrong* include:

(a) **Line management** – a performance management system is primarily the concern, not of experts in the personnel/HRM department, but of the managers responsible for driving the business.

(b) **Specific** – as each organisation has unique issues to face, performance management systems cannot really be bought off the shelf.

(c) **Future-based** – performance management is forward looking, based on the organisation's future needs and what the individual must do to satisfy them.

1.3 The process of performance management

A systematic approach to performance management might include the following steps.

Step 1 From the business plan, identify the requirements and competences required to carry it out.

Step 2 Draw up a performance agreement, defining the expectations of the individual or team, covering standards of performance, performance indicators and the skills and competences people need.

Step 3 Draw up a performance and development plan with the individual. These record the actions needed to improve performance, normally covering development in the current job. They are discussed with job holders and will cover, typically:

- The areas of performance the individual feels are in need of development
- What the individual and manager agree is needed to enhance performance
- Development and training initiatives

Step 4 Manage performance continually throughout the year, not just at appraisal interviews done to satisfy the personnel department. Managers can review actual performance, with more informal interim reviews at various times of the year.

High performance is reinforced by praise, recognition, increasing responsibility. Low performance results in coaching or counselling. Work plans are updated as necessary.

Deal with performance problems by identifying what they are; establish the reasons for the shortfall; take control action (with adequate resources); and provide feedback.

Step 5 Performance review – at a defined period each year, success against the plan is reviewed, but the whole point is to assess what is going to happen in future.

Activity 1 **(10 minutes)**

What are the advantages to employees of introducing such a system?

1.4 Goal setting

People are 'purposive' – that is, they act in pursuit of particular goals or purposes. The goals or objectives of an individual influence:

(a) What (s)he **perceives,** since we filter out messages not relevant to our goals and objectives and select those which are relevant

(b) What (s)he **learns,** since learning is a process of selecting and analysing experience in order to take it into account in acting in future, so that our goals and objectives may be more effectively met

(c) What (s)he **does,** since people behave in such a way as to satisfy their goals. This is the basis of motivation, since organisations can **motivate** people to behave in desirable ways (effective work performance) by offering them the means to fulfil their goals.

In order for learning and motivation to be effective, it is essential that **people know** exactly **what their objectives are.** This enables them to do the following.

(a) **Plan and direct their effort** towards the objectives

(b) **Monitor their performance** against objectives and adjust (or learn) if required

(c) Experience the **reward of achievement** once the objectives have been reached

(d) Feel that their tasks have **meaning and purpose**, which is an important element in job satisfaction

(e) Experience the **motivation of a challenge**: the need to expend energy and effort in a particular direction in order to achieve something

(f) Avoid the **de-motivation** of impossible or inadequately rewarded tasks. As we have in the chapter on motivation, there is a calculation involved in motivated performance. If objectives are vague, unrealistic or unattainable, there may be little incentive to pursue them: hence the importance of SMART objectives.

Some principles for devising performance measures are as follows.

Principle	Comment
Job-related	They should be related to the actual job, and the key tasks outlined in the job description
Controllable	People should not be assessed according to factors which they cannot control
Objective and observable	This is contentious. Certain aspects of performance can be measured, such as volume sales, but matters such as courtesy or friendliness which are important to some businesses are harder to measure
Data must be available	There is no use identifying performance measures if the data cannot actually be collected

Activity 2 **(10 minutes)**

A senior sales executive has a job that involves: 'building the firm's sales' and maintaining 'a high degree of satisfaction with the company's products and services'. The firm buys sports equipment, running machines and so on, which it sells to gyms and individuals. The firm also charges fees to service the equipment. Service contracts are the sales executive's responsibility, and he has to manage that side of the business.

Here are some possible performance indicators to assess the sales executive's performance in the role. What do you think of them?

(a) Number of new customers gained per period
(b) Value of revenue from existing customers per period
(c) Renewal of service contracts
(d) Record of customer complaints about poor quality products
(e) Regular customer satisfaction survey

2 BENCHMARKING

2.1 Types of benchmarking

Definition

> **Benchmarking** is a continuous, systematic, process for evaluating the products, services, and work processes of organisations that are recognised as representing best practices for the purpose of organisational improvement.

Through benchmarking, organisations learn about their own business practices and the best practices of others. Benchmarking enables them to identify where they fall short of current best practice and determine action programmes to help them match and surpass it.

Any activity that can be measured can be benchmarked. However, it is impracticable to benchmark every process and organisations should concentrate on areas that:

- Tie up most cash
- Significantly improve the relationship with customers, *and*
- Impact on the final results of the business

The choice of the activity to be benchmarked will determine the approach that needs to be taken. There are three primary types of benchmarking that are in use today.

(a) **Internal benchmarking** – in most large companies there are similar functions in different business units. One of the simplest benchmarking exercises is to compare these internal operations. It assumes there are differences in the work processes of an organisation as a result of geographical differences, local organisational history, customs, differences among business units, and relationships among managers and employees. The advantages include the information sharing that accompanies internal benchmarking and the immediate gains that can be obtained by identifying the best internal practices and transferring those to other parts of the organisation. The disadvantage of internal benchmarking is that it fosters an introverted view. It is all too easy to ignore that other organisations have the edge on you if you are concentrating on outperforming internal rivals.

(b) **Competitive benchmarking** concerns the identification of specific information about a competitor's products, processes, and business results to make comparisons with those of its own organisation. Direct competitors are the most obvious to benchmark against. The objective is to compare companies in the same markets that have competing products or services or work processes, eg Coca Cola and Pepsi.

The advantage of competitive benchmarking is that you can see what your relative performance is. The main disadvantage is that information is very hard to obtain, beyond that in the public domain. Where information may be commercially sensitive an appropriate third party can be used.

(c) **Process or activity benchmarks** – makes comparisons with organisations in different, non-competing product/service sectors but with similar core operations. They involve the identification of state-of-the-art products, services, or processes of an organisation that may or may not be a company's direct competitor. The objective of this type of benchmarking is to identify best practices in any type of organisation that has established a reputation for excellence in specific business activities such as manufacturing, marketing, engineering, warehousing, fleet management, or human resources eg, the recruitment process. The big advantage of this benchmarking is that it is easier to identify willing partners, since the information is not going to a direct competitor. The disadvantages are cost and the fact that the most renowned companies are beginning to feel overwhelmed with benchmarking visits and some are even charging a fee for access.

2.2 Benchmarking objective setting

Firms like Rank Xerox have developed employee involvement in setting their own objectives by encouraging them to benchmark their own activities against the best practice for doing their job. This is a very different approach from that used in some companies, where benchmarking is used as a 'stick' to set objectives. In the Xerox case, employees are encouraged to investigate the best practice for their activity and not only to find out what is achieved in terms of a numerical benchmark but also to discover *how* it can be achieved. The involvement is necessary to get the commitment to change required to achieve top performance.

This technique has been used to make substantial changes to systems and processes used not only in the main operational areas like sales, manufacturing and distribution but also in central areas like administration, finance and information systems.

3 FEEDBACK

3.1 Effective feedback

Definition

> **Feedback** is communication, which offers information to an individual or group about how their performance, results or behaviours are perceived or assessed by others.

Feedback relates closely to goal setting. Goals serve as targets for performance. When employees understand how they are attaining those goals, they can adjust their behaviour to perform more. Effective and timely feedback should motivate, encourage, and guide, while creating a positive environment.

Recognition, praise and encouragement create feelings of confidence, competence, development and progress that enhance the motivation to learn.

3.2 Types of feedback

There are two main types of feedback, both of which are valuable in enhancing performance and development.

(a) **Motivational feedback:** used to reward and reinforce positive behaviours and performance by praising and encouraging the individual, and allowing him or her to celebrate positive results, progress or improvements. Its purpose is to increase **confidence** and **motivation.**

(b) **Developmental feedback:** given when a particular area of performance needs to be improved, helping the individual to identify what needs to be changed and how this might be done. Its purpose is to increase **competence** and aid **learning.**

Feedback is a crucial tool in managing people – as in any control system.

(a) Positive feedback acts as a **reinforcer** or reward, which aids motivation and commitment.

(b) Negative feedback – delivered constructively provides **information for learning** processes: it supports goal setting and improvement planning.

(c) Feedback on performance **enriches work** by giving it meaning. It helps to integrate individual goals with team and organisational goals, adding to employees' satisfaction and commitment by giving them a sense of how their work is contributing to the whole.

(d) Feedback on progress helps employees to manage and adjust their **performance;** they know 'where they are' in relation to standards and targets.

(e) Ongoing feedback contributes to an effective **management style.** Rewards, sanctions and corrections are perceived to be more fair (and are less stressful for employees) if they are based on known performance standards and attainments. Feedback empowers employees to diagnose and solve their own performance problems.

Constructive feedback is designed to widen options and support development. This does not mean giving only encouraging or positive feedback when a person has done something well: feedback about undesirable behaviours or performance shortfalls, given skilfully, is in many ways more useful to the individual.

3.3 Giving feedback

Giving constructive feedback is an important leadership skill. It requires:

(a) **Assertiveness**. You must be prepared to give difficult messages and confront difficult issues where required.

(b) **Respect for others**. While being honest about other people's development/improvement needs, you must consider their right to be treated with respect.

(c) **Skill**. Giving effective feedback is a complex interpersonal skill.

The following are some general guidelines for giving constructive feedback.

(a) **Choose the right time**. Feedback should be given close to the event, so that the details are fresh in both parties' minds – but with sensitivity to the appropriate time and setting. Feedback is best given calmly and confidentially.

(b) **Start with positives**. People will more readily accept criticism as constructive if it is balanced with acknowledgement of positive aspects.

(c) **Focus on the behaviour**. Feedback needs to refer clearly to behaviours, actions and results – not the person or their personality. ('Tough on the problem, soft on the person' is a good general rule.)

(d) **Be accurate**. Feedback needs to be specific, avoiding vague and global statements (for example, not 'you're always late!' but 'on two occasions this week you have been more than fifteen minutes late for work') and avoiding inferences and assumptions.

(e) **Don't tackle everything at once**. Give the person one or two priority areas to deal with at a time.

(f) **Close with encouragement.** Balance negative feedback with positive encouragement that change is possible and will be supported by you and the organisation.

Activity 3 **(10 minutes)**

Consider how easy or difficult you find it to receive feedback. See if you can come up with some guidelines for yourself on how to receive (possibly negative) feedback assertively, and how to make use of it constructively for your learning and development.

4 APPRAISAL PROCESSES

4.1 The purpose of appraisal

The process of appraisal is part of the system of performance management.

Definition

Performance appraisal is the process whereby an individual's performance is reviewed against previously agreed goals, and where new goals are agreed which will develop the individual and improve performance over the forthcoming review period.

The general purpose of any appraisal system is to improve the efficiency of the organisation by ensuring that the individuals within it are performing to the best of their ability and developing their potential for improvement.

(a) **Reward review.** Measuring the extent to which an employee is deserving of a bonus or pay increase as compared with his or her peers.

(b) **Performance review**, for planning and following up training and development programmes, ie identifying training needs, validating training methods and so on.

(c) **Potential review,** as an aid to planning career development and succession, by attempting to predict the level and type of work the individual will be capable of in the future.

4.2 Uses of appraisal

Jeannie Brownlow has decided to leave Gold and Silver where she has worked for five years as a supervisor. When the personnel manager asked for her reasons she said, 'I'm fed up. You don't know where you are here. No one tells you if you're doing the job well, but they jump on you like a ton of bricks if anything goes wrong. Talk about "no news is good news" – that's the way it is here'.

Monitoring and evaluating the performance of individuals and groups is an essential part of people-management. It has several uses.

(a) Identifying the current level of performance to provide a basis for informing, training and developing team members to a higher level.

(b) Identifying areas where improvement is needed in order to meet acceptable standards of performance.

(c) Identifying people whose performance suggests that they might be suitable for promotion in future.

(d) Measuring the individual's or team's level of performance against specific standards, to provide a basis for reward above the basic pay rate (in other words, individual or group bonuses).

(e) Measuring the performance of new team members against the organisation's (and team's) expectations, as a means of assessing whether selection procedures have been successful.

(f) Improving communication about work tasks between managers and team members, as a result of discussing the assessment.

(g) In the process of defining what performance should be, establishing what key results and standards must be reached for the unit to reach its objectives.

It may be argued that a particular, deliberate stock-taking exercise is unnecessary, since managers are constantly monitoring and making judgements about their subordinates and (theoretically) giving their subordinates feedback information from day to day.

4.3 Why have a system?

It must be recognised that, if no system of formal appraisal is in place:

(a) Managers may obtain random impressions of subordinates' performance (perhaps from their more noticeable successes and failures), but not a coherent, complete and objective picture

(b) Managers may have a fair idea of their subordinates' shortcomings – but may not have devoted time and attention to the matter of improvement and development

(c) Judgements are easy to make, but less easy to justify in detail, in writing, or to the subject's face

(d) Different managers may be applying a different set of criteria, and varying standards of objectivity and judgement, which undermines the value of appraisal for comparison, as well as its credibility in the eyes of employees

(e) Managers rarely give their subordinates adequate feedback on their performance. Most people dislike giving criticism as much as receiving it

Activity 4 **(15 minutes)**

List four disadvantages to the individual of not having an appraisal system.

4.4 The process of appraisal

A typical system would therefore involve:

(a) Identification of **criteria** for assessment

(b) The preparation of an **appraisal report**

(c) An **appraisal interview**, for an exchange of views about the results of the assessment, targets for improvement, solutions to problems and so on

(d) The preparation and implementation of **action plans** to achieve improvements and changes agreed, *and*

(e) **Follow-up**: monitoring the progress of the action plan

Definition

A **criterion** (plural: **criteria**) is a factor or standard by which something can be judged or decided. For example, 'meeting output targets' is one criterion for judging work performance.

We will now look at each stage in turn. First of all, what is the basis of appraisal going to be?

4.5 What should be monitored and assessed?

Managers must broadly monitor and assess the same things, so that comparisons can be made between individuals. On the other hand, they need to take account of the fact that jobs are different, and make different demands on the jobholder. If every individual were rated on 'communication skills' and 'teamworking', for example, you might have a good basis for deciding who needed promoting or training – but what about a data inputter or research scientist who does not have to work in a team or communicate widely in your organisation?

Activity 5 **(20 minutes)**

Think of some other criteria which you would want to use in assessment of some jobs – but which would not be applicable in others.

There is also the important question of whether you assess **personality** or **performance**: in other words, do you assess what the individual is, or what (s)he does? Personal qualities like reliability or outgoingness have often been used as criteria for judging people. However, they are not necessarily relevant to job performance: you can be naturally outgoing, but still not good at communicating with customers, if your product knowledge or attitude is poor. Also, personality judgements are notoriously vague and unreliable: words like 'loyalty' and 'ambition' are full of ambiguity and moral connotations.

In practical terms, this has encouraged the use of competence or results-based appraisals, where performance is measured against specific, job-related performance criteria.

Choosing assessment criteria

So how does a manager choose what criteria to base the assessment on? Most large organisations have a system in place, with pre-printed assessment forms setting out all the relevant criteria and the range of possible judgements. (We reproduce such a form later in this chapter). Even so, a team manager should critically evaluate such schemes to ensure that the criteria for assessment are relevant to his or her team and task – and that they remain so over time, as the team and task change.

Relevant criteria for assessment might be based on the following.

(a) **Job analysis**: the process of examining a job, to identify its component tasks and skill requirements, and the circumstances in which it is performed.

Analysis may be carried out by observation, if the job is routine and repetitive it will be easy to see what it involves. Irregular jobs, with lots of 'invisible' work (planning, thinking, relationship-building and so on) will require interviews and discussions with superiors and with the job holders themselves, to find out what the job involves.

The product of job analysis is usually a **job specification** which sets out the activities (mental and physical) involved in the job, and other factors in its social and physical environment. Many of the aspects covered – aptitudes and abilities required, duties and responsibilities, ability to work under particular conditions (pressure, noise, hazards), tolerance of teamwork or isolation and so on – will suggest criteria for assessment.

(b) **Job descriptions**: more general descriptions of a job or position at a given time, including its purpose and scope, duties and responsibilities, relationship with other jobs, and perhaps specific objectives and expected results. A job description offers a guide to what competences, responsibilities and results might be monitored and assessed.

(c) **Departmental or team plans, performance standards and targets**. These are the most clear-cut of all. If the plan specifies completion of a certain number of tasks, or production of a certain number of units, to a particular quality standard, assessment can be focused on whether (or how far) those targets have been achieved. (Personality and environmental factors may be relevant when investigating why performance has fallen short – but do not cloud the assessment of performance itself.)

Let us now look at some of the performance monitoring and reporting methods used in organisations.

5 APPRAISAL PROCEDURES

5.1 Monitoring and reporting

Overall assessment

This is much like a school report. The manager simply writes narrative judgements about the appraisee. The method is simple – but not always effective, since there is no guaranteed consistency of the criteria and areas of assessment from manager to manager (or appraisal to appraisal). In addition, managers may not be able to convey clear, precise or effective judgements in writing.

Guided assessment

Assessors are required to comment on a number of specified characteristics and performance elements, with guidelines as to how terms such as 'application', 'integrity' and 'adaptability' are to be interpreted in the work context. This is a more precise, but still rather vague method.

Grading

Grading adds a comparative frame of reference to the general guidelines. Managers are asked to select one of a number of levels or degrees (Grades 1–5 say) which describe the extent to which an individual displays a given characteristic. These are also known as rating scales, and have been much used in standard appraisal forms (for example, see the diagram of an appraisal form on the following page). Their effectiveness depends to a large extent on two things.

(a) **The relevance of the factors chosen for assessment**. These may be nebulous personality traits, for example, or clearly-defined work-related factors such as job knowledge, performance against targets, or decision-making.

(b) **The definition of the agreed standards or grades**. Grades A–D might simply be labelled 'Outstanding – Satisfactory – Fair – Poor', in which case assessments will be rather subjective and inconsistent. They may, on the other hand, be more closely related to work priorities and standards, using definitions such as 'Performance is good overall, and superior to that expected in some important areas', or 'Performance is broadly acceptable, but the employee needs training in several major areas and motivation is lacking'.

Numerical values may be added to gradings to give rating scores. Alternatively a less precise graphic scale may be used to indicate general position on a plus/minus scale.

Personnel Appraisal: Employees in Salary Grades 5–8

Date of Review	Time on Position Yrs Mths	S.G.	Age Yrs	Name
Period of Review	Position Title			Area

Important: Read guide notes carefully before proceeding with the following sections

Section One	Performance Factors NA	U	M	SP	E	O	Section Two	Personal Characteristics 1	2	3	4	5
Administrative Skills							Initiative					
Communications – Written							Persistence					
Communications – Oral							Ability to work with others					
Problem Analysis							Adaptability					
Decision Making							Persuasiveness					
Delegation							Self-Confidence					
Quantity of Work							Judgement					
Development of Personnel							Leadership					
Development of Quality Improvements							Creativity					

Section Three — Highlight Performance Factors and particular strengths/weaknesses of employee which significantly affect Job Performance

Overall Performance Rating (taking into account ratings given)

Prepared by: Signature .... Date .... Position Title ....

Section Four — Comments by Reviewing Authority

I R Review Initial

Signature .... Date .... Position Title .... Date

Section Five — Supervisor's Notes on Counselling Interview

Signature .... Date .... Position Title ....

Section Six — Employees Reactions and Comment

Signature .... Date ....

Performance Classification

Outstanding performance is characterised by high ability which leaves little or nothing to be desired.

Personnel rated as such are those who regularly make significant contributions to the organisation which are above the requirements of their position. Unusual and challenging assignments are consistently well handled.

Excellent performance is marked by above-average ability, with little supervision required.

These employees may display some of the attributes present in 'outstanding' performance, but not on a sufficiently consistent basis to warrant that rating. Unusual and challenging assignments are normally well handled.

Satisfactory Plus performance indicates fully adequate ability, without the need for excessive supervision.

Personnel with this rating are able to give proper consideration to normal assignments, which are generally well handled. They will meet the requirements of the position. '**Satisfactory plus**' performers may include those who lack the experience at their current level to demonstrate above-average ability.

Marginal performance is in instances where the ability demonstrated does not fully meet the requirements of the position, with excessive supervision and direction normally required.

Employees rated as such will show specific deficiencies in their performance which prevent them from performing at an acceptable level.

Unsatisfactory performance indicates an ability which falls clearly below the minimum requirements of the position.

'**Unsatisfactory**' performers will demonstrate marked deficiencies in most of the major aspects of their responsibilities, and considerable improvement is required to permit retention of the employee in his current position.

Personal Characteristics Ratings

1 – Needs considerable improvement – substantial improvement required to meet acceptable standards.
2 – Needs improvement – some improvement required to meet acceptable standards.
3 – Normal – meets acceptable standards.
4 – Above normal – exceeds normally acceptable standards in most instances.
5 – Exceptional – displays rare and unusual personal characteristics.

Figure 10.2: Example of an appraisal form

Results-oriented schemes

All the above techniques may be used with more or less results-oriented criteria. A wholly results-oriented approach sets out to review performance against specific targets and standards of performance, which are agreed – or even set – in advance by a manager and subordinate together. This is known as **performance management**.

5.2 Correcting under-performance

Employees do not always perform according to expectations. When there is evidence that an individual is not performing at an acceptable level, the manager should investigate the circumstances without delay and try to ascertain the reasons for the unsatisfactory performance. If, following this examination, the manager considers that the individual's performance is deficient in some material respect; an informal discussion with the member of staff will be arranged. At this meeting the manager will:

(a) Make clear the areas in which the individual's performance is below expectations (explaining the grounds/evidence for this view) with the aim of identifying any problems or reasons for the under-performance, which could be resolved. Solutions to the problem could include additional training, providing a mentor, coaching or some other kind of ongoing support to the individual.

(b) Give the individual the opportunity to explain their under-performance and to raise any concerns they may have about the job, or the support and guidance they have been given to do it. There are many reasons why people fail to deliver what is required of them. A previously good employee may be experiencing problems at home or the job may have become too tedious. The reasons for poor performance could significantly affect how this matter is resolved.

(c) Ensure that the member of staff is aware of the level of performance/ productivity required in relation to each element of the duties about which there is a concern.

(d) Set a reasonable timeframe within which improvement is expected and arrange a further meeting at the end of this time to review the situation. When establishing 'reasonable timescales' for improvement, managers must consider the complexity of the tasks involved in relation to the qualifications and experience of the individual.

The content and outcome of this meeting will be confirmed by the manager/supervisor in writing to the individual, including the type of improvement required, any additional support or training that will be provided, any other agreed actions and the timescale for improvement and review.

When discussing under-performance managers must be specific about their concerns and must demonstrate evidence and/or give examples to support their assertions. The consequences of continued under-performance need to be explained to the individual. For example, it could result in a freeze in salary, demotion or no opportunity to take part in new projects. It may be serious enough to warrant dismissal.

In introducing 'performance management', we have raised the possibility that an employee might be involved in monitoring and evaluating his or her own performance. If targets are clear, and the employee is able to be honest and objective, self-assessment may be both effective and satisfying.

5.3 Who does the appraising?

Organisations have begun to recognise that the employee's immediate boss is not the only (or necessarily the best) person to assess his or her performance. Other 'stakeholders' in the individual's performance might be better, including the people (s)he deals with on a day to day basis:

(a) The current (and perhaps previous) boss (including temporary supervisors)
(b) Peers and co-workers (peer appraisal)
(c) Subordinates; (upward appraisal)
(d) External customers or
(e) The employee him or herself (self appraisal)

5.4 360 degree feedback

360-degree feedback is an approach which collects comments and feedback on an individual's performance from all these sources (usually anonymously using questionnaires) and adds the individual's own self-assessment.

The advantages of 360-degree feedback are said to be as follows.

(a) It highlights every aspect of the individual's performance, and allows comparison of the individual's self-assessment with the views of others. (Rather revealing, in most cases.)

(b) Feedback tends to be balanced, covering strengths in some areas with weaknesses in others, so it is less discouraging.

(c) The assessment is based on real work – not artificial (eg interview) situations. The feedback is thus felt to be fairer and more relevant, making it easier for employees to accept the assessment and the need for change and development.

Activity 6 **(20 minutes)**

Peter Ward, who introduced 360-degree feedback at Tesco in 1987, gives an example of the kinds of questionnaire that might be used as the instrument of 360-degree feedback. 'A skill area like "communicating", for example, might be defined as "the ability to express oneself clearly and to listen effectively to others". Typical comments would include "Presents ideas or information in a well-organised manner" (followed by rating scale); or: "Allows you to finish what you have to say".'

Rate yourself on the two comments mentioned above, on a scale of 1–10. Get a group of friends, fellow-students, even a tutor or parent, to write down, anonymously, on a piece of paper their rating for you. Keep them in an envelope, unseen, until you have a few.

Compare them with your self-rating. If you dare... What drawbacks did you (and your respondents) find to such an approach?

5.5 Upward appraisal

A notable modern trend, adopted in the UK by companies such as BP, British Airways and some television companies, is upward appraisal, whereby employees are rated not by their superiors but by their subordinates. The followers appraise the leader.

The advantages of this method might be as follows.

(a) Subordinates tend to know their (one) superior better than superiors know their (many) subordinates.

(b) Instead of the possible bias of an individual manager's ratings, the various ratings of several employees may reflect a rounded view.

(c) Subordinates' ratings have more impact, because it is less usual to receive feedback from below: a manager's view of good management may be rather different from a team's view of being managed!

(d) Upward appraisal encourages subordinates to give feedback and raise problems they may have with their boss, which otherwise would be too difficult or risky for them.

Activity 7 **(15 minutes)**

Imagine you had to do an upward appraisal on your boss, parent or teacher. Suggest the two major problems that might be experienced with upward appraisal.

Having reported on an individual's performance – whether in a written narrative comment, or on a prepared appraisal form – a manager must discuss the content of the report with the individual concerned.

5.6 The appraisal interview

There are basically three ways of approaching appraisal interviews.

(a) The **tell and sell** method. The manager tells the subordinate how (s)he has been assessed, and then tries to 'sell' (gain acceptance of) the evaluation and any improvement plans.

(b) The **tell and listen** method. The manager tells the subordinate how (s)he has been assessed, and then invites comments. The manager therefore no longer dominates the interview throughout, and there is greater opportunity for counselling as opposed to pure direction. The employee is encouraged to participate in the assessment and the working out of improvement targets and methods; change in the employee may not be the sole key to improvement, and the manager may receive helpful feedback about job design, methods, environment or supervision.

(c) The **problem-solving** approach. The manager abandons the role of critic altogether, and becomes a counsellor and helper. The discussion is centred not on assessment of past performance, but on future solutions of the employee's work problems. The employee is encouraged to recognise the problems, think solutions through, and commit himself to improvement. This approach is more involving and satisfying to the employee and may also stimulate creative problem-solving.

EXAMPLE

A survey of appraisal interviews given to 252 officers in a UK government department found that:

(a) Interviewers have difficulty with negative performance feedback (criticism), and tend to avoid it if possible

(b) Negative performance feedback (criticism) is, however, more likely to bring forth positive post-appraisal action, and is favourably received by appraisees, who feel it is the most useful function of the whole process, if handled frankly and constructively

(c) The most common fault of interviewers is talking too much

The survey recorded the preference of appraisees for a 'problem-solving' style of participative interview, over a one-sided 'tell and sell' style.

Many organisations waste the opportunity represented by appraisal for **upward communication**. If an organisation is working towards empowerment, it should harness the aspirations and abilities of its employees by asking positive and thought-provoking questions.

(a) Do you fully understand your job? Are there any aspects you wish to be made clearer?

(b) What parts of your job do you do best?

(c) Could any changes be made in your job which might result in improved performance?

(d) Have you any skills, knowledge, or aptitudes which could be made better use of in the organisation?

(e) What are your career plans? How do you propose achieving your ambitions in terms of further training and broader experience?

5.7 Follow-up

After the appraisal interview, the manager may complete his or her report with an overall assessment and/or the jointly-reached conclusion of the interview, with recommendations for follow-up action. This may take the following forms.

(a) Informing appraisees of the results of the appraisal, if this has not been central to the review interview. (Some people argue that there is no point making appraisals if they are not openly discussed, but unless managers are competent and committed to reveal results in a constructive, frank and objective manner, the negative reactions on all sides may outweigh the advantages.)

(b) Carrying out agreed actions on training, promotion and so on.

(c) Monitoring the appraisee's progress and checking that (s)he has carried out agreed actions or improvements.

(d) Taking necessary steps to help the appraisee to attain improvement objectives, by guidance, providing feedback, upgrading equipment, altering work methods or whatever.

If follow-up action is not taken, employees will feel that appraisal is all talk and just a waste of time, and that improvement action on their side will not be appreciated or worthwhile.

5.8 Assessing potential

Definition

> **Potential review** is the use of appraisal to forecast where and how fast an individual is progressing.

Potential review can be used as feedback to the individual to indicate the opportunities open to him or her in the organisation in the future. It will also be vital to the organisation in determining its management promotion and succession plans.

Information for potential assessment will include:

(a) Strengths and weaknesses in the employee's existing skills and qualities

(b) Possibilities and strategies for improvement, correction and development

(c) The employee's goals, aspirations and attitudes, with regard to career advancement, staying with the organisation and handling responsibility

(d) The opportunities available in the organisation, including likely management vacancies, job rotation/enrichment plans and promotion policies for the future

No single review exercise will mark an employee down for life as 'promotable' or otherwise. The process tends to be on-going, with performance at each stage or level in the employee's career indicating whether (s)he might be able to progress to the next step. However, an approach based on performance in the current job is highly fallible. *L J Peter* pointed out that managers tend to be promoted from positions in which they have proved themselves competent, until one day they reach a level at which they are no longer competent – promoted 'to the level of their own incompetence'!

Moreover, the management succession plan of an organisation needs to be formulated in the long-term. It takes a long time to equip a manager with the skills and experience needed at senior levels, and the organisation must develop people continuously if it is to fill the shoes of departing managers without crisis.

Some idea of **potential** must therefore be built into appraisal. It is impossible to predict with any certainty how successful an individual will be in what will, after all, be different circumstances from anything (s)he has experienced so far. However, some attempt can be made to:

(a) Determine key **indicators of potential:** in other words, elements believed to be essential to management success; these include past track record, and also administrative, interpersonal and analytical skills; leadership; orientation towards work, and a taste for making money; or a suitable mix of any of these

(b) Simulate the conditions of the position to which the individual would be promoted, to assess his or her performance. This may be achieved using case studies, role plays, presentations or team discussions and so on. An alternative approach might be to offer some **real** experience (under controlled conditions) by appointing the individual to assistant or deputy positions or to committees or project teams, and assessing his or her performance. This is still no real predictor of his or her ability to handle the **whole** job, on a continuous basis and over time, however, and it may be risky, if the appraisee fails to cope with the situation

6 INTERPERSONAL SKILLS AND FEEDBACK

6.1 Interpersonal behaviour

Interpersonal behaviour describes interaction between people – a two way process such as communicating, delegating, negotiating, resolving conflict, persuading, selling, using and responding to authority. It is also a way of defining an individual's behaviour in relationship to other people.

The way you behave in response to other people includes:

(a) How you perceive other people
(b) Listening to and understanding other people
(c) Behaving in a way that builds on this understanding
(d) Giving and receiving feedback

We use feedback information on the results of past behaviour to make rational decisions about whether to maintain successful behaviours or modify unsuccessful behaviours in the future, according to our goals and our plans for reaching them.

Development options that improve employees' effectiveness in their current jobs are called 'position related' while those that develop opportunities for career advancement are called 'career related'.

We are going to explain three activities that could be considered appropriate for employee development – coaching, mentoring and counselling.

6.2 Coaching

Managers help employees achieve objectives on a daily basis. Coaching is a behavioural control technique used by the manager to give on-going guidance and instruction, to follow day-to-day progress, and to give feedback.

Coaching is the ability to improve the job performance of employees. It is active, instead of passive, and is involved with guiding performance. Managers, who emphasise formal training and day-to-day coaching, reap the benefits of competence, high performance, commitment and cooperative behaviour.

The coaching process includes the following steps.

(a) **Establish learning targets** – the areas to be learned about should be identified and specific, realistic goals, eg completion dates or performance standards stated by agreement with the trainee

(b) **Plan a systematic learning and development programme** – this will ensure regular progress and appropriate stages for consolidation and practice

(c) **Identify opportunities for broadening the trainee's knowledge and experience** – eg by involvement in new products, placement on inter-departmental committees, suggesting new contacts or simply extending the job by adding more tasks, greater responsibility etc

(d) **Take into account the strengths and limitations of the trainee** in learning, and take advantage of learning opportunities that suit the trainee's ability, preferred style and goals.

(e) **Exchange feedback** – the coach will want to know how the trainee sees his or her progress and future and will also need performance information to monitor the trainee's progress, adjust the learning programme if necessary, identify further needs which may emerge and plan future development for the trainee

6.3 Mentoring

Mentoring is a process where one person offers help, guidance, advice and support to facilitate the learning or development of another.

Mentors can assist in:

(a) Drawing up personal development plans
(b) Advice with administrative problems people face in their new jobs
(c) Help in tackling projects, by pointing people in the right direction

Mentoring should not be seen as an additional or supplementary management task. It is an approach to management that puts the learning and development of the person at the heart of the process, offering advice and guidance to facilitate development. It is a good way of breaking down internal barriers between departments or groups and promoting equal opportunities. Mentoring offers a constructive alternative to the more traditional development methods by:

(a) Giving structure and continuity to development in the workplace

(b) Providing learners with a sounding board and facility for trust and confidentiality

(c) Focusing learning on the learner, not the tutor

(d) Transferring knowledge and skills

(e) Enabling quicker and more effective induction on new employees

(f) Providing structure for improved succession planning

(g) Enabling learners to focus on their own experience

(h) Allowing failure to be tolerated and used as a learning tool

(i) Helping the learner to solve real problems and make real decisions

(j) Providing continuous personal support and motivation

6.4 Counselling

Unlike mentoring, which focuses on learning and supporting the learner through the learning process, and coaching which focuses on the task and ensuring that the learner gains competence, counselling focuses on the person and enabling an individual to explore situations and responses.

Counselling can be defined as 'a purposeful relationship in which one persons helps another to help himself. It is a way of relating and responding to another person so that that person is helped to explore his thoughts, feelings and behaviour with the aim of reaching a clearer understanding. The clearer understanding may be of himself or of a problem, or of one in relation to the other' (*Rees*).

The need for workplace counselling can arise in many situations, eg:

(a) during appraisal
(b) in grievance or disciplinary situations
(c) following change, such as promotion or relocation
(d) on redundancy or dismissal
(e) as a result of personal or domestic difficulties
(f) in cases of sexual harassment or violence at work

Effective counselling is not merely a matter of pastoral care for individuals but is very much in the organisation's interests. The benefits include the following.

(a) Prevents underperformance, reduces labour turnover and absenteeism and increases commitment from employees

(b) Demonstrates an organisation's commitment to and concern for its employees

(c) Gives employees the confidence and encouragement necessary to take responsibility for self and career development

(d) Recognises that the organisation may be contributing to the employee's problems and therefore provides an opportunity to reassess organisational policy and practice

7 DISCIPLINARY SITUATIONS

7.1 Discipline

Definition

> **Discipline** can be considered as: 'a condition in an enterprise in which there is orderliness in which the members of the enterprise behave sensibly and conduct themselves according to the standards of acceptable behaviour as related to the goals of the organisation'.

Another definition of 'positive' and 'negative' discipline makes the distinction between methods of maintaining sensible conduct and orderliness which are technically cooperative, and those based on warnings, threats and punishments.

(a) **Positive (or constructive) discipline** relates to procedures, systems and equipment in the work place which have been designed specifically so that the employee has **no option** but to act in the desired manner to complete a task safely and successfully. A machine may, for example, shut off automatically if its safety guard is not in place.

(b) **Negative discipline** is then the promise of **sanctions** designed to make people choose to behave in a desirable way. Disciplinary action may be punitive (punishing an offence), deterrent (warning people not to behave in that way) or reformative (calling attention to the nature of the offence, so that it will not happen again).

The best discipline is **self discipline.** Even before they start to work, most mature people accept the idea that following instructions and fair rules of conduct are normal responsibilities that are part of any job. Most team members can therefore be counted on to exercise self discipline.

7.2 Types of disciplinary situations

There are many types of disciplinary situations which require attention by the manager. Internally, the most frequently occurring are these.

- Excessive absenteeism
- Poor timekeeping
- Defective and/or inadequate work performance
- Poor attitudes which influence the work of others or reflect on the image of the firm
- Breaking rules regarding rest periods and other time schedules
- Improper personal appearance
- Breaking safety rules
- Other violations of rules, regulations and procedures
- Open insubordination such as the refusal to carry out a work assignment.

Managers might be confronted with disciplinary problems stemming from employee behaviour *off* the job. These may be an excessive drinking problem, the use of drugs or some form of narcotics, or involvement in some form of law breaking activity. In such circumstances, whenever an employee's off-the-job conduct has an impact upon performance on the job, the manager must be prepared to deal with such a problem within the scope of the disciplinary process.

7.3 Disciplinary action

The purpose of discipline is not punishment or retribution. Disciplinary action must have as its goal the improvement of the future behaviour of the employee and other members of the organisation. The purpose obviously is the avoidance of similar occurrences in the future.

The suggested steps of progressive disciplinary action follow ACAS guidelines.

Step 1 **The informal talk**

If the infraction is of a relatively minor nature and if the employee's record has no previous marks of disciplinary action, an informal, friendly talk will clear up the situation in many cases. Here the manager discusses with the employee his or her behaviour in relation to standards which prevail within the enterprise.

Step 2 **Oral warning or reprimand**

In this type of interview between employee and manager, the latter emphasises the undesirability of the subordinate's repeated violation, and that ultimately it could lead to serious disciplinary action.

Step 3 **Written or official warning**

These are part of the ACAS code of practice (shown later in this chapter). A written warning is of a formal nature insofar as it becomes a permanent part of the employee's record. Written warnings, not surprisingly, are particularly necessary in unionised situations, so that the document can serve as evidence in case of grievance procedures.

Step 4 **Disciplinary layoffs, or suspension**

This course of action would be next in order if the employee has committed repeated offences and previous steps were of no avail. Disciplinary lay-offs usually extend over several days or weeks. Some employees may not be very impressed with oral or written warnings, but they will find a disciplinary layoff without pay a rude awakening.

Step 5 **Demotion**

This course of action is likely to bring about dissatisfaction and discouragement, since losing pay and status over an extended period of time is a form of constant punishment. This dissatisfaction of the demoted employee may easily spread to co-workers, so most enterprises avoid downgrading as a disciplinary measure.

Step 6 **Discharge**

Discharge is a drastic form of disciplinary action, and should be reserved for the most serious offences. For the organisation, it involves waste of a labour resource, the expense of training a new employee, and disruption caused by changing the make-up of the work team. There also may be damage to the morale of the group.

Activity 8 **(15 minutes)**

How (a) accessible and (b) clear are the rules and policies of your organisation/office: do people really know what they are and are not supposed to do? Have a look at the rule book or procedures manual in your office. How easy is it to see – or did you get referred elsewhere? is the rule book well-indexed and cross-referenced, and in language that all employees will understand?

How (a) accessible and (b) clear are the disciplinary procedures in your office? Are the employees' rights of investigation and appeal clearly set out, with ACAS guidelines? Who is responsible for discipline?

7.4 Relationship management in disciplinary situations

Even if the manager uses sensitivity and judgement, imposing disciplinary action tends to generate resentment because it is an unpleasant experience. The challenge is to apply the necessary disciplinary action so that it will be least resented.

(a) **Immediacy**

Immediacy means that after noticing the offence, the manager proceeds to take disciplinary action as *speedily* as possible, subject to investigations while at the same time avoiding haste and on-the-spot emotions which might lead to unwarranted actions.

(b) **Advance warning**

Employees should know in advance (eg in a Staff Handbook) what is expected of them and what the rules and regulations are.

(c) **Consistency**

Consistency of discipline means that each time an infraction occurs appropriate disciplinary action is taken. Inconsistency in application of discipline lowers the morale of employees and diminishes their respect for the manager.

(d) **Impersonality**

Penalties should be connected with the act and not based upon the personality involved, and once disciplinary action has been taken, no grudges should be borne.

(e) **Privacy**

As a general rule (unless the manager's authority is challenged directly and in public) disciplinary action should be taken in private, to avoid the spread of conflict and the humiliation or martyrdom of the employee concerned.

7.5 Disciplinary interviews

Preparation for the disciplinary interview

(a) **Gathering the facts** about the alleged infringement

(b) **Determination of the organisation's position:** how valuable is the employee, potentially? How serious are his offences/lack of progress? How far is the organisation prepared to go to help him improve or discipline him further?

(c) **Identification of the aims of the interview**: punishment? deterrent to others? improvement? Specific standards of future behaviour/performance required need to be determined.

(d) **Ensure that the organisation's disciplinary procedures have been followed**

(i) Informal oral warnings (at least) have been given.

(ii) The employee has been given adequate notice of the interview for his own preparation.

(iii) The employee has been informed of the complaint against his right to be accompanied by a colleague or representative and so on.

7.6 The content of the disciplinary interview

Step 1 The manager will explain the purpose of the interview.

Step 2 The charges against the employee will be delivered, clearly, unambiguously and without personal emotion.

Step 3 The manager will explain the organisation's position with regard to the issues involved: disappointment, concern, need for improvement, impact on others. This can be done frankly – but tactfully, with as positive an emphasis as possible on the employee's capacity and responsibility to improve.

Step 4 The organisation's expectations with regard to future behaviour/performance should be made clear.

Step 5 The employee should be given the opportunity to comment, explain, justify or deny. If he is to approach the following stage of the interview in a positive way, he must not be made to feel 'hounded' or hard done by.

Step 6 The organisation's expectations should be reiterated, or new standards of behaviour set for the employee.

(a) They should be specific and quantifiable, performance-related and realistic.

(b) They should be related to a practical but reasonably short time period. A date should be set to review his progress.

(c) The manager agrees on measures to help the employee should that be necessary. It would demonstrate a positive approach if, for example, a mentor were appointed from his work group to help him check his work. If his poor performance is genuinely the result of some difficulty or distress outside work, other help (temporary leave, counselling or financial aid) may be appropriate.

Step 7 The manager should explain the reasons behind any penalties imposed on the employee, including the entry in his personnel record of the formal warning. He should also explain how the warning can be removed from the record, and what standards must be achieved within a specified timescale. There should be a clear warning of the consequences of failure to meet improvement targets.

Step 8 The manager should explain the organisation's appeals procedures: if the employee feels he has been unfairly treated, there should be a right of appeal to a higher manager.

Step 9 Once it has been established that the employee understands all the above, the manager should summarise the proceedings briefly.

Records of the interview will be kept for the employee's personnel file, and for the formal follow-up review and any further action necessary.

Activity 9 **(20 minutes)**

Outline the steps involved in a formal disciplinary procedure (for an organisation with unionised employees) and show how the procedure would operate in a case of:

(a) Persistent absenteeism

(b) Theft of envelopes from the organisation's offices

7.7 The ACAS Code of Practice

This highlights the features of a good disciplinary system.

ACAS Code of Practice

Disciplinary and grievance procedures should:

- be in written form*
- specify to whom they apply (all, or only some of the employees?)
- be capable of dealing speedily with disciplinary matters
- indicate the forms of disciplinary action which may be taken (such as dismissal, suspension or warning)
- specify the appropriate levels of authority for the exercise of disciplinary actions
- provide for individuals to be informed of the nature of their alleged misconduct
- allow individuals to state their case, and to be accompanied by a fellow employee (or union representative)
- ensure that every case is properly investigated before any disciplinary action is taken
- ensure that employees are informed of the reasons for any penalty they receive
- state that no employee will be dismissed for a first offence, except in cases of gross misconduct
- provide for a right of appeal against any disciplinary action, and specify the appeals procedure

** The ACAS code of practice does not extend to informal 'first warnings', but these are an important part of the organisation's policy: don't forget them!*

8 GRIEVANCE

Definition

A **grievance** occurs when an individual thinks that he is being wrongly treated by his colleagues or supervisor; perhaps he or she is being picked on, unfairly appraised in his annual report, unfairly blocked for promotion or discriminated against on grounds of race or sex.

When an individual has a grievance he should be able to pursue it and ask to have the problem resolved. Some grievances should be capable of solution informally by the individual's manager. However, if an informal solution is not possible, there should be a formal grievance procedure.

8.1 Grievance procedures

Formal grievance procedures, like disciplinary procedures, should be set out in **writing** and made available to all staff. These procedures should do the following things.

(a) State what **grades of employee** are entitled to pursue a particular type of grievance.

(b) State the **rights of the employee** for each type of grievance. For example, an employee who is not invited to attend a promotion/selection panel might claim that he has been unfairly passed over. The grievance procedure must state what the individual would be entitled to claim. In our example, the employee who is overlooked for promotion might be entitled to a review of his annual appraisal report, or to attend a special appeals promotion/selection board if he has been in his current grade for at least a certain number of years.

(c) State what the **procedures for pursuing a grievance** should be.

Step 1 The individual should discuss the grievance with a staff/union representative (or a colleague). If his case seems a good one, he should take the grievance to his immediate boss.

Step 2 The first interview will be between the immediate boss (unless he is the subject of the complaint, in which case it will be the next level up) and the employee, who has the right to be accompanied by a colleague or representative.

Step 3 If the immediate boss cannot resolve the matter, or the employee is otherwise dissatisfied with the first interview, the case should be referred to his own superior (and if necessary in some cases, to an even higher authority).

Step 4 Cases referred to a higher manager should also be reported to the personnel department. Line management might decide at some stage to ask for the assistance/advice of a personnel manager in resolving the problem.

(d) **Distinguish between individual grievances and collective grievances.** Collective grievances might occur when a work group as a whole considers that it is being badly treated.

(e) Allow for the **involvement of an individual's or group's trade union** or staff association representative. Indeed, many individuals and groups might prefer to initiate some grievance procedures through their union or association rather than through official grievance procedures. Involvement of a union representative from the beginning should mean that management and union will have a common view of what procedures should be taken to resolve the matter.

(f) **State time limits** for initiating certain grievance procedures and subsequent stages of them. For example, a person who is passed over for promotion should be required to make his appeal within a certain time period of his review, and his appeal to higher authority (if any) within a given period after the first grievance interview. There should also be timescales for management to determine and communicate the outcome of the complaint to the employee.

(g) **Require written records** of all meetings concerned with the case to be made and distributed to all the participants.

8.2 Grievance interviews

The dynamics of a grievance interview are broadly similar to a disciplinary interview, except that it is the subordinate who primarily wants a positive result from it. Prior to the interview, the manager should have some idea of the complaint and its possible source. The meeting itself can then proceed through three phases.

Step 1 **Exploration**. What is the problem: the background, the facts, the causes (manifest and hidden)? At this stage, the manager should simply try to gather as much information as possible, without attempting to suggest solutions or interpretations: the situation must be seen to be open.

Step 2 **Consideration**. The manager should:

(a) Check the facts

(b) Analyse the causes – the problem of which the complaint may be only a symptom

(c) Evaluate options for responding to the complaint, and the implication of any response made

It may be that information can be given to clear up a misunderstanding, or the employee will – having 'got it off his chest' – withdraw his complaint. However, the meeting may have to be adjourned (say, for 48 hours) while the manager gets extra information and considers extra options.

Step 3 **Reply**. The manager, having reached and reviewed his conclusions, reconvenes the meeting to convey (and justify, if required) his decision, hear counter-arguments and appeals. The outcome (agreed or disagreed) should be recorded in writing.

Grievance procedures should be seen as an employee's right. To this end, managers should be given formal training in the grievance procedures of their organisation, and the reasons for having them. Management should be persuaded that the grievance procedures are beneficial for the organisation and are not a threat to themselves (since many grievances arise out of disputes between subordinates and their boss).

Activity 10 **(20 minutes)**

Find your organisation's grievance procedures in the office manual, or ask your union or staff association representative. Study the procedures carefully. Think of a complaint or grievance you have (or have had) at work. Have you taken it to grievance procedures? If so, what happened: were you satisfied with the process and outcome? If not, why not?

9 RELEVANT LEGISLATION

As with other areas of employment, there are statutes that cover the disciplinary and grievance procedures in an organisation. These include dismissal and the termination of employment.

9.1 Termination of employment

The Employment Rights Act 1996 lays down minimum periods of notice for both employer and employee. A contract of employment may not permit either side to give less than the minimum period of notice. However, either party may waive his right to notice or take a payment in lieu, and the Act does not affect the right to terminate a contract without notice in the event of gross misconduct.

The contract of employment may be terminated by either party for any reason or for no reason upon giving notice of a reasonable length, unless the contract is one for a fixed term or unless it specifically restricts the reason for which it may be terminated.

At common law either party may lawfully terminate the contract summarily, eg sacking without giving any notice, if the other party has committed a serious breach of the contract. The general principle justifying summary dismissal is that the employee's conduct prevents further satisfactory continuance of the employer-employee relationship, eg misconduct including disobedience, insolence and rudeness, committing a criminal act such as stealing, or causing injury through practical jokes.

9.2 Dismissal

Dismissal is the ultimate sanction in any disciplinary procedure. However, dismissals occur most frequently in the form of redundancy. Statistics published by the Department of Employment list the major reasons for dismissal as redundancy, sickness, unsuitability and misconduct in that order. Legislation in Britain during the 1970s, notably the Industrial Relations Act 1971, the Trades Unions and Labour Relations Act 1974 and the Employment Protection Act 1975, the Employment Protection (Consolidation) Act 1978 and the Employment Rights Act 1996, makes it a difficult and costly business to dismiss employees because of the provisions for employees to challenge the employer's decision. However, in recent statistics published by the Department of Employment it was revealed that only a proportion of cases of unfair dismissal actually reach employment tribunals; the majority are dealt with by some form of conciliation and arbitration.

Dismissal may be fair or unfair:

Fair dismissal – there is a statutory obligation for an employer to show that a dismissal is fair. In this case a dismissal is fair if it is related to:

(a) **A lack of capability or qualifications** – where the employee lacks the qualifications, skill, aptitude or health to do the job properly. However, in all cases the employee must be given the opportunity to improve the position or in the case of health be considered for alternative employment.

(b) **Misconduct** includes the refusal to obey lawful and reasonable instructions, absenteeism, insubordination over a period of time and some criminal actions. In the last case, the criminal action should relate directly to the job; it can only be grounds for dismissal if the result of the criminal action will affect the work in some way.

(c) **A statutory bar** occurs when employees cannot pursue their normal duties without breaking the law, eg drivers who have been banned.

Unfair dismissal – in all cases there are two stages of proof. First, the circumstances that represent fair grounds for dismissal must be established, and second, the tribunal must decide whether dismissal is fair in the circumstances of the case in question.

For dismissal to be automatically unfair, it must be for one of the following reasons.

(a) Trade union membership or non-membership
(b) Pregnancy
(c) Sex or race discrimination
(d) Revelation of a non-relevant spent conviction

9.3 Provisions for unfair dismissal

Where employees feel that they have been unfairly dismissed they have the right to take their case to the industrial tribunal. The tribunal will normally refer the case to ACAS (Advisory Conciliation and Arbitration Service) in the hope of gaining an amicable settlement. The possible solutions or remedies for unfair dismissal include:

(a) **Withdrawal of notice** by the employer. This is the preferred remedy as stated in the Employment Rights Act.

(b) **Reinstatement (order of industrial tribunal)** – this treats the employee as though he or she had never been dismissed. The employee is taken back to his old job with no loss of earnings and privileges.

(c) **Re-engagement (order of industrial tribunal)** – the employee is offered a different job in the organisation and loses continuity of service. Both reinstatement and re-engagement were provisions introduced by the Employment Protection Act 1975.

(d) **Compensation (order of industrial tribunal)** – if an employer refuses to re-employ then the employee receives compensation made up of a penalty award of 13 to 26 weeks' pay (more in the case of discrimination), a payment equivalent to the redundancy entitlement and an award to compensate for loss of earnings, pension rights and so on. Some form of compensation may also be appropriate in cases of reinstatement and re-engagement.

9.4 Prevent discrimination and value diversity

The practical implications of the legislation for employers are set out in **Codes of Practice**, issued by the Commission for Racial Equality and the Equal Opportunities Commission. These do not have the force of law, but may be taken into account by employment tribunals, where discrimination cases are brought before them. Many organisations now establish their own policy statements or codes of practice on equal opportunities: apart from anything else, a statement of the organisation's position may provide some protection in the event of complaints.

Every business wants the best person for the job. Unequal treatment, prejudice or harassment discredits the business – and can be very costly. An employee may hold the owner or manager responsible for any discriminatory action.

It is unlawful to discriminate on the grounds of someone's sex (including gender reassignment), sexual orientation, marital status, race, colour, nationality, ethnic origin, religion, beliefs or because of a disability, pregnancy or childbirth or because they are a member or non-member of a trade union. From 1 October 2004 the Government will extend the currently available protection to disabled people.

If a person feels they are discriminated against unlawfully, they may take a case to an employment tribunal. This could lead to heavy penalties for the employer and in the absence of an appropriate explanation, employment tribunals are required to infer that discrimination has occurred. It is also important to bear in mind that anti-discrimination legislation applies equally to part-time workers. It's against the law to discriminate against them because of their part-time status.

To prevent discrimination in day-to-day working practices means finding it.

- **Direct discrimination** is generally easily recognisable, where someone is denied employment because of race, gender, sexual orientation etc.
- **Indirect discrimination,** however, can be harder to detect and may often be unintentional.

Anti discriminatory practices consists of four elements.

(a) **Knowledge** – knowing and recognising how prejudice and discrimination work and understanding the processes at work. How our culture has influenced our thinking.

(b) **Values** – understanding our personal values and how this affects our attitudes and behaviour. Recognising personal prejudices and seeking to overcome them. Recognising where personal and organisational values differ. Performance can suffer and stress levels can rise.

(c) **Skills** – applying knowledge and values to practice. Using communication skills appropriately. Being self aware and dealing with people appropriately despite prejudices. Reflecting on performance.

(d) **Experience** – continuous development through experience and increased knowledge. Reflecting on experiences, both positive and negative, and learning from them. Learning from experiences of others.

Employer's responses

Most employers produce policies that set out the rules and procedures their staff need to know. A policy statement may help employees to understand what the employer expects of them, and their legal rights and obligations.

Some organisations make minimal efforts to avoid discrimination, paying lip service to the idea only to the extent of claiming 'We are an Equal Opportunities Employer' on advertising literature. To turn such a claim into reality, the following are needed.

(a) **Support** from the top of the organisation for the formulation of a practical policy

(b) A **working party** drawn from – for example – management, unions, minority groups, the HR function and staff representatives. This group's brief will be to produce a draft Policy and Code of Practice, which will be approved at senior level

(c) **Action plans and resources** (including staff) to implement and monitor the policy, publicise it to staff, arrange training and so on

(d) **Monitoring**. The numbers of women and ethnic minority staff can easily be monitored

(i) On entering (and applying to enter) the organisation
(ii) On leaving the organisation
(iii) On applying for transfers, promotions or training schemes

(It is less easy to determine the ethnic origins of the workforce through such methods as questionnaires: there is bound to be suspicion about the question's motives, and it may be offensive to some workers.)

Another response by employers is to take positive action.

Definition

Positive action: the process of taking active steps to encourage people from disadvantaged groups to apply for jobs and training, and to compete for vacancies. (Note that this is not positive discrimination.)

Examples of positive discrimination might be: using ethnic languages in job advertisements, or implementing training for women in management skills. The **Race Relations (Amendment) Act 2000** requires larger public organisations (more than 150 employees) to draw up detailed plans for achieving racial equality in all employment practices, for example.

Chapter roundup

- Performance management suggests that people must agree performance standards, that the responsibility for performance management is principally that of line management and that it is a conscious commitment to developing and managing people in organisations. It is a continuous process.
- Benchmarking is a continuous systematic process for evaluating the products, services and work processes of organisations that are recognised as representing best practices for the purpose of organisational improvement.
- Feedback is communication, which offers information to an individual or group about how their performance, results or behaviours are perceived or assessed by others.
- There are two main types of feedback – motivational feedback and developmental feedback.
- Giving feedback requires assertiveness, respect for others and skill.
- Appraisal is part of the system of performance management, including goal setting, performance monitoring, feedback and improvement planning.
- Appraisal can be used to reward but also to identify potential, and to plan training, development and improvement programmes.
- A variety of appraisal techniques can be used to measure different criteria in different ways.
- New techniques of appraisal aim to monitor the appraisee's effectiveness from a number of perspectives, including self-appraisal, upward appraisal and 360-degree feedback.
- Coaching is a behavioural control technique used by the manager to give on-going guidance and instruction, to follow day-to-day progress and to give feedback.
- Mentoring is a process where one person offers help, guidance, advice and support to facilitate the learning or development of another.
- Discipline has the same end as motivation – ie to secure a range of desired behaviour from members of the organisation.
- Progressive discipline includes the following stages – informal talk, oral warning, written/official warning, lay-off or suspension and dismissal.
- Grievance procedures embody the employee's right to appeal against unfair or otherwise prejudicial conduct or conditions that affect him and his work.
- Grievance interviews follow: exploration, consideration, reply.
- Legislation that applies to discipline and grievance relates to dismissal and termination of employment as set out in the Employment Rights Act 1996.

Quick quiz

1 Define performance management.

2 List the steps in performance management.

3 What are the purposes of appraisal?

4 What bases or criteria of assessment might an appraisal system use?

5 Outline a results-oriented approach to appraisal.

6 What is the difference between performance appraisal and performance management?

7 What is a 360-degree feedback, and who might be involved?

8 When a subordinate rates his or her manager's leadership skills, this is an example of:

(a) Job evaluation
(b) Job analysis
(c) Performance management
(d) Upward appraisal

9 The most empowering style of appraisal interview is the 'tell and listen' approach. True or false?

10 What follow-up should there be after an appraisal?

11 How can appraisals be made more positive and empowering to employees?

Answers to quick quiz

1 **Performance management** is: a means of getting better results by managing performance within an agreed framework of goals, standards and competence requirements. It is a process to establish a shared understanding about what is to be achieved, and an approach to managing and developing people.

2 The steps in performance management

(a) From the business plan, identify the requirements and competences required to carry it out.

(b) Draw up a performance agreement

(c) Draw up a performance and development plan with the individual

(d) Manage performance continually throughout the year

(e) Performance review

3 Identifying performance levels, improvements needed and promotion prospects; deciding on rewards; assessing team work and encouraging communication between manager and employee.

4 Job analysis, job description, plans, targets and standards.

5 Performance against specific mutually agreed targets and standards.

6 Appraisal on its own is a backward-looking performance review. But it is a vital input into performance management, which is forward-looking.

7 Refer to paragraph 5.4 for a full answer.

8 (d). ((a) is a technique for grading jobs for salary-setting purposes. (b) is the process of analysing jobs for job evaluation and job description. Make sure you know what (c) is!)

9 False. The most empowering style is 'problem-solving'.

10 Appraisees should be informed of the results, agreed activity should be taken, progress should be monitored and whatever resources or changes are needed should be provided or implemented.

11 Ensure the scheme is relevant, fair, taken seriously, and cooperative.

Answers to activities

1 The key to performance management is that it is forward looking and constructive. Objective-setting gives employees the security in knowing exactly what is expected of them, and this is agreed at the outset with the manager, thus identifying unrealistic expectations. The employee at the outset can indicate the resources needed.

2 These measures do not all address some of the key issues of the job.

- Number of new customers. This is helpful as far as it goes but omits two crucial issues: how much the customers actually spend and what the potential is. Demand for this service might be expanding rapidly, and the firm might be increasing sales revenue but losing market share.
- Revenue from existing customers is useful – repeat business is generally cheaper than gaining new customers, and it implies customer satisfaction.

- Renewal of service contracts is very relevant to the executive's role.
- Customer complaints about poor quality products. As the company does not make its own products, this is not really under the control of the sales manager. Instead the purchasing manager should be more concerned. Complaints about the service contract are the sales executive's concern.
- Customer satisfaction survey. This is a tool for the sales manager to use as well as a performance measure, but not everything is under the sales executive's control.

3 The following are just some suggestions.

- Stay open: listen actively and demonstrate your willingness to be receptive.
- Clarify and test your understanding of what is being said. Feedback may be non-specific, ambiguous or unfair. You need to find out exactly what the problem (learning opportunity) is, by asking questions:
  - 'What do you mean by...?',
  - 'Could you give me some specific examples?'
- Don't be too quick to reject or deny. It will be your choice whether you act on the feedback or not: you can afford to hear and reflect on it first.
- Don't be too quick to defend or justify: remember it is to your benefit to learn how your behaviour or performance is perceived by others, whether or not you think it fair.
- Monitor your feelings. We usually react to negative (and sometimes positive) feedback as a threat to our self image and competence: be aware that you may feel refusal, anger and defensiveness before you move on to acceptance and problem-solving.
- Thank the person for the feedback. Giving feedback is a tough job!

4 Disadvantages to the individual of not having an appraisal system include the following. The individual is not aware of progress or shortcomings, is unable to judge whether s/he would be considered for promotion, is unable to identify or correct weaknesses by training and there is a lack of communication with the manager.

5 You will have come up with your own examples of criteria to assess some jobs but not others. You might have identified such things as:

- Numerical ability (applicable to accounts staff, say, more than to customer contact staff or other non-numerical functions)
- Ability to drive safely (essential for transport workers – not for deskbound ones)
- Report-writing (not applicable to manual labour, say)
- Creativity and initiative (desirable in areas involving design and problem-solving not routine or repetitive jobs in mass production or bureaucratic organisations).

6 Drawbacks to 360-degree appraisal include:

- Respondents' reluctance to give negative feedback to a boss – or friend
- The suspicion that management is passing the buck for negative feedback, getting people to 'rat' on their friends
- The feeling that the appraisee is being picked on, if positive feedback is not carefully balanced with the negative

7 Problems with upward appraisal include fear of reprisals or vindictiveness (or extra form-processing). Some bosses in strong positions might feel able to refuse to act on results, even if a consensus of staff suggested that they should change their ways.

8 Your own research.

9 Apart from the outline of the steps involved – which can be drawn from the chapter, this question raises an interesting point about the nature of different offences, and the flexibility required in the handling of complex disciplinary matters.

- There is clearly a difference in kind and scale between
  - unsatisfactory conduct (eg absenteeism)
  - misconduct (eg insulting behaviour, persistent absenteeism, insubordination) and
  - 'gross misconduct' (eg theft or assault).
- The attitude of the organisation towards the purpose of disciplinary action will to a large extent dictate the severity of the punishment.
  - If it is punitive it will 'fit the crime'.
  - If it is reformative, it may be a warning only, and less severe than the offence warrants.
  - If it is deterrent, it may be more severe than is warranted (ie to 'make an example').

The absenteeism question assumes that counselling etc. has failed, and that some sanction has to be applied, to preserve credibility. The theft technically deserves summary dismissal (as gross misconduct), but it depends on the scale and value of the theft, the attitude of the organisation to use of stationery for personal purposes (ie is it theft?) etc. Communicating the situations given might best be done as follows.

(a) Telephone, confirmed in writing (order form, letter)

(b) Notice board or general meeting

(c) Fact-to-face conversation. it would be a good idea to confirm the outcome of the meeting in writing so that records can be maintained.

(d) Either telephone or face-to-face.

10 Your own research.

Bibliography

Adair, J. and Allen, M. (1999) *Time Management and Personal Development*. London: Hawksmere.

Beck, U. (1994) *Reflexive Modernization: Politics, Tradition, and Aesthetics in the Modern Social Order* Stanford University Press

Bryce, L. (1989) *The Influential Woman: How to Achieve Success without Losing Your Femininity*. Piatkus Books

Buchanan and Huczynski. (2004) *Organizational Behaviour: An Introductory Text*. Financial Times/ Prentice Hall; 5th edition

De Bono, E. (1990) *Six Thinking Hats*. Penguin Books Ltd

Drucker, P. (2007) *The Practice of Management*. A Butterworth-Heinemann Title; 2nd edition

Festinger, L. (1957). *A Theory of Cognitive Dissonance*. Stanford University Press

Gardner, H. (1993) *Frames of Mind: The Theory of Multiple Intelligence*. Basic Books; 10th edition

Goleman, D. (1998) *Working with Emotional Intelligence*. London: Bloomsbury.

Guirdham, M. (1995) *Interpersonal Skills at Work* (2nd ed.) Harlow, Essex: Prentice Hall.

Handy, C. (1993) *Understanding Organisations*. Penguin; Fourth Edition

Herzberg, F. (2008) *One More Time: How Do You Motivate Employees?* Harvard Business School Press

Higgs and Dulewicz (2002) *Making Sense of Emotional Intelligence*. National Foundation for Educational Research; 2nd Revised edition

Honey, P. and Mumford, A. (1992) *The Manual of Learning Styles*. Maidenhead: Peter Honey.

Kolb (1984) *Experiential Learning*. New York: Prentice Hall.

Koontz, O'Donnell, Weihrich. (1980) *Management*. McGraw-Hill Education; 7th edition

Kotter, J. (1988) *The Leadership Factor*. The Free Press; 1st Edition.

Krol, E and Ferguson, P. (1 Nov 1995) *The Whole Internet for Windows 95*. O'Reilly Media

Likert, R (1961) *New patterns of Management*. McGraw-Hill Inc., US

Luft, J. (1961) The Johari window, *Human Relations Training News*, No. 5.

Maslow, A. H.(1998) *Toward a Psychology of Being*. John Wiley & Sons; 3rd Edition

Pareto, V. (1980) *Manual of Political Economy*. Kelley, USA; Reprint edition

Pedler, M., Burgoyne, J. and Boydell, T. (2001), *A Manager's Guide to Self Development* (4th ed.) Maidenhead: McGraw Hill.

Peter, L. (1972) *The Peter Principle*. Bantam

Rodger, A. (1952) *The seven point plan*. London NIIP

Rogers, C. (1961) *On Becoming a Person*. Boston: Houghton Mifflin.

Tannenbaum, R. and Schmidt, W.H. (2009) *How to Choose a Leadership Pattern*, Harvard Business School Press; Reprint edition

Whetten, D. and Cameron, K. (2002) *Developing Management Skills* (5th ed.) New Jersey: Prentice Hall.

Yukl, G.A (2009) *Leadership in Organizations*. Pearson Education; 7th edition

Index

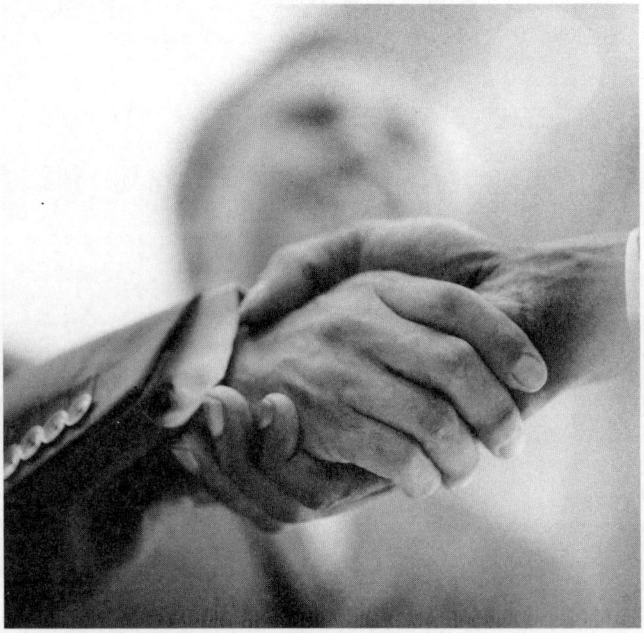